Fulfilling the Sacred Ancestral Prophecy of the Triple Nine:
Unveiling the Prophetic 2012 Meltdown of the Lost and Astray Pale State of Mind

by High Priest Kwatamani

The Most Supreme Spirit of All That There Is of Supreme Love

A Divine Body of Flesh, He and She

A Divine Mind of Thought Of the Most Supreme Spirit of

Published by the Kwatamani Holistic Institute of Brain Body & Spiritual Research & Dev., Inc.

Email: kwatamani@earthlink.net
kwatamani@livefoodsunchild.com
kwatamani@triplenineninepr ophecy.tv
Website: http://www.livefoodsunchild.com
http://www.triplenineprophecy.tv
http://www.myspace.com/kwatamani

Editors:
High Priest Kwatamani and
Royal Priestess Gail Kwatamani
*Feminine Spirit Translator for the
High Priest Kwatamani*:
Royal Priestess Gail Kwatamani
Technical Editor: Queen Bea Kwatamani

MANIFESTING THE EXPRESSIONS OF SUPREME LOVE, RIGHTEOUSNESS & THE HOLISTIC LIVING TRUTH ABOUT SUPREME LOVE

First Edition
Release Date January 9, 2009 9:00 p.m.
Copyright © 2008. All rights reserved.

Warning:

Please be advised that this text has been forwarded through the sacred ancestral codes and decodes of the Most Supreme Seen and Unseen Essence of Life and Supreme Love.

Be further advised that the planet Earth has entered the second phase of its shifting into the sacred ancestral prophecy of the triple nine and that this text serves to anoint the Sacred Temple of Kwa Ta Man I.

Be further advised that this text would indeed be rated Triple X within the toxic parallel and thus is rated **TRIPLE NINE 999** in the parallel divine.

Therefore this text is for those who truly wish to resurrect the most supreme ancestral spirit presence of Man, He and She, and divine spirit consciousness within every phase of one's existence.

Thus it is a guarantee that this book is not like any other that you have seen, heard or read, and so we urge that you do not expect it to be or evaluate it the same, or you will drive yourself insane.

Be totally aware of the fact that no two opposite energies can occupy the same space at the same time, so we warn that this text might indeed blow a fuse within a weak and feeble state of mind.

Intense Divine Spirit Conscious Energy At Work:

Thus this book is not for the casual reader or those locked in the various stages and phases of pale thought and reasoning, and so we urge and warn that you do not enter the pages of this text unless you have the will, want or desire, and/or are prepared, to take the challenges of entering the safety zone of the divine parallel. And even with that, please know fo' sho that only a divine and sacred few will indeed pass go.

Please know for sure that only a divine and sacred few will amass the sacred energy to endure and take those steps necessary to go beyond Chapter Nine and apply the divine actions that will speak louder than the words that one memorize, plagiarize, capitalize and improvise on from the profound words and supreme energy of expression within this text.

Please read the fine print

This text is written within the vibration of spirit code to resurrect divine spirit consciousness within the sacred presence of Man, He and She. For best results, with the least amount of interpersonal conflict, it is a prerequisite that one consume of whole life energy that begins with the consumption of raw and living fruits, vegetables, seeds and nuts in order to achieve divine clarity. Additionally, this text should be read three times - -one for the brain, one for the body and one for the spirit.

Let
The
Most
Supreme
Spirit
Of
Love
Be
Your
Guide

The Wholly Messenger

High Priest Kwatamani

Dedication

Prelude:
Ancestral Libation

**Song 1 from "Conjuring Ancestral Spirit Consciousness"
Kwatamani musical CD release, 2007**

<u>Royal Priestess vocals:</u>
Ancient, original, indigenous, native Man
Suntanned Children of the Sun across every land
The sacred garden origin of Man, He and She
From the deep, dark essence of our sacred ancestry
The glorious solarized tan of the divine family tree
Shades of the earth, black as the soil, rich brown golden hues and terra-cotta red
Listen Children to what is being said
Sacred ancestral gathering deep in the tropical rainforest
Deep in the tropical rainforest, ancestral...
Sacred ancestral gathering
deep in the tropical rainforest

<u>High Priest vocals:</u>
This is dedicated to the sacred suntanned tribes and clans who ascended and descended
from the original Man, He and She
Devoted to their sacred garden culture ancestry
This is dedicated to you and me—
Nok, Nubian, Kushite, Dravidian, Shang Li
This is dedicated to our trip across the sea
Olmeks moving divinely
This is dedicated to the offspring Children who would come to be—Carib, Taino, Seminole and Cherokee
This is dedicated to the Children who were sold

FULFILLING THE SACRED ANCESTRAL PROPHECY OF THE TRIPLE NINE: UNVEILING THE PROPHETIC 2012 MELTDOWN OF THE LOST AND ASTRAY PALE STATE OF MIND

and enslaved from across the sea
Maroone, Garifune, suntanned Children
refusing to be doomed
This is dedicated to those who escaped on the shore and
ran into the rainforest of Panama, Columbia
Venezuela and Ecuador
Breaking chains, hiding in the rain
moving swiftly from the aches and pain
This is dedicated to the suntanned Children
with no tribal name, Afrikan Americans all the same
This is dedicated to the Children
who sprung off the Inca vein
This is dedicated to the Zambo thang
This is dedicated to the suntanned Children
moving fast and swiftly on their heels
This is dedicated to the Palmare
and the other suntanned Children of Brazil
This is dedicated to the Mayan
and the Aztec who got all mixed up
trapped in the tricks of the invader rut
This is dedicated to the suntanned Children of every land
every Afrikan descendant, every tribe and every clan
of the He and She of Man
This is dedicated to the Children of the Sun
who suffered the fate of murder, rape, steal and take at
the hands of the Children of the Sun who lost their tan
This is dedicated to the pale Children who suffered too
and all of the Children of the Earth
who no longer want to maintain this pale doo doo
And so to remove you from these cold-blooded lies that
are disguised as true

PRELUDE: ANCESTRAL LIBATION

We now bring to you a Supreme Love vibe of spirit juju
Musical voodoo, a live Kwatamani home brew
dedicated to you

Royal Priestess vocals:
Children of the Sun with a golden tan
Ancient, original, indigenous native Man
Basking in the sun of the divine garden plan
Consuming raw and living fruits, vegetables, seeds and
nuts, herbs and spice
Green and lush, grown with ease
the fruits of the trees of life
Invaded by the vicious, pale
bloodthirsty Children from the pits of hell
The ice-cold, barren lands
freezing caves and brutal warring clans
Animal slaughter and bloodspill
carnivorous predator mind
of the hunting and herding kind
Every where you look across the land
you will come to understand
the story of the sacred garden culture
of the original suntanned Man, He and She

High Priest vocals:
Ancestral spirit juju
melting down toxic, mind-bending doo doo
With pulsating hearbeat musical voodoo
aimed directly at you

Dedication

*This is dedicated to
the holistic living process of elimination
detoxing and purging
to prevent the continuation
of the opposite energy's manifestation
of mutation and degeneration
that is geared to alter Man, He and She's
divine spirit conscious destination.
In other words, this is dedicated
to resurrecting
the sacred ancestral spirit presence
of the Divine Children of the Sun and
the Sacred Garden Culture
from which we come.*

Innerlude:
Is It Yo Thang?

Song 11 from "12th Hour Prophecy: The Pale Curse and the Solarized Energy Shift," Kwatamani musical CD release, 2008

Royal Priestess vocals:
It's yo thang, do what you want to do
I can't tell you who to give your thang to
It's yo thang, it's yo thang, it's yo thang

High Priest vocals:
Is this your thang that is going around
and coming around like a boomerang
Zap, sapping, trapping the mental essence of the brain
like a predator with a fang
Sucking the entire population of the Earth
into a spiritual drain

Royal Priestess vocals:
It's yo thang, it's yo thang
And you're full grown, and you're full grown
Doing what you want to do, got a mind of your own
And you didn't even know that when you submitted
 you became committed to uphold this thang as yo thang
The religious, social economic schemes
You continue to uphold the pale-male-war god dreams
And you so with it, you can't quit it
And you so with it, you can't quit it
So addicted that you claim it as yo thang

FULFILLING THE SACRED ANCESTRAL PROPHECY OF THE TRIPLE NINE: UNVEILING THE PROPHETIC 2012 MELTDOWN OF THE LOST AND ASTRAY PALE STATE OF MIND

<u>High Priest vocals:</u>
The thing that is really insane is you think
this is yo thang
Consuming every deception
the lost and astray mind can bring
Without stress strain or panic
and taking nothing for granted
I'm a take a little time and educate you about this thang
that's a threat to the planet Earth
and everything on the earthly turf
Listen very closely to every riddle and every rhyme
Then take a little time, check out your mind, and let's see
if you can figure out what is the bottom line

<u>Royal Priestess vocals:</u>
It's yo thang, do what you want to do
I can't tell you who to socket into
You are body, spirit and brain and it's up to you
Who you gonna devote your whole life essence to?

<u>High Priest vocals:</u>
Submit or die, murder, rape, enslave
Kill the infidel, send the heathen to the grave
The pale-male-war god would self install
Using sex and violence
to pin the Children against the wall
He would play the game of top dog and spell it reverse
Using vengeance, war and wrath to inflict his black curse
And deep within the mind, the death culture'd be at work
Breeding lust, lies, illusions; seeding harm and hurt
This energy would be bred in a white-blight zone

INNERLUDE: IS IT YO THANG?

Degenerating and mutating the lost and astray Children
of the Sun until they'd become a deadly breed unknown
They would bust out of them caves
leaving a bloodstained trail
Showing the Children of the Sun
the tricks and treats of hell
There'd be nothing but gruesome stories to tell
since the Children of the Sun met
the Children who were pale
And they would bring forward
this death-consuming energy
Because they knew not of the fruits of the tree
And they knew not of spirit conscious energy
So they would work to break down
the Sacred Garden Culture ancestral family tree
These pale Children would breed
greed, vengeance, war and spite
Taking lies, illusions, lust, confusion
death and deadly destruction to a brand new height
And as this deadly and destructive pale energy
came to be
It would bring forward the essence of this war-god deity
And they would declare this deity to be a god of love
burnt offering, first choice
consumer of flesh and blood
Thus would be the nature of the energy of the cold
death culture in its own image
mutating DNA code
But the sacred suntanned Children
would be on another roll
Earth, wind, rain and sun
is what we would behold

FULFILLING THE SACRED ANCESTRAL PROPHECY OF THE TRIPLE NINE: UNVEILING THE PROPHETIC 2012 MELTDOWN OF THE LOST AND ASTRAY PALE STATE OF MIND

Of the most supreme ancestral DNA code
as the Most Supreme Unseen had long ago unfold
Then we would meet up with
that completely opposite energy
that the pale-male-war god would unfold
And there's never been a more sorrowful story told
Submit or die, murder, rape, enslave
Kill the infidel, send the heathen to the grave
The pale-male-war god would self-install
Polluting the earth, water and air;
threatening the life of us all
Divine spirit consciousness would be cursed and reversed
Love would become a game of harm and hurt
Deep within and all around the white-blight zone
A spiritual war would be going on
turning Man, He and She into clones and worker drones
And the sacred suntanned Children started flipping,
slipping, tripping 'til their mind was blown
Weakened and depleted spirits stone-cold to the bone
Deep in the place the ancestral spirit roam
Becoming steeped knee-deep in the white-blight zone
Feeling that integration and assimilation
would make it so much easier to get a groove on
Hypnotized and mesmerized and living in disguise
Becoming a major component pushing white–blight lies
Styling, smiling, profiling on the cell phone
Internet connections to the brain
blamed for things going wrong at home
Cocky, arrogant and vain, ego-tripping off the thang
you eat, snort and smoke to ease the pain
of the brain drain that's driving you insane

INNERLUDE: IS IT YO THANG?

As the ancestral spirit is more intensely denied
one shuffles and scoot in an attempt to plant a new root
as the spook sitting by the door that hide
the last remains of an ancestral spirit
said to have been uprooted and died
The projection of the cloning program is going very well
Producing carbon copies of the energy that is pale
And within this spiritual war, the energy that was
opposite would use every player
to inflict a fatal wound or scar
But as the horn would blow for the final hoop
one would still be a spook or the F-troop
or sitting on the side line or in the prison cell
trying to make bail
Sitting on the dock of the bay, watching time roll away
Wasting time, finding a new way to pray
Or somewhere within the bloodstained trail
consuming toxic taste and smell
within the gates of hell
And within the gates of hell
one's worship of one's god is well-defined
by one's ability to rack, stack and pack cash money
the bottom line
And there's a method to the madness
of this pale-male-war god's cry
Whose objective is to get you to submit and to deny
Your most supreme ancestral presence
and watch your spirit die
This piece is dedicated to the mothers and the fathers
and the sisters and the brothers
and my daughters and my sons
and my granddaughters and grandsons

FULFILLING THE SACRED ANCESTRAL PROPHECY OF THE TRIPLE NINE: UNVEILING THE PROPHETIC 2012 MELTDOWN OF THE LOST AND ASTRAY PALE STATE OF MIND

and any other one wishing to resurrect
the sacred ancestral presence
of the Divine Children of the Sun
and the Sacred Garden Culture
from which we come

Table of Contents

Prelude: *Ancestral Libation* 9
Dedication 13
Innerlude: *Is It Yo Thang?* 15
Table of Contents 21
Prelude: *Sweet Ancestral Memory* 29
Forward: Coming Whole and Clean: Reclaiming the Unconquered Spirit 35
Innerlude: *Free to Change* 43
Prelude: *We'll Take You There* 49
Introduction: The Coming of a Sacred Ancestral Soothsayer 53
   The Divine Intervention 53
Innerlude: *Undeniable Truth: Lesson One* 59
Chapter 1 Prelude: *Ancestral Prophecy* 67
Chapter One: A Most Supreme Unseen Movement 75
   The Raw and Living Vibration 76
   The Greatest Weapon 77
   The Gathering Time of the Sacred Few 82
   Divine Mission 85
   The Triple Nine 86
   The Test of Time 89
   2009: The Second Cycle 90
   The Era of 2012 91
   The Steps to Resurrection 94
   Divine Reasoning 99
Chapter 1 Innerlude: *Same Game, Different Name* 105
Chapter 2 Prelude: Introduction to the 12th Hour Prophecy 113
Chapter Two: Spiritual War 117
   The Divine Parallel 120

FULFILLING THE SACRED ANCESTRAL PROPHECY OF THE TRIPLE NINE: UNVEILING THE PROPHETIC 2012 MELTDOWN OF THE LOST AND ASTRAY PALE STATE OF MIND

    The Coming of the Toxic Parallel 122
    Exposing the Nature of the Toxic Parallel 126
    Pale Privileges, Benefits and Rewards 133
    Suntanned Disciples and Followers of Paleness 135
Chapter 2 Innerlude: *The Nature of the Beast* 147
Chapter 3 Prelude: *The Ooh's and the Aah's of a Love Supreme* 155
Chapter Three: The Divine Origin of Man, He and She
.... 161
    Sacred Ancestral Memory: The Unknown and the All-Knowing 161
    The Beginning 162
    The Void 164
    The Sacred Ancestral Coming upon the Seen 168
    The Dividing Line 178
    The Warning 180
Chapter 3 Innerlude: *The Soothsayer Speaks* 185
Chapter 4 Prelude: *Do You Know What It Took and What It Will Take?* 193
Chapter Four: The Division of Race 199
    Telling the Supreme Truth 199
    Division and Separation in Black and White 200
    Millennial Movements within the Divine Parallel ... 201
    A Recent Breed of Mutation and Degeneration 205
    The Predator 211
    Fight or Flight 214
    The Mental Mindset of Paleness 218
Chapter 4 Innerlude: *0 to 12 Degrees* 223
Chapter 5 Prelude: *Keep on Pushing* 235
Chapter Five: Running the Pale Master Plan Against the Sacred Suntanned He and She of Man 239

TABLE OF CONTENTS

Verse One: Breeding the Pale State of Mind into a Partnership of Crime 239
   The Suntanned Children Became Lost and Astray 239
   The Flood 241
   The Suntanned Male and Female United 243
   Cold and Pale Games 245
   The Pale False and Fake Superiority Trait 247
Verse Two: A Painful Story to Tell 250
   A Turning Point 250
   Nearly 6,000 Years 252
   Power Would Concede Nothing Without a Struggle 254
   A New Beginning and a New Ending As Well ... 256
Verse Three: The White Blight and the White-Lady Syndrome 258
   It's Just a Program 259
Verse Four: Spreading the Pale Plague into the Chattel Slavery Days 263
   Master Program 266
Verse Five: The Protection Divide 268
Verse Six: Indulging in the Treats and the Tricks of the Triple-Six Fix 275
   An Analysis of a Very Serious Time 275
Verse Seven: Sister True 282
Verse Eight: Ancestral Spirit Call 289
Chapter 5 Innerlude: *Helluva Program* 297
Chapter 6 Prelude: *Something to Step to* 307
Chapter Six: Religions and the Deities of Death 313
   The First and the Second Coming 313
   Religion: A Way of Life 316

FULFILLING THE SACRED ANCESTRAL PROPHECY OF THE TRIPLE NINE: UNVEILING THE PROPHETIC 2012 MELTDOWN OF THE LOST AND ASTRAY PALE STATE OF MIND

    The Dominant Religious Orders of the Toxic Parallel 325
    Secret Societies and Sacred Orders 328
    The Favor and Blessings of the Pale-Male-Warlord Deity 337
Chapter 6 Innerlude: *Submit or Die* 349
Chapter 7 Prelude: *What's Up* 357
Chapter Seven: The White Blight Zone 363
    Herd Mentality of the Hunting and Herding Culture 364
    The Appearance of Change 368
    Crying for a Little Relief 371
    On the Fringe of the Social Order 375
    The Truth Shall Set You Free 379
    The Subconscious: Far Below Whole Life Awareness 385
    The Highs of the Low 388
Chapter 7 Innerlude: *Divided Union* 395
Chapter 8 Prelude: *Hear We Stand* 403
Chapter Eight: Sacred Ancestral Prophecy 407
    Beyond Speculation 407
    Current Affairs and Global Issues 415
    Crisis for the Consumers of the Death Culture 419
    Fossil Fuels 427
    Coming Out of the Cold 429
    Stem Cells 434
Chapter 8 Innerlude: *Changing Tide* 445
Chapter 9 Prelude: *Lies in Disguise* 455
Chapter Nine: The Changing of the Guard 461
    Recycling and Reciprocation 461
    Spirits Who Choose To Live 467

TABLE OF CONTENTS

    More than a Cause 473
    Checks and Balances 475
    Deliverance 481
    The Known and the Unknown Factors 495
    Matters of Life and Death 502
    The Forward Multiplication of Divinity 508
    Divine Social Economic Family Community 512
    Melting Down 515
Chapter 9 Innerlude: *Emergence of a Divine Intervention* 525
Holistic Living Resource Materials 535

Forward

Prelude:
Sweet Ancestral Memory

**Song 7 from "Conjuring Ancestral Spirit Consciousness"
Kwatamani musical CD release, 2007**

<u>Royal Priestess vocals:</u>
*Sweet ancestral memory. There was a time
when the sacred garden culture flourished
Sweet ancestral memory. And the sacred spirit presence
of Man, He and She, was nourished
Sweet ancestral memory. Man, He and She
would embrace each other in the warmth of the sun
Man, He and She, consuming of the fruits of the trees
of Life and moving to the sacred ancestral drum
To the sacred ancestral drum
Spirits, spirits come again
When will those times come again, gone so long
We come again in this sacred ancestral song
Sweet ancestral memory*

<u>Royal Priestess vocals:</u>
Every good-bye ain't gone no matter how long
you been doing wrong. Sweet ancestral memory
With a focus on right now and how your mind
will allow you to feel about the real deal
All that has come before is the door for your spirit to soar
Beyond this deep-freeze state of mind
learn the lessons of time and realign
with divine spirit consciousness of mind
Ancestral memory is the key
to remember all that you have divinely come to be
Set your spirit free

FULFILLING THE SACRED ANCESTRAL PROPHECY OF THE TRIPLE NINE: UNVEILING THE PROPHETIC 2012 MELTDOWN OF THE LOST AND ASTRAY PALE STATE OF MIND

<u>High Priest vocals:</u>
From the earliest time you got scarred
When the death culture got its start
And you played the wrong card
Now it's time to show some heart
And to break that invested connection
with that deep-freeze biblical cord
The I in I come to you from a divine spirit consciousness
of mind and invoke that you emerge
deep into this sacred ancestral spirit
as it unwinds and realign
The time has long passed
for you to be stale, pale and sad
Hooked on the good, ugly and the bad
Steeped in fantasies, fashions and fads
Knee-deep in the book revised, stolen and took
and fed to you like a bait on a hook
And you follow blindly behind
this lost and astray mind because of a dollar sign
Talking games of divinity while selling and buying this
ice-cold, deep-freeze insanity
Feeding toxic stuff and things to the brain
while becoming more addicted to the misery, aches and
pains that this death culture bring
And your mind continues to focus on the big bang
a con game, to pacify things
And the artifacts, facts and findings
continue to show the lame brain that the evolution of
Man, He and She, goes far beyond the ape or the
orangutan
And the genesis of the Children of the Sun

PRELUDE: SWEET ANCESTRAL MEMORY

goes far beyond the pale-male-war god
or the disciples and the followers
that keep the lost and astray Children in a nod
Hoping to maintain this façade
And mothers continue to consume this deceit
giving birth to lust, lies, and illusions, while singing
"oh, baby, don't you weep"
Hope your mind makes room so that you can get in tune
with what the I in I have to say and to convey
during this spirit interplay
We come to introduce you to the essence of Life
and not to prepare you for doomsday
Look Dick, look Jane, look the misery, aches and pains
Playing slick, wicked and quick
Flick a dollar, flick a bick, turn a trick
slip a mick, talking trash
sniffing, snorting, drinking, smoking, having a bash
while the fibers of your brain crash
And it must be the stuff that you eat
that's causing your lifeline to spring a leak as your body,
brain and spirit go feeble and weak
And your big bang, another sex and violence game
And the deep-freeze mentality is planted so deep that you
can not feel, hear or see
the spirit calling of the ancestral family tree
The I in I have come to identify
and to melt down this deep-freeze lie
and in context the I in I have come to resurrect
the sacred spirit presence of the Olmeks
Enough of this deep-freeze pitter and patter
that causes the mind to chitter and chatter
making your brain not matter

FULFILLING THE SACRED ANCESTRAL PROPHECY OF THE TRIPLE NINE: UNVEILING THE PROPHETIC 2012 MELTDOWN OF THE LOST AND ASTRAY PALE STATE OF MIND

as your body gets fatter and your spirit does the latter as
these cold-blooded, deep-freeze relationships shatter
Enough of being out of focus with reality
playing the game of bestiality or getting in the flow
up high or down low, playing the game of homo
and then to react, getting in touch with necrophiliac
or some other toxic plan that prohibits
the spirit growth of the He and She of Man
We come at you like a light beam
from the Most Supreme Unseen
Resurrecting the sacred ancestral spirit of Love
beyond your wildest dream
And within this text
we bring to you divine spirit consciousness
to break this deep-freeze hex
And to connect with your supreme ancestral memory that
is stored away in your DNA
Want you to know that if you blow and don't show
or if you falter and don't alter
this cold-blooded deep-freeze way
the most fatal dues you will have to pay
forever more until doomsday
Yet no matter how Man, He and She
stumble, fumble and fall, if one pays any attention at all
one can still hear the supreme ancestral call
And so within the I in I confess
that we have come to resurrect
the most supreme ancestral spirit of the Olmeks
And all the rest of those who have been or will be
of this most supreme ancestral family tree

PRELUDE: SWEET ANCESTRAL MEMORY

And in case you haven't heard
children learn by the example
that goes beyond the word

<u>Royal Priestess vocals:</u>
Sweet ancestral memory

Forward:
Coming Whole and Clean:
Reclaiming the Unconquered Spirit

When anyone first encounters the vibrations and sensations of whole life energy, the spirit presence stirs within, and a vague sense of inner recognition is awakened. While the spirit whispers faintly, "Here I am," the lost and astray mind remains momentarily stunned and overwhelmed. This unexpected meeting is the only way that a lifeline of connection can get past the mental traps and alarms installed by the opposite energy to keep one locked down forever in the toxic parallel. However, if an individual hesitates and does not grab hold quick, hanging on for dear life to the holistic living truth about Supreme Love, the rallying forces of that opposite energy will soon overtake one's thinking and reasoning to capture one's full attention once again. If this takeover occurs, one may never able to regain an inner focus on resurrection. And one becomes just another casualty in this spiritual war....

Everyone who has gathered within the safety zone of divine spirit consciousness remembers their first encounter with the High Priest Kwatamani. Many, many years ago, there was a heartfelt question presented to the High Priest Kwatamani. The question was, "How do we escape the cycles of our mothers and our mothers' mothers and those before them?" Let's be real here, the question was addressing the plight of the suntanned female and the vibrations of bitterness, frustration, loneliness, and hurt that have haunted her experiences

FULFILLING THE SACRED ANCESTRAL PROPHECY OF THE TRIPLE NINE: UNVEILING THE PROPHETIC 2012 MELTDOWN OF THE LOST AND ASTRAY PALE STATE OF MIND

within the death consuming culture. The High Priest Kwatamani had been encountered for the first time, and during that brief contact there was a noticeable quickening of the spirit, a welcomed breath of life to revive a sense of hope. Oh, but the mind of thought was ready to debate, ready to dismiss the entire possibility that a presence of real change existed. And the High Priest Kwatamani, in his supreme soothsayer way, answered that question with his own question. "Have you met the Sisterhood?," he asked.

Well, those questions still echo in my memory. Within the movement of the divine intervention, I was introduced to the Kwatamani Royal Sisterhood, and the warm and encouraging expressions of suntanned femininity that I encountered were so profound that I was compelled to align within the greater wholeness of sisterhood. I found out later from the Queen Mother that she, too, had been compelled to align within the ancestral vibrations of Sisterhood many years earlier as a result of the same radiating warmth and welcoming embrace that she met among the Sisterhood of an earlier phase. And through the years, with the divine guidance and divine protection provided by the High Priest Kwatamani, the Kwatamani Royal Sisterhood has brought forward a stronger and more unified presence of the divine nurturing essence that is indeed the strength of the sacred ancestral mother spirit. And this is the radiant glory that we have to pass on to our daughters who, themselves, continue to emerge within a more refined presence of divine femininity and to our sons who have a new definition of feminine presence to experience and a new

FORWARD: COMING WHOLE AND CLEAN: RECLAIMING THE UNCONQUERED SPIRIT

sense of respect and honor for their own masculine presence to uphold.

This divine intervention of resurrecting the sacred ancestral mother spirit did not emerge because of rhetoric, theory, or idle wishful thinking. As a matter of fact, it would have been impossible without the sacred ancestral spirit presence of High Priest Kwatamani and his bringing forward the Most Supreme Seen and Unseen Essence of Life and Supreme Love upon the seen to be nurtured. The task is tremendous. Can one comprehend what it took to drag the sacred suntanned feminine presence from her magnificent height of divine nurturer and beat her down so low that she now wallows in the toxic parallel of a disconnected, depleted and confused state of being? And where is her mate, the sacred suntanned masculine presence?

The tragic and toxic nature that has befallen the suntanned female within the death-consuming culture was actually inflicted thousands and thousands of years before the Trans-Saharan and Trans-Atlantic slave trade began and has been impacting every generation that has been birthed since those earlier times. And what must be done to resurrect the sacred ancestral mother spirit again upon the seen directly relates to an entire toxic parallel of experiences that must be addressed by looking at the adverse effects upon generation after generation after generation of suntanned mothers, daughters and sisters.

These cycles of abuse and violation and toxic consumption have almost completely destroyed, and have indeed devastated, the nurturing essence of femininity by corrupting that divine essence into the breeding ground for lust, lies, illusions, confusion, death and deadly

FULFILLING THE SACRED ANCESTRAL PROPHECY OF THE
TRIPLE NINE: UNVEILING THE PROPHETIC 2012 MELTDOWN
OF THE LOST AND ASTRAY PALE STATE OF MIND

destruction. And the suntanned female has indeed been used and abused as the mammy of the death-consuming culture – and the whore. How has she come to now honor and lust after those cold and pale values, attitudes and behaviors of a foreign invader culture that has never held, and will never hold, any regard for her sacred ancestral spirit presence? When, at first, in her natural and innate unconquered state of being, the very thought of ever forsaking her divine nurturing responsibilities was inconceivable.

No, this is not the way it was meant to be within the divine master plan of the He and She of Man. However, the painful memories of destruction and devastation do not simply fade away into the paleness of the toxic parallel; those painful memories fester within a consciousness of fright and fear. And the suffering, wailing cries of the suntanned feminine presence were never truly silenced even as those cries are now pacified by the values, attitudes and behaviors that keep one obedient and submissive to a lost and astray state of mind. The gut-wrenching pain of witnessing brutal attacks upon one's beloved suntanned mate, watching in disbelief as he is violently struck down, and then having one's own tears turn into screams of horror and disgust as one is stripped naked and brutally raped at the hands of the same vicious invader. These echoing cries of having one's sons or daughters stolen away and families torn apart are imprinted in the ancestral memory of the suntanned female. And then the bitterness sets in…the blame and accusations against the suntanned masculine presence for his absence, leaving her empty, lonely, sad

FORWARD: COMING WHOLE AND CLEAN: RECLAIMING THE UNCONQUERED SPIRIT

and blue. And so, in truth and reality, what else should the primary nurturer be expected to nurture other than the vibrations of lust, lies, illusions, confusion, death and deadly destruction that have surrounded her disconnected existence. And as the first teacher, these toxic vibrations would be all that she is left to nurture into each and every offspring born off of her.

And the suntanned feminine presence is left to reason with her own fright and fear, left to figure out her own means of survival as she does whatever she can to protect herself and her children. And so she turns to that opposite energy, because it appears to provide the only guidance and protection available to her. However, this guidance leads deeper into the attitudes, values, beliefs and behaviors of the death-consuming culture—protected by the fantasies, illusions, delusions and dreams of a better day. And as the circumstances become worse, the more one wishes, hopes and prays for a better day.

This is about the ancestral memories regarding the coming of the mutated and degenerated pale breeds who invaded, raided, raped and slaughtered after the most recent ice age period, leaving the Divine Children of the Sun and the Sacred Garden Culture from which we come in ruins. Despite her strength to endure and survive the ordeals that have befallen her, the suntanned female has indeed become a weak and feeble remnant of her sacred ancestral spirit presence. This is about the sacred ancestral mother spirit of all of Man, He and She, as expressed in the divine and original presence of the sacred suntanned female and how she became a target of manipulation in the games of domination and control.

FULFILLING THE SACRED ANCESTRAL PROPHECY OF THE TRIPLE NINE: UNVEILING THE PROPHETIC 2012 MELTDOWN OF THE LOST AND ASTRAY PALE STATE OF MIND

Throughout the pages of this sacred text, the reader will indeed encounter the divine reality of fulfilling the sacred ancestral prophecy of the Triple Nine.

And as a prelude to the disconnected self...all that mental chatter and all those old songs that keep repeating over and over inside the head, all those memories that get re-played again and again, and all those scenes from old shows and movies that keep flashing from time to time while one becomes fascinated by a daydream or a re-run scene or the latest scheme to keep one tuning into the toxic parallel. And in the midst of all that mental noise and static, how can one ever expect to receive a thought of divine spirit consciousness?

So many ways to become distracted and drift off into fantasies, illusions, delusions and dreams, so many ways for one's attention to wander, so many ways to stay hypnotized, mesmerized and addicted to the death-consuming culture. So many ways in the way of change...

Only a divine intervention could possibly penetrate the haze of the mind maze that keeps one entrapped in the familiar mental habits of toxic consumption. And even then, one must exercise the will and tenacity to consume the holistic living truth about Supreme Love by making a concentrated effort to listen, focus and respond to the inner movements of whole life energy.

The prophesied second cycle of the divine intervention is well underway. Those who have already taken major steps to exit the opposite energy and its toxic parallel now stand as frontrunners in fulfilling the sacred ancestral prophecy of the Triple Nine. This sacred

FORWARD: COMING WHOLE AND CLEAN: RECLAIMING THE UNCONQUERED SPIRIT

pathway has been cleared and secured by the High Priest Kwatamani as he established the Kwatamani Royal Family and as he anoints the Sacred Ancestral Temple of Kwa Ta Man I. The supreme essence of masculinity and femininity are realigning within the Divine Union of One to divinely guide, protect and nurture the resurrection of the sacred ancestral spirit presence of the Divine Children of the Sun and the Sacred Garden Culture from which we come.

While the hectic rush and rumble of the death-consuming culture keep so many individuals busy, dizzy and dazed, there is a quiet and profound emergence happening. This emergence will not be televised, nor will it make the headlines of the daily papers, nor will it hit the top ten list on the radio; however, it will be delivered in divine order to the Sacred Few. Stay divinely tuned.

Royal Priestess Gail Kwatamani
Oshami of the Kwatamani Royal Sisterhood

Innerlude:
Free to Change

**Song 5 from "Conjuring Ancestral Spirit Consciousness,"
Kwatamani musical CD release, 2007**

<u>Royal Priestess vocals:</u>
Free, free to live in harmony
with earth, wind, rain and sun. To live in harmony...
Earth, wind, rain and sun
Free, free to reclaim the divine union
of Man, He and She
Free to consume of the fruits of the trees of life
in a tropical rainforest paradise
Free to reclaim the divine glory, free
The sacred garden culture
the original Supreme Love Story
The sacred garden culture, the original way of life...
Free to reclaim the suntanned glory
of the original Supreme Love story

<u>High Priest vocals:</u>
Deep, deep within the ancestral glory
Upon the sacred garden culture of the rainforest story
And the essence of the sacred soil and seed
Would breed the deep-seated roots
of the fruits of the tree and the glorious vegetation
from the fruits of the trees would indeed
provide Man, He and She, all their basic needs
And the bark and the flowers and the stem
root and leaves would be the guarantee
that Man, He and She, had fresh air to breathe
And to maintain mental and physical and spiritual health

FULFILLING THE SACRED ANCESTRAL PROPHECY OF THE TRIPLE NINE: UNVEILING THE PROPHETIC 2012 MELTDOWN OF THE LOST AND ASTRAY PALE STATE OF MIND

Herbs would provide Man, He and She, much wealth
And the water would be crystal clear and fine
And Man, He and She, would live divine
And consuming of these sacred tastes and smells would
cause Man, He and She, to live very well
Until they were introduced to the pits of hell
where the bloodstained trail
of the death-consumption culture would be the story the
deep-freeze mentality would tell
Where an animal's life became a game of prey
Where hunting and herding became
a social economic mainstay
And the strangers were outsiders, and they would prey
They were hunters and herders, and they would prey
Mothers would be raped, and the strangers would pray
Fathers would be slain, and the strangers would pray
The Children began to adopt these cold-blooded ways
and means and means and way
and they would soon learn to pray
And they would prey on each other
as they learned to pray
They would pray themselves into their own doomsday
And they would stink and they would smell, praying to
resurrect from this cold-blooded hell
And this lost and astray mind that degenerated outside
would plot and scheme and connive, capitalizing on
anything, taking all of Man, He and She, for a ride
into the pits of a hellish disguise
And the sugar-coated, cold-blooded
materialistic lies would pull the wool
over Man, He and She's, eyes

INNERLUDE: FREE TO CHANGE

leaving them sitting in harm's way
watching, witnessing and waiting
for their own demise
And the Children of the Sun
would learn to plot and scheme
and the Children of the Sun would have bad, bad dreams
over this cold-blooded, deep-freeze mentality thing
In the midst of these vibes
the Children would become divided
and deceived into taking sides
on the right-side or the left-side
of these cold-blooded lies
And to think this was meant to be a love story
need I confide
But I continue to hear the wailing cries
and the rainforest facing its demise
Resurrecting the sacred ancestral culture
Is left with me and you
Listen very careful to this music juju
And let divine action be the thing that we do

<u>Royal Priestess vocals:</u>
Free to choose, free to maintain
the death consumption culture game
Free to change, free to make a divine change
Free to win and free to lose, free to choose
Free to go, free to stay, free to see a better day
Free to make a better way
And when your back is up against the wall
Know some freedom isn't free at all
With your back up against the wall
Free to reclaim your divine identity as a Child of the Sun
Free to consume of the fruits of the trees of Life

FULFILLING THE SACRED ANCESTRAL PROPHECY OF THE TRIPLE NINE: UNVEILING THE PROPHETIC 2012 MELTDOWN OF THE LOST AND ASTRAY PALE STATE OF MIND

Free to choose a better way
Free to live in a tropical rainforest paradise
Sacred garden culture paradise, paradise

Introduction

Introduction

Prelude:
We'll Take You There

**From Song 7, "Supernatural Healing Serum: Dose One,"
Kwatamani musical CD release, 2005**

<u>*Royal Priestess vocals:*</u>
We know a place, we know a place
Ain't nobody crying
Ain't nobody dying
Ain't nobody lying
Wearing false faces
Spreading confusion about the races
No more confusion
Ain't nobody fighting, ain't nobody fighting
Ain't nobody busy back biting
We know a place, we know a place
We know a place
And if you're ready, if you're ready
detox your mind and see
We'll take you there
We'll take you there, with a Kwatamani flair
We'll take you there
We'll take you there
We'll take you there, with a Kwatamani flair
We know a place, we know a place
We know a place, we know a place
That houses the fruits of the trees of life
Houses the fruits of the trees of life
Where you nurture on the herbs and spice
We'll take you there
Where life is a glorious groove

FULFILLING THE SACRED ANCESTRAL PROPHECY OF THE TRIPLE NINE: UNVEILING THE PROPHETIC 2012 MELTDOWN OF THE LOST AND ASTRAY PALE STATE OF MIND

And where Man, He and She
don't give each other the low down dirty blues
We'll take you there
Where birth is a natural thing
We know a place
And the birds have a song to sing
We know a place
And the natural colors, tastes and smells
are what the flowers bring
We'll take you there
We know a place
Are you ready? We know a place
And if you're ready, if you're ready
We'll take you there
If you're ready, if you're ready
We'll take you there, if you're ready
We'll take you there, if you're ready
We'll take you there

<u>High Priest vocals:</u>
A change of pace, a change of pace
We put the Supreme Love Spirit
Right up in your face
Tell me if Man, He and She's, not living in disgrace
Living on freebase insanity without a trace
A change of pace, a change of pace
I know a place where Man, He and She
don't have to live in disgrace
A place where there is no jive
A place where Man, He and She
don't murder, rape, steal and take

PRELUDE: WE'LL TAKE YOU THERE

to get themselves by
Oh, it's a fact
I know a place where the children or the adults
do not smoke crack
Where the lonely hearts don't sit at the dock of the bay
Watching their life slip away
A place where one don't worry
about the dues they have to pay
A place where pimps and whores don't stay
No dog, no dog
A change of pace, a change of pace
Rise up, roll call
A place where there's clean water and air
And if you're ready, we'll take you there
And don't just sit there and stare
Unwind inside your mind and leave this insanity behind
Feel the flow, 'cause this not just another religious show
You know the game, blame
You know the game, insane
You know the game, misery, aches and pains
The same game with another name
Like a pet dog trained to forget
A Divine Child of the Sun from which you came
A change of pace, a change of pace
There's a toxic place that begins inside your mind
And it will end when
you leave the death consumption culture behind
A change of pace, a change of pace
And if you're ready, we'll take you there

FULFILLING THE SACRED ANCESTRAL PROPHECY OF THE TRIPLE NINE: UNVEILING THE PROPHETIC 2012 MELTDOWN OF THE LOST AND ASTRAY PALE STATE OF MIND

<u>Royal Priestess vocals:</u>
We know a place, we know a place
We know a place
Are you ready?
And if you're ready, we'll take you there
We'll take you there
We'll take you there
Are you ready? Are you ready?
Are you ready inside your mind?
Divine spirit consciousness of mind

Introduction:
The Coming of a Sacred Ancestral Soothsayer

The Divine Intervention

Somewhere in and around the mid-1800's, a beautiful and young Afrikan daughter called Annie Nash would receive what she described as a sacred message from the ancestors giving her orders and directions. These directions related how she was to proceed in preparation for the birth of a specific child. Annie Nash would give birth to a daughter, Essie. As best as she could, Annie Nash held on to her ancestral ties, maintaining a deep connection to her glorious motherland. Annie Nash suffered the wounds and scars of so many others who had been shipped as slave cargo from the glorious land of the Divine Children of the Sun called Afrika.

You see, Annie Nash and her mother before her, as well as so many of her peers, had endured the battle cries of a blood-thirsty war god. This pale-male-war god was called upon and used to sanction the enslavement of the suntanned Children. This pale-male-war god was prayerfully worshipped by those who scorned, degraded and reduced the suntanned Children to 3/5 of a human being as slaves to a master who had mutated and degenerated in the ice-cold caves of the deep freeze called the Ice Age.

Great-grandmother Annie Nash would speak the words of a prophecy to the I in I generations later; she

FULFILLING THE SACRED ANCESTRAL PROPHECY OF THE TRIPLE NINE: UNVEILING THE PROPHETIC 2012 MELTDOWN OF THE LOST AND ASTRAY PALE STATE OF MIND

would simply smile and say, "He done come, ya." Somehow the I in I would comprehend these words; somehow, based on the social environment and cultural influences of the time, these words rang mysteriously. Great-grandma Annie Nash spoke in broken English with many words of Twi, an Akan dialect of the Kwa language group, and the huh's and utterances that reflected a communication far beyond any language spoken. The I in I would learn to comprehend her well. Great-grandma Annie Nash would, in fact, make it clear to the I in I a time of spiritual reckoning had come. She explained that the I in I would suffer many battles. In a language that I came to understand she made it very clear that indeed a spiritual war was underway. This war was actually a war against the Most Supreme and Most Sacred Ancestors and Great-grandma Annie Nash explained that the I in I would stand as a physical representation of the Most Supreme Unseen ancestral spirit presence.

The way that this story would go is that Great-grandma Annie Nash, pronounced "Anu" would mate with a masculine presence of love and give birth to many offspring. One of their daughters was called Essie, pronounced "Esi." Essie's name would reflect her Fanti ancestry from what the pale invader culture would call the Gold/Slave Coast of Afrika and what the Kwame Nkrumah regime later renamed as Ghana. Essie would indeed be noted as very hardworking, devoted, dedicated and sincere. She would remain as the keeper of her mother, Annie Nash. Essie would eventually find herself

INTRODUCTION: THE COMING OF A SACRED ANCESTRAL SOOTHSAYER

outside of St. Louis, Missouri on a little island called the Island.

Essie would be identified as a seer and healer. These gifts had been passed on to her, and she would transmit them to a grandson who would eventually be born from her lineage. Essie would note quite often to the I in I that it was a strange kind of healing vibration that she had inherited. It was an unseen and a spirit-healing vibration, and she did not really comprehend the nature of this vibration. All she knew was that she would have to transmit it to the I in I, her grandson. Essie eventually met up with a handsome, dark and vibrant, stud-strong male called Charlie Williams. Essie would be powerful enough to cause him to join her in union. Indeed, by Grandpa Charlie's accounts to the I in I, Essie was a very charming and mysterious woman who overpowered him upon first sight.

Grandma Essie and Grandpa Charlie Williams had many offspring. One of the sons called Gilbert would meet up with a tenacious and strong-willed young sister named Bessie May. During the days of emancipation and the rush for freedom, Bessie's mother, Lizzie Evans, and many others found their way up from the New Orleans and Mississippi area into the crossing of the Mason-Dixon Line. Traveling the routes of the Mississippi River eventually led them to the coastal area called the Island: Madison, Venice, Newport, etc.

Lizzie would marry Grandpa Reginald Robinson whose family lineage was of the Black Seminoles with ancestral ties to the Maroons or Garifuna who settled in the areas which would now be called Belize and southern Mexico. Lizzie's mother, Viola, had ascended from the

FULFILLING THE SACRED ANCESTRAL PROPHECY OF THE TRIPLE NINE: UNVEILING THE PROPHETIC 2012 MELTDOWN OF THE LOST AND ASTRAY PALE STATE OF MIND

suntanned tribe who were identified as Cherokee. Viola's family line had ascended from the coastal area in what is now called Vera Cruz. This ancestral lineage had existed long before the coming of the 15th century invaders of the pale culture.

Grandma Viola united with Grandpa Rankin whom she continued to describe as a beautiful, dark-skinned man with a radiant charm of warmth, love and compassion. And this is exactly how the I in I experienced him. Grandma Viola and Grandpa Rankin came from the area known as the Louisiana Purchase. Somehow Grandma Viola, who was also a great grandmother to the I in I, would have similar kinds of insight regarding the birth and presence of the I in I. She would share everything she knew about her ancestral past, her shaman father and foresight regarding a great spiritual coming out of his lineage. Thus puts together the ancestral lineage that would identify the physical birth route from which the I in I would come forward upon the seen.

One hot summer day in 1945, Bessie and Gilbert found themselves in a most auspicious position, and in the ebb and flow of call and response, the divine intervention would begin upon the seen. As the Most Supreme Unseen would have it occur on the seen, the revealing that was brought forward through Great-grandma Nash, Grandma Viola, Grandpa Rankin and others would come into fruition. Amazingly the I in I can recall each and every visit with these ancestral spirit beings, and they would indeed ratify the divine duty, obligation and responsibility that would mark the I in I's

INTRODUCTION: THE COMING OF A SACRED ANCESTRAL SOOTHSAYER

birth rites…A birth rite that the I in I have a divine duty, obligation and responsibility to go forward and multiply upon the seen.

High Priest Kwatamani, Supreme soothsayer, soul seer and spiritual healer

Innerlude:
Undeniable Truth: Lesson One

Song 3 from "Conjuring Ancestral Spirit Consciousness, " a Kwatamani musical CD release, 2007

<u>Royal Priestess Vocals:</u>
*What you gonna do when you come
to get your final lesson?
Can you figure out what's going on?
Player, player, play it well
Been passing, but you still fail
Somebody handed you a pile of lies that you consumed
and now you can't tell right from wrong
No clue about divine spirit consciousness
Completely unaware that something else is there
Beyond your superficial profile
Class is in session
And if you don't study well during these school days
You may wind up stuck in a mind maze
Stiff as a board, lost in a haze
Unable to raise your consciousness
To the next phase
And now with divine expression
I bring to you the High Priest Kwatamani who is in charge of the lesson
And class is now in session*

<u>High Priest Vocals:</u>
*Zig zag, new fashion, new fad
She gotta have it, and he got it bad
Seeking to get the things mama and daddy never had*

FULFILLING THE SACRED ANCESTRAL PROPHECY OF THE TRIPLE NINE: UNVEILING THE PROPHETIC 2012 MELTDOWN OF THE LOST AND ASTRAY PALE STATE OF MIND

Steeped knee-deep in misery, aches and pains
Playing off of new sex and violence games
And now hard-core violence is just not enough
to replace the lusting desire for new things and stuff
Sick, afflicted, diseased, mind scattered
Obese populations growing fatter and fatter
Wait a minute, wait a minute, let's stop the chitter and the chatter
Let's cut to the chase and get to the heart of the matter
Although a racist ideology has been pushed in your face
Let's uncover the face that's behind the lace
and I'm sure we'll be able to solve this case
with style and grace
And when we follow the funk and the stanky smell of the bloodstained trail
It will lead us straight to the feet
Of the power base of deceit
And that will tell us a lot about the stuff we eat
And when we follow the rot and the stench
of this bloodstained trail
It will lead us straight to the pits of hell
Where the Children of the Sun turned pale
And heads would swell
due to the mutation of the feeder cell
Right now, right up until this day
We all wish that those lost and astray Children
had not lost their way
And turned the entire planet into a victim of prey
Now, if we could just keep moving with style and grace
And move real fast, we can crack this case
And not get all hung up in race

INNERLUDE: UNDENIABLE TRUTH: LESSON ONE

So, now, let's just keep moving on
And examine new habits, new addictions and old jones
Now, let's talk about supply and demand
And what one would do to get all that they can
And let us not forget that when demand exceeds supply
Somebody will die
Regardless of how much Mother Earth wails and screams and moans and cry
And there would be absolutely too much misery, aches and pains
At the core of this supply-and-demand game
And there would be too much toxic sound
And too many trees would continue to be cut down
Until the ground itself would frown
The laws of supply and demand
Would ignore the Children of the Sun's basic needs
The rainforest would be destroyed
Just to prepare a place
for the hunters and herders' cows to feed
And to control supply and demand
One would mastermind terminator seeds
And to further control one's lusting greed
One would mastermind a clone breed
Comprised of a materialistic lusting population that would do anything indeed
And it would not matter how much toxins is spread in the air
And it would not matter how much misery, aches and pains one could bear
It would not matter how much sex and violence is there
It would not matter if all things are fair
It would not matter how the Children of the Sun

FULFILLING THE SACRED ANCESTRAL PROPHECY OF THE TRIPLE NINE: UNVEILING THE PROPHETIC 2012 MELTDOWN OF THE LOST AND ASTRAY PALE STATE OF MIND

scream and holler
In the death consumption culture
the bottom line is all about the dollar
And in the cesspool and the shadows
of toxic waste and greed
Is where all the disciples and the followers feed
Stripped, ripping and raping the land
Controlling the supply and manipulating the demand
Implanting gods and demons up inside your head
And you swear to these gods and hope to die
Creating a demand for graveyards and a casket supply
And there's nothing the I in I have said that you can deny
Now that the I in I have exposed the various degrees of
stuff and things that keep you locked down
in this masterful con game
Now that we've exposed the bloodstained trail and the
cold of the death-consumption culture born and bred in
the deep-freeze mentality of the pits of hell
We're going to close this session with Priestess Gail

<u>Royal Priestess Vocals:</u>
Study well and learn the nature of the energy
 that moves through history
Energy that moves through history
History
The nature of the original man, do not fail to understand
Understand
And learn the lesson well, lesson
The tests of time do tell, time do tell
The golden rule: The energy that you consume
The energy that you consume is your fuel

INNERLUDE: UNDENIABLE TRUTH: LESSON ONE

Is all that you can live and all that you can give
To foe and friend
To foe or friend
It's all that can return
It's all that will return to you again
Children of the Sun, comprehend
the movement that was begun
When the lost and astray wandered
from the Sacred Garden Culture way

Chapter One:
A Most Supreme
Unseen Movement

Chapter 1 Prelude:
Ancestral Prophecy

Song 2 from "Supernatural Healing Serum, Dose Two," Kwatamani musical CD release, 2006

<u>Royal Priestess vocals:</u>
Prophecy, it was foreseen
Mother spirit cried for this time to arrive
There would come a time upon the earth when the
Children would awaken
When the spirit presence would be shaken to rise above
the rubble and decay of a mind lost and astray
A sacred one would come to be
Amassing from cycles and cycles and cycles of recycled
whole-life energy to return a presence upon the earth,
long forgotten, but long foretold from times of old
A wholly messenger to sound the call
High Priest Kwatamani, aah
Answering the mother spirit's call

<u>High Priest vocals:</u>
Self-define, realign, reject the vibrations
of a lost and astray mind
Trying to atone and figure out what went wrong
and why divine spirit consciousness
been gone for so long
Time to reject the death-consumption-culture tribe
Time to resurrect the sacred garden culture
and come alive
Plots, schemes, tricks, connive
disconnected from the spirit vibe

FULFILLING THE SACRED ANCESTRAL PROPHECY OF THE TRIPLE NINE: UNVEILING THE PROPHETIC 2012 MELTDOWN OF THE LOST AND ASTRAY PALE STATE OF MIND

Ancestral patience grown very thin
Lust, lies, illusions, dominating sin, understand the trend
Remind me of a time just before the sacred garden
culture was on its rapid decline
And just after the Most Supreme Seen and Unseen had
shown the Divine Children of the Sun the danger signs
Before these times, we did not see or understand
the lost and astray mind
Before these times, we did not understand
a flesh-eating man
We certainly did not understand
a man who would rape, murder, steal or kill
We certainly did not understand
a Man, He and She, honoring a bloodspill
We could not understand
a man who eat of blood, flesh and bone and skin
We could not understand
a man who would waver and bend
We knew of no man who would use tricks and deception
to enslave and abuse and misuse another man
The Children of the Sun had no idea of what that
northern wind would blow in
But they would be properly introduced
to the lost and astray Children of the Sun
with the pale skin, the Children
who would introduce them to sin
And so these pale Children would fake and murder
rape and steal and take
And play a game of innocence, or so it would seem to be
Doing everything they possibly could
to get the mother spirit to side with He and She

CHAPTER 1 PRELUDE: ANCESTRAL PROPHECY

Although innocent on the real
they seemed to have understood the deal
Whoever controls the hands that rock the crib
controls the Children for real
Mother looking innocently to get the Children
to come back in
But the Children were lost and astray in the mind full of
lust, lies, illusions, confusion, death and deadly
destruction, oh my, these Children were full of sin
But mother spirit had compassion
Supreme Love Spirit feel
The mother spirit would do every single thing she could
to get these Children to heal
Father spirit listening to mother spirit's cry
And for father spirit, mother spirit he could not deny
Father spirit opens the door
lost and astray Children come in
Short notice, everybody learned
they were dealing with a beast of sin
Murder, rape, steal and take, kill, and mother spirit still
would beg the ancestors to give her an answer and give
her the key to heal these Children
from the ice-cold, deep-freeze insanity
And mother spirit could not understand why it was
so difficult for these Children to realign, to train
And mother spirit could not understand why these
Children perpetuated lust, lies, illusions, confusion, death
and deadly destruction against everything
So the mother spirit would consult the High Priest
Yes, the mother spirit would consult the Chief
And so, all of the master healers would gather
to provide some divine relief

FULFILLING THE SACRED ANCESTRAL PROPHECY OF THE TRIPLE NINE: UNVEILING THE PROPHETIC 2012 MELTDOWN OF THE LOST AND ASTRAY PALE STATE OF MIND

Queen Mother, mother spirit of the land, mother spirit
the mother of every He and She of Man
Mother spirit, the mother of
the sacred garden culture clan
Mother is the nature of the land
Mother is the nature of the fruits of the trees of Life
in fact, mother is the nature
of the Most Supreme master plan of Man
But not only did these lost and astray Children
have no honor for sisters or brothers
these lost and astray Children had no honor for mother
Rape, murder, steal and take, kill
to serve a worshipping blood spill thrill
And although the High Priest and elders would do
everything they would come to know
It had become very clear
that these lost and astray Children had to go
Simply because the ancestral spirit of the sacred garden
culture could not tolerate this anymo'
Not only would these lost and astray Children kill
an animal to consume of its blood and bones and flesh
and skin and feet and hand
These lost and astray Children would kill
to consume another man
These lost and astray Children
would know no divine laws, no divine rules
The only thing these Children would come to know
is to implement the vibrations and sensations
of the low, down, dirty blues
And although these Children
would have eventually been forced to go

CHAPTER 1 PRELUDE: ANCESTRAL PROPHECY

They would have left some seeds
in many violent rape attacks
And like a thief in the night, their ghosts and goblins
would find their way back through the DNA track
And the mother spirits would beg and beg and beg
the High Priest for mercy
The mother spirit would beg the High Priest
to find the missing key to heal these Children eternally
And then one sad and dreary day
the death blow would come, and it would not delay
But this time it would be the High Priest
these Children would slay
But during these days and times the High Priest
would leave a prophecy well-defined
And the High Priest would foresee many wars
rape and murder and violent attacks
The High Priest would foresee integration and
assimilation and many, many suntanned Children
getting lost and off track
And those who were responsible to take the lead
would adopt the ways and the means
of the ice-cold, deep-freeze seed
And although the boundaries of this bloodstained trail
had come directly from the ice-cold, deep-freeze hell
The Children of the Sun would join forces
with the Children that were pale
and expand the boundaries of hell
And in this hell the death consumption culture
would be the reality, and it would be led
by the ice-cold, deep-freeze mentality
And they would pollute the water, the soil and the air
and would push Mother Nature 'til she could not bear

FULFILLING THE SACRED ANCESTRAL PROPHECY OF THE TRIPLE NINE: UNVEILING THE PROPHETIC 2012 MELTDOWN OF THE LOST AND ASTRAY PALE STATE OF MIND

These Children would pollute their own holy temples,
altering and burning their hair and skin
working desperately to blend in
And sometimes they were foe
and sometimes they were friend
in fact, the only thing that divided the suntanned Children
and the pale Children was the color of their skin
During the last days and times of this lost and astray
mind, they would become so blind
that they could not even see the danger sign
And sickness and disease would show
that the lost and astray mind was pleased
And they would become so big and fat
sick and affliction walking on feet
all because of toxicity that they would eat
And the Man, He and She, relationship would become so
scarred being torn apart
And the cure to these relationship games would be
homosexuality as a cure to the pain
From physical slavery to mental slavery
from Crusades to Holy Wars
from political to economic wars
Man, He and She, ripped and torn and scarred
But out of all this conflict would come harmony
as mother has asked it to be
And the ice would begin to melt, and the water would
begin to rise in the sea
And Mother would speak from hurricanes and tornadoes
and desert storms
All of the earth would begin to warm

CHAPTER 1 PRELUDE: ANCESTRAL PROPHECY

And the lost and astray Children would be forced to deal
with the Holistic Living Truth about Supreme Love
or the consequence of rejecting divinity
And then in the last breath
the High Priest said to the mother spirit
"Mother, although it looks to you like I'm about to go
in fact, the I in I will return back
with a divine intervention
to put the Sacred Garden Culture
and the Divine Children of the Sun back on track."

<u>Royal Priestess vocals:</u>
Divine Children of the Sun, prophecy has been fulfilled
The sacred one has come

Chapter One: A Most Supreme Unseen Movement

The movement within the Most Supreme Unseen had to be forwarded upon the seen, and the I in I emerged as a whole life presence to fulfill this divine intervention. The first of three 9's upon the planet were spent getting adjusted to the fact that the I in I was a supreme soothsayer, soul seer and spiritual healer who had no priority greater than resurrecting the sacred ancestral spirit presence of the Divine Children of the Sun and the Sacred Garden Culture from which we come. Although preparation for the emergence of the I in I was secured and nurtured within a soothsayer lineage, comprehending this mission was a tremendous task for a young sunchild during the 1950's and 60's.

Yes, the I in I would have a tremendous task on my hands. However, the I in I would not hold it against any of my ancestral family for being steeped knee-deep in the death consumption culture. As for my mother Bessie, as so many other struggling suntanned mothers, she would be left to raise her children in keeping with the patterns and programs of the old slavery days. However, the physical shackles and chains were replaced with mental shackles and chains. Her role, as was the role of every other suntanned mother, was to keep the male child in his place and to teach each daughter to take care of "massa's" big house and the social economic structure of the plantation.

FULFILLING THE SACRED ANCESTRAL PROPHECY OF THE TRIPLE NINE: UNVEILING THE PROPHETIC 2012 MELTDOWN OF THE LOST AND ASTRAY PALE STATE OF MIND

By the age of nine, the I in I was beginning to get a grip on the unique qualities and abilities in my connection with the Most Supreme Unseen. In almost every instance, people would ask, "Boy, what's wrong with you? You talking blasphemy. Don't you believe in god?" What they did not understand was that the I in I had no connection with the pale-male-war-god deity. This is indeed a jealous god of vengeance, war, greed and spite. In fact, it was clear to the I in I that the pale-male-war-god deity was a manifestation of an energy that is opposite of Supreme Love and the Essence of Life.

The Raw and Living Vibration

As a very young child, whenever my parents would force me to eat depleted and devitalized substances, the I in I would become sick and afflicted, creating an extensive medical record. There was much concern in identifying the ailment and the condition. The analysis was based on the fact that the I in I would get massive and sudden fevers which the medical specialists had no cure for or comprehension of. It later became very clear that the I in I was suffering from an overdose of the death consumption culture. When the I in I had to be hospitalized, my grandmother had enough ancestral spirit comprehension to observe that eating fresh, raw fruits, vegetables, seeds and nuts allowed me to regain my health. The strange phenomena was that any time the I in I was on the verge of collapse, Grandma Essie would collect me from my sick-bed, take me to her house and nurture me with fresh-picked garden vegetables, such as apples, berries, tomatoes, greens and cucumbers. The I

CHAPTER ONE: A MOST SUPREME UNSEEN MOVEMENT

in I consumed raw and living fruits, vegetables, seeds and nuts as a conscious consumption from a very young age. Unquestionably, my grandparents and great-grandparents were not raw and living foodists. They were simply suntanned country folk who remained on the farm down South, growing vegetables and eating what they grew.

It seemed that no one truly understood what was going on except the I in I and the sacred ancestral spirit presence of Grandma Essie and Great-grandma Nash and Grandma Viola. "Son, don't worry, you've got a special mission. They just don't know, huh," Great-grandma Nash would say just before she started muttering in an unknown tongue. Just think, everybody thought that Old Nash was senile, because she would just stare without speaking and then look at me and smile like we had a <u>serious</u> secret going on between us...

Although it appeared to be a mission impossible, it was a mission ordained by the Most Supreme Seen and Unseen ancestral spirit presence of Man, He and She.

The Greatest Weapon

The truth of the matter is that the greatest weapon of the Divine Children of the Sun is, was and has always been divine spirit consciousness. It is unquestionable that the loss of divine spirit consciousness manifested the lost and astray pale state of mind. In truth and reality, the lost and astray pale state of mind has never been about the resurrection of the sacred ancestral spirit presence of the Divine Children of the Sun and the Sacred Garden Culture from which we come. In truth and reality, the lost and astray pale state of mind continues to be about the I-me-my-mine syndrome. It is nothing short of mind consciousness: "mind" or "mine" consciousness, a consciousness of selfishness, a consciousness of disconnection from the sacred ancestral spirit presence of Man, He and She; a consciousness that actually despises the whole life presence, actually despises the holistic living truth about Supreme Love; a consciousness that despises wholesome mental, physical, and spiritual health and well-being; a consciousness that does not, in any way, perpetuate the Essence of Life and Supreme Love.

Yes, the I in I would grow to comprehend much, too much for others to appreciate. Each and every encounter would provide a positive learning experience as the I in I emerged from childhood into adolescence and adulthood. As Great-grandma Annie Nash had spoken, the I in I was obligated to survive nine battles of the six attacks, and then, nine years after that, the sacred ancestral prophecy would be revealed. Never again to be concealed.

My maturing years occurred during a historical period which spanned segregation, the Civil Rights Movement, women's liberation, hippies, flower children, Black Panthers, COINTELPRO, the Vietnam Conflict, and many other social eruptions within the death consumption culture. These events served to show the I in I how cold-blooded, vicious and chaotic all of the disciples and followers of the opposite energy can be. My objective would be to survive the tracks and traces of the bloodstained trail.

During these earlier periods of time when the general population was completely unaware of raw and living foods, the I in I was seen as weird, insane and from outer space. However, those who tasted the raw-and-

CHAPTER ONE: A MOST SUPREME UNSEEN MOVEMENT

living-foods dishes that the I in I created such as the Original Pyramid Loaf and the Original Klem Burger, i.e. the Cabbage Sandwich could not deny that they were delicious. The foothold of this whole life energy was birthed in the mid 60's in Malaysia where the I in I created the Original Kwatamani Kush made from legumes. Not only was a spiritual war being waged during that time, the so-called Vietnam Conflict was also being waged.

The destructive forces of the energy that is opposite of Supreme Love and the Essence of Life were expressed in the brutal acts of violent bloodshed and the atrocities of the war mentality. Within a tropical environment blighted by the cold and pale acts of military aggression, the I in I experimented with various exotic fruits, such as lychee, jackfruit, durian, mangoes, coconuts and assorted leafy green vegetables, including sea vegetables, seeds and nuts. Exquisite earth and sea vegetable dishes began to manifest, such as the popular Kwatamani Seaweed Roll.

Upon returning the U.S. in 1969, the consciousness era had started to emerge with radicals, revolutionaries and hippies. Yet, no one was truly on the sacred ancestral mission of divine spirit conscious change from deep within. The supreme solar relationship had been completely interrupted within suntanned communities where descendants of former slaves and sharecroppers, had completely forgotten their sacred ancestral ways of divine consumption. The I in I maintained a specific focus on attempting to sway the malnourished minds of my soul-food-eating kin, i.e. dead, devitalized, and soulless food-eating kin. However, it seemed that the

FULFILLING THE SACRED ANCESTRAL PROPHECY OF THE TRIPLE NINE: UNVEILING THE PROPHETIC 2012 MELTDOWN OF THE LOST AND ASTRAY PALE STATE OF MIND

mentally and spiritually enslaved suntanned Children had become so adjusted to eating toxic waste, slave scraps and the other consumption patterns of the hunting and herding culture that they were too addicted and afflicted to change.

There were only a few surviving lineages of ancestral consciousness that endured the brutal breaking process and insidious assimilation process inflicted upon the suntanned Children during the era of the savage and vicious invasions of the pale ones from the Caucasus mountain and steppe regions. These first cold-blooded waves of pale invasions would be followed by more of the same that would include the Trans-Saharan Slave Trade, the Trans-Atlantic Slave Trade, Reconstruction and the Jim Crow era. These lines of ancestral consciousness had managed to endure the many historical acts of invasion, conquest, colonization, and religious contamination that had been inflicted upon the Children of the Sun since the emergence of the energy that is opposite of Supreme Love and the Essence of Life.

The I in I would continue to focus on identifying and appealing to the Sacred Few. The vigor and vitality of my holistic living mission centered on divine consumption for the brain, the body and the spirit with divine expression in words and action. During this time, the I in I was engaged in serious street research. Known as the Griot, wearing a buba and dashiki, styling a large afro, dark shades and walking staff, the I in I would throw down truth lyrics that called upon the suntanned Children to re-connect with their sacred ancestral spirit consciousness. This was a time when "black pride" was

CHAPTER ONE: A MOST SUPREME UNSEEN MOVEMENT

making a ripple in the mass consciousness. Black nationalists, black militants and revolutionaries were at the forefront of demands for social change. Spoken-word artists, such as Gil Scott Heron, the Watts Prophets, the Last Poets, Bodacious Boo-gorillas, Amiri Baraka, Nikki Giovanni and others were expressing a need for change in the social scene.

One of my popular pieces, *So Many Ways in the Way of Change*, echoed the fact that there was very little change going on beyond the appearance of things. This was before COINTELPRO did its thing and before the drug culture would reign and the social welfare programs would become the primary plot and scheme to further divide the suntanned family unit, further devastating the mental mindset of the suntanned youth.

All the while, the I in I continued to create delicious raw and living recipes such as the Original Live Sweet Potato Pie, Marinated Collard Greens, Live Okra and those profound dishes that the I in I have kept within the secret places – the ever-popular Ol-Meks Supreme, the Nile Valley, Kwa-Touli and the Kwa-Tamale. Since there is a heavy Cajun accent in the family, the I in I created Jumba-Liva and Live Gumbo. The challenge of transitioning individuals to a raw and living vibration became a daily practical focus. It was clear that individuals who are functioning with a malnourished brain would never be able to reason divinely or even address resurrecting the sacred ancestral spirit presence of the Divine Children of the Sun and the Sacred Garden Culture from which we come.

This sacred man-child would spend over twenty years outside of the land called the U.S.A. It would truly

FULFILLING THE SACRED ANCESTRAL PROPHECY OF THE TRIPLE NINE: UNVEILING THE PROPHETIC 2012 MELTDOWN OF THE LOST AND ASTRAY PALE STATE OF MIND

be a time of learning, a time of study, a time to comprehend the necessities for divine spirit consciousness. From the anchorages of Alaska through Canada down through the Americas and into the various elements of Central and South America, the Malaysias, Japan and Asia, Europe and Afrika, it became clearly understood that the death consumption culture was dominant in the lost and astray mind. The energy that is opposite of Supreme Love and the Essence of Life continues to dominate the earth and threaten the existence of all of Man, He and She, and every other living thing. Every sign and every twist and every turn was a signal that divine intervention was an urgent necessity for all of Man, He and She, who were being dominated by the death consumption culture and suffocated by the energy that is opposite of Supreme Love and the Essence of Life. The I in I would speak of a time when Greenland would truly become a green land as the earth would begin to show a new direction for the He and She of Man. During these times, many would chuckle at the I in I.

All this was preparation for the prophetic time of the gathering.

The Gathering Time of the Sacred Few

Three cycles of 9, marking the second 27 years leading up to 1999 would be especially intense for the I in I as High Priest Kwatamani. In order to fulfill the sacred mission of resurrecting the sacred ancestral spirit presence of the Divine Children of the Sun and the Sacred Garden Culture from which we come, the I in I

CHAPTER ONE: A MOST SUPREME UNSEEN MOVEMENT

had to develop the skills and acquire the tools to spiritually mastermind neutralizing the energy that is opposite of Supreme Love and the Essence of Life. Although the ninth battle of six would indeed occur during my return to the U.S., it would oftentimes appear to be impossible for the I in I to escape the trials and tribulations of the war-torn areas of Sierra Leone and Liberia.

During all of this struggle and strife, there was indeed a mother spirit, a presence who stood toe-to-toe through the grudging situations. This magnificent young feminine presence had been left to care for this sacred man-child by his Queen Mother who had in fact met up with unforeseeable circumstances that occurred due to a car accident. Although, this young mother spirit would not be allowed to travel with this glorious man-child and his children, the I in I made a promise, an oath of allegiance with her as we prepared to depart so that she would later make the sojourn. She had shown the loyalty, the strength and the might to stand as a mother spirit within a divine interventionary presence. She would serve as the bridge between the old and the new emergence of the Kwatamani Royal Family.

In late 1997, the I in I and my family would somehow miraculously escape the blood diamond areas of Sierra Leone and Liberia and return back to the U.S.A. to prepare for the Divine Gathering of the Sacred Few. This first cycle of the Triple Nine, 1999, would lead to a course of comprehension that would affect the sacred few so deeply that the sacred ancestral spirit presence would be forwarded eternally. However, 1997 would only be the beginning of seeing the after-effects, the adverse

FULFILLING THE SACRED ANCESTRAL PROPHECY OF THE TRIPLE NINE: UNVEILING THE PROPHETIC 2012 MELTDOWN OF THE LOST AND ASTRAY PALE STATE OF MIND

effects of the death consumption culture and the ice-cold, deep-freeze mentality upon massive populations throughout the U.S.

Needless to say, the rampant effects and side-effects of crack, AIDS, homosexuality; the sick, the fat and the obese; toxic masculine-feminine relationships; single-parent families and so on would be overwhelming. These depleted states of being would simply be a norm within the death consumption culture. This sacred man-child would have the duty, obligation and responsibility to re-seed divine spirit consciousness within a Sacred Few. This sacred man-child, therefore, had a mighty task of putting the family structure and all of its elements back together. Indeed, this man-child had suffered many losses in the process of this cold-hearted spirit war inflicted by the disciples who followed that opposite energy. However, there was a changing of the guard that had been foretold years before, and it had now come time for the sacred ancestral feminine spirit presence to re-emerge out of the rubble and decay of the death consumption culture.

The sacred man-child had expected this gathering of a very powerful family order long, long before. The I in I would indeed open the gateway of divine spirit consciousness in order to have the opportunity to glorify in the Divine Union of One with the sacred ancestral mother spirit. Among these feminine nurturers that would surround the I in I as the Kwatamani Royal Sisterhood, there would be a spiritually dynamic and sensuous Royal Priestess who would emerge to become the sacred ancestral feminine spirit voice, that is, if she

CHAPTER ONE: A MOST SUPREME UNSEEN MOVEMENT

could survive the battle cries of the lost and astray mind. You see, strangely enough, this priestess had witnessed setbacks in times prior to now, lifetimes, one would say, where she was given the opportunity to birth the resurrection of this glorious man-child, but fright and fear would cause her to neglect her divine duties, obligations and responsibilities. Thus, during the divine intervention, this Royal Priestess would emerge again upon the earthly seen with the opportunity to nurture the sacred ancestral spirit presence of the I in I as well as the opportunity to divinely align within the Most Supreme Seen and Unseen Essence of Life and Supreme Love.

Divine Mission

In order to fulfill the divine mission of resurrecting the Divine Children of the Sun and the Sacred Garden Culture from which we come, the I in I had to come forward as a divine example. Clearly, at this point in time, there is no need for a lot of rap, rhetoric, or fanfare. The divine example of all that the I in I bring forward must be nurtured and multiplied within the Kwatamani Royal Family in order for that divine example to be secured within the seen. The I in I am not above the divine laws of whole life energy. As the High Priest Kwatamani, the I in I must embody the divinity of whole life energy in action, or I will be unable to connect with the Most Supreme Unseen essence of all that I am. Therefore, my first and foremost duty, obligation and responsibility as a masculine presence is to divinely submit to the sacred ancestral guidance and protection of the Most Supreme Seen and Unseen in maintaining the Divine Union of One within self. The behaviors,

FULFILLING THE SACRED ANCESTRAL PROPHECY OF THE TRIPLE NINE: UNVEILING THE PROPHETIC 2012 MELTDOWN OF THE LOST AND ASTRAY PALE STATE OF MIND

attitudes and values that are experienced within the energy that is opposite of Supreme Love and the Essence of Life do not, and can not, exist within divine spirit consciousness at all. The Divine Union of One within self means that the brain, body and spirit remain within the vibrations and sensations of whole life energy in complete and total obedience to the Most Supreme Seen and Unseen Essence of Life and Supreme Love.

The Triple Nine

Many may wonder what all this talk about divine spirit consciousness has to do with the sacred ancestral prophecy of the era of 2012. First and foremost, let us make it clear that the sacred ancestral prophecy deals with a significant movement of natural occurrences that coincide with the orchestrated movements of Man, He and She. The interplay of various cycles of energy will manifest events in and around 2009 that reflect a changing tide. This dramatic process of change began within the era of the Triple Nine when the energy of this prophecy was intensified upon the seen. In 1999, during what the I in I have called the Gathering Time, there was an amassment of energy that would proceed through the cycle of nine bringing divine clarity to a most sacred ancestral spirit presence.

For many individuals, 1999 was filled with various rumors about the end of the millennia, rumors about Y2K, rumors about a new age. There was talk about possible end-of-the-world scenarios, scares about massive power outages or computer crashes and predictions about some sort of collapse within the social

CHAPTER ONE: A MOST SUPREME UNSEEN MOVEMENT

order. So-called survivalists started stocking food and water; some individuals headed away from the big cities, and others went to church to pray for safety and salvation during the coming apocalypse. However, within the Most Supreme Unseen, there was an entirely different movement going on. After several generations of intense preparation, 1999 was spiritually year-marked as the Divine Gathering of the Sacred Few in order to forward the resurrection of the sacred ancestral spirit presence of the Divine Children of the Sun and the Sacred Garden Culture from which we come.

During the height of movement in 1999, a steady procession of the curious, the mystified, the truly-inspired, and more than a few skeptics and critics found their way to Kwatamani Royal Feasts of Raw and Living Foods that were held in the West End of Atlanta. As a matter of fact, those weekly community gatherings magnetized a network of individuals, both nationally and internationally, who formulated within the so-called raw-and-living-foods movement as it came to be known in Atlanta. Furthermore, there would be those magnificent gatherings through festivals, such as the International African Arts Festival in New York and the African World Festival in Detroit, as well as through new age/ consciousness raising expos throughout the U.S. Individuals from all walks of life, regardless of race, creed, color, religion or nationality attended, sitting before the I in I asking questions, absorbing as much information as they could consume. These individuals were newcomers to the concepts of divine consumption and did not comprehend even the basics of transitioning from their standard diets of dead, devitalized and depleted food substances, be they meat-eaters, vegetarian or vegan. Many expressed their amazement and delight at the unique, original and totally delicious gourmet dishes of raw and living foods that were acclaimed as the Kwatamani Divine Healing Cuisine.™

The Kwatamani Royal Family would use their project, Kwatamani Raw and Living Foods on the Move™ to spread this vibration nationally and internationally. A primary attraction for many individuals became how to capitalize on what appeared upon the seen as a profitable new social trend, the premiere of a health conscious cuisine with wide appeal. In the midst of the plots and schemes of the pale lost and astray state of mind, the Gathering Time actually signaled the emergence of several sacred spirits who would witness their lives dramatically and divinely changed.

These gatherings even drew the offspring of those who had gathered at the First Innercourse in Philadelphia during the late 1970's, early 80's. The messages that the I in I delivered were taken as an intriguing viewpoint, to say the least, and for a brief time, it appeared to the unsuspecting on-looker that the Kwatamani vibration was the new fad in town. Divine consumption was even becoming a popular phrase spoken with authority by those who enjoyed posing as experts and profound thinkers.

CHAPTER ONE: A MOST SUPREME UNSEEN MOVEMENT

The Test of Time

Although many would come, only the Sacred Few would be able to emerge into the safety zone of divine spirit consciousness. Among the many who would come, there would be masters of the art of fake and pretentious behavior who were very adept at dealing within the death consumption culture. However, their pretense of being humble and ready to follow the vibrations of whole life energy would not serve to disguise their hidden agendas. Their sideline motives did not allow them to stand the test of time.

The emergence of the Kwatamani Royal Family continues to stand the test of time. The divine guidance and protection of ancestral spirits through the I in I as High Priest Kwatamani to the Kwatamani Royal Sisterhood to the offspring is a strong and undeniable demonstration of obedience to the Supreme Laws of whole life energy: divine union, divine consumption and going forward to multiply divinity in the offspring. The Kwatamani Royal Family symbolizes the shape of things to come within the sphere of the Sacred Ancestral Temple of Kwa Ta Man I.

Only after a threshold level has been reached does it appear that events just happen out of thin air, but in truth and reality the unseen process has been well underway in the unseen, only crossing over into the seen after an extensive birthing process. The process of earth shifts and energy changes has already been happening, and now the appearance of things is obvious enough for even the most unaware to begin to see. Over the course of years and many direct challenges, the I in I strengthened within

FULFILLING THE SACRED ANCESTRAL PROPHECY OF THE TRIPLE NINE: UNVEILING THE PROPHETIC 2012 MELTDOWN OF THE LOST AND ASTRAY PALE STATE OF MIND

divine spirit consciousness in order to break through the toxic mental barricades and barriers that have locked down the sacred ancestral spirit presence within. Patience would be the primary lesson that the most supreme ancestral spirit presence would bring to the I in I. And patience would forward the principles and practices of divine humility. When all was said and done, the impossible would be made possible, and the I in I would find myself live and in living color upon the seen to deal with the Divine Gathering whole and clean.

2009: The Second Cycle

Within the many happenings that are connected within the forward movement of divine intervention, 2009 signals the second cycle of the Divine Gathering. This second cycle is marked by expansion upon the seen and the emergence of the Kwatamani Divine Social Economic Family Community. The sacred ancestral prophecy signifies a time of transition, a time when the emerging cycle of whole life energy causes ripple effects of change upon the seen. Within the cycle of life there are no endings and beginnings as one might reference in the toxic parallel. While there is a death consciousness of finite and limited existence within the opposite energy, there is a life consciousness of infinite and unlimited existence within the divine parallel. Therefore, we speak of transition from one phase of energy expression to another. We speak in terms of the garden where there are cycles of planting and harvesting, where old compost becomes new fertilizer, and each ripe fruit carries the seed of its rebirth.

CHAPTER ONE: A MOST SUPREME UNSEEN MOVEMENT

The number nine represents the vibrations of maturity and fruition within any cycle, and signals the forward multiplication of all that has gone before. The alignment of the triple nine that occurred in 1999 marked a circulation of whole life energy for the brain, the body and the spirit moving to the 9th degree in order to prepare for the greater movement of Divine Oneness into divine spirit consciousness. This circulation of whole life energy would continue and enter into a second cycle of nine, beginning in 2009. The first phase of energy amassment will manifest as many events upon the seen that mark the era of 2012. However, the year 2012 will only be one third of the way into the forthcoming whole life earth-shift change that will cause mass effects upon the social, economic and religious orders of the opposite energy.

Although the supreme anointing of the Sacred Ancestral Temple of Kwa Ta Man I will occur on the ninth day of the ninth month of the ninth year, those within the apocalypse syndrome will remain focused on predictions of dramatic changes that are expected to occur in or around 2012. There would be no way for another model of reality to be seen, heard or focused upon, because there would be no divine spirit conscious reasoning. Only the Sacred Few among the few would be able to reason with the nature of the energy shifts that are occurring.

The Era of 2012

As we move into the era of what is called 2012, the bottom would start to fall out of hell. Hell would indeed be experienced by the lost and astray pale state of mind.

FULFILLING THE SACRED ANCESTRAL PROPHECY OF THE TRIPLE NINE: UNVEILING THE PROPHETIC 2012 MELTDOWN OF THE LOST AND ASTRAY PALE STATE OF MIND

Hell would be engineered within the social, economic, political and religious structures of the death-consuming culture. The disciples and followers would bring about hell on earth as they glorified in the all mighty and omnipotent pale-male-war-god deities. The disciples and followers of the opposite energy would not be able to fake and pretend their way into divine spirit consciousness, into divine clarity, or into the divine parallel.

The I in I have come to bring Supreme Truth. The I in I have come to resurrect the Sacred Ancestral Temple of Kwa Ta Man I and call forward the royal ancestral priestesses and priests upon the seen to bring divine guidance, divine protection and divine nurturing once again to the most supreme ancestral spirit presence of Man, He and She. The focus of all that one will read within this text is actually to prepare one to enter a greater thought and reasoning, to be able to identify the toxic thoughts, tastes and smells of the toxic parallel if one has the divine will to come forward. The wholly trilogy, *The Holistic Living Truth About Supreme Love, Book One, Book Two* and *Book Three*, was to prepare a sacred few for a greater comprehension presented from 1999 up until this point in time. Yes, the *Holistic Living Truth About Supreme Love, Book One, Book Two*, and *Book Three* provide an introduction to the attitudes and behaviors that have been perpetuated within the death-consuming culture of paleness. These texts are accompanied by the *Supernatural Healing Serum* CD series, featuring musical expression, traditional rhythms and spoken word to bring forward truth lyrics. As well

CHAPTER ONE: A MOST SUPREME UNSEEN MOVEMENT

as the powerful Kwatamani presentations *Conjuring Ancestral Spirit Consciousness* and *12th Hour Prophecy: The Pale Curse and the Solarized Energy Shift*.

The concepts, definitions and historical overview that were laid out in the wholly trilogy were given to provide a new framework of thought and reasoning. This introduction paved the way for an even greater exploration of the opposite energy in the comprehensive text, *Exposing the Ice-Cold, Deep-Freeze Mentality and Whole Life Healing of Sexual Energy within the Divine Parallel*. And then there is the comprehensive reference source, entitled *Raw and Living Foods: The First Divine Act and Requirement of a Holistic Living Way of Life*. The focus of this text is to address the need to consume whole life energy, because without the ability to fuel and nourish the body, one's whole life movement is severely limited. Yes, the consumption of raw and living fruits, vegetables, seeds and nuts is the first divine act and requirement of a holistic living way of life. One must begin to nourish the brain, body and spirit with raw and living fruits, vegetables, seeds and nuts to begin an infusion of whole life energy. Without divine fuel, it is impossible for a malnourished brain to function beyond the weak and feeble thoughts and reasoning of the opposite energy. So long as one is a consumer of dead, devitalized and depleted energy, there is no way to have enough strength to move beyond the toxic parallel.

It is time to move far beyond the lost and astray mind and begin to examine every possible way to exit this cold and pale state of being entirely. This is the time to open completely to divine knowledge, wisdom and understanding and enter the advanced stages of detoxing and purging so that one can approach the divine parallel whole and clean.

The Steps to Resurrection

If the I in I were to ever practice impatience, irritation, anger, condemnation, arrogance and acts of ego gratification, then the I in I am in no position to bring forward anything to anyone else except contradictions and confusion. The male presence has practiced these misdeeds for too long with terrible consequences in his relationships with the feminine presence. In order to even speak of providing divine guidance and protection to the feminine presence so that divinity can be nurtured, the masculine presence must apply a tremendous amount of self-correction through detoxing and purging.

The steps that the I in I have taken are the only steps that can lead one out of the energy that is opposite of Supreme Love and the Essence of Life. In fact, the steps that the I in I have taken can and must be followed tenaciously in order for any resurrecting spirit, masculine or feminine, to enter within divine spirit consciousness. Any other route will definitely lead one deeper into the many ego trips of that opposite energy. It can be very easy for the masculine presence to get side-tracked on a pale ego trip where he can "big-up" on someone else and feed his lost and astray ideas of how big and strong he is.

Divine humility appears to be especially difficult for the masculine presence, because, in a disconnected state of being, there are so many physical and superficial ways to define strength that have absolutely nothing to do with divine spirit consciousness. The requirements of divine

CHAPTER ONE: A MOST SUPREME UNSEEN MOVEMENT

humility call for one to swallow an awful lot of false pride and show obedience to a supreme ancestral spirit presence that is far greater than the individual self. To bring this point home, once one swallows false pride, one must be divinely conscious of not spitting it back out on someone who appears to deserve it because of their toxic reactions, lack of comprehension, or utter disrespect for one's presence. Yes, indeed, that false pride must be released as toxic waste from the root of one's behind, i.e. one's toxic mental, physical and spiritual past.

Once finding out that the I in I was responsible for securing a divine mission, it could have been possible within the opposite energy to allow certain information to feed an ego vibration and develop a cocky, arrogant and vain presentation to bring great personal gain. For instance, the I in I have been told that my eyes and voice are hypnotic and can cause a feminine presence to melt. It could have been easy enough to get on a serious ego trip within the opposite energy. However, ego-tripping only leads deep into the far reaches of the emptiness of an over-inflated ego. Claims of spiritual enlightenment and higher consciousness are especially appealing to those within the lost and astray state of mind, because there is a vague notion that the mind has the ability to control the spirit presence. Even if one has money and physical strength within the death consumption culture, it is even more appealing to have access to a power boost of supernatural and unseen energy...that is the egotistical reasoning within the energy that is opposite of Supreme Love and the Essence of Life.

Within the opposite energy, the image of masculine leadership always falls within definitions of power and strength to dominate others, either with greater access to money, knowledge, military might or superhuman abilities. Followers follow leaders and join movements to satisfy their own personal plots and schemes of ego gratification. These kinds of power games and popularity contests occur on a daily basis within the death consumption culture and contaminate every social movement within the history of the opposite energy. The I in I have absolutely nothing to do with those toxic matters of fact.

    The message that the I in I bring forward relates to a holistic living way of life and the necessity for divine social economic family community. If the I in I bring forward this message, and yet the I in I am unable to bring forward a divine example that extends beyond myself, then my message is fruitless. The defining elements of divine masculine presence look very different from the profile that has developed within the opposite energy. Within divine spirit consciousness, the masculine presence is completely obedient to the Most Supreme Seen and Unseen Essence of Life and Supreme Love, working to follow the movement of whole life energy and communicating first through divine action. The requirements of divine humility, patience, the ability to listen, caring compassion, self-discipline and self-control and a steadfast focus on the consumption of whole life energy are the same for both the masculine and feminine presence. In order for the divine social economic family community to grow within whole life energy, the basic qualities of all parts working together for the benefit of the whole must be practiced as a

CHAPTER ONE: A MOST SUPREME UNSEEN MOVEMENT

holistic living way of life. The masculine presence must therefore embody the spiritual principles and practices as a steadfast focus in order for these qualities to be nurtured by the feminine presence.

The I in I have worked by every divine means available to divinely guide and protect the resurrection of the sacred ancestral mother spirit presence within the vibrations of Queen Mother, Queen and Royal Priestess as a collective feminine entity of sisterhood. Without the resurrection of the sacred ancestral mother spirit, there can be no resurrection of the Divine Children of the Sun and the Sacred Garden Culture from which we come. It is only at this phase within the gathering cycle that the I in I am able to communicate whole and clean regarding the Divine Union. It is only at this phase that the Kwatamani Royal Sisterhood can now communicate whole and clean regarding the resurrecting sacred ancestral spirit presence of femininity. It is only at this time that divine social economic family community is possible. In the midst of global warming and other earth-shifting changes, it is only at this time that a land base with the capacity to support and maintain divine social economic family community has been secured and occupied as the Sacred Ancestral Sanctuary of the High Priest Kwatamani and the Kwatamani Royal Family.

Make no mistake about it, the only reason why the I in I am able to speak whole and clean is that the I in I continue to maintain a tenacious focus on detoxing and purging the opposite energy from within the environmental presence in which I stand. The key point to remember here is that nobody, absolutely nobody, within the social economic environment of what has been

FULFILLING THE SACRED ANCESTRAL PROPHECY OF THE TRIPLE NINE: UNVEILING THE PROPHETIC 2012 MELTDOWN OF THE LOST AND ASTRAY PALE STATE OF MIND

declared as "civilized" culture or any other culture influenced or intruded upon by "civilized" culture has been left uncontaminated by that opposite energy, directly or indirectly. Contamination occurs, regardless of one being blonde or bald or natty, natty dread, regardless of the color of one's skin.

And now it is resurrection time for the Children of the Sun, and it requires every available energy of divine intervention in order to implement this sacred mission. Therefore, for the I in I to even have the nerve to undertake the task of gathering a divine and sacred few, the I in I must have enough divine humility and patience to understand the level and degree of damage inflicted by the lost and astray mind that consumes of the death consumption culture and its opposite energy.

If a masculine presence who has enough will to undertake this challenge does not fully comprehend the damage that has been done, there is no way for that masculine presence to lead himself out this insanity let alone lead the ancestral mother spirit or any offspring that are born of this death-consumption culture experience. In truth and reality, the ancestral mother spirit, or should I say the essence of femininity, is a natural and innate nurturer. The reason why the Children of the Sun are in such a horrifying state of being at this time is because that opposite energy has been brought forward for her to nurture. This will go on until all of Man, He and She, has perished from the face of the earth unless the sacred ancestral father spirit can humble himself to the Most Supreme Seen and Unseen ancestral spirit presence in order to provide divine guidance and

CHAPTER ONE: A MOST SUPREME UNSEEN MOVEMENT

protection. This can not and will not ever be done through the foul acts of sex and violence, war and crime. No, no, none of the acts of lust, lies, illusions, confusion, death and deadly destruction will allow the ancestral masculine spirit to penetrate the whole life presence of the sacred ancestral mother spirit.

For these reasons, it is necessary that the I in I bring forward a divine example to set the pace for the masculine presence and the feminine presence. Bringing forward the Kwatamani Royal Family is therefore a necessity for the survival of the sacred ancestral spirit presence of the Divine Children of the Sun and the Sacred Garden Culture from which we come. A divine example demonstrates that the resurrection of the sacred ancestral spirit presence of the Divine Children of the Sun and the Sacred Garden Culture from which we come is indeed possible.

Divine Reasoning

Sitting here thinking about all the blood that was spilled down in old Ethiopian mud, sitting here thinking about all the land that was occupied by He and She of the old Ethiopian man, sitting here thinking about Egypt and Sudan, having flashbacks about Iraq and Iran, sitting here thinking about the glorious suntanned peaks, having a glorious flashback on Italy and Greece, sitting here thinking about the time when the earth was sane and the suntanned He and She of Man, occupied Portugal, France, England and Spain, pumping the Supreme Love spirit that the suntanned Man, He and She, once claimed.

Yes, sitting here thinking about the old Ethiope when old Europe had a solarized ray of hope, and then

FULFILLING THE SACRED ANCESTRAL PROPHECY OF THE TRIPLE NINE: UNVEILING THE PROPHETIC 2012 MELTDOWN OF THE LOST AND ASTRAY PALE STATE OF MIND

there is a flashback of all the southeastern land, from China to Malaysia, East Asia and into Japan, and the glorious time spent there by the original dark and lovely He and She of Man.

It is my ancient memory on which I rely. I sometimes break down and cry about the Black Untouchable lie and the glorious Indus Valley that my glorious sisters and brothers did once proudly occupy. A glorious ancient land where the pale ones would rally, the glorious ancient land where massive suntanned death tolls would be tallied. There was massive suffering, misery and dread as the pale male warlords arrived with savage cries of "slaughter the black head" and another innocent and unaware father or son was left dead amidst the thrill of the kill and the blood spill. Did these sacred ones die, or did they simply resurrect into the sacred ancestral spirit presence of the I in I?

When I look deep into divinity, it becomes easy for the I in I to see, the great irrigation lands, the magnificent planting and harvesting, and that wonderful Sacred Garden Culture that spread throughout the land of these Kushite Nubian people of the dark and lovely Dravidian suntan. Oh the Ethiopian land, oh, the dark and lovely He and She of Man.

What a Most Supreme master plan until the dark and lovely He and She of Man met up with the stale, pale lost and astray Children who lost divine spirit consciousness of mind, their sacred ancestral spirit and their golden tan. When I tap into my memory bank, there is absolutely no way to end the text without the glorious reflections of the Ethiopian He and She of Man in the

CHAPTER ONE: A MOST SUPREME UNSEEN MOVEMENT

Australian land and all of the South Seas and the glorious Olmeks of all the other America land, the first He and She occupants, Divine Children of the Sun with the golden tan.

Then comes the time when I get a little vexed as I move on through my memory text and begin to encounter the massive stale and pale lie, all the blood-spilling deception that no one can deny. Even with all emotions under control, even the Most Supreme Seen and Unseen have to break down and cry. So where do you think that leaves the I in I? Somebody has got to correct all that this opposite energy holds as status and success. And this death consumption culture, Man, He and She, must correctly address, because it is simply a cold-blooded killer's mess where murder, rape, steal and take would be at its best. And this would be what the pale-male-war god himself would bless. This deception of love can fill a heart with sad emptiness, especially witnessing the opposite energy and the death consumption culture claiming lost and astray minds so easy to impress.

When I look from ancient ancestral eyes, it becomes so easy to see these cold and pale deceptions and lies. It seems that the religious fanatics just cannot reconcile the days of the cold and frozen times of the Ice Age and then connect with the Sacred Garden Culture fertile crescent mud and the melting of the ice and the floods that would come during the day by night and then would be followed by the great white flight, trying to escape that cold frostbite of the white blight, a vicious and deadly cold-blooded kin who lost their melanin, their mind and their connection to the sacred ancestral spirit within. So they would bring with them another flood as they would

FULFILLING THE SACRED ANCESTRAL PROPHECY OF THE TRIPLE NINE: UNVEILING THE PROPHETIC 2012 MELTDOWN OF THE LOST AND ASTRAY PALE STATE OF MIND

carry out blood spill in the old Ethiopian mud. And the war-god spirit that was once the primary occupant of hell, would rape, murder, steal and take, pollute and dilute, leaving a lost and astray pale state of mind to dwell.

The dwelling place of this toxic seed would be the toxic offspring of a confused warlord half-breed who would forsake the sacred ancestral spirit and reject the Sacred Garden Culture creed to uphold the cold-blooded invaders and their pale-male-war-god lead to become grand masters of deceit. These half-breed warlord tribal clans would call themselves the chosen ones with great storytelling plans. They would steal the sacred ancestral texts of the Divine Children of the Sun with a golden tan. They would honor the pale-male-war god's bloodstained trails and alter the original texts to run their sneaky little tales and call these deceptions holy books based on the appearance of how a thing looks. And what a story they had to tell; they would run their lies and deceptions so well that the stories they told on parchments of animal skin would be the story of how the downfall really did begin, tracing every step of lust, lies, illusions, confusion, death and deadly destruction to the bitter end. Strangely enough, it would be through these texts, that Man, He and She, would be led to Armageddon, an apocalypse trail straight back into the gates of hell.

When the suntanned Children did not want to follow this most deceptive plan, things did not go too well. The disciples and followers of this war god would slaughter and behead them as infidels. If believers had any questions or had anything else to say, they would simply

CHAPTER ONE: A MOST SUPREME UNSEEN MOVEMENT

be told to pray and they would get their glory by and by, after they die one day. Oh, what a cold-blooded means and way to play with the most supreme ancestral spirit presence of Man, He and She. Oh my, what a load of dues to pay. All of those who would follow these rules would lose.

The I in I do not mean to bring you any bad news, but there are fatal consequences for the disciples and followers of these pale lowdown dirty blues. It's a healing time, a most supreme healing time, and what is required is a divine spirit conscious state of mind. It's a most supreme healing time to leave the lost and astray mind behind. It is indeed a time to realign with divine knowledge, wisdom and understanding of a divine spirit consciousness state of mind. It is indeed a time to resurrect the most supreme ancestral spirit presence and reconnect then and now with now and then beyond the mind of thought and the body of flesh and blood and bones and skin. The time is now to go deep within reversing the pale and toxic attitudes, behaviors and color-coded plots, schemes and trends that adversely affect the planet Earth now and that adversely affected the planet Earth then. It's time for a change beyond the change game, where ain't nothing changed except the name of the game while the mass majority make no change beyond praying and hoping for this hellish, pale game to change.

Chapter 1 Innerlude:
Same Game, Different Name
Original version 2006, unreleased

<u>Royal Priestess vocals</u>
Same game, different name
Same game, different name
Same game, different name

<u>High Priest vocals</u>
Same game with another name played the same
Bip, bam, it's a scam
Driving the Children insane
And while you sit and worry about UFO's and chemtrails
The toxic stuff you drink and eat retards your
taste and smell
As the fat, sick and addicted lead you down this
bloodstained trail
Deep within your mental tomb, you dream of
doom and gloom
While the ghosts that live inside your head seek and
search the stuff you read
Causing you to hallucinate on the resurrection of the dead
Same game that you've been fed, born again and inbred
Flocking, stocking and jocking
Seeing divine spirit consciousness as cock-blocking
Living in dread, hearing absolutely nothing the I in I
have said
In truth and reality you scared
Trapped in the tricks and the deceptions of the same
game with a another name you've constantly been fed
Same game with another name altered and changed

FULFILLING THE SACRED ANCESTRAL PROPHECY OF THE TRIPLE NINE: UNVEILING THE PROPHETIC 2012 MELTDOWN OF THE LOST AND ASTRAY PALE STATE OF MIND

Alacazam it's a scam, retarding your brain
Different name for the same game rearranged
Lust, lies and illusions driving the Children insane

<u>Royal Priestess vocals</u>
Same game, different name
Same game, different name
Same game, different name

<u>High Priest vocals</u>
Same game with another name played the same
Using lies and deceptions to keep things the same
Same game, different name under a freedom claim
Taking the shackles and the chains from the feet and hands
And then placing them on the brain
Fueled by every stroke that one sniff, snort and smoke
And every toxic treat that one drinks and eat
Same game, different name
Pale religions claim
Using a different name to play the game to gain fortune and fame
Same game, different name
Over and over, I've traced this thing
And every track and every trace
The Children of the Sun face disgrace
Same game, different name
Played the same
Using a different name for the same game while expecting thangs to change
Same game with another name pushed in your face

CHAPTER 1 INNERLUDE: SAME GAME, DIFFERENT NAME

Within this track and its trace, no ancestral base
Different name for the same game, religion and race
Brother trapped in a prison cell
Sister trying to get play
Different name, down-low game altered and changed
Bip bam, thank you ma'am was the name of this game
Different name for the same game of opposite
energy fame
A mind of your own is what you claim
Continuing to play this game
Different name for the same game, perpetuating this lie
Stuff and things you sell and buy
To get you a piece of the pie

<u>Royal Priestess vocals</u>
Bip bam, bip bam, it's a scam
Same game, different name
Took the shackles from your feet and hands and put them
on your brain
And put them on your brain
Same game, different name
Driving the Children of the Sun insane

<u>High Priest vocals</u>
It's a cold and spiritless game
It blinds, cripples and maims the brain
Feasting off the death-consuming values of misery,
aches and pains
A suffering, capitalizing game
Using many different names
Offspring born, bred and trained
To play this deep-freeze game
Seeking and searching for someone to blame

FULFILLING THE SACRED ANCESTRAL PROPHECY OF THE TRIPLE NINE: UNVEILING THE PROPHETIC 2012 MELTDOWN OF THE LOST AND ASTRAY PALE STATE OF MIND

OD'ing off the mainframe of this thang
Struggling and striving to maintain this game
Feeling that if it is color-coded, it will change
Nipped and tugged, feeling truly humbugged and calling it love
While on the prison rug
Two tough thugs kiss and hug
And in the meantime, the revolutionary mind
Is well defined by the thoughts that come from a deep-freeze state of mind
And the lost and astray mind that is deaf, dumb and blind
Leave no ancestral generation for the next future time
And the generation next on a jones stone cold to the bone
Trapped knee-deep in the fright and the fret and the deception and the regret

But, wait a minute
Wait a minute, wait a minute, wait a minute
Wait a minute, we ain't done yet?!
We ain't done yet!

Continuing to play the same game
With the same and different names
Pale, color-coded fallacies
Deceptions sugar-coating a toxic reality
And ain't nothing changed, but the name of the game
And for those trapped within that cold-blooded vicious circle
It is a guarantee that things will remain the same

CHAPTER 1 INNERLUDE: SAME GAME, DIFFERENT NAME

<u>Royal Priestess vocals</u>
Same game, different name
But no one said you had to play
Nobody said you had to stay
You are the one who makes it that way
And, in truth, the game is done
Nobody won
Sacred ancestral resurrection has now begun
In the midst of the confusion
With the Children lost and astray
The High Priest Kwatamani has returned to show the way
Sacred ancestral spirits from the Most Supreme Unseen
Supreme emergence upon the seen
The ancestral root, bearing the tree
That bears the fruit that sends forward the seeds of divinity
Sending forward the seed of divinity

**Chapter Two:
Spiritual War**

Chapter 2 Prelude:
Introduction:
12th Hour Prophecy

Song 1 from "12th Hour Prophecy: The Pale Curse and the Solarized Energy Shift, Kwatamani musical CD release, 2008

<u>Royal Priestess vocals:</u>
Time to heed the sacred ancestral call
To the supreme soothsayer, soul seer
and spiritual healer, High Priest Kwatamani
Exposing the pale cold of the rising fall

<u>High Priest vocals:</u>
There'd be a war going on, a spiritual war that turn the entire planet Earth into a white blight zone
Yes, indeed there'd be a spiritual war and the opposite energy would appear to be winning so far
And the signs of the times would show
that the lost and astray mind
Was handcuffed and bind by spiritual crime
And the gray ghost would wine and dine
on a confused state of mind
And the victims of prey would get high and get drunk
And would pray in his name
Jamming the lanes of the fast food chains
While the mentally insane would walk about, raping and stealing and taking people out

FULFILLING THE SACRED ANCESTRAL PROPHECY OF THE TRIPLE NINE: UNVEILING THE PROPHETIC 2012 MELTDOWN OF THE LOST AND ASTRAY PALE STATE OF MIND

And you couldn't really tell if these were human beings,
clones or worker drones
Even if you were standing right next to one
on the telephone

And every thug and gangster rap
and every song that one sang
would make it very clear that a love supreme
would have nothing to do with this
although it would become very clear
that there was a deep-seated love
for the pain game and just one more hit
of that toxic addiction that one just can not quit
And this pale insane game of pain
is driving the ancestral mother spirit insane
Once such a sweet, fine sexy thang
Now growing sick, fat, obese toting this monkey
on her back trying to gain fortune and fame
And as the first teacher who would install
the mental and physical attitudes and behaviors of all
She would become the primary target
used by this cold-blooded, pale opposite energy
to self-install paleness into all
And the ejaculation trail of this cold-blooded energy
stale and pale would lead the Children of the Sun
straight to hell
And sacred ancestral masculinity
had become completely minimized
No divine guidance, no divine protection
no supreme ancestral affection
And neither he nor she had any recollection

CHAPTER 2 PRELUDE: INTRODUCTION TO THE 12^(TH) HOUR PROPHECY

that would pinpoint the divine knowledge, wisdom, and
understanding of their most supreme ancestral connection
And so the Children of the Sun would spend an entire
life wishing and hoping and praying to the energies of
hell
Until the Children of the Sun themselves would turn pale
And from these days well seen
They would produce offsprings who would sing
and dance and rap a different theme
calling each other "ice" and whoes and niggas
bitches and dogs during the days of the final fall
And stuff would begin to move fast and furious
within the gates of hell out there
And the rot and the stink and the funky smell would
pollute and contaminate the fresh air
But this was a spiritual war and all would be fair in this
stale and pale game of love and war
And every disciple and follower
would seek to be a super star
And although one would feel vague and empty within
The deceptive ability to front, fake and pretend
Would make it very easy for one to produce
a cocky, arrogant and confident grin
And although esteemlessness and insecurity
would be at its greatest height
All would be seen as well
within this white blight

Chapter Two: Spiritual War

Yes, it's a spiritual war, and the opposite energy appears to be winning so far. Deception and disguise have kept the energy that is opposite of Supreme Love and the Essence of Life in full operation, and so long as one remains entangled in the death consumption culture, one continues to be an instrument of that opposite energy. The ancestral prophecy that is brought forward within this text is a prophecy of resurrecting the Divine Children of the Sun and the Sacred Garden Culture from which we come.

There is a prophecy that directly relates to that energy that is opposite of Supreme Love and the Essence of Life. The opposite energy has its own paths to its own truth. It has been made divinely clear from the Most Supreme Seen and Unseen Essence of Life and Supreme Love that all entanglement with that toxic parallel must cease and desist. The toxic parallel is the sum total of the death-consuming culture that has been bred by the energy that is opposite of Supreme Love and the Essence of Life.

A mighty struggle is occurring within the toxic parallel as the suffocating effects of depletion squeeze the last breaths of life energy out of the weak and feeble consciousness of Man, He and She. The truth and the consequences is that as the squeeze occurs within the lost and astray mind, the ego flares with explosive reactions and defensive attacks and emotional breakdowns. Perhaps, one has experienced these symptoms of residing within the hostile environment of the toxic parallel within self. Whether one lives in the obvious urban war zone of

FULFILLING THE SACRED ANCESTRAL PROPHECY OF THE TRIPLE NINE: UNVEILING THE PROPHETIC 2012 MELTDOWN OF THE LOST AND ASTRAY PALE STATE OF MIND

ghetto life or the comfortable suburban gated communities of covert war games or somewhere in between, one's living space within the death consumption culture is a mind field of hostile aggression. Every bit of life energy within the toxic parallel gets preyed upon, and so it appears that the weak get weaker while the strong get stronger.

Blatant ignorance and common deception are still dominating the minds of Man, He and She, at this late date of self-destruction within the death consumption culture. Daily headlines and personal accounts of stress and strain, conflict and confusion in everyday encounters are the signs of the times. Even as the symptoms of social disorder and disorder within individuals become more and more obvious, the mass majority of Man, He and She, continues with business as usual. The complaints of mental, physical and spiritual dis-ease and disorder become more widespread, and the energy that is opposite of Supreme Love and the Essence of Life continues to cause a depletion of life energy.

The vibrations of deterioration are now even more obvious in the overweight and bloated bodies and within the troubled outcries of emotional instability. When an obese individual continues to eat yet another meal of devitalized food substances, and a smoker takes yet another puff of his or her cigarette, and a devoted religious believer gives in to yet another temptation of sin, the addictive and depleting effects of the energy that is opposite of Supreme Love and the Essence of Life can be identified. Depletion and deterioration are key vibrations within the energy that is opposite of Supreme

CHAPTER TWO: SPIRITUAL WAR

Love and the Essence of Life, and the mental, physical and spiritual signs of breakdown and imminent collapse are common sights.

Within the toxic parallel, master predators do exploit mass populations and feed their gnawing hunger for power, control and domination through manipulations that keep the mass majority of Man, He and She, enslaved to the energy that is opposite of Supreme Love and the Essence of Life.

There are two separate and distinct energy fields that are presently upon the earth. These energy fields form and define two completely opposite states of being. The consciousness of Man, He and She, is the war zone, and the outcome is a matter of life and death. Only a sacred few will emerge from the rubble and decay of the final conflict where the opposite energy will inflict every means of attack to gain and maintain greater control and domination within the minds of Man, He and She. And the manifestations of violence, war and hostile aggression are the outer projection of the unseen movements of the energy that is opposite of Supreme Love and the Essence of Life. Thus are the signs of these days and times.

There is a definite earth-shift divide between the toxic parallel of that death-consuming energy that is opposite of Supreme Love and the Essence of Life and the divine parallel of the solarized whole life energy that is the Most High Essence of Life and Supreme Love. We must take time to identify this divide so that one does not get caught in the tricks and traps of deception while assuming that one is walking an imaginary thin line between the two parallels. We must fully identify the

FULFILLING THE SACRED ANCESTRAL PROPHECY OF THE TRIPLE NINE: UNVEILING THE PROPHETIC 2012 MELTDOWN OF THE LOST AND ASTRAY PALE STATE OF MIND

problem so that the divine solution can be comprehended. The problem is that there is a spiritual war and the intruding and invading vibrations of that opposite energy are constantly on the attack. In order for the Divine and Sacred Few to resurrect, they must remove themselves from the toxic parallel and stay out of harm's way as that opposite energy feasts upon its death-consuming culture until the bitter end. That is the nature of the beast.

This text reveals the sacred ancestral prophecy that has been preserved within divine spirit consciousness. Therefore, this text will be very different and unique for the reader, especially if one is still impressed and intoxicated by one's indulgences in the death consumption culture. The fulfillment of the sacred ancestral prophecy will usher in the next phase of the Gathering of the Divine and Sacred Few who have recognized the sacred ancestral call to resurrect the Divine Children of the Sun and the Sacred Garden Culture from which we come.

The Divine Parallel

The divine origin of Man, He and She, began within the energy of the Most High Essence of Life and Supreme Love. The Most High energy is the energy which creates, sustains and reproduces life as a whole life presence. The whole life presence is represented by brain, body and spirit—the divine union of consciousness, physical form and life energy. The I in I reference this Most High energy as whole life energy. Within the solar system of Man, He and She, the sun

CHAPTER TWO: SPIRITUAL WAR

generates whole life energy for all life upon the planet Earth.

The term Divine Children of the Sun, i.e. the sacred suntanned Man, He and She, describes Man, He and She, within the wholeness of his and her natural and innate state of being within the divine order of earth, wind, rain and sun. Living within the divine order of a natural and innate connection with the sun indeed creates a presence that reflects this supreme solar relationship. The natural and innate consumption patterns of the Divine Children of the Sun reflect this supreme solar relationship beginning with the consumption of raw and living fruits, vegetables, seeds and nuts.

The green leafy plants are the first-level food producers for the planet. The food chain begins at the source of the sun with the green plants converting solar energy for food. The consumption of raw and living fruits, vegetables, seeds and nuts provides the optimum fuel to nourish the whole life presence of Man, He and She, as the supreme creation of divine spirit consciousness.

The green pigment in the plants reflects a supreme solar relationship where whole life energy is absorbed, consumed and transformed into divine fuel. The black, brown, red and yellow melanin pigments of the solarized suntanned complexion reflect a supreme solar relationship within the Divine Children of the Sun. These earth tone pigments that range from the terra-cotta reds, the rich blacks and browns and golden hues absorb, consume and transform whole life energy into divine fuel. The color pigments of the fruits of the trees of life and the color pigments of the Divine Children of the Sun bring home the theme that the natural color scheme of the Sacred Garden Culture from which we come is black, red, gold and green.

The natural and innate environment of the Divine Children of the Sun reflects a supreme solar relationship. The tropical and sub-tropical climate regions of the planet represent the unity of earth, wind, rain and sun that provides the natural habitat for Man, He and She. Within the tropical and sub-tropical environments, the fruits of the trees of life provide a garden paradise. The Sacred Garden emerged within the solarized ecology of abundant plant vegetation, thick tree growth – producing clean, oxygen-rich air, sparkling mineralized waterways, warm temperature range and, of course, plenty of sunshine. The culture or way of life within the Sacred Garden reflects the supreme solar relationship of earth, wind, rain and sun and upholds the principles and practices of divine consumption, i.e. the mental, physical and spiritual consumption of whole life energy.

The Coming of the Toxic Parallel

The sacred ancestral prophecy foretold of a time in the existence of the Divine Children of the Sun when a completely different and opposite cycle of energy would emerge upon the planet. All that was known within the Sacred Garden Culture was the nature of whole life energy. All that was known was the divine order of earth, wind, rain and sun and Man, He and She, living with a sense of cooperation, collective responsibility and respect for all living things. Communications received from the Most Supreme Seen and Unseen Essence of Life

CHAPTER TWO: SPIRITUAL WAR

and Supreme Love revealed the movements of whole life energy so that the divine social economic family community could remain in sync, in tune and in time with the rhythms of life.

The prophecy that foretold of the coming of the energy that is opposite of Supreme Love and the Essence of Life was received with reverence, but the comprehension of what was meant was not whole. It was not possible for the Divine Children of the Sun to know what the opposite energy was all about, although the warning was to leave it alone and move away from its manifestation upon the planet Earth. Throughout time upon the earth, there have been cycles of cooling and warming that have caused drastic changes in certain environmental regions. The center land of the Earth, nearest the equator, is more moderately affected during these times of climate change and environmental fluctuations. During the various migrations that had occurred, sea-faring travels and land expeditions were conducted by the Divine Children of the Sun. The migrations populated the planet with the suntanned presence of Man, He and She. The movements of the Divine Children of the Sun were coordinated through the energy movements of the Most Supreme Seen and Unseen.

Sacred ancestral warnings to prevent unfavorable movement into life-threatening regions obviously went unheeded, and groups of Children of the Sun ended up far from their natural and innate environment in the midst of global changes. These unaware and isolated groups became stranded in a changing environment that turned snowy white and icy cold within an Ice Age ordeal that

FULFILLING THE SACRED ANCESTRAL PROPHECY OF THE TRIPLE NINE: UNVEILING THE PROPHETIC 2012 MELTDOWN OF THE LOST AND ASTRAY PALE STATE OF MIND

lasted for hundreds of generations. This snowy white and icy cold environment is what we call the White Blight. The prophecy foretold of the coming of the energy that is opposite of Supreme Love and the Essence of Life, and it also foretold of the ending of this pale and toxic energy cycle. However, in truth and reality, the unseen essence of this prophecy foretold of the resurrection of the sacred ancestral spirit presence of the Divine Children of the Sun and the Sacred Garden Culture from which we come.

The energy that is opposite of Supreme Love and the Essence of Life reflects the paleness of separation from the solarized environment of the Sacred Garden Culture. The vibrations of life are easily visible in the colorful vegetation within the garden. On the other hand, the cold and lifeless absence of solarized vibrations is easily visible in the white blight of the freezing ice and snow. The absence of whole life energy over an extended period of time would eventually breed, seed and feed mutation and degeneration producing a pale state of being. The lack of whole life consumption would cause mental, physical and spiritual depletion. For example, the physical manifestation of paleness resulted from DNA error or mutation and a lack of solarized relationship.

The energy that is opposite of Supreme Love and the Essence of Life originated in a deep-freeze environment that was opposite from the natural and innate habitat of Man, He and She, where the divine order of earth, wind, rain and sun was severely interrupted. Consequently, the mental, physical and

CHAPTER TWO: SPIRITUAL WAR

spiritual consumption of whole life energy of Man, He and She, was severely interrupted causing a disconnection from divine spirit consciousness.

Disconnection from the whole life energy causes an interruption in the forward movement of life. When forward movement is interrupted, stagnation begins to produce a degenerating state of being. The truth and the consequences of the emergence of the energy that is opposite of Supreme Love and the Essence of Life gave birth to a harsh and cruel reality of violence, bloodshed, war and crime. This opposite energy has festered into the current trends of the death consumption culture where sex and violence, war and crime are the signs of the time.

Getting an understanding of the attitudes and behaviors that are manifested by this opposite energy is only the first step. One will not be able to follow the tracks of the opposite energy as it now exists during these modern times without having a historical overview of how this mutated and degenerated vibration came to be in the first place. However, what must be understood is that all points of standard historical reference have been distorted and contaminated by the lost and astray, opposite state of mind. Therefore, it is absolutely necessary that the I in I call upon the Most Supreme Seen and Unseen ancestral spirit presence of Man, He and She, in order to provide divine clarity to you. Be clear that all that the I in I bring to you within this text is of the wholeness of a divine set-up. Through the grace of the Most Supreme Seen and Unseen ancestral essence of the Sacred Temple of Kwa Ta Man I, the I in I shall dig deep in order to provide a greater level and degree of divine spirit conscious insight.

FULFILLING THE SACRED ANCESTRAL PROPHECY OF THE TRIPLE NINE: UNVEILING THE PROPHETIC 2012 MELTDOWN OF THE LOST AND ASTRAY PALE STATE OF MIND

Exposing the Nature of the Toxic Parallel

Our goal and objective is to provide a way to expose the nature of the opposite energy so that it can be seen and identified for what it is—a foreign, toxic, depleting, mutated and degenerated presence. Once seen and identified, it becomes easier for one to identify the many different disguises and deceptions that have manifested through time and continue to plague the lives of the mass majority of Man, He and She, to this very moment. The disguises and deceptions of the toxic parallel are all fueled by an energy that is completely opposite of the sacred ancestral spirit presence of Man, He and She, an energy that is opposite of the Sacred Garden Culture from which we come. This energy is opposite of the divine creation that is our origin as the Divine Children of the Sun. What is being said here is that the opposite energy is completely opposite of the Most Supreme Spirit of Love and the Essence of Life.

In order for such a cold and pale vibration to manifest from a toxic unseen energy into a toxic physical form, the environmental conditions would have to be completely opposite of the Sacred Garden Culture. In other words, it is impossible for a opposite energy to be expressed within the whole life energy of the divine parallel. Indeed, this opposite energy had to come from somewhere else that was totally foreign and opposite of the sunny and warm climate of the region that gave birth to the Divine Children of the Sun. During Ice Age cycles upon the planet Earth, certain vast regions of the planet became desolate frozen wastelands where snow and ice

CHAPTER TWO: SPIRITUAL WAR

were all that showed upon the horizon. The barren cold of this deep-freeze environment was the icy birthplace of the cold and dank vibration that filled the northwest Caucasus cave areas and then eastward to the Russian steppe region. The Children of the Sun became lost and astray and then entrapped within these icy lands for thousands of years.

The first generations of lost and astray Children who experienced the snow and ice were totally unprepared mentally or physically for the icy howling winds and the frozen white blight. The mutation and degeneration of the Children of the Sun was a torturing ordeal of starvation, malnutrition, disease and nutritional deficiencies resulting from the lack of sunshine and raw and living fruits, vegetables, seeds and nuts. The first cycles of complete disconnection from the sacred ancestral spirit presence were an inner torment of misery. Generation after generation, the natural and innate presence of these lost and astray Children became degraded and deformed over time as the DNA coding deteriorated into the errors of massive mutation and degeneration. The wretched screams of the lost and astray Children echoed in the cold caves that became the festering womb of the opposite energy upon the seen.

Within ancient times, sacred ancestral soothsayers, royal priestesses, and priests foretold of the coming of the energy that is opposite of Supreme Love and the Essence of Life within the consciousness of Man, He and She, before its first appearance in physical form. The energy that is opposite of Supreme Love and the Essence of Life can be described as an absence of whole life energy or a lifeless state of being. The act of opposing

FULFILLING THE SACRED ANCESTRAL PROPHECY OF THE TRIPLE NINE: UNVEILING THE PROPHETIC 2012 MELTDOWN OF THE LOST AND ASTRAY PALE STATE OF MIND

the natural and innate movement of whole life energy causes an opposite energy movement to occur. When one disconnects from the whole life energy by going a separate and opposite direction outside of divine spirit consciousness, then one enters an entirely opposite parallel of energy in mind consciousness.

Mind consciousness is that consciousness of thought and reasoning that focuses on domination and control over all living things regardless of the consequences, i.e. mind over matter. It may easily be referred to a "mine" consciousness or "mind" consciousness, and it is the source of the I-me-my-mine syndrome. It is indeed that source of thought and reasoning that was consumed and projected by such personalities as Genghis Khan when he expressed that his greatest thrill in life was conquest via the destruction of the defeated males and the taking of their wives and the other females as concubines. It is that selfish and greedy consciousness that causes a raping, raiding savage to declare himself as civilized while declaring those that he preys upon to be uncivilized heathens. It is only through the concepts of mind consciousness that one can claim the will of a god as one's justification for invading and enslaving innocent populations. It is only through the disguises of mind consciousness that one can claim spiritual enlightenment while maintaining the attitudes of racial superiority.

It is through this penetrating vibration of mind consciousness that a female can prostitute her body and a male can pimp this ordeal or become a low-profile gigolo. And the breeding, seeding and feeding of mind consciousness is a necessity in order for one to become a

CHAPTER TWO: SPIRITUAL WAR

drug-addict, alcoholic, or a consumer of the death consumption culture while becoming fat, obese and bloated with sickness and disease. Although we are using the term mind consciousness here, another way to identify this consciousness is the lost and astray pale state of mind. This mind consciousness is at work instigating water pollution, air pollution, soil pollution and depletion of Earth's natural and nonrenewable resources. The pollution and depletion caused by mind consciousness can, and does indeed, cause hazardous and life-threatening earth-shift changes. This mind consciousness is truly of the toxic parallel, because it represents all movement that negates, opposes and endangers the natural and innate essence of life and supreme self-love. In other words, this mind consciousness is the fueling source of thought and reasoning with the death consumption culture.

The sacred ancestral spirit presence of whole life energy is completely different from anything that one could possibly encounter within the opposite energy of the death-consuming culture. It is as though one has been living within a toxic ocean and can not even comprehend that one is drowning in toxic vibrations and sensations even as one's life presence grows weaker and more feeble. Often an individual will fall prey to the commonly accepted idea that one can simply focus on positive energy and somehow elevate one's consciousness beyond the opposite energy that one consumes. It seems difficult for many individuals to comprehend that one is a sum total of the energy that one consumes mentally, physically and spiritually. Mind consciousness is fueled by toxic mental consumption,

FULFILLING THE SACRED ANCESTRAL PROPHECY OF THE TRIPLE NINE: UNVEILING THE PROPHETIC 2012 MELTDOWN OF THE LOST AND ASTRAY PALE STATE OF MIND

toxic physical consumption and toxic spiritual consumption.

The savage and brutal acts of a survival-of-the-fittest mentality grew in the freezing cold. Mind consciousness grew out of the intense desperation and emotional trauma of being isolated and trapped within a hostile environment, initially separated from one's ancestral family community, vulnerable to attacks from human and animal predators, and in a constant struggle to secure one's survival. Out of this starving desperation grew a cold-blooded-like carnivorous, cannibalistic breed of mankind that mutated and degenerated deep within the core of the DNA. This breed would declare itself as a superior breed based on savage aggression and mercilessness, and the cunning, conniving and swift ability to slaughter, rape, raid or invade as a way of life. These were the factors that created severe mental stress and strain leading to extreme mental disorder. This way of life lasted for hundreds of generations, day by day, breeding a mankind that became more and more of a reflection of the cold and pale mutation and degeneration.

The death consumption culture was born and bred in acts of slaughter and conquest, combat and warfare where physical might and the ability to swiftly kill positioned a violent and aggressive mentality at the top of the social order. Slavery, domination and stealing from the weak, hording the booty and plunder of raids, human and animal sacrifices, and killing as a daily means to survive are the death-consumption-culture ways and means. Many may insist that the death consumption culture is their innate and natural way of life. The death

CHAPTER TWO: SPIRITUAL WAR

consumption culture is not the natural and innate way of life for Man, He and She; it is a culture born and bred of an energy that is completely opposite of our most supreme ancestral spirit presence as the Divine Children of the Sun.

It is not coincidental, nor is it by chance, that the Sacred Ancestral Temple of Kwa Ta Man I, as the centerpiece of the Sacred Ancestral Sanctuary of the High Priest Kwatamani and the Kwatamani Royal Family, is located in the same region once occupied by the ancestral Olmeks and their Mayan offspring. In January 2008, an archeological team ushered past the Kwatamani Sacred Ancestral Sanctuary to begin excavation of ruins that have been identified as housing a royal family and temple complex of an ancient population. These ruins have been reported as one of the most significant finds of its kind. The excavation site borders a rainforest jungle preserve which happens to be next to the land base for the Sacred Ancestral Sanctuary of the High Priest Kwatamani and the Kwatamani Royal Family. Only a tiny strip of land that serves as a jaguar path in the jungle now separates the two properties. Is this all by coincidence, or is there an unseen relationship between the sacred Ancestral Temple of Kwa Ta Man I and the ancestral prophecy of 2012?

There are no coincidences within the universe of the Most Supreme Seen and Unseen Essence of Life and Supreme Love. Within the divine order of whole life energy, each incident is a significant event that reveals some part of a whole pattern of unseen energy within the seen. The Sacred Temple of Kwa Ta Man I symbolizes the spiritual strength of the Sacred Garden Culture where

FULFILLING THE SACRED ANCESTRAL PROPHECY OF THE TRIPLE NINE: UNVEILING THE PROPHETIC 2012 MELTDOWN OF THE LOST AND ASTRAY PALE STATE OF MIND

the sacred ancestral spirit presence is amassed in the seen and communicated and preserved within divine spirit consciousness for the divine guidance, protection and nurturing of the Divine Children of the Sun. The Temple, the High Priest, royal priestesses and priests were the first targets of destruction when it became clear and evident that the Divine Children of the Sun could not be conquered by mere physical violence and threat of slaughter. Divine spirit consciousness could not be penetrated until the connection between the Most Supreme Seen and Unseen was broken. Once those who embodied the Most Supreme Seen connection with the Most Supreme Unseen were removed as the center strength of the Sacred Garden Culture, conquest was only a matter of time. The ultimate breaking occurred when Man, He and She, began consuming the energy that is opposite of Supreme Love and the Essence of Life and began to submit to the pale-war-god deity of the toxic parallel.

The I in I carry forward an ancestral promise of return to divine order. Therefore, the ancestral prophecy surrounding the era of 2012 is no less than the revealing of a pattern of whole life energy. The correction of errors which have indeed run their course was only a matter of time. The I in I am present to carry forward a sacred mission as ordained within the Most Supreme Unseen, and that mission is the resurrection of the Divine Children of the Sun and the Sacred Garden Culture from which we come. All things in and around this mission are the acts of divine order.

CHAPTER TWO: SPIRITUAL WAR

The energy that is opposite of Supreme Love and the Essence of Life is depleted and devitalized energy that is unwhole because the vital connection with the Most Supreme Seen and Unseen Essence of Life and Supreme Love has been totally broken. In a very real sense, the disciples and followers of the opposite energy have become separated and disconnected from the whole life unifying force which is the Essence of Life and Supreme Love. It is not seen that one's consciousness exists within a toxic parallel of energy that is opposite of Supreme Love and the Essence of Life and that no power of thought, visualization, or affirmation will actually move one anywhere except deeper within the toxic parallel. The only way to exit the toxic parallel and to move into divine spirit consciousness is to release the toxic disorder, i.e. to detox and purge the attitudes, values, beliefs and habitual ways and means of consuming toxic mental, physical and spiritual energy. We make note that this process must be in sync, in concert and in alignment with the consumption of whole life energy, mentally, physically and spiritually.

Pale Privileges, Benefits and Rewards

The idea of resurrecting one's sacred ancestral spirit presence is an unheard of proposition with no intrinsic value within the death-consuming culture. If one could imagine the vibrations and sensations of resurrecting one's sacred ancestral spirit presence, there is no incentive to even consider such an idea. One is kept busy in a false life of faking, shaking and pretending to be the image of success.

FULFILLING THE SACRED ANCESTRAL PROPHECY OF THE TRIPLE NINE: UNVEILING THE PROPHETIC 2012 MELTDOWN OF THE LOST AND ASTRAY PALE STATE OF MIND

So long as there is another credit plan, the lost and astray pale state of mind becomes very complacent and pacified in being maintained as a well-used pawn within the death-consumption-culture plan. Unfortunately, there are enough different games to keep one hopping from one game to another, seeking to be a player's player. So, like well-trained clones and worker drones, the suntanned Children continue to follow behind the lost and astray pale state of mind all the way into the hell and damnation of their doom and gloom.

What indeed would be necessary at this time is for the suntanned Man, He and She, to cease and desist maintaining loyal allegiance to the disciples and followers of this opposite energy and take a divine leadership role. However, the delusions and illusions of fortune and fame and success have caused them to maintain the same thinking and reasoning as the pale-skinned Children who mutated and degenerated in the ice. There may indeed be a sacred few among the mutated and degenerated pale breeds of Man, He and She, who desire to resurrect the sacred ancestral spirit presence of the Divine Children of the Sun. The mass majority are deep-seated in seeking to attain and acquire the assumed rights of passage that the white-racist ideology is supposed to provide them for being of the white race.

CHAPTER TWO: SPIRITUAL WAR

Suntanned Disciples and Followers of Paleness

The mass majority of suntanned Children have become deep-seated in the death-consuming culture and its materialistic games of success, fortune and fame. These suntanned disciples and followers have actually entrusted the religions and social economic systems of the death-consuming culture to maintain their lives and the lives of their offspring. Many fantasies, illusions, delusions, and dreams have kept so many suntanned individuals entrapped in a lifetime of trivial pursuits and toxic consumption with the hopes that someday, somehow he or she will make it big like the powerbrokers of the death-consuming culture.

Listening to the gullible, the ignorant and innocent who speak of their big plans and their big deals, one would get the impression that living large is the death-consuming-culture way. While one is busy following the formulas for success, one can not see how the death-consuming culture actually works. There is no desire to even consider that the entire death-consuming game is a losing proposition. If things do not materialize as desired within the toxic parallel, one finds yet another way to come up with yet another formula for success for one's self or one's offspring.

Many suntanned Man, He and She, experienced the effects and after-effects of the social, economic and political movement within the death consumption culture referred to as the Civil Rights Movement. The generation that inherited the outcome of this movement was led to believe that education and employment opportunities would open a whole new road to success

FULFILLING THE SACRED ANCESTRAL PROPHECY OF THE TRIPLE NINE: UNVEILING THE PROPHETIC 2012 MELTDOWN OF THE LOST AND ASTRAY PALE STATE OF MIND

within the death consumption culture. However, the results of integration and assimilation that were key elements within the civil rights doctrine produced children of the movement who completely melted into a pot of paleness, adopting the image of the dominant culture and further rejecting their sacred ancestral spirit presence. Those who best upheld the cultural values of the death-consuming culture found that they received the favors and benefits of being accepted as the new color-coded clones and worker drones, i.e. the "new house slaves."

This description may cause offense to those who proudly claim that they now have attained the class and status and credentials to be looked at as suntanned powerbrokers within the death-consuming culture. The fact remains that only those who jump through the approved hoops and perform the required tricks receive the desired treats of fortune, fame and success within the death-consuming social order. Every hoop and every trick is determined from within the thought and reasoning of a state of mind that was born and bred within the energy that is opposite of Supreme Love and the Essence of Life. With such a focus on imitating the image of the lost and astray pale Children and submitting to the values, attitudes, beliefs and behaviors that define the death-consuming culture, one is never, ever able to gain a focus on one's sacred ancestral spirit presence. One actually surrenders all of one's mental, physical and spiritual being to the vibrations and sensations that originated in the mutation and degeneration within the

CHAPTER TWO: SPIRITUAL WAR

energy that is opposite of Supreme Love and the Essence of Life.

Only a being who has completely disconnected from his or her sacred ancestral spirit presence could ever bow down and worship the image of those who worked to destroy the presence of his or her ancestors. Only a being who has no ancestral memory could disregard the historic invasions, rape, murder, stealing and the brutal taking of life that destroyed one's sacred ancestral ways. Only a broken and pitiful being could imitate the degenerated ways and means that originated in a breed of mankind that represented the dominant expressions of the energy that is opposite of Supreme Love and the Essence of Life. Only a wretched being could practice the self-hate of rejecting one's natural and innate presence that shows a solar relationship such as melaninated skin tone and natural hair texture to copy every mutated and degenerated characteristic possible.

The superficial, fake and artificial beauty standards and cultural values of the death-consuming culture are foreign and dishonorable expressions of an opposite state of being that manifested out of mutation and degeneration in the harsh, cold and freezing ice. And yet, there are those who will remain stuck within the physical identifications of so-called "racial" categories and will not be able to comprehend that the opposite energy is not identified merely by color. The I in I must work to bring forward this clarity so that the Sacred Few will be able to recognize themselves.

There are many questions that pop into the head. Questions such as, "Will there be any white people among the Sacred Few?" and "I feel like I am one of the

FULFILLING THE SACRED ANCESTRAL PROPHECY OF THE TRIPLE NINE: UNVEILING THE PROPHETIC 2012 MELTDOWN OF THE LOST AND ASTRAY PALE STATE OF MIND

Sacred Few, how can I tell for sure?" Within the toxic parallel, these questions are completely understandable and are to be expected. Questions from vibrations of bitterness and suspicion and contempt that were produced by the pain and suffering and misery historically inflicted upon suntanned populations by those lost and astray pale Children. Questions from fright and fear. Questions from vibrations of denial, avoidance, feigned innocence and deception that serve as a pale cover-up for the lost and astray Children of mutation and degeneration who refuse to acknowledge their historical role within the opposite energy. Questions from vibrations of arrogance and selfish greed that keep the disciples and followers of the opposite energy feeling as though one is more entitled to privileges, benefits, and rewards based on the color of one's skin or one's ability to assimilate or break the color line of the paleness state of mind.

The historical impact of the invasions, conquests, murder, rape, enslavement, colonialism, and the violent attacks of pale religious orders committed by the lost and astray Children of mutation and degeneration is an ugly bloodstained trail that charts the complete destabilization of the Divine Children of the Sun and the Sacred Garden Culture from which we come. In fact, the entire scope of the atrocities and brutality committed against Man, He and She, defines the cycle of the energy that is opposite of Supreme Love and the Essence of Life. As the final days of the meltdown play themselves out, one can sense the demise of that opposite energy right before one's eyes. As that opposite energy comes to an end, there must be a divine spirit conscious rise.

CHAPTER TWO: SPIRITUAL WAR

The question, "Will there be any white people among the Sacred Few?" is easily understood when one reviews the historical events that mark the bloodstained trail of the pale breed of mankind. The accounts of what happened when the Taino were invaded by the pale mutated and degenerated breed of mankind reveal the exact same patterns of murder, rape, steal, take and enslavement that have befallen many other suntanned populations of the planet Earth. A Taino chief once expressed the sentiment very clearly:

> Hatuey was a Taino Indian Chief from the island of Hispaniola who was a witness to the atrocities the Spaniards were committing upon his people.
> The Hispaniola Tainos had received Columbus and his fellow Europeans with open arms, and the Spaniards had brutalized the Indians in return. Hatuey sailed to neighboring Cuba and warned the Cuban Tainos about the Europeans.
> When Columbus and his ships showed up, they were received not with open arms but with armed resistance. Eventually Hatuey was captured by the Spaniards and prepared for burning at the stake.
> A Spanish priest asked Hatuey if he wanted to repent from his sins and be baptized before being burned at the stake. The baptism, promised the priest, would ensure that Hatuey go to heaven and live happily among the Christians. Hatuey asked if the bearded white men would go to heaven when they too died. The priest nodded yes and said that the Spaniards would go to heaven because they were good Christians.
> *"In that case,"* replied Hatuey as the flames began to lick at his feet, *"I want to go to hell."*
> Michael Auld at Fondo del Sol: An Art Review
> By F. Lennox Campello, originally published in *Visions Magazine for the Arts*

FULFILLING THE SACRED ANCESTRAL PROPHECY OF THE TRIPLE NINE: UNVEILING THE PROPHETIC 2012 MELTDOWN OF THE LOST AND ASTRAY PALE STATE OF MIND

Many scholars explain the annihilation of the Taino by pointing to the introduction of European diseases in the Americas. Indeed, the introduction of small pox, measles, whooping cough, bubonic plague, typhoid, influenza, Malaria, and yellow fever wiped out an important section of the Taino population whose immune system was not accustomed to those diseases. For example, the outbreak of the small pox epidemic in Espanola in Dec 1518 extinguished about one third of the native population in a few weeks. What must however be understood is that the decline of the population also occurred in years when there was no epidemic.

The main factor in the Taino population reduction directly results from Spanish obsession for gold and the establishment of the Encomienda and the Repartimiento, which destroyed the rhythm of their lives, and their social structure. The Taino family structure was broken up as the men were sent to work on gold mines all over the island. They suddenly faced the obligation to spend most of their day working for a master whose cruelty and punishments were swift and justified by greed. Malnutrition quickly developed and the Taino suffered from protein deficiency and overwork. Another factor was the deliberate cruelty the Spaniards displayed towards the Indians. In their inexorable march for conquest in the island, the Spanish destroyed and burned entire villages. The treacherous massacre of the Taino of Xaragua was one of the most cruel and complete mass killings of Taino on the island.

An Indian chief who was being executed was about to be baptized. The priest promised him that if he did get baptized, he would go to paradise. He asked the priest: "Are there any Spaniards in your heaven?". The priest responded that only good ones go to heaven. At

CHAPTER TWO: SPIRITUAL WAR

> those words, the chief refused the baptism retorting that "even the best one of them is worth nothing; I do not want to go to any heaven where I stand to meet one"

One thing is for sure: there will definitely not be anyone of the lost and astray state of mind who can transition into the holistic living presence of the divine parallel, regardless of the color of one's skin. There is no entry into the divine parallel for anyone who maintains the ways and means of the opposite energy. In fact, one will not even be able to connect with the movement of resurrecting the sacred ancestral spirit presence of the Divine Children of the Sun and the Sacred Garden Culture from which we come unless one detoxes and purges the lost and astray mentality that breeds, seeds and feeds the death-consuming culture of the opposite energy.

The truth of the matter is that once one has detoxed and purged the opposite energy, then the entire nature of one's presence divinely changes, mentally, physically and spiritually. However, the process of detoxing and purging is impossible for anyone who remains steeped knee-deep in the opposite energy. The paleness factor then has always been, and remains, a question of energy. The question has indeed been answered within this text. The only question is whether the answer is suitable to the lost and astray mind and those disciples and followers of the paleness kind.

The mental disorders and impairments that create such concepts as "white racist ideology" reflect the limitations and shortcomings of having absolutely no way to connect with the Most Supreme Seen and Unseen

FULFILLING THE SACRED ANCESTRAL PROPHECY OF THE TRIPLE NINE: UNVEILING THE PROPHETIC 2012 MELTDOWN OF THE LOST AND ASTRAY PALE STATE OF MIND

Essence of Life and Supreme Love. Not only are we speaking about "white racist ideology" where those of pale skin seek to maintain domination and control by using color to justify the privileges, advantages and benefits that were claimed by invasion, conquest, rape, murder, steal and take. We are also speaking about a unique kind of paleness ideology where suntanned Children use the same vibrations, thoughts, and reasoning born and bred off of "white racist ideology" to maintain color-coded class and caste systems against other suntanned Children. Such superficial concepts that dwell on the outer appearance of things are a flashing sign that one is dwelling in the outer zone of consciousness, within the white blight of an exiled state of being, a state of separation, deep in that opposite energy.

When the I in I use the description "flashing sign," let it be comprehended that we are not speaking about a physical sign. Therefore, if one is only able to deal with what can be seen with the physical eye, one is going to have great difficulty processing this information that addresses unseen senses that are not only unknown but are severely damaged, distorted or dormant. Individuals do not even know that the thoughts that they think carry an energy code and that their entire mental activity within the toxic parallel is contaminated by the energy that is opposite of Supreme Love and the Essence of Life. Therefore, there are many loud and clear flashing signs that identify the lost and astray state of mind, always busy calculating, looking for an issue to debate, vying for position; ready to jump defensive, aggressive or hostile, and always working to maintain domination and control

CHAPTER TWO: SPIRITUAL WAR

within the energy that is opposite of Supreme Love and the Essence of Life.

There is no way to capture the full scope of agonizing pain that was inflicted upon the Divine Children of the Sun at the hands of the lost and astray Children who mutated and degenerated in the ice-cold deep freeze. No words are available to provide a sense of the tragedy that was enacted again and again as the Sacred Garden Culture from which we come became more and more de-stabilized. So many individuals within the toxic parallel have become so numb to the brutality that is practiced by the disciples and followers of the opposite energy that they have very little feeling for the suffering of others. Just as the hunter has no remorse for the hunted, many individuals have become so cold-blooded and pale inside that they can dismiss the most gruesome and vicious acts with cold indifference. Those of the lost and astray state of mind may be anxious to forget, ignore and dismiss the long list of atrocities committed at the hands of the disciples and followers of the energy that is opposite of Supreme Love and the Essence of Life.

It is often reasoned within the depleted state of mind that one can not place blame for historical crimes against humanity that happened hundreds or even thousands of years ago. The concepts of crime and punishment, justice and the judgments of guilt and innocence are tossed around by those who think and reason from the toxic parallel. Every attempt is made by the disciples and followers of the energy that is opposite of Supreme Love and the Essence of Life to be innocent of all wrong-doing and completely justified in the values, attitudes and behaviors of the paleness ideology. How can there be a call for justice that will address the foul and wretched acts that have been committed within the death culture? Do not expect that the masters and grand masters of deceit who are the power brokers and privileged elite of the death-consuming culture will ever acknowledge any fault. The mental mindset of this group of individuals is obsessed with maintaining domination, control and financial wealth by any means necessary. Every social structure within the death-consuming culture is devised as a means to maintain dominance, control and financial wealth for those of the family lines who occupy the power base of deceit.

The legal systems that maintain the law and order of the death-consuming culture, the educational systems that maintain the teaching and learning elements of the death-consuming culture, the religious systems that maintain the morality and values of the death-consuming culture, and every other system and sub-system of the death-consuming culture all work in concert to uphold the disciples and followers of the opposite energy. The entire structure of the social order was erected to validate, support and promote the paleness ideology. Therefore, those who actively indulge in the lost and astray state of mind feel justified, and even glorified, in the death-consuming culture. The death-consuming culture will not change, because the energy of its origin is well-installed.

One cannot remain within the culture of death consumption and expect to be anything more than a disciple and follower of that opposite energy. It was

CHAPTER TWO: SPIRITUAL WAR

amazing that so many individuals have actually read the text, *Exposing the Ice-Cold, Deep-Freeze Mentality and Whole Life Healing of Sexual Energy within the Divine Parallel* and still remain deeply entrenched in the death-consuming culture. As a matter of fact, some of these individuals still communicate with the I in I and speak as if the death-consuming culture is all around them, but they are not actually within the death-consuming culture. This is a grave error in thinking and reasoning, and it is a primary way that the opposite energy continues to infect and infest the mass majority of Man, He and She. It is amazing how individuals can walk around feeling like they are somehow outside of that herd that continues to blindly follow the opposite energy. In truth and reality, these individuals are unwilling to detox and purge and are so deep in the herd that they are actually lost in the crowd.

It is indeed a spiritual war, and the opposite energy appears to be winning so far. The divine duty is to learn the lessons, retrieve the blessings and move back into the essence of the Divine Union of One, and the ooh's and aah's of a Love Supreme. In other words, one must connect with every way and means of applying divine spirit conscious thought and reasoning. It is an absolute necessity for Man, He and She, to reject the superficial, artificial, and surface thought and reasoning and go deep within, regardless of one being blonde or bald or natty, natty dread, regardless of the color of one's skin. Keep this in mind as we enter Chapter 3 where we will indulge in a Most Supreme Seen and Unseen telling. Be reminded that the goal and objective here is to bring

FULFILLING THE SACRED ANCESTRAL PROPHECY OF THE TRIPLE NINE: UNVEILING THE PROPHETIC 2012 MELTDOWN OF THE LOST AND ASTRAY PALE STATE OF MIND

forward divine clarity regarding the nature of energy consumption.

Chapter 2 Innerlude:
The Nature of the Beast

Song 7 from "Supernatural Healing Serum: Dose Three," Kwatamani musical CD release, 2006

<u>Royal Priestess vocals</u>:
Cold, starving afraid and alone
Beware, beware....
The lost and astray mind in the deep-freeze zone
Beware, beware....
Always ready to take from somebody else to get its own
Beware, beware....
That's the nature of the beast, nature of the beast
All the talk has come before about the final days of a spiritual war
What it looks like and what will it be, what will it be
Began in the ice-cold caves of the deep-freeze mentality
Upon the earth, there was no conflict and strife until the pale vibration wandered from the darkness of life
Which is a richness of hue, deep intensity
of whole life energy
Disconnected from the source,
 isolated in the ice-cold caves
Pale as the snow, lost in the ice, the lost and astray mind became a killing device
Slaughter to eat and kill to survive
That's the nature of the beast, nature of the beast
A culture of death consumption
can only do what is done before
That's the nature of the beast
And the beast tries to destroy the sacred spirit presence

FULFILLING THE SACRED ANCESTRAL PROPHECY OF THE TRIPLE NINE: UNVEILING THE PROPHETIC 2012 MELTDOWN OF THE LOST AND ASTRAY PALE STATE OF MIND

Every time you consume the pale vibrations
of the ice-cold, deep-freeze mentality,
you consume the nature of the beast

<u>High Priest vocals:</u>
There'd be an eternal memory bank left in the mud
of the old Ethiopian land after the flood
And the footprints still have tracks of blood
within the bloodstained trails that came after the flood
Yes, there would indeed be a first coming
of this lost and astray mind, and all of the disciples
and followers would carry the beastly mark
of the death-consumption-culture crime
And the ice-cold, deep-freeze mentality
would indeed be the signs of the time
And the stale and pale reflections would transcend
every color line
Be one blonde or bald or nappy head, straight-laced,
mixed race or natty dread
And the pale ghosts and goblins of the living dead
would be the primary occupants in almost every head
And the signature mark of everything seen, heard or read
leaving the whole life presence of Man, He and She,
hanging on a thin, thin thread
And the sick and afflicted, fat and obese body would
hang heavy like a ton of lead
Reflecting the misery, aches and pains of the
bloodstained trail and the flood
of mental, physical and spiritual blood
that was continuously bled

CHAPTER 2 INNERLUDE: THE NATURE OF THE BEAST

It would have indeed been the first coming of this lost and astray mind, and it would have occurred during the time of the ice-cold, deep-freeze story line
And mental, physical and spiritual mutation would indeed be the signs of these times
And the pale blood-spilling Children would be how the lost and astray mind was defined
And murder, rape, steal and take is how these pale Children would unwind
And the glorious suntanned Children would soon find themselves in a bind
And the Sacred Garden Culture would be on a rapid decline
As the whole of the planet Earth would meet up with these pale Children of mind
You see, during the meltdown, the Children that were pale would find their way down
and leave a blood-stained trail
And would march themselves all the way into these modern times, raising hell
And the Children that were pale would cause much harm and hurt and much hate and self hate
And the suntanned Children would try to integrate or separate, but they would never have worked to purge or to detox the deep-freeze mental state
And so the death consumption culture would continue to be the bait to control their mental fate
And so they would pay many dues and pay many mental, physical and spiritual costs
As the deep-freeze mentality
would continue to be their boss
And this would leave the offsprings

FULFILLING THE SACRED ANCESTRAL PROPHECY OF THE TRIPLE NINE: UNVEILING THE PROPHETIC 2012 MELTDOWN OF THE LOST AND ASTRAY PALE STATE OF MIND

without much of anything
And the suntanned Children would learn to lean
and to cling to a dream and the fantasies and illusions
and delusions of a heavenly religious scheme
All of which would merely be an orchestrated plot and
scheme of the ice-cold, deep-freeze mentality
and the death consumption culture that it bring
And it really wouldn't be too hard to disguise
if the suntanned Children would simply open their eyes
to the bloodstained trail of these cold-blooded lies
There would quickly arise during the cold-blooded days
of going lost and astray, spending much time
in a homeless, starvation-like phase
crawling around in a cold, dank, maze-like cave,
not knowing if one is delusionary or in a daze
Where blood and guts and bones and septic waste is what
one would learn to crave, and from birth to death
not once would one have bathed
except in the blood and guts and puke and septic waste
that one would learn to crave
And these would be the means and the ways to breed the
lost and astray mind during the deep-freeze days
And this would be the nature of the beast and how the
stale and pale mind would behave
But these suntanned Children would absolutely refuse
to open their eyes
And so they would become all caught up
in the ice-cold, deep-freeze vibe
And what they would eat, drink and smoke would
basically be nothing but toxic waste and dope
And now the lost and astray mind

CHAPTER 2 INNERLUDE: THE NATURE OF THE BEAST

would be where they would put their hope
And although there would indeed have been the first
coming of the lost and astray mind
And although the pale Children
was how the lost and astray mind was initially defined
And although mutation and degeneration was indeed the
signs of the time of the ice-cold, deep-freeze story line
And although the pale Children would continue to rock,
there would now indeed be a new kid on the block
And the suntanned Man, He and She
would pull out every stop
And they would rock and they would roll
until the suntanned Man, He and She, would become ice
cold
And hell would be re-defined to include
these lost and astray suntanned Children of mind
And although the six-thousand year old history had
already unfold
You would think that these lost and astray suntanned
Children had never, ever been told
And so these stubborn, pale-minded suntanned Children
had become so cocky, arrogant, bold and cold
Their position would be, "These are modern times
and that stuff is old."
And so the suntanned Children would honor and worship
the deities of hell
And would add more blood
to their own bloodstained trail
The confusion would be massive;
the confusion would be insane
In fact, the word for this confusion
would not even have a name

FULFILLING THE SACRED ANCESTRAL PROPHECY OF THE TRIPLE NINE: UNVEILING THE PROPHETIC 2012 MELTDOWN OF THE LOST AND ASTRAY PALE STATE OF MIND

But the basic facts of this confusion
is that now you only have yourself to blame

Chapter Three:
The Divine Origin
of Man, He and She

Chapter 3 Prelude:
The Ooh's and the Aah's of a Love Supreme

Song 2 from "12th Hour Prophecy: The Pale Curse and the Solarized Energy Shift," Kwatamani musical CD release, 2008

<u>Royal Priestess vocals:</u>
Our most sacred ancestral presence
is the essence of a love supreme
And the radiant glory of the Divine Children of the Sun is
a supreme love story, seen and unseen

<u>High Priest vocals:</u>
This is about the essence of a love supreme
The most supreme essence seen and unseen
And out of the ooh and the aah
came our most supreme ancestry, seen and unseen
The Ta and the Tat giving birth to all living things
For the sake of time, let's call this most supreme
Ta and Tat the sacred ancestral presence
Man, He and She, Osiris and Auset
Osiris and Auset, the most supreme ancestral spirit
essence, Man, He and She
Divine union, divine consumption
And going forward to multiply ancestral divinity
And out of this glorious manifestation of the gatherings
of the matters of the earth, wind, rain and sun
The ooh's and the aah's would show that they're pleased
And they would come giving birth
to the Divine Children of the Sun

FULFILLING THE SACRED ANCESTRAL PROPHECY OF THE TRIPLE NINE: UNVEILING THE PROPHETIC 2012 MELTDOWN OF THE LOST AND ASTRAY PALE STATE OF MIND

And they would nurture off divine spirit conscious insight
And the raw and living fruits, vegetables, seeds, nuts, herbs and spice would be their gift
from the Tree of Life
And so upon the Earth had emerged a love supreme
Coming from the essence of the Most Supreme
Seen and Unseen
And the Children of the Sun
would continue to want some
So they were given the gift of the Sacred Garden Culture
from which we come
And the Children of the Sun would have so much joy
that we would dance and sing and drum
and do our thing, enjoying the ooh's and the aah's
of every single pleasure a love supreme would bring

<u>Royal Priestess vocals:</u>
Ooh aah

<u>High Priest vocals:</u>
And the sacred ancestral mother spirit would nurture the most supreme essence of femininity
And she would give birth to Man, He and She
And the sacred ancestral father spirit would give divine guidance and protection and that would maintain masculinity keeping in tune
with our most supreme ancestral connection
And so it was and so it continues to be, eternally
And only through the breaking
of this most supreme ancestral tie

CHAPTER 3 PRELUDE: THE OOH'S AND THE AAH'S OF A LOVE SUPREME

Will the sacred ancestral spirit presence
of Man, He and She, die
Yeah, we was on it baby, whole and clean
A manifestation of the most supreme ancestral essence
and honoring all living things
Keeping it simple, baby, yeah
keeping it whole and clean upon the seen
Preparing for their own return back
from the Most Supreme Unseen to the Seen
To once again be heard and seen
expressing the ooh's and the aah's of a love supreme

<u>Royal Priestess vocals:</u>
Ooh aah, a love supreme, Divine Children of the Sun
and the Sacred Garden Culture from which we come
As it was in the beginning and so it shall be
a love supreme

<u>High Priest vocals:</u>
But somewhere out there within the deep-freeze
unknown
An opposite energy was lurking waiting to get it on
Weaving its web, casting a spell, baiting a trail
To draw the lost and astray mind deep into its pits of hell
Cunning tricks, masterminding a quick fix
You see, this energy was a sadomasochist
Misery, aches and pains was its primary gain
But the Children of the Sun
would totally ignore this opposite energy
that consumes of blood spill and flesh and bones
Instead of consuming of the fruits of the tree
And so this energy would lurk outside
of the energies of the sun

FULFILLING THE SACRED ANCESTRAL PROPHECY OF THE TRIPLE NINE: UNVEILING THE PROPHETIC 2012 MELTDOWN OF THE LOST AND ASTRAY PALE STATE OF MIND

Seeking to search and find anything or anyone
That it could draw outside to create a bond
And lo and behold one day, some Children of the Sun
lost their way and were led deep into the pits of hell
Where they would become scavengers and predators and consume of death and cave dwell
And that stale and pale opposite energy
would quickly go to work, doing its thing
Mutating and degenerating them, spirit, body and brain
And out of these experiences
came a cold-blooded, pale breed of mankind
Thinking from a cold-blooded, pale
opposite-energy state of mind
And they would learn to carry a monkey on their back
And they would call this monkey the god of love
A god of vengeance, war and wrath
A jealous god, inflicting the energy of a thug
And this god of vengeance, war and wrath
that they could never see
Would be a manifestation of that opposite energy
And they would seek and search to find a place
to put this god of love
And out of a cold-blooded pale state of mind
They would choose to place this pale-male-war god
into a heaven above
And they would become confused about every single thing
And they would learn to worship this death culture
and the opposite energy from which it came
So they would learn to inflict lust, lies, illusions, confusion, death and deadly destruction

CHAPTER 3 PRELUDE: THE OOH'S AND THE AAH'S OF A LOVE SUPREME

on every living thing
And they would hunt and herd
and they would utilize animal husbandry
to breed their feast
Yeah, they would murder, rape, steal and enslave
to satisfy their sexual pleasure
and their blood-spilling crave
Yeah, these lost and astray Children of the Sun
had indeed become a cold-blooded predator
and a scavenger-like beast
And this is what the Divine Children of the Sun
would meet
When they would encounter their pale, lost and astray kin
Who would continue to consume
of this stale opposite energy
that had mutated and degenerated them
from outside and within
And Ta and Tat would look upon this
and the ancestors would not be pleased
There were many, many lessons that had to be learned
And unless the Divine Children of the Sun
maintain divine spirit consciousness
they too would mutate and degenerate
taking their own turn
And although it was prophesied
that the Children of the Sun
would suffer many heartaches, heart breaks and regrets
It was also prophesied
that the opposite energy would seal its own tomb
through its own energy of doom and gloom
And the lesson would be learned, locking that pale,
opposite energy out forever

FULFILLING THE SACRED ANCESTRAL PROPHECY OF THE TRIPLE NINE: UNVEILING THE PROPHETIC 2012 MELTDOWN OF THE LOST AND ASTRAY PALE STATE OF MIND

Never again to be able to return
Clearing the pathway for the sacred ancestral presence
of the Divine Children of the Sun
to return upon the Seen from the Unseen
To again become a most supreme expression
of the ooh's and the aah's of a Love Supreme

<u>Royal Priestess vocals:</u>
Ooh Aah, a Love Supreme

<u>High Priest vocals:</u>
And now that we've brought this thing to you
whole and clean
Examine this white blight; learn the lessons that come
from dealing with this thing

<u>Royal Priestess vocals:</u>
High Priest Kwatamani leading us through the pathway into a Love Supreme

Chapter Three: The Divine Origin of Man, He and She

Sacred Ancestral Memory:
The Unknown and the All-Knowing

There are complete unknowns that are indeed a total mystery within the toxic parallel, actually beyond the capacity of individuals within the lost and astray state of mind to fathom. Sacred ancestral memory is a vast collection of divine knowledge, wisdom and understanding that preserves and records the movement of the Most Supreme Seen and Unseen Essence of Life and Supreme Love. One must seriously exercise one's ability to stretch one's mental boundaries so that one can conceive of time and space that extends into the millions of years and extends far beyond the physical state as projected by the paleness of the lost and astray mind. For millions of years, the Divine Children of the Sun advanced the glory of whole life energy within the Sacred Garden Culture from which we come.

This revealing is the primary step in moving into greater comprehension about the nature of energies that occupy the existence of Man, He and She. We are speaking of a sacred and ancient presence of divine knowledge, divine wisdom and divine understanding. The code of this divine communication is secured and protected by the energy of a Love Supreme, and cannot be de-coded or broken by anything or anyone not of a Love Supreme. This sacred ancestral revealing has been carefully designed within the most supreme spirit of

FULFILLING THE SACRED ANCESTRAL PROPHECY OF THE TRIPLE NINE: UNVEILING THE PROPHETIC 2012 MELTDOWN OF THE LOST AND ASTRAY PALE STATE OF MIND

Divine Oneness. In order to gain greater comprehension about this telling and all that is revealed in prophecy, we must start at the beginning.

The Beginning

Before the time of time, in the deep dark wholeness of the Most Supreme Unseen, the sacred ancestral spirit presence of He and She joined in Divine Oneness. The ripe and radiant energies of the most supreme masculine essence and the most supreme feminine essence embraced each other, caressing every inner and outer space, rocking and grooving to the universal rhythms of divine innercourse. This Most Supreme Union of Oneness of masculine and feminine energy, He and She, is a natural high and stimulating rush, arousing a tremendous surge of excitement within the vibrations and sensations of Love Supreme. The most supreme masculine essence pulsated in the warm and wet sensuousness of a strong magnetic pull within the black whole of the most supreme essence of femininity.

Within this most supreme essence of the Union of One, the invigorating heat would produce the intensity of a breath of life; the pouring hot wetness from the deep penetration of masculine energy would cause tight-gripping movements deep within the feminine birth canal as both masculine and feminine intensity would throb and swell. As the intensity of masculine penetration would create the heat sensation of solarization, the feminine response to this solarized vibration would be so exact and in sync that her breath of expression would be the fuel to infuse the heat of light upon the seen. At that

CHAPTER THREE: THE DIVINE ORIGIN OF MAN, HE AND SHE

moment, both he and she came, and that would give birth to the physical presence of rain. Out of feminine panting sticky hot wetness, her essence as Mother Earth came. And each time she came, another formulation of earth-like presence, would manifest from the masculine solar energy who would bring her climaxing pleasures that formulated the elements of earth, wind and rain.

The nature of that intense pleasure from the masculine climax caused his magnetic and invigorating vibration to intensify. Things had gotten so intense that both the masculine and feminine energies were starting to manifest whole life presence upon the seen. Now that the supreme glory of the elements of earth, wind, rain and sun had begun, a sacred place for the divine union of masculine and feminine energy was ripe to materialize under the sun. The most supreme masculine and feminine ecstasy was how all planetary bodies would come to be. Thus would be the manifestation out of the most supreme union of masculine and feminine energy.

The Most Supreme laws of the universe apply across the board, in every instance, in every existence of whole life matters. Therefore, in order for any matters of whole life energy to manifest whole and clean upon the seen, the most supreme ancestral spirit presence of masculine and feminine energy would indeed have to be forwarded from the Most Supreme Unseen to the seen whole and clean. Within the Most Supreme Law of the universe, any matter that does not manifest from the most supreme masculine and feminine energy upon the seen is a clear indication that the life matter in question is not of the Most Supreme Essence of Life and Supreme Love. These are the laws of the universe of the Most High

FULFILLING THE SACRED ANCESTRAL PROPHECY OF THE TRIPLE NINE: UNVEILING THE PROPHETIC 2012 MELTDOWN OF THE LOST AND ASTRAY PALE STATE OF MIND

Essence of Life and Supreme Love. These are the laws of the Most Supreme Seen and Unseen ancestral spirit presence of masculine and feminine energy. These are the sacred laws of the divine parallel.

The Void

There has never been and shall never be a void or a state of disorder within the universal sphere of whole life energy. However, outside of the divine parallel, there is a void within a sphere of energy that opposes the Most High Essence of Life and Supreme Love. This void of disorder and chaos exists outside of the divine order of whole life energy. The opposite energy is a lifeless matter that lurks outside of the divine parallel attempting to penetrate divine spirit consciousness again and again.

However, it is a supreme law of the universe that no two energies of an opposite nature can occupy the same space at the same time. Based on the opposite nature of the energy, there is absolutely no way for the energy that is opposite of Supreme Love and the Essence of Life to enter the divine parallel. The most Supreme Laws of the Most Supreme Unseen Essence of Life and Supreme Love eternally prohibit any possibility of that opposite energy from having any entry into the Most Supreme Unseen. Only a total energy transformation through divine humility could change the nature of the opposite energy and correct the massive disorder, thus allowing entry into the divine parallel. However, given the arrogant nature of the opposite energy, it stubbornly refused to submit to the process of detoxing and purging, and violently rejected the divine order of whole life

CHAPTER THREE: THE DIVINE ORIGIN OF MAN, HE AND SHE

energy. The pale opposite energy of the toxic parallel would remain in the outer zone.

You see, there is a most supreme state of awareness that provides an all-knowing sight of matters seen and unseen within divine spirit consciousness. This all-knowing state of divine spirit consciousness allows the opposite energy to be immediately exposed, identified and clearly seen within the unseen. As a result, the Most Supreme Unseen ancestral spirit presence of the High Priest warned that, although the lifeless void was a sphere of nothingness, it existed as a low-level, conscious-like state of being in the unseen. In other words, the opposite energy would exist as a consciousness that was completely opposite from divine spirit consciousness in every way and of every matter of fact.

The opposite energy lurked and festered in the frustration, impotence, anger and rage because of its inability to penetrate the divine parallel, inability to penetrate the Most Supreme Unseen Essence of Life and Supreme Love, inability to enter the Divine Union of One, inability to manifest within the most supreme glory of life matters. The energy that is opposite of Supreme Love and the Essence of Life can never experience the creative glory of divine innercourse nor experience the deep and abiding climax of natural and innate pleasure that originates within the Most Supreme black whole.

The opposite energy can never be made whole in and of itself. There is no whole life feminine energy to nurture its existence within the unseen—only a void of nothingness, a frigid empty un-wholeness serving the stub-like puniness that ejaculates toxic waste. The

FULFILLING THE SACRED ANCESTRAL PROPHECY OF THE TRIPLE NINE: UNVEILING THE PROPHETIC 2012 MELTDOWN OF THE LOST AND ASTRAY PALE STATE OF MIND

opposite energy cannot produce beyond the nothingness of its unseen sterile and empty existence. The lifeless energy of the toxic parallel can only express frustration and rage as it explodes in a destructive and violent fury, ejaculating nothingness, returning to the cold, pale nothingness within the enlarged blighted hole of nothingness.

Jealousy and envy churned within the energy that is opposite of Supreme Love and the Essence of Life as it witnessed the fruitful manifestations of whole life energy. The churning jealousy and envy instigated fierce hatred within the core of the toxic parallel, and the opposite energy became obsessed with destroying the target of its deepest longing and greatest desire. Due to the nature of the opposite energy, it would seek to destroy what it could not dominate, control and possess. The mere existence of the Divine Union of One between the Most Supreme ancestral masculine and feminine energy was a nagging reminder that a supreme state of being existed that was far beyond the reach of the opposite energy.

Within the toxic parallel, ambition was entertained along with horrible, ugly and brutal intentions of reducing the most supreme masculine essence to an inferior state of being. In this way, the most supreme feminine essence could be tricked and deceived and used at its own free will as a result of divine femininity not having divine guidance and protection. That opposite energy had become well-aware that the supreme feminine presence was the key in the Most Supreme Union of One, simply because she was the point of birth of all living

CHAPTER THREE: THE DIVINE ORIGIN OF MAN, HE AND SHE

things. It had become very clear that the Most Supreme ancestral mother spirit was the first source, i.e. the first teacher, and if the codes could be broken to rip her apart from the most supreme masculine presence within this Most Supreme Union of One, the toxic master plan could begin to run. However, as it was within the Most Supreme Unseen, there was absolutely no point of entry for that energy that is opposite of Supreme Love and the Essence of Life. The opposite energy was in a powerless state due to the nothingness of its existence, but this cold and pale reality fueled its power-hungry predatorial nature even more.

Vibrations of slaughtering, raping rage and conquest stormed within the opposite energy, feeding a consciousness of lust, lies, illusions, confusion, death and deadly destruction. The energy that is opposite of Supreme Love and the Essence of Life was entrapped by its own cold and pale nature in the freezing pit of its own hell within the toxic parallel. In all of its ugly and wretched foul vibrations, the opposite energy was naked to the all-knowing unseen sight of the Most Supreme ancestral spirit presence, and it was known that the opposite energy aimed to spread the vibrations and sensations of the toxic parallel like a plague.

Let us keep in mind that there is no force or power or presence in existence within the universe that is greater than the Most Supreme Essence of Life and Supreme Love. Whole life energy can never be stopped or conquered by any other energy of an opposite or unwhole nature. Therefore, even though the vicious predatory nature of the opposite energy was clearly exposed, the forward movement of the Most High

FULFILLING THE SACRED ANCESTRAL PROPHECY OF THE TRIPLE NINE: UNVEILING THE PROPHETIC 2012 MELTDOWN OF THE LOST AND ASTRAY PALE STATE OF MIND

Essence of Life and Supreme Love did not waver or bend, and could not be intimidated, bullied or conquered by fright and fear. The Most Supreme Unseen would be ever-vigilant and continue to push a Love Supreme.

The Most Supreme ancestral spirit presence of the masculine and feminine essence intensified the Supreme Love vibrations expressed in the Divine Union of One, becoming stronger and manifesting as the Most Supreme Seen presence of masculine and feminine energy. The Most Supreme Unseen had indeed called together the sacred elements of whole life energy in a supreme unification of the earth, the wind, the rain and the sun within the solarized system of the whole life presence of all living things. Within that, the most supreme ancestral spirit presence of masculine and feminine energy did indeed call forward their own presence upon the seen as the sacred ancestral spirit presence of Man, He and She.

Out of the inner sphere of the Sacred Ancestral Temple of Kwa Ta Man I of the Most Supreme Unseen did indeed come the first expressions of Man, He and She upon the seen, whole and clean.

Kwa—of the Most
Ta—Supreme Thought and Reasoning
Man—Supreme Body of Flesh
I—Supreme Ancestral Spirit Presence of Man, He and She

The Sacred Ancestral Coming upon the Seen

She was indeed of a most supreme ancestral manifestation of femininity upon the planet Earth, just as

CHAPTER THREE: THE DIVINE ORIGIN OF MAN, HE AND SHE

he was in his fullness and expression of the most supreme ancestral manifestation of masculinity. Within their sacred ancestral spirit presence as the Divine Union of One, He and She would indeed go forward and multiply divinity within their offspring as Divine Children of the Sun. Yes, she had given birth to many again and again and was, in fact, the grand, great, great, grandmother to Queen Mother Zebeka whose archaeological ruins would be recovered by pale lost and astray minds far, far, far later in time.

> Archaeologist finds Queen Mother Zebeka of the Original Garden Culture and Calls Her Lucy.
>
> The earliest 'hominid' to be widely studied to date is identified as *Australopithecus afarensis,* best known from a nearly complete skeleton found in Ethiopia in 1974, known popularly as 'Lucy.' Nearly all authorities agree that *Australopithecus afarensis* was the earliest member of the upright-walking line that led, some four million years later, to modern humans. While disputing details, authorities tend to agree that these earliest humans were vegetation eaters and developed in body to resemble long-distance runners. Two primary points of divine clarity emerge from this communication: 1) A common melaninated lineage of all the tribes of Man, He and She, hence only one race of Man. This is a clear indication that Man, He and She, had a divine solar relationship upon the Earth and a direct relationship with the garden culture; and 2) A definitive case is made here that the original and earliest known consumption pattern of Man, He and She, is the divine consumption of raw and living fruits, vegetables, seeds and nuts.
> *Book One* of *The Holistic Living Truth About Supreme Love,* Sixth Edition, page 207.

FULFILLING THE SACRED ANCESTRAL PROPHECY OF THE TRIPLE NINE: UNVEILING THE PROPHETIC 2012 MELTDOWN OF THE LOST AND ASTRAY PALE STATE OF MIND

And although those of the pale lost and astray state of mind that emerged out of the toxic parallel did not have the ability to comprehend the holistic living truth about supreme love, they would have to acknowledge her existence. You see, for the few thousand years that those of a lost and astray pale state of mind had been upon the earth, they had sworn to a toxic energy of racist ideology.

You see, they were actually the proponents of the toxic parallel. They had been mutated and degenerated into a lost and astray pale state of being as a result of falling into the traps and the tricks of deception of the opposite energy. In fact, there was no divine spirit consciousness anywhere within. There was no divine clarity, so all that they could come up with was the toxic thought and reasoning that had manifested from the blood spill, the raping raids, and invasions upon the Sacred Garden Culture from which we come.

In the death-consuming culture, power comes from a crushing stone or a blazing sword or the barrel of the gun or the hang man's noose. In other words, to these pale ones, power would come from the swift ability to kill, torture or maim by any means necessary. And lust, lies, illusion, confusion, death and deadly destruction were the determining factors of all things. This would simply be the truth and consequences that befell the lost and astray Children of the Sun who mutated and degenerated in the deep-freeze ice cold. Like the massive plague that it is, this devastating virus would spread among all disciples and followers, regardless of the color of their skin.

CHAPTER THREE: THE DIVINE ORIGIN OF MAN, HE AND SHE

This would make it nearly impossible to conceive of Queen Mother Zebeka and an ancient ancestral sisterhood upon the planet millions and millions of years prior the mutation and degeneration that produced the cold-blooded and pale breed of mankind, let alone the story of her great, great, great grandmother as the coming of the Most Supreme ancestral spirit presence of Man, He and She, upon the seen. Two parts to one whole, She, the divine femininity and He, the divine masculinity—the unification of Divine Oneness upon the seen, whole and clean. You see, as it was within the most supreme unseen, so it had come to be among the most sacred ancestral spirit presence upon the seen. For that reason, the forwarding of this most supreme ancestral telling now comes to you whole and clean.

There she was standing in deeply suntanned solarized glory. Her beautiful brown-eyed virgin innocence shone as a radiant reflection of the Sacred Garden Culture from which she comes. Soft, sensuous warmth flowed in her every expression of a Love Supreme from deep inside. She moved with grace and style, and her firm shapeliness spoke the invigorating and enticing language of femininity. She would warmly embrace the true nature of a Love Supreme from the divinity of the masculine essence. You see, deep inside the inner walls of her feminine essence re-cycled the Most Supreme ancestral spirit presence of Man, He and She, preparing for that most magnificent trip from the Most Supreme Unseen to the seen. The Divine Union of One would go forward to multiply divinity upon the seen through the offspring.

FULFILLING THE SACRED ANCESTRAL PROPHECY OF THE TRIPLE NINE: UNVEILING THE PROPHETIC 2012 MELTDOWN OF THE LOST AND ASTRAY PALE STATE OF MIND

Yes, the most supreme ancestral mother spirit had been forwarded in tact, statuesque, straight back, breasted, stomach flat, small waist, smoothly curving hips, never a dull moment from the tip of her tongue to the wetness of her inner cheeks and sweet expressions of her voluptuous lips. She would speak the language with such gentle, warm and soothing ancestral intensity. This strong and vibrant suntanned feminine presence would be the embodiment of divine humility by decree. Within herself, she would be the excitement of whole life stimulation which would cause his nature to rise and come alive from sensing the sight and sound of her sacred ancestral feminine vibe. She would indeed nurture all that He would bring to her, and He would bring to her all that was whole and clean.

You see, divinely guiding and protecting his and her sacred ancestral spirit presence was the joy of the supreme ancestral father spirit. And going forward to multiply divinity within the offspring is what He would bring with every breath that He would take while upon the seen. He was indeed divine masculinity at its best, and He too would stand strong and straight, deeply solarized with a firm statuesque build of athletic skill, broad chest and muscular physique. You see, his sacred suntanned presence indeed fulfilled the supreme unseen ancestral feminine request. It was her decision that if She was going to come upon the seen, She wanted to be divinely guided and protected by the very best. So this gentle, yet firmly compassionate expression of masculinity would bring divine spirit consciousness by decree. Yes, He was naturally and innately an athlete,

CHAPTER THREE: THE DIVINE ORIGIN OF MAN, HE AND SHE

fast and swift on his feet. However, it would be his divine spirit consciousness that he would bring with every pulsating vibe of his heartbeat.

During gatherings of harvest within the Sacred Garden Culture, He and She would feast upon the raw and living fruits, vegetables, seeds and nuts as a daily delight. There would be a time and a place for everything divine. When it was time for He and She to unwind, he would bring his firm masculine presence to her well-matured divine spirit conscious state of mind. His greatest desire would be to bring the joys and pleasures of life to her in divine order. Just as it was her greatest desire to bring the joys and pleasures of life to him in divine order. So, they would dance and sing and make body music to celebrate their sacred ancestral spirit presence upon the seen as they indulged in the Divine Union of One. And they would glorify the essence of whole life presence as manifested within the supreme elements of earth, wind, rain and sun. As it was within the Most Supreme Unseen between the sacred ancestral masculine and feminine energy, so it would come to be upon the seen with the sacred ancestral spirit presence of Man, He and She. They would go forward to multiply divinity and the joys and pleasures of life as the Divine Children of the Sun and the Sacred Garden Culture from which we come. This Love Supreme was so whole and true that nothing of the opposite energy could break this bond of Divine Union or find its way through. And this sacred ancestral bond of Divine Union would have an ever-lasting seal, divine spirit consciousness, and this would keep things whole and real.

FULFILLING THE SACRED ANCESTRAL PROPHECY OF THE TRIPLE NINE: UNVEILING THE PROPHETIC 2012 MELTDOWN OF THE LOST AND ASTRAY PALE STATE OF MIND

No fantasies, no delusions, no dreams; no lust, lies, illusion, confusion, death and deadly destruction; no cold-blooded predatorial plots and schemes, no hunting and herding ways and means. In fact, nothing of a dead and devitalized, depleted kind grew within the Sacred Garden Culture from which we come. Divine union, divine consumption, and going forward to multiply divinity in the offspring were indeed the sacred signs of the times—these would be the divine laws that the Most Supreme Unseen ancestral spirit presence of the Divine Children of the Sun, had self-installed. And so, from the Most Supreme Unseen to the seen had come the Sacred Ancestral Temple of Kwa Ta Man I to forward divine knowledge, divine wisdom and divine understanding of the Most Supreme Essence of Life and Supreme Love.

Within this most sacred ancestral coming, the Most Supreme Unseen would secure their physical presence in divine order as Man, He and She. As it began, so shall it be within every movement and expression of whole life energy. The Divine Union of One was the beginning of all life matters within the seed vibrations of unity, oneness and all parts working together to forward a greater wholeness. Now, Man, He and She, was called forward as a manifestation of the sacred elements of earth, wind, rain and sun. And the sacred ancestral seeds of Man, He and She, would indeed be planted upon the earth, whole and clean, a sacred suntanned presence, forwarded as the Divine Children of the Sun, rooted in the Sacred Garden Culture from which we come.

From the very first expressions of divine oneness, the fruits of the trees of life carried forward the seed

CHAPTER THREE: THE DIVINE ORIGIN OF MAN, HE AND SHE

vibrations from the Most Supreme Unseen to the seen. And in order for this whole life movement to keep on pushing a Love Supreme upon the seen, divine consumption of whole life energy would be the absolute fuel requirement. While the Divine Children of Sun glorified in the feasts of the garden and the fruits of the Trees of Life, the raw and living fruits, vegetables, seeds, nuts, herbs and spice provided a communion of the sacred elements of earth, wind, rain and sun. And the mental, physical and spiritual consumption of whole life energy goes even deeper into the unseen roots of divine spirit consciousness.

The cycles of the seeds growing roots and the trees bearing fruits would intensify the forward multiplication of the sacred elements of earth, wind, rain and sun. From the Most Supreme Unseen to the seen, the whole life presence would be maintained whole and clean, each presence forwarding itself in offspring vibrations, again and again. From the Most Supreme Unseen to the seen, over cycles and cycles of time, a forward manifestation of divine spirit consciousness prepared a greater space for the return of the sacred ancestral spirit presence. All that the Divine Children of the Sun harvested within divine spirit consciousness upon the seen would be recycled as they returned to the Most Supreme Unseen. And upon this return to the Most Supreme unseen womb of the divine parallel, an even stronger and more abundant sacred ancestral spirit presence would be divinely guided, protected and nurtured to accelerate the most supreme master plan, forwarding again and again upon the seen to intensify divine spirit consciousness among the He and She of Man.

FULFILLING THE SACRED ANCESTRAL PROPHECY OF THE TRIPLE NINE: UNVEILING THE PROPHETIC 2012 MELTDOWN OF THE LOST AND ASTRAY PALE STATE OF MIND

However, somewhere out there within the deep-freeze unknown, the opposite energy would be lurking, waiting to get it on, casting its spell, weaving its web, hoping to draw the lost and astray mind deep into its deep-freeze pits of hell. You see, that cold-blooded opposite energy truly had no life of its own. So it would play on fright and fear as it attempted to spook folks, because, come hell or high water, that opposite energy would need a host. The only way for the opposite energy to maintain and spread its existence would be to pollute, dilute and contaminate divine spirit consciousness. In fact, this would be the only way to deplete whole life energy to a weak and unwhole state where it could be preyed upon by the opposite energy. This was a very desperate matter for the energy that is opposite of Supreme Love and the Essence of Life, because if that opposite energy did not expand and spread, then it would simply wither farther and farther into the decay of nothingness from which it comes.

So after many unsuccessful attempts to invade the Most Supreme Unseen Essence of Life and Supreme Love, the opposite energy would lurk like a cold-blooded predator awaiting the opportunity to launch its attack upon the seen. That opposite energy would study well, becoming the grand master of deceit as well as the grand master of disguise, hiding deep within every fantasy, delusion, illusion, dream and lie. The pale objective would be to capture the attention of an unsuspecting host long enough to destabilize the whole life presence of Man, He and She.

CHAPTER THREE: THE DIVINE ORIGIN OF MAN, HE AND SHE

Using every deadly weapon at its disposal, every temptation and distraction, every manipulation, every sly, slick and wicked strategy, the opposite energy set its sight upon the sacred ancestral spirit presence of Man, He and She. Watching and waiting like the cruel and merciless predator that it is, setting trap after trap, launching attack after attack, the opposite energy was relentless and vicious in its lust for conquest and victory. For millions of earth cycles around the sun, this vicious lurking vibration would go on and on, unsuccessfully. Yet, generation after generation, this opposite energy would work desperately, seeking and searching to find a wandering or distracted mind to serve as a host. The mission would be to use this host as a breeding ground of mutation and degeneration, producing a violent and cruel pale breed of mankind.

The pale master plan was to enter the physical world and accomplish in the seen what it could not accomplish in the unseen. Namely, occupy the physical presence of Man, He and She; invade, enslave and contaminate the sacred ancestral spirit presence; and degrade divine spirit consciousness into a consciousness of the opposite energy. Once installed within the consciousness of Man, He and She, the opposite energy reasoned that it could return to the unseen and slip unrecognized into the divine parallel. The pale master plan of the opposite energy was to wage a massive cover-up of artificial, fake and false presentations like a wolf in sheep's clothing to camouflage its true nature. The weak and toxic reasoning was that if the deception was skillful enough, then the Most Supreme Unseen would be deceived into allowing the opposite energy to enter into the divine parallel. The primary mission of this opposite energy would be to reduce the Most Supreme Essence of Life and Supreme Love to a weakened, depleted and disconnected state of being. A state of being that worships the dead, where dying is the kingdom, the power and the glory.

The Dividing Line

There is a mighty universal force that separates the opposite energy of the toxic parallel from the sacred ancestral spirit presence within the divine parallel. This boundary divides and separates the two parallels so that the nature of both becomes easy to identify within divine spirit consciousness. This means that one is either of a most <u>Serious</u> state of being within divine spirit consciousness, or one is at different levels and degrees of a cold and pale state of being within mind consciousness.

The opposite energy has no power, except the power that one grants it through consuming of it. The sacred ancestral ones observed the nature of the opposite energy and comprehended that, once consumed, this toxic energy embeds itself in every membrane and fiber of the consumer and depletes the life energy of its host.

This weak and depleted energy only gains strength when it is allowed to enter the consciousness of Man, He and She, upon the seen and feed upon the life presence. The only way for this opposite energy to enter into the mental and physical experience of Man, He and She, is for one to consume of the toxic energy through willing consent. Lies, illusions, lust, confusion, death and deadly

CHAPTER THREE: THE DIVINE ORIGIN OF MAN, HE AND SHE

destruction are how this opposite energy ejaculates itself into a mental conception.

There are many methods that have been used by the disciples and followers of the opposite energy to influence the will of Man, He and She. These vicious methods of domination and control serve to break and corrupt the will so that one submits and consents to consuming the energies of the toxic parallel. In every instance, deception, violent force, rape, fright and fear and the threat of death are key weapons in the weakening of one's mental stability. Once de-stabilized in one's thoughts, divine focus is lost, divine reasoning becomes impossible, and one is left vulnerable to the mental pollution of the toxic parallel.

The spirit presence becomes so depleted by the toxic waste of the opposite energy that the spirit presence actually deteriorates. The deterioration of spirit-life energy causes mutation and degeneration in the whole life presence of Man, He and She, and installs a false and deceptive presentation referred to as the lost and astray pale state of mind. The massive deterioration that was caused by the consumption of the opposite energy was foreseen and foretold by the sacred ancestral ones.

It was foreseen that the toxic parallel presented a real danger of massive contamination and corruption through mental distraction and the use of deception and deadly force. The sacred ancestral spirit presence of the High Priest revealed that so long as the Supreme Laws were kept, then divine guidance, protection and nurturing would safeguard divine spirit consciousness. The requirements of the Supreme Laws are a very <u>Serious</u> matter of maintaining divine union, divine consumption and the forward multiplication of divinity in the offspring. Obeying these supreme laws would be the ever-lasting guarantee that, come what may, the opposite energy would indeed be powerless in its efforts to overthrow divine spirit consciousness. The sacred ancestral spirit presence of Man, He and She, would remain embraced in the ooh's and aah's of a Love Supreme, whole and clean within the Most Supreme Seen and Unseen.

The Warning

The Divine Children of the Sun were warned to never consume of the opposite energy, because the deceptions of the toxic parallel would draw them into the mental mindset that indulges in a death culture. Timing was critical; remaining in sync and in tune was critical. Although the warnings of a sacred ancestral prophecy were well known, the message went unheeded by a few distracted ones who began wandering in the outer zone of the opposite energy, ignorant and innocent of the consequences.

The moment these few distracted ones opened their thoughts to stepping away from the divine guidance, protection and nurturing of the Most Supreme Seen and Unseen, they immediately became disconnected from divine spirit consciousness. These disconnected ones stepped into the nothingness of the toxic parallel and became lost and astray in the opposite energy. The more these few distracted Children of the Sun entertained thoughts of disobedience, the more they became unwhole. The more these few distracted Children

CHAPTER THREE: THE DIVINE ORIGIN OF MAN, HE AND SHE

became unwhole, the more they became separated from the Sacred Garden Culture from which we come and the more they experienced separation, division, and alienation. In this way, the few distracted Children removed themselves from the Sacred Garden Culture and were drawn deeper into the web of division, separation, conflict, confusion and disconnection.

Through this methodology, the opposite energy would be successful in turning the lost and astray Children of the Sun into a host. It would be those of these lost and astray suntanned Children who would mutate and degenerate into a pale breed of mankind. The opposite energy would lead these distracted, disobedient and lost Children down a path of lust, lies, illusions, confusion, death and deadly destruction. Death and dying would become the honor, the glory, the power and the might of these Children of the Sun who had become lost and astray. Unfortunately, the sacred ancestral spirit presence that once occupied the physical existence of these lost and astray Children of the Sun would now become trapped within the deep-freeze pits of hell known as the toxic parallel.

These distracted Children of the Sun began to weaken in their sense of duty, obligation and responsibility to the divine social economic family community. They began to focus on the individualized pursuits of the I-me-my syndrome and attempted to move outside of divine order. As a result of following the leadership of the unclear and the disconnected, these distracted Children of the Sun would eventually end up lost and astray in the outer northern regions of the planet. As time unfolded, the opposite energy further confused

FULFILLING THE SACRED ANCESTRAL PROPHECY OF THE TRIPLE NINE: UNVEILING THE PROPHETIC 2012 MELTDOWN OF THE LOST AND ASTRAY PALE STATE OF MIND

these lost and astray Children, and they became entrapped during a severe energy shift that caused periods of ice glaciers and freezing. Several periods of freezing white blight upon the earth have come and gone. These times of white blight are referred to in modern times as the coming of the Ice Age.

The lost and astray Children consumed of the opposite energy; they consumed dead and decomposing animal flesh and bones and blood and guts and skin. The lost and astray Children fed upon their own mutation and degeneration. They scavenged the rotting remains of corpse and carcass. They slaughtered to survive. They would rape and raid and learned to seek the thrill of the kill, becoming the embodiment of the opposite energy. Eventually a pale breed of mankind would fester in the icy caves, a breed of scavengers, hunters, herders, warlords, and nomadic invaders.

Once divine order was interrupted and the divine social economic family community was divided and destabilized through the acts of toxic consumption, a spiritual seal was immediately put in place. The sacred ancestral spirit presence of the High Priest Kwatamani foretold of a time when the Most Supreme ancestral spirit presence of Man, He and She, would remain within the Most Supreme Unseen, unable to return to the seen, because the passageway to and from the divine parallel would be closed.

Only a time of divine intervention, would signal the opening of the spiritual lock and allow the barrier to be removed between Most Supreme Unseen and the seen presence of Man, He and She. The sacred ancestral spirit

CHAPTER THREE: THE DIVINE ORIGIN OF MAN, HE AND SHE

presence of the High Priest Kwatamani would return to the seen during the final days of melting down the energy that is opposite of Supreme Love and the Essence of Life to gather the Sacred Few. Only when the High Priest Kwatamani had succeeded in unifying the sacred ancestral elders within the Sacred Ancestral Temple of Kwa Ta Man I by securing the first and second generation of the Kwatamani Royal Family and calling forward the sacred ancestral spirit presence of the royal priestesses and priests would the fulfillment of the prophecy of the era of 2012 be secured.

Within the scope of this powerful prophecy, the era of 2012 marks the final phases of the White Blight upon the planet when the masculine and feminine presence would be strangers and hostile enemies to each other and the only thing birthed upon the seen again and again would be toxic disorder. The signs of the time expose how completely opposite from divine order Man, He and She, has become. The critical state of affairs within the life and times of the mass majority of Man, He and She, would reach a fatal and futile point of extreme danger. A secured port of entry was preserved for the Sacred Few who come forward during these final days of the White Blight.

<u>High Priest vocals:</u>
And although it was prophesied
that the Children of the Sun
would suffer many heartaches, heart breaks and regrets
It was also prophesied that the opposite energy
would seal its own tomb
through its own energy of doom and gloom

FULFILLING THE SACRED ANCESTRAL PROPHECY OF THE TRIPLE NINE: UNVEILING THE PROPHETIC 2012 MELTDOWN OF THE LOST AND ASTRAY PALE STATE OF MIND

And the lesson would be learned
locking that pale, opposite energy out forever
Never again to be able to return
Clearing the pathway
for the sacred ancestral presence
of the Divine Children of the Sun
to return upon the Seen from the Unseen
To again become a most supreme expression
of the ooh's and the aah's of a Love Supreme

<u>*Royal Priestess vocals:*</u>
Ooh Aah
A Love Supreme

<u>High Priest vocals:</u>
And now that we've brought this telling to you
whole and clean
Examine this white blight;
learn the lessons that come from dealing with this thing

Chapter 3 Innerlude:
The Soothsayer Speaks

Song 3 from "12th Hour Prophecy: The Pale Curse and the Solarized Energy Shift," Kwatamani musical CD release, 2008

<u>Royal Priestess vocals:</u>
How did the Children come
to such a sad state of being
Not knowing and not seeing
And what would the soothsayer say

<u>High Priest vocals:</u>
Divine Children of the Sun
A statement of our most supreme ancestral presence head to toe
Melanination, a statement of solarization
Earth, wind, rain and sun
The essence of our most supreme ancestral presence,
Supreme Love flow
And our ancestral link to the Sphinx would endure
to make sure Supreme Love is kept, whole and pure
An imprinted statement of our existence long befo'
The hell and high water would begin to flow
And the sacred ancestral soothsayer
told of this story long befo'
That cold-blooded, opposite energy appeared at our do'
Disguised as lost and astray pale kin, looking hapless and helpless and wearing animal skin
A reflection of a savage rage
Smelling of a foul funk that offend to no end
Looking piss-poor and depraved

FULFILLING THE SACRED ANCESTRAL PROPHECY OF THE TRIPLE NINE: UNVEILING THE PROPHETIC 2012 MELTDOWN OF THE LOST AND ASTRAY PALE STATE OF MIND

Showing that there was no spirit consciousness saved
A cold-blooded scavenger/predator, consumer of flesh
and blood, bones and skin
Be it fish, foul, or animal or the He and She of Men
It would be extremely difficult, almost impossible to
determine that these lost and astray pale Children
were of our kin
You see, they had mutated and degenerated
from outside and within
A reflection of that cold-blooded opposite energy that
was nothing less than a Satanic Jinn
And although the sacred ancestral soothsayers had
warned us about the coming of these cold-blooded,
pale kin
We would open our doors and let them in
You see, we were about divine social economic
family community
But that would mean nothing to these cold-blooded kin
of the opposite energy
And ooh if the Children of the Sun could see what the
sacred ancestral soothsayers did see
They could have avoided experiencing this cold-blooded
opposite energy and its cold-blooded pale
manifest destiny
But the sacred ancestral soothsayers really didn't have a
whole lot of time for the chit chat
Only had enough time to bring forward divine spirit
consciousness
Where action speaks louder than words
and holistic living is an absolute fact

CHAPTER 3 INNERLUDE: THE SOOTHSAYER SPEAKS

And at anytime the Divine Children of the Sun did not
take heed to the divine knowledge, wisdom and
understanding that the sacred soothsayers did see
Indeed, experience would let the Children of the Sun
know for sho'
The nature of this cold-blooded, opposite energy
and how the freezing fires of hell do flow
You see, the Sun Children reasoned and thought
that should the pale ones thaw their brain, body
and spirit out
Surely, there would be a divine conscious turn about
We would do every thing we could
to get these pale Children to rise
We would teach 'em civil laws
and they would turn to civil lies
Taking the course of deadly force
Murdering, raping, stealing to enslave
Using sex and violence, war and crime to disguise
the civil lies
In order to manipulate the suntanned Children's demise
And so, although we would deal
with supreme ancestral truth up front and be for real
The lost and astray pale kin would seek the thrill
that they would feel from the kill
and to live the lies and deceptions
of this opposite energy
And would worship the mentality of this energy
as a deity
Control freak, seeking to search and destroy and enslave
anything and anyone that they would meet
Breeding, seeding, feeding off this cold-blooded
opposite energy

FULFILLING THE SACRED ANCESTRAL PROPHECY OF THE TRIPLE NINE: UNVEILING THE PROPHETIC 2012 MELTDOWN OF THE LOST AND ASTRAY PALE STATE OF MIND

Spreading the plague of the suffering and grueling
harsh and cruel pains that would cause this mutating
degeneration to come to be
Having a keeny nose and small breathing holes
That reflected acclimation of living
in cave-dwelling ice cold
And so to see the sacred garden culture
of the Children of the Sun from these pale eyes, well
This holistic living truth had no way to be
comprehended, interpreted or internalized
Except through deceptions and lies
You see, from jump street
these pale Children had a death wish
Rejecting the most supreme seen and unseen essence of
Life and Supreme Love, Ta and Tat
Yeah, those of that pale mentality truly have a death wish
Aligning with that cold-blooded, opposite energy and its
pale-male-war god twist
The sacred ancestral soothsayer said
there'd be days like this
And this cold-blooded opposite energy of doom and
gloom would adversely affect anyone
caught up in the midst

<u>Royal Priestess vocals:</u>
The warning came before
 but the Children did not comprehend
And the warning comes again
As the cycle of the cold-blooded opposite energy
  comes to an end

CHAPTER 3 INNERLUDE: THE SOOTHSAYER SPEAKS

<u>High Priest vocals:</u>
And during those earlier times
before the Children of the Sun would trip
And become trapped in the deep-freeze cold
and turn pale
The sacred ancestral soothsayers would warn
about the coming of this cold-blooded freezing storm
Yeah, they were advised and warned to take heed
about the coming of the deep freeze
Sort of like being warned
about the coming of global warming
Except during those times
the freezing fires of hell would be storming
Yeah, these Children of the Sun was on a mind trip
and would become lost and astray
because the weather would flip
Yeah, they would ignore the sacred ones
now, they would look at the sacred ancestral soothsayers
in disbelief
Forgetting that the soothsayers were sent
from the Unseen to the Seen to give them relief
Yeah, they would disobey and ignore
As the freezing fires of hell would pour
And they would breed, seed and feed
off of this opposite energy
And the entire planet would have to pay the price
As this cold-blooded, scavenger-like predator would
emerge from the ice
And about that the sacred ones had long ago given advice
About the coming of the pale ones, the spreading of hell
and the high waters that follow melting down of the ice
But the Children of the Sun could not hear well

FULFILLING THE SACRED ANCESTRAL PROPHECY OF THE TRIPLE NINE: UNVEILING THE PROPHETIC 2012 MELTDOWN OF THE LOST AND ASTRAY PALE STATE OF MIND

You see, they had no experiences with the energy of hell
You see, the suntanned Children's focus was on the Most Supreme Spirit of Love
What they were about to experience of that opposite energy, they could not conceive of
And so what went down in the ice
seeded by innocence and ignorancy and not taking advice
Would go around and come back around
and bite the Children of the Sun twice
Yeah, because those who were in power
to call the roll of the dice
Had personal missions and wouldn't take advice
The mass majority would have to bite the ice
Yeah, that same egotistical energy
that emerged back then
Is the same egotistical energy
that causes the lost and astray Children of the Sun
to continue to waver and bend
Yeah, the sacred ancestral soothsayers
said there'd be days like days like this
During the last days and times
the last level and degree of melting down
that ice-cold, deep-freeze state of mind
And the I in I now warn it to be a fatal mission
if this supreme truth is ignored, disregarded or dismissed
And the I in I speak to you from deep within
Regardless of you being blonde or bald or natty dread
Regardless of the color of your skin

Chapter Four:
The Division of Race

Chapter 4 Prelude:
Do You Know What It Took and What It Will Take?

Song 2 from "Dose Three: Supernatural Healing Serum," Kwatamani musical CD release, September 2006

<u>Royal Priestess vocals:</u>
Do you know what it took?
Just take a look, got your mind shook
It got you off your source, took you way off course
You've got to understand, it was a mighty fall that came
to He and She of Man
How many times did you have to crawl
and lick the toxic filth off the floor
Until you cried and cried for more?
Do you know what it took?
Do you know what it took?
Do you know what it took to tie your mind
into a knot until you get what you got?
That's why you get what you got
Do you know what it took to contaminate your brain 'til
every thought and reasoning drives you insane?
It's a massive shame how you entertain
this massive game
that continues to be played on you
and you play it too
There was a cave-dwelling crew
that grew and grew in their pale, stale cold blooded ways
of toxic consumption
And then to make it worse, you fell to the curse

FULFILLING THE SACRED ANCESTRAL PROPHECY OF THE TRIPLE NINE: UNVEILING THE PROPHETIC 2012 MELTDOWN OF THE LOST AND ASTRAY PALE STATE OF MIND

and you started craving it, raving it
Playing it like it was yo' thang
Will somebody please tell me what it took?
Do you know what it took?

<u>High Priest vocals:</u>
Do you know what someone would look like and what
their life would come to be
if they were spiritually disconnected
from their divine ancestry and locked down
in the vibrations and the sensations of toxic insanity?
Can you imagine someone so weak and depleted
that they take their instructions
from the ghosts and the goblins that live in their head?
Can you imagine a whole-life energy source consuming
of the weak and feeble toxic energy of the dead?
And do you know what it took to contaminate
your body, your spirit and your brain?
And do you know what it takes
to cause an animal to break?
Do you know the tricks and deceptions
and the games used to infuse misery, aches and pains
and the technique used to misuse and abuse
so that one can train and tame?
And after you've done all that, in fact
I want you to multiply the con game
and multiply the misery, aches and pains
And what will remain is the toxic deceptions
that you now claim
And what do you think it would take
to cause you to change?

CHAPTER 4 PRELUDE: DO YOU KNOW WHAT IT TOOK AND WHAT IT WILL TAKE?

Do you know what it took to cause you to change
and about the violent attacks and the blood-gushing
misery, aches and pains and fright and fear
that was installed in your brain?
Do you know what it would take
to cause you to change?
Do you know about this fate
and the rape of your mate
And do you know about your life that it would take
And do you know about the color-coded game
of bone-crushing hate?
Do you have any idea of the Sun Children's fate?
Or are you simply lost and astray in the mind
and just cannot relate?
And maybe you think that
your thoughts are first rate
and that there are pale Children
who suffer the same kind of fate
in the toxic vibrations of white-on-white hate
And maybe you just can't feel the gaps of time, 'cause
your focus is on black-on-black crime
and you do not realize that there is much more
to this story of mind
Do you know what it would take
to cause you to change?
Do you know how much DNA degeneration it would
take to mutate your body and your brain?
Do you think there's any possibility that your spirit
energy would remain the same
not being toxicly affected by the mutation and
degeneration of your body and your brain?
Do you know what it took to cause you to change?

FULFILLING THE SACRED ANCESTRAL PROPHECY OF THE TRIPLE NINE: UNVEILING THE PROPHETIC 2012 MELTDOWN OF THE LOST AND ASTRAY PALE STATE OF MIND

Do you have any idea about the suffocating misery and
the grueling aches and pains?
Can you imagine the violent rage of a blood-sucking
pack on the attack or the tearing and ripping fangs of a
blood- and bone- and flesh-eating gang?
Can you imagine the mental and physical pain of being
tied and chained and crippled and maimed simply
because you are trying to escape this thang?
Can you imagine being used and abused, then used as
trade until you reach a ripe old age?
Can you imagine the cold-blooded deception of the
mentally insane?
How much of this it would take
to cause you to change?
Can you imagine how much a brother was shook having
all of his jewels took
turning him into a eunuch?
Can you imagine a queen mother, priestess or princess
being misused and abused
from front and behind
turned into a cold-blooded killer's concubine?
Can you imagine the life of a brother
after having his jewels took
and then given somebody's religious book
and a ray of hope that after he died the invader god
would replace all that was took
so long as he followed the ways and the means
of the keepers of the book?
Imagine the fright and the fear and the wailing cries and
the illusions and delusions
and the cold-blooded lies

CHAPTER 4 PRELUDE: DO YOU KNOW WHAT IT TOOK AND WHAT IT WILL TAKE?

and know that they received nothing
after they had died
from the grueling aching pains that came
because they were spiritually disconnected
from the Most Supreme Ancestral Presence
from which they had came
Can you comprehend the strategy
of the mentally and spiritually insane
the slick and wicked and cunning games
that take the chains from the feet and hands
and then place them on your brain?
Do you know what it took to cause you to change?
Do you know what it took to drive you
mentally and physically and spiritually insane?
Do you know what it took
to cause this massive brain drain?
Do you know what it took to cause you to worship this
death-consumption culture game?
Do you know what it took to cause you to seek
fortune and fame
in this cold, blood-thirsty and heartless game?
Do you know what it took to cause you to move
into the fast-lane of going lost and astray
moaning and groaning while you play and pray, crying
the blues because of the self-inflicted dues
that you've got to pay?
Do you know what it took to cause you to change?
Do you know what it would take to cause you to purge
and to detox this cold-blooded, ice-cold, deep-freeze
game and change in divine order?

Chapter Four: The Division of Race

Telling the Supreme Truth

This telling may not be pleasing to those who are consumers of that opposite energy. Nevertheless, this telling must be told. This is not about personal likes and dislikes. This is not about having a vivid imagination and making up tales. This telling is straight from the Most Supreme Seen and Unseen Essence of Life and Supreme Love. Although many will have their own interpretation about what this is all about, any interpretation that is given will be based upon the energy of one's consumption. The Most Supreme Seen and Unseen ancestral spirit presence of the Divine Children of the Sun now speaks in this telling as the expressions forwarded through the essence of the I in I.

Therefore, we are not dealing with matters of interpretation or personal preference, but rather we are dealing with being able to identify the nature of the energy that one consumes. Beyond that, we are dealing with the ability to identify the energy that has been consumed all along one's ancestral line. As one begins to reason with the nature of one's energy consumption, one will begin to understand how the energy works and moves in one's own existence. One will begin to reason with the nature of one's own energy and how one happens to be a sum total of the energy that one consumes, mentally, physically and spiritually.

When one becomes serious about the nature of the energy that one has consumed, one will be able to make a clear determination about whether or not one seeks more of the same results or whether one is ready for a divine change. One can determine whether one wants to continue consuming of that opposite energy or whether one wants to forward the consumption of the Most Supreme ancestral energies of the divine parallel. When that determination has been made by the individual, the host who decides to consume of whole life energy must immediately begin to detox and purge with an ancestral spirit surge. Learn the lessons, retrieve the blessings and move forward into the essence of the Divine Union of One, emerging into the ooh's and the aah's of a Love Supreme.

Division and Separation in Black and White

Mutation and degeneration did divide Man, He and She, into two parallels of thought and reasoning, two parallels of existence upon the planet Earth. In fact, a division became clearly pronounced as distinct as the difference between the color vibrations of black and the absence of color called white. Black is the unification of all vibrations within whole life energy as the Most Supreme Essence of Life and Supreme Love. The wholeness of black is the source of all life as it emerged within the Most Supreme Seen and Unseen essence of masculine and feminine energy, deep inside the divine parallel. Black also represents the unification of the earth, wind, rain and sun as the supreme elements of the sacred ancestral spirit presence of the Divine Children of the Sun. Color is clearly a reflection of light. The

CHAPTER FOUR: THE DIVISION OF RACE

absence of color indicates that the solar rays are not being absorbed whole and clean.

In the opposite parallel, white is considered as pure. However, there are no thoughts by those who consume of the opposite energy regarding what the purity of white is all about. White is the pure absence of color and thus the absence of the essence of life and Supreme Love. Therefore, white represents the vague and lifeless emptiness of the energy that is opposite of Supreme Love and the Essence of Life. The coldness of white would then be considered pale. The absence of life energy and the unwhole state of white is the source of all the cold and pale vibrations of lust, lies, illusions, confusion, death and deadly destruction that emerged from the toxic parallel. White also represents separation and isolation from life energy where there is no feminine energy to co-create with the angry, vengeful, jealous and violent pale-male-war-god deity. The white blight also represents the coming of the tribes and clans of a breed of mankind who mutated and degenerated in that cold and pale white blight environment where the deep-freeze ice cold dominated.

Millennial Movements within the Divine Parallel

Let us track the nature of this division as written in black and white. For millions of years, the Divine Children of the Sun inhabited this glorious earth, moving and grooving within the Divine Union of One, recycling within higher and more intense phases of divine spirit consciousness. From the infant stage of growth and development into millions of years of experience and expressions, the sacred ancestral spirit presence was

FULFILLING THE SACRED ANCESTRAL PROPHECY OF THE TRIPLE NINE: UNVEILING THE PROPHETIC 2012 MELTDOWN OF THE LOST AND ASTRAY PALE STATE OF MIND

strong, intact and beyond penetration by the opposite energy.

From the sunbathed center lands of the earth, the Divine Children of the Sun traveled and navigated, making the glorious earth a most enjoyable and pleasant home. The Divine Children of the Sun were secure in the divine knowledge that the Most Supreme Unseen would never leave us to do this thing along. As we emerged into higher levels and degrees of spirit conscious energy, the Divine Children of the Sun experienced a most supreme ancestral spirit surge, a natural high within the vibrations and sensations of whole life energy.

As the whole life presence continued to emerge and intensify, great wonders would manifest as divine creative expressions of thought and reasoning within the Most High plan. The Divine Children of the Sun would dwell deep within the melaninated pleasures of their golden tan as the essence of the He and She of Man. And the original DNA codes of melanin were the dominant genetic expression of a solarized physical presence within the Sacred Garden Culture from which we come. These sacred suntanned Children would move freely, learning the various landscapes, studying the patterns of whole life energy upon the seen. The Divine Children of the Sun would uphold that holistic living respect, honor and divine humility for earth, wind, rain and the glory of that golden sun that bathed and baptized them in their divinity.

As the Divine Children of the Sun would learn they would teach within the Most Supreme essence of One, and as they would teach, they would learn. Maintaining

CHAPTER FOUR: THE DIVISION OF RACE

the fruits of the trees of life was a key focus within the Sacred Garden Culture from which we come. Whole life energy provided the most essential and nutritional consumption pattern within the raw and living fruits, vegetables, seeds, nuts, herbs and spice.

For millions of years of getting acquainted with the earth's space and place, the Divine Children of the Sun would start to create at an amazing pace. As a top priority within the essence of life, the Divine Children of the Sun would continue to hold the glory, the joy, pleasures and the utmost divine humility for earth, wind, rain and sun.

The Divine Children of the Sun were very wise in comprehending that the elements of earth, wind, rain and sun were the essence of their being. The essence of their being was a reflection of divine creation, the most supreme creative force of all that there is of Supreme Love. The soil was maintained as a most precious resource within the Sacred Garden Culture from which we come. Trees were honored as a source of whole life energy. For example, the simple matter of cutting a tree down would require the rituals and rites of ancestral request. Any time there was the taking of a tree, a new tree would be planted a season prior to the taking of that tree to honor the recycling of whole life energy.

The Most Supreme Seen presence of Man, He and She, honored the connection with the most Supreme Unseen and worked to maintain the Divine Oneness of the whole life presence. As it is, as it was and as it must be, all living things were honored as sacred within the cycles of whole life energy. All living creatures mated and related with their own kind and kin in the divine

FULFILLING THE SACRED ANCESTRAL PROPHECY OF THE TRIPLE NINE: UNVEILING THE PROPHETIC 2012 MELTDOWN OF THE LOST AND ASTRAY PALE STATE OF MIND

union of masculine and feminine energy. The Sacred Garden Culture from which we come had no concept or practice of animal husbandry, bestiality and no vibrations of hunting and herding. The Divine Children of the Sun would encounter these cold and pale practices in the mutated and degenerated clans and tribes who emerged from the white blight of the deep-freeze environment. The ways and means of animal husbandry, bestiality, hunting, herding and scavenging defined the predatory nature of the death-consuming culture and were identified as a clear contradiction to the most Supreme spirit of love for all living things. Additionally, the consumption of flesh and bones and blood and guts of animals or humans showed a grave disrespect for the fruits of the trees of life that were given to Man, He and She, to consume divinely.

The Divine Children of the Sun had no way to relate to the nature of the opposite energy. When the mutated and degenerated lost and astray Children emerged upon the seen of the planet Earth, they were an unknown and foreign presence. The Divine Children of the Sun had no concern for the opposite energy. Without concern for those toxic energies, the sacred suntanned Children would glorify in their sacred ancestral spirit presence by building great monuments and sacred temples. The Divine Children of the Sun would glorify in the Divine Union of One by expressing the sacred sexuality of the masculine and feminine essence. It was comprehended that there could never be a masculine presence without the birthplace of femininity, nor could there be a feminine presence without the ejaculation of masculinity.

CHAPTER FOUR: THE DIVISION OF RACE

The divine innate requirement for the sacred ancestral spirit presence is, was and will always be Divine Union of the masculine and feminine energy. Man, He and She, would be two parts to one whole. If ever there was a state of division, conflict and separation between the masculine and feminine energy, such a divided state would be a contradiction to the most Supreme Seen and Unseen Essence of Life and Supreme Love.

The Divine Children of the Sun had no thought or reference for stepping outside of Divine Oneness. Therefore, acts of inflicting hurt and harm upon another were seen as inflicting hurt and harm upon self. Likewise, thoughts and behaviors of inflicting hurt and harm upon the Earth, were not even conceivable within the Sacred Garden Culture from which we come. Such thoughts would be unthinkable within whole life energy, because there were no vibrations present to process such thoughts. As time would unfold, creations of the physical seen would emerge as great temples and social economic family community structures within the ancient lands. These sacred ancestral temples and structures were built to glorify the Most Supreme Seen and Unseen Essence of Life and Supreme Love. Therefore, in honor of the Sacred Garden Culture from which we come, the Divine Children of the Sun would anoint great irrigation systems and gardens and magnificent ways and means of recycling whole life energy.

A Recent Breed of Mutation and Degeneration

The lost and astray Children of the Sun would mutate and degenerate into scavenger-like predators who would learn to cave dwell. These cave-dwelling clans

FULFILLING THE SACRED ANCESTRAL PROPHECY OF THE TRIPLE NINE: UNVEILING THE PROPHETIC 2012 MELTDOWN OF THE LOST AND ASTRAY PALE STATE OF MIND

would emerge out of the freezing ice, transforming into nomadic warring clans. From the core and essence of these mutated and degenerated breeds would come the extension of the brutal and savage predatorial mentality that initially emerged within their cave-dwelling days. This would be the mentality that followed the melting ice into the lands of the sacred suntanned He and She of Man.

This recent period of time upon the planet has been a very trying time for Man, He and She, although time has passed in just the blink of an eye. When one takes a deep-seated look at the last 12,000 years or so, one can not even truly begin to fathom the degree of damage that occurred within the mental, physical, and spiritual presence of Man, He and She. The experiences of the recent millennia have brought forward mutation and degeneration within one's DNA, errors within one's genetic codes, and a severe decrease in the ability to tap into the unseen connections of whole life energy. There has been an extreme amount of interference and interruption with the genetic codes that express the sacred ancestral spirit presence of Man, He and She. The DNA codes have lost the divine order of whole life energy, and as a result, genetic defects, hereditary diseases, physical deformities, retardation, and mental illness are passed along in mutated and degenerated DNA codes. With many unfortunate, vicious and violent events, the opposite energy has spread like a plague, completely deteriorating and degrading the presence of masses of Man, He and She. The toxic parallel is the reflection of Man, He and She, at the lowest possible

CHAPTER FOUR: THE DIVISION OF RACE

state of being before complete self-destruction is activated.

The ugliest and most wretched examples of Man, He and She, within the death-consuming culture are in truth and reality the most telling embodiments of the opposite energy. And even the hidden lives of most individuals reveal the nature of the opposite energy in secret and shameful places of the lost and astray mind. While many individuals posture and proclaim righteousness in the public presentation, many of these same individuals have a private closet full of the ghosts and goblins of their personal affairs with the opposite energy. It becomes a general social attitude within the death-consuming culture to condemn those who wallow at the bottom of the social order—the prostitutes, drug addicts, mentally deranged, petty criminals, the poor, the illiterate, etc. As if those who do not have the same circumstances and actions are not still consuming of the exact same opposite energy. As if that opposite energy is not the same energy that fueled the horrors and brutality of the first lost and astray Children who mutated and degenerated in the deep-freeze pits of hell. And this same opposite energy continues to feed those who manipulate and orchestrate from positions of domination and control within the social, economic and religious infrastructures. These are same infrastructures that were born and bred from the death-consuming culture mentality.

First and foremost, it must be clear that each and every one of Man, He and She, originally off sprang from the sacred ancestral spirit presence of the Divine Children of the Sun and the Sacred Garden Culture from

FULFILLING THE SACRED ANCESTRAL PROPHECY OF THE TRIPLE NINE: UNVEILING THE PROPHETIC 2012 MELTDOWN OF THE LOST AND ASTRAY PALE STATE OF MIND

which we come. The first expression of Man, He and She, upon the seen was a divine expression of the Most Supreme Seen and Unseen essence of masculinity and femininity. One must begin to know, understand and comprehend that one has a divine duty, obligation and responsibility to uphold one's sacred ancestral spirit presence regardless of the color of one's skin, regardless of one being blonde or bald or natty, natty dread.

Translations and interpretations related to race and variations of racist ideology come from the mentality of the energy that is opposite of Supreme Love and the Essence of Life. The state of mind that emerges from consuming the opposite energy has absolutely no access to divine knowledge, wisdom and understanding, no ability to translate whole life energy. One must understand that those who consume of the opposite energy will only be able to translate and interpret based on their depleted mentality. Once one begins to reason with energy consumption, it becomes easier to understand why and how the death-consuming culture is a culture that worships, idolizes, and feasts upon the dead and depleted energies of the toxic parallel. These death-worship concepts include the resurrection of the dead and looking forward to dying and death in order to enjoy a heavenly afterlife.

The only way of reasoning within the toxic parallel is the reasoning of toxic order. This is why we say that one sinks steeped knee-deep in the toxic parallel. One can only consume of the nature of the energy that is provided by the toxic parallel. As the vicious cycle goes back around, the toxic parallel provides a culture born

CHAPTER FOUR: THE DIVISION OF RACE

and bred off of a energy that is opposite of Supreme Love and the Essence of Life. That would immediately let one know that the toxic parallel is a parallel that perpetuates, and will continue to perpetuate, a death-consuming culture, a culture that is based on the energies of lust, lies, illusions, confusion, death and deadly destruction, mentally, physically and spiritually. And when one makes a numerical translation on the vibrations and sensations of the opposite energy, one ends up with a triple-six vibration.

Within the number system, the number six is a part of the counting process as one advances to the number nine. Nine represents the state of completion and wholeness. The triple-six vibration represents an incomplete movement, standing, in and of itself, as an unwhole expression within the disguises and deceptions of the toxic parallel. The first six represents all that is unwhole, incomplete and deceptive within the mind of thought and reasoning. The second six represents all that is unwhole, incomplete and deceptive within one's physical presentation and appearance. The third six represents all that is unwhole, incomplete and deceptive within one's connection to spirit consciousnesss. This is the incomplete, unwhole and deceptive nature of the triple-six vibration. This 666 mark of the beast is the continuous perpetuation of the vibrations of lust, lies, illusions, confusion, death and deadly destruction.

Within the triple-six vibrations, one experiences feelings of being incomplete and unwhole while projecting the deceptions of being superior, righteous and advanced in one's state of being. Understandably, the nature of this triple-six syndrome would actually cause one to experience hidden self-doubt and self-hate, to experience feelings of inferiority within self while projecting that inferiority upon others. However, one actually feels inadequate and weak within self, and, at all points in time, one feels afraid of having one's true weakness exposed. The nature of the opposite energy produces a defensive and reactionary state of mind where one constantly guards against perceived and imaginary threats and challenges. One may feel paranoid or suspicious, constantly under attack, vulnerable to having one's weaknesses targeted by others who function within the same predatory energy. You see, the whole nature of the opposite energy is to take the depletion that one feels inside about self and then translate it as an outside happening so that one can always point the finger at someone else.

Within the toxic parallel, one can imagine that one is right and correct in one's thinking and reasoning. What becomes unpleasant or uncomfortable within self can easily be pushed on others so that someone else can be blamed and identified as the bad guy. Once one begins to project one's inner toxic waste on others, one becomes so focused outside of self that one is unable to see how the opposite energy is actually feeding deep inside one's thoughts and reasoning. An individual will sink deeper and deeper into the deception that everyone and everything else is the blame for one's hurtful and painful life experiences, rather than ever being able to evaluate the energy of one's consumption. One will never even believe that one's consumption of the opposite energy is causing the arrogant, self-righteous, defensive and stubborn attitudes and behaviors. The opposite energy will be actively running the games of lust, lies, illusions, confusion, death and deadly destruction on an individual, and the individual will have every excuse for what is happening in their life while never addressing the true cause, source and origin of his or her problems. In this way, the hosts and consumers of the opposite energy are enslaved within a mental consciousness that keeps them unaware and submissive to the opposite energy.

The Predator

The predatory nature of the opposite energy fuels a mentality that targets others as possible hosts and consumers. You see, within the toxic parallel others are seen as objects, either objects of desire, objects to be controlled and dominated, or objects to be used and abused to serve one's personal will. The opposite energy seeks to take possession of the life presence of the individual who serves as a host, claiming every thought and behavior, demanding complete obedience and loyalty, and always requiring more and more toxic consumption to maintain the deceptions and disguises of the death-consuming culture.

An error was made by the Divine Children of the Sun. In their state of innocence and ignorance, they could not conceive of the danger or the consequences that would come from consuming this cold-blooded and pale opposite energy. The error was based on having no frame of reference in dealing with the completely foreign and totally opposite energy that manifested far outside the vibrations and sensations of whole life energy. We have come to learn, know and understand that the opposite energy is a brutal, vicious, predatory energy that manifests in vibrations and sensations of lust, lies, illusions, confusion, death and deadly destruction.

When one is dealing with opposite energy, one must begin to understand that the nature of a predator is sly, slick, wicked, cold-blooded and without compassion. The predator masters in disguise and deception. In order for a predator to lure its prey for a deadly attack, the predator will do anything, by any means necessary. The nature of the predator is to prey upon its victims. While the prey may feel that the predator is merciless and cruel, the predator feels quite comfortable within the hostile and unfeeling predatory energy from which it is bred. As a matter of fact, those who have been mesmerized and hypnotized by fright and fear, or who have been impressed by materialistic dreams of fortune, fame and success, may even feel that the predatory nature is honorable, brave and appealing. One can then begin to interpret this predator mentality of the opposite energy as being a progressive and glorified way of life. In this way, many within the death-consuming culture can honor war heroes and military killers while praising the historic bloodbaths of invasion and conquest. Many have come to completely uphold the predator nature of the opposite energy as the values of hostile aggression, violence, slaughter and inflicting pain and suffering are seen as the means to securing a better life for one's self.

Indeed, the predator is a master of disguise reflecting the deceptive nature of the energy within the toxic parallel. Amazingly, those who assimilate,

CHAPTER FOUR: THE DIVISION OF RACE

integrate and associate with the cold and pale predatorial mentality very quickly align with the attitudes, values and beliefs of the energy that is opposite of Supreme Love and Essence Life. These same individuals who become a host to the energy of mutation and degeneration within the toxic parallel begin to reduce their mental and physical presence to a cold and pale state of being. The opposite energy can only manifest in the image of its nature, and, therefore, the marks of mutation and degeneration, although first expressed in the deep-freeze pits of hell, are now self-inflicted in the sunshine.

The nature of the opposite energy is to spread like a plague once it enters the mental consciousness of a host. The host will actually become a missionary to spread the toxic vibrations and sensations, passing on the these toxic attitudes, values, perceptions and behaviors like a fatal and contagious disease. Within the toxic parallel one can do anything and everything to alter and corrupt one's physical appearance. Visible changes start to occur when one consumes of the opposite energy. Remember, the nature of the opposite energy is to destroy any expressions of the sacred ancestral spirit presence of Man, He and She, and to turn everything that it touches into a depleted state of being.

One can bleach and blonde one's hair to appear more pale. One can perm and press one's hair to make it conform to the images of mutation and degeneration. One can paint and powder one's face and lips, pierce, cut and tattoo one's body. One can undergo cosmetic surgery and re-make one's slanted eyes to appear more round, one can add or subtract body parts. The body simply becomes the breeding ground for the opposite energy, so one can treat it like a beast of burden as one bends and twists to satisfy the demands, values and standards of the lost and astray state of mind. One can bloat into a fat and obese mass of toxic consumption or shrink into a withered drug-addicted fiend; one can dress in the costumes of bondage and domination, and wear the designer suits of financial manipulation – all in humble service to the opposite energy and its death-consuming culture. It really does not matter, because one has become steeped knee-deep in hopes and dreams of being accepted and praised by the grand masters of deceit who specialize promoting the values, attitudes and behaviors of the opposite energy.

Fight or Flight

The Children of the Sun did not even realize that the plague of the opposite energy had been spread by the offspring seeds who were produced by rape and the raging raids, intrusions and interruptions. Fright and fear was imprinted in those who witnessed the offspring males being brutally slaughtered. Fright and fear was imprinted in the minds of the survivors who witnessed vicious pale warlords call upon angry pale-male-war gods who were appeased by violence, bloodshed and human sacrifice. The vicious and brutal ways of the opposite energy were strange and unknown to the existence of the sacred suntanned Children.

The Divine Children of the Sun endured wave after wave of invasions, endured slaughter, raping raids and constant acts of hostile aggression. Generations and

CHAPTER FOUR: THE DIVISION OF RACE

generations of the sacred ancestral spirit presence were inflicted and infected by the mutated and degenerated breed of mankind that wielded the death blow of the opposite energy. The Divine Children of the Sun found that, although divine spirit consciousness could not be penetrated, the physical presence was vulnerable to attack after attack. The offspring seeds of rape were born; these mixed breeds came upon the seen, carrying the genetic codes of mutation and degeneration born of sacred suntanned mothers who had been violated and contaminated by the opposite energy. Consumption that was completely foreign and opposite from the Sacred Garden Culture was adopted and assimilated and integrated by those who were enslaved by the pale lost and astray mentality. The nature of this cold and pale mentality continued to be inflicted generation after generation upon suntanned Children who had already suffered a mental, physical and spiritual breakdown. These offspring suntanned Children would eventually begin to accept these savage, brutal and hostile acts as a part of their own existence, such as the eating of flesh and bones and blood and guts and skin, consuming of cow and goat milk, consuming of burnt offerings. These death-consuming-culture ways and means seeped into their existence as the suntanned Children fled from the areas where that opposite energy became dominant.

    The historical invasions inflicted by the vicious nomadic warring clans clearly show the predatory nature of the opposite energy. It is clear that, from the earliest times of the raging raids of rape and slaughter, the Children of the Sun were faced with either being slaughtered and annihilated or finding a way to defend

FULFILLING THE SACRED ANCESTRAL PROPHECY OF THE TRIPLE NINE: UNVEILING THE PROPHETIC 2012 MELTDOWN OF THE LOST AND ASTRAY PALE STATE OF MIND

themselves against the savage nomadic warlord invaders. Although the acts of slaughter and blood spill were alien to the Divine Children of the Sun, it became clear after time that the choice was either life or death, fight or flight. The lost and astray Children brought the vibrations of slaughter, death and blood spill with them from their origins in the white blight of the northern deep freeze. This mutated and degenerated breed of mankind embodied the hellish vibrations of the toxic parallel and spread the consequences of this pale ordeal like a plague.

The Divine Children of the Sun would either flee or stand their ground to fight. A mass movement of fleeing suntanned populations created a large displacement southward and westward in the ancestral motherland. The pale breed of mankind invaded throughout the suntanned lands of the He and She of Man, burning, pillaging, raiding temples, destroying intricate systems of the Sacred Garden Culture. Those suntanned Children who did not run began to fight back, and they began to adopt the vicious, cold-blooded nature of the opposite energy in order to fight fire with fire. As the Children of the Sun waged a defense against the savage nomadic warlords, they became skilled in the cold-blooded and pale ways of slaughter and warfare. In this way, the opposite energy continued to contaminate the consciousness of Man, He and She.

The Children of the Sun would amass the strength and might to force these cold-blooded, raping, raging savage scavengers and killers out of the Sacred Garden Culture environment. However, these invading tribes and clans would be ever-lurking just outside of the

CHAPTER FOUR: THE DIVISION OF RACE

remaining areas of divine social economic family community, burning, destroying and attacking to force a way back inside. When these vicious hordes were pushed back, they would camp to amass more of their kind as waves of these invaders came from the Caucasus steppe region and moved with savage rage to attack the Sacred Garden Culture. The raping raids became an overwhelming horror upon the seen.

The predatory nature of the opposite energy does not change. The greedy, vengeful, brutal, and selfish nature of this energy that is opposite of Supreme Love and the Essence of Life does not change. In fact, since its recent emergence upon the seen, the opposite energy has remained true to its white-blight origin. The pale invaders were obsessed with stealing, claiming, dominating and controlling the wealth of the Sacred Garden Culture, the mineral wealth, the beautiful garden lands of a solarized paradise, the enchanting dignity of the suntanned feminine presence and the glorious strength of the suntanned masculine presence. The vampire-like hunger of the mutated and degenerated breed of mankind could not be satisfied as that opposite energy kept on fueling vibrations of depletion and devitalization.

As the Sacred Garden Culture became more destabilized, the Children of the Sun became more polluted and diluted in their energy consumption and more mutated and degenerated in their genetic codes. To deal with the relentless invasions, these weakened remnants of the Divine Children of the Sun engaged in acts of surrender, submission, appeasement, integration, assimilation and association with the disciples and followers of that opposite energy. What this looked like upon the seen was a sorrowful sight as the sacred ancestral spirit presence of Man, He and She, actually was reduced to the weak and feeble vibrations and sensations of a cold and pale state of mind.

The invasions from the northern Nordic tribes would totally destabilize the suntanned land that has been identified as Old Europe, just as the brutal Semitic tribes would invade from the east. As these vicious tribes would crisscross, they would establish the nature of today's global warfare. In clear and simple terms, the global-warfare syndrome of the savage and brutal nomadic warlords of the East and the West of the northern hemisphere, today declared as Europe, would set the stage for a final conflict. The nature of the opposite energy is self-destructive. That cold-blooded and pale toxic nature has become a dominant force upon the planet Earth, squeezing the sacred ancestral spirit presence of Man, He and She, in a death grip. Savage, brutal and hostile aggression coupled with a lack of compassion for the essence of life will lead the disciples and followers of the opposite energy to a final conflict within the toxic parallel.

The Mental Mindset of Paleness

The mental mindset that continues to dominate the lives of Man, He and She, upon the earth is the paleness ideology that has divided Man, He and She, into physical categories of skin color, social class and caste systems where the paleness of skin or one's allegiance to the paleness ideology determines the pecking order. Such

CHAPTER FOUR: THE DIVISION OF RACE

manifestations of a superiority complex where those of the lost and astray pale state of mind project themselves as superior only serve to compensate for gnawing insecurities and mental, physical and spiritual inadequacies that are the direct result of being disconnected from the most supreme ancestral spirit presence of Man, He and She.

False, fake, and pretentious categories of race are simply another ugly face of the same vibrations of division, conflict, opposition and hostile aggression that fuel every relationship within the energy that is opposite of Supreme Love and the Essence of Life. The paleness ideology is interwoven within the fabric of all thinking and reasoning among every group and sub-group, every class and caste, every religious theology, scientific methodology, new age philosophy and modern technology. The paleness ideology is the true nature of every mission and every task of all who consume of the death culture that feeds so-called modern civilized social order.

Regardless, of the many paths of the paleness ideology that one may travel, one is never able to go beyond paleness. In fact, the more one assimilates and integrates the pale ideologies born out of suffering mutation and degeneration, the deeper one ventures into the white-blight zone of the death consumption culture. One's presence becomes pale and lifeless, like a walking corpse or a clone or a worker drone as one follows the paths of paleness seeking success, fortune and fame to the bitter end.

Whenever the claim of many paths is offered, it is a red flag to signal that the individual is steadfast in his or her position and does not truly desire to be disturbed. For, one has invested in a pathway within the death consumption culture that promises success, fortune and fame in the form of either economic power, political power, religious power or intellectual power. Power plays and power struggles line every pathway within the energy that is opposite of Supreme Love and the Essence of Life while the deception continues that one is seeking some greater good beyond feeding an overblown ego. With any level and degree of exposure to supreme truth, one will become very defensive and stubborn in justifying one's chosen path.

Finding the truth and living the truth are two different pursuits. One may intellectualize about truth up inside one's head, playing all kinds of mental games, speaking as an expert while one's behaviors and actions stand as a complete contradiction. For example, one can find out the truth about their consumption patterns and how what they are eating, drinking or smoking is causing their body to become sick, addicted and afflicted. However, after finding out the truth, this same individual can still continue to knowingly consume the same dead, devitalized and depleted substances over and over again, becoming sicker and sicker. Or, one may decide to focus on the part of the truth that is most appealing and soothing to the mind while quickly ignoring other parts and resisting the whole truth. This "pick-and-choose" method of truth-seeking is quite common, and obviously very appealing, to the lost and astray mind.

Let us not ignore the fact that one may consciously search for the truth about the nature of the lost and astray

CHAPTER FOUR: THE DIVISION OF RACE

pale state of mind while glorifying the cunning and deceptive ways that express the true nature of the energy that is opposite of Supreme Love and the Essence of Life.

The hateful scorn expressed in sexist and racist ideologies; the humiliating and degrading sexual acts of bestiality, homosexuality, sadomasochism, rape and necrophilia; the brutality of violent crimes, and the cold-blooded plots and schemes of social economic and religious exploitation are all examples of the true nature of the energy that is opposite of Supreme Love and the Essence of Life. It is sad to say, but there are those who wallow in these truths as a way of life.

While deep-freeze environmental conditions and consumption patterns have absolutely nothing to do with the natural and innate presence of Man, He and She, they have everything to do with the paleness ideology that is indeed based upon the hunting and herding vibrations of the energy that is opposite of Supreme Love and the Essence of Life. The truth is that those who seek the truth about the paleness ideology and seek to uphold that truth must indeed continue to consume of the depleted and devitalized vibrations of the energy that is opposite of Supreme Love and the Essence of Life. The "caveman diet," as it has been called, is indeed the original consumption plan to maintain the lost and astray pale state of mind, and there are many paths to this truth.

Chapter 4 Innerlude:
0 to 12 Degrees

Song 4 from "12th Hour Prophecy: The Pale Curse and the Solarized Energy Shift," Kwatamani musical CD release, 2008

<u>Royal Priestess vocals:</u>
*Children of the Sun, our excuse has been
we didn't know who, what, when, why, where or how
Oh, oh, oh; but we should have learned
should have learned our lesson by now*

<u>High Priest vocals:</u>
Millions of years, Divine Children of the Sun
Yeah, that's our story
Masters of the Sacred Garden Culture, builders of pyramids, monuments and temples of glory
And although going through different changes different times
The ooh's and the aah's of a Love Supreme would remain constant as the bottom line all the time
There was those times when the northern hemisphere would become ice cold
And the energy of the opposite would unload its load
And during those times, Divine Children of the Sun
supposed to roll and get their dark behinds
up out of that ice cold
Because resistance or stubbornness of any kind
would feed the opposite energy
and breed the lost and astray mind
And the essence of Life is that as the world turn
The Divine Children of the Sun

FULFILLING THE SACRED ANCESTRAL PROPHECY OF THE TRIPLE NINE: UNVEILING THE PROPHETIC 2012 MELTDOWN OF THE LOST AND ASTRAY PALE STATE OF MIND

had many lessons to learn
But regardless of how those lessons come
and how they would go
Our divine responsibility is to move on and stay strong
and to know that the Most Supreme Unseen would never
leave us to do this thing alone
Yeah, we were master gardeners, mastering every
mathematical equation
Breeding, seeding, feeding off of the tree of life
Nurturing and protecting our earthly paradise
Mastering the herbs and every energy used to heal
Having no relationship with a red or blue pill
And the ankh would indeed be our unified seal
Divine union of Man, He and She, into one
The Most Supreme equation and the real deal
And the I is the essence of all that I am
The Most Supreme Seen and Unseen
no deception, no lies, and no scams
Having no divine ancestral relationship with a jealous
god of vengeance, war and wrath
who is declared as a god of love
However, we would indeed learn about a Grand Master
of Deceit who would speak with a forked tongue
Perpetuating deceptions and lies under the veil of pale
skin, pale hair, pale eyes
Yeah, we were far beyond the outside
where the opposite energy thrived
Honoring our most supreme ancestral presence
in living color and live
Whole and clean, seen and unseen

CHAPTER 4 INNERLUDE: 0 TO 12 DEGREES

But there would come a time upon this glorious earth
When the pale ones would raid and invade
our garden culture turf
And as the sun would melt down the icy hell
where the pale ones would birth
They would ride the tides of high water
and bring us harm and hurt
And to seal the deal, they would leave the rot and stench
of blood spill
And they would rock and roll and reel
and get a thrill from the kill
And the stench of the dead, raped and innocent would
leave ghosts and goblins in our head
And this would be our experience as we encountered the
death culture of the dread
And we would become confused
as the pale ones would abuse
And a divine spirit conscious tool could not be used
So we would establish a new lesson plan
and drive out this pale beastly clan
And the residue of this experience
would cause us to lose our blessing
If we made the slightest mistake and not learn our lesson
As the blessings would go, the lessons would come
And it is now our divine and innate responsibility
To detox and purge with a spiritual surge
Learn our lesson, retrieve our blessing
Return back to the essence of the divine union of one
Yeah, we've been upon this earth for millions of years
And after witnessing and watching that cold-blooded,
opposite energy self-install
We have seen it all

FULFILLING THE SACRED ANCESTRAL PROPHECY OF THE TRIPLE NINE: UNVEILING THE PROPHETIC 2012 MELTDOWN OF THE LOST AND ASTRAY PALE STATE OF MIND

We should know better now
should have known better then
But we were so confused by the fact that these lost and
astray pale Children had mutated and degenerated
from ancestral kin
We did not know, neither did we comprehend
the level and degree of mutated degeneration
or the extreme damage that was caused
once that cold-blooded opposite energy
had found itself in
Yeah, that first hour of the prophecy
really caught us off guard
We were young, dumb and full of come
Deaf, dumb and blind to the nature of the deadly, beastly
predatory pale mind

As the clock struck two, we would find ourselves steeped
knee-deep in hell and high water
And we would come to know things about ourselves we
never, never knew
We would also come to know what a cold-blooded stale
and pale mind will do
And the raping rage would leave stains and pained birth
And the pains would be encoded into DNA signals
sent to the brain
And the raped and abused mothers would breed
confusion and optical illusion and give birth to a strain
that would break the ancestral chain
And the offspring Children would arrive
carrying a semi-pale vibe
And semi-pale tribes like Semites and Hittites

CHAPTER 4 INNERLUDE: 0 TO 12 DEGREES

would begin to thrive
By the time the clock struck three, we would begin to see
through the veil of these cold stale and pale lies
Regain our composure, have a strong turn about and
drive the pale ones back out

But by the time the clock struck four, they would snuck
their sneaky little tales in through the back door
Using a color-coded vibe to disguise
their stale and pale lies
And once under cover
more stale and pale lies would pour
And now they would arrive
under a Semite and Hittite vibe
And they would attack, but we would survive
and drive them back outside
But by the time the clock struck five
they would be back on it
Seeking color-coded vibes to capitalize
Many an ancestral mother had grown very weak
Because they had given birth to this deceit
Now they're back on it, running their pale plan
and had the ancestral mother eating from their hand
And upon their table flesh and blood would be a treat
As this would be what the Children of the Sun
would learn to eat
And as the Children would consume
half alive and half dead
This would be the stamp to approve
the death culture of dread
And the ghosts and the goblins were au-feasting and
au-festering deep inside their heads

FULFILLING THE SACRED ANCESTRAL PROPHECY OF THE TRIPLE NINE: UNVEILING THE PROPHETIC 2012 MELTDOWN OF THE LOST AND ASTRAY PALE STATE OF MIND

And the ancestors were not pleased
But the Children of the Sun
were being led lost and astray
No longer following their ancestral lead

And before we could reach hour six
we were already in a hell of a fix
Something wicked, cold, pale and cruel was going on
You see, a sister named Cleo was on the throne
And a plot and a plan was there to seize her
Because a guy named Julius wanted to control her throne
This minute it was done, the triple-six vibe was on
Need I mention the other things going on
The pale ones who would call themselves Aryan/Hindu
would tighten up the screw
And the Indus Valley they would undo, and the Children
of the Sun were trapped in their plot
With the fires of hell freezing hot
The plan was to turn Blacks into untouchables
within our own land
Yeah, every where you look there was a pale master plan
Vicious cruel and whack and every kind of attack
The plan, to control the Children of the Sun
and their land

And you couldn't really tell where the fifth hour end
and the sixth hour begin
But somewhere within was born another vibe as the pale-
male-war god had his son crucified
Some say it was because he was on our side
But anyway it went, they said the brother man died

CHAPTER 4 INNERLUDE: 0 TO 12 DEGREES

And as it was with the paleness of the Hindu, so it would
be with the Jew, and so it was with the Christians, and
now so it would be with the Arab/Muslims
as they begin to tighten up the screw
Leading the fatal attack, knock us off our feet
and break our back
Yeah, they would all begin to get together and tighten up
the screw
And squeeze our butts and balls so tight
we turned pale blue

And by the time the seventh hour had arrived
we were struggling and striving
with tears in our eyes, trying to survive
And those who would not submit
would be inflicted with gruesome misery aches and pains
until they had died
Yeah, during the seventh hour we were captured
bought and sold as slaves
During the time of the Arab/Muslim, trans-Saharan trade

By the time of hour eight, we had suffered lust, lies,
illusions, confusion, death
and deadly destruction first rate

And so by hour nine
we had almost completely lost our mind
Divided and conquered along tribal lines
Raided and invaded by color-coded kin
under the guidance of a Satanic Jinn
Who disguised himself as confused white men
Color-coded Jinn, transferring the slave trade

FULFILLING THE SACRED ANCESTRAL PROPHECY OF THE TRIPLE NINE: UNVEILING THE PROPHETIC 2012 MELTDOWN OF THE LOST AND ASTRAY PALE STATE OF MIND

from the Muslims to the Christians
as the trans-Atlantic slave trade would begin
Yeah, this would be the hour where the freezing fires of
hell would burn 96 degrees
A cold-blooded freeze on the mind that would leave the
Children of the Sun completely blind
During these times, the triple-six program would be
stamped and engraved in our mind
And it would become the stamp of approval through time
And unless one is able to detox and purge
Lust, lies, illusions, confusion, death and deadly
destruction will become the action
that speaks louder than words
Now we're in the eleventh hour about to come to an end

Hitler cleared all confusions and illusions
about the nature of the Aryan/White men
The eleventh hour, north, south, east and west
Those of the lost and astray pale state of mind doing
everything they can to fail this final test
And sex and violence and war and crime is maintained
and supported by the lost and astray mind
And the South African pale game was played so well
That most folks think that paleness failed
Because it can not see the residue of this paleness trail
And India's pale mindset has produced
a nuclear weapon plan
Causing the Black Untouchables
to become scared as hell
diffusing any idea about trying to rebel
And within the ancestral Nubian land

CHAPTER 4 INNERLUDE: 0 TO 12 DEGREES

now called the Sudan
Well, the pale Children are now running
a master genocidal plan
And they righteously call this pale surge a religious purge
A cold-blooded, pale opposite energy
turning up the deep-freeze heat
Not giving those who love this earth any relief
As those of the lost and astray pale state of mind
show the nature of the beast
And the suntanned Children should know better than this
Continue to live their life
as though they have a death wish
Caught up in a capitalistic trait of this pale fate
Wheeling and dealing, thinking they jelling
When in truth and reality they're simply paling
And the pale Children, well
this cold-blooded opposite energy game
was how they were born, bred and trained
But, in order to secure their survival
one would think they would want to give up
that opposite energy and its cold-blooded
death-consuming cultural game
However, more and more toxic pollutions
are being produced to pollute polluted air, water and soil
As the Earth continues to be ripped, stripped and raped
to feed a lusting, capitalistic greed for oil
And mental, physical, spiritless sickness and disease
go insane as toxins boil
And the rot and the stench and the toxic taste and smell
Make it very, very clear
that the bottom is about to fall out of hell
And the Ta and the Tat would look upon this

FULFILLING THE SACRED ANCESTRAL PROPHECY OF THE TRIPLE NINE: UNVEILING THE PROPHETIC 2012 MELTDOWN OF THE LOST AND ASTRAY PALE STATE OF MIND

and the ancestors would not be pleased
And the only way the sacred ancestral spirit
of Man, He and She, will be retrieved
Is for a few among the few
to quickly emerge and quickly move
into an ancestral spirit surge, detox and purge
Learn those lessons, retrieve them blessings
move quickly back into the essence
of the divine union of one
and then indulge in the ooh's and the aah's
of a Love Supreme

<u>Royal Priestess vocals:</u>
Ooh Aahs of a Love Supreme

Chapter Five:
Running the Pale Master Plan Against the Sacred Suntanned He and She of Man

Chapter 5 Prelude:
Keep on Pushing

Song 5 from "12th Hour Prophecy: The Pale Curse and the Solarized Energy Shift," Kwatamani musical CD release, 2008

<u>Royal Priestess vocals:</u>
Keep on pushing this thing, High Priest Kwatamani
Let's keep on pushing this thing until the sacred
suntanned Children release this cold-blooded game
Let's keep pushing a Love Supreme

<u>High Priest vocals:</u>
Keep on pushing, can't stop now
Push a little harder some way, somehow
Keep on pushing the Supreme Love Vibe
Or the sacred suntanned Children will not survive
Gotta keep on pushing, and that ain't no jive
Ain't pushin' no dope, no delusions no illusions
no false ray of hope
No fright and fears, no blood, sweat and tears
No delusions or illusions orchestrated to spook folks
No, we gotta keep pushing, and you can't stop
Gotta keep on pushing to breed an ancestral stock
Ain't talking about pushing upon no sister's hips or
thighs
To satisfy that lustful greed for pleasure in your eyes
Hoping your esteemless secrets are very well kept
While you plot and scheme
to put another notch on your belt
Thinking that would give your weak
and depleted manhood some help

FULFILLING THE SACRED ANCESTRAL PROPHECY OF THE TRIPLE NINE: UNVEILING THE PROPHETIC 2012 MELTDOWN OF THE LOST AND ASTRAY PALE STATE OF MIND

Gotta keep pushing against these stale and pale lies
That are pulling the essence of life from the Earth
causing a cold-blooded demise
Gotta keep on pushin' or the dues we have to pay
is that our mental, physical and spiritual presence
will return DOA
Yes, here it is coming from the great I Am
Running it down, no lies, no illusions
no deceptions and no scams

Royal Priestess vocals:
Keep on pushing a Love Supreme
Run it down, run it down
Where were you at when I was young gifted and Black
Having no idea
where my sacred ancestral presence was at?
Where were you at
when I was shackled, chained and bound
Bent down, stripped, ripped and raped
and left on the ground
Bought and sold pound for pound
And with no help around
had to watch you hunted down by howling bloodhounds?
And the sounds of my wailing cries
Where were you at
as I suffered so many heartbreaks
regrets and set backs?

High Priest vocals:
Somewhere close to where you were at, ducking and dodging all along this bloodstained trail

CHAPTER 5 PRELUDE: KEEP ON PUSHING

Trying to get you to escape from this stale and pale hell
Rapping facts through my words and my acts
using a lot of ancestral style, grace and tact
Avoiding the social and religious contradictions that
breed a mental whack attack
Keeping the Children of the Sun at bay
lost and astray off track
Suffering psychological delay
I pushed real hard to avoid the way that cause one to feel
they about to escape this maze
Surefooted and arrogant within their tracks
Only to find out they've been led right back
Causing one to become even more arrogant
and set in their ways
Reaction off track, another spirit blindsided
with false facts
And the shackles and chains
that were placed on my balls and brain
Caused all that I am to become pale in your womb
Orchestrated to become an ancestral tomb
And you were spoon-fed on this death-culture dread
And then misled to nurture every child on this doom and
gloom and the worship of the dead
And where was I at, huh!! I was struggling up inside
your womb, and with no two energies able to occupy the
same space at the same time
For nine months, I went almost out of my mind
I keep on pushing, despite the signs of the times, striving
to resurrect Supreme Love and an ancestry divine

FULFILLING THE SACRED ANCESTRAL PROPHECY OF THE TRIPLE NINE: UNVEILING THE PROPHETIC 2012 MELTDOWN OF THE LOST AND ASTRAY PALE STATE OF MIND

<u>Royal Priestess vocals:</u>
Keep on pushing, keep on pushing deep inside of me
Raise up my divine spirit consciousness
so the inner I can see
While you were deep inside my womb
couldn't you see the insanity pushed upon me?
Wouldn't let my spirit, my spirit be free
Could you not see that I too wanted to escape
this pale fate
That caused me to be mentally and physically
and spiritually raped?
Could you not sense my bitterness, anger
scornful hate and self-hate?
How can I be expected to survive
left empty, lonely sad and blue
Without an ancestral mate by my side?
And it seemed it was all a part of a pale plan
to divide and conquer
the sacred suntanned He and She of Man
Keep on pushin', keep on pushin'
Can't stop now

<u>High Priest vocals:</u>
Gotta keep on pushin' the Supreme Love vibe
For without this push, neither you nor I will survive
Gotta keep on pushin'
there's too much to detox, purge and heal
Gotta push until
our most supreme ancestral spirit presence
is all that we can feel

Chapter Five:
Running the Pale Master Plan Against the Sacred Suntanned He and She of Man

Verse One: Breeding the Pale State of Mind into a Partnership of Crime

<u>The Suntanned Children Became Lost and Astray</u>

Although all that was and is to be
has already been foretold
There would be no experience
that could express the coming
Of the mutating and degenerating freezing cold
Oh, yeah, that opposite energy
would be big, bad and bold
And its objective would be to conquer
the sacred ancestral mother
Rip, strip and raping the spirit essence of her soul
Creating fright and fear, deep inside her mind
Manipulating and orchestrating her
into becoming a partner
To breed the manifestation of this hellish, palish crime
inflicting a death toll on the ancestral male
slaughtering him as an infidel
Weakening the ancestral mother spirit's state of mind
Turning her into a sex toy, a whore or a concubine
The suntanned Children became lost and astray
from their most supreme ancestral mold
Yeah, degeneration and mutation

FULFILLING THE SACRED ANCESTRAL PROPHECY OF THE TRIPLE NINE: UNVEILING THE PROPHETIC 2012 MELTDOWN OF THE LOST AND ASTRAY PALE STATE OF MIND

had indeed become a beastly mark
within that deep-freeze ice cold
and out of the ice-cold hell
the Children of the Sun would mutate and degenerate
becoming mentally, physically and spiritually pale
Without the glory of the sun
a cold-blooded, deadly insanity would start to run
Yeah, that cold and freezing ice
was something to behold
in the northern part of the earth
the white-blight syndrome would take its toll
Degeneration and mutation deep within the DNA
Turning everything that it would meet
into a victim of prey
as the last vestige of divine spirit consciousness
would become lost and astray
and the victims of prey would spread
this cold and pale virus-like plague
as they would seek and search
to find every means and way
to turn anything that they would meet into a
victim of prey
Their primary focus would be
to spread this pale state of mind
seeking and searching in every means and way
to self-define while being aligned
with that opposite energy
as it continues its decline into doomsday
Yeah, there was much mutation and degeneration
within that ice cold
the pale male's penis had shrunk

CHAPTER FIVE: RUNNING THE PALE MASTER PLAN AGAINST THE SACRED SUNTANNED HE AND SHE OF MAN

as if it had been tucked and rolled
And the pale female, well, yeah, she had also suffered
from that cold and freezing sting
Her vagina wall had grown big and wide
in order for her to give birth to this big-headed
mutated and degenerated offspring
And it would be a heck of an experience
for the pale male and female
who had mutated and degenerated
within the deep-freeze pits of hell
Yeah, it would be a heck of an experience
for their kind and kin
who had mutated and degenerated from deep within

The Flood

Now what had come to be
was that the icy hell was on a meltdown
and the thawing ice brought the flooding of the Black Sea
And the high waters caused the pale Children to meet up
with the sacred ancestral spirit presence of Man,
He and She
the Divine Children of the Sun
the essence of our most supreme ancestry
as it had come to be
No, the pale Children had no recollection
of any of what they would see
For too long they had been disconnected
from their most supreme ancestry
Within the pale state of mind there was no recollection
of the glory of the fruits of the tree
the white blight would mark

FULFILLING THE SACRED ANCESTRAL PROPHECY OF THE TRIPLE NINE: UNVEILING THE PROPHETIC 2012 MELTDOWN OF THE LOST AND ASTRAY PALE STATE OF MIND

every place and space of the pale memory
Now the pale Children would see a sight
to baffle their eyes
Being in the midst of the glory and the essence
of a magnificent sunset and sunrise
There would be much that they would sneak and peek
knowing not of the experience
nor having the ability to understand
the sacred suntanned essence of the He and She of Man
especially seeing the suntanned He and She
laying so intimately
expressing thanks, praise and appreciation
to each other so delicately
No, the pale male had no recollection of experiencing
such firm, tight-gripping vagina lips
and such smooth, soft and sensuous, solarized hips
butt and thighs
And likewise
the pale female had never experienced
such a penetrating rise
deep up inside the vagina walls of her inner thighs
And since the mutation and degeneration
had made her thick, flat and wide
there was nothing within her imagination
to cause her to feel a desire for such a penetrating vibe
And besides, whenever the pale male was on his plots
and schemes to connive
she would be left somewhere behind or outside

CHAPTER FIVE: RUNNING THE PALE MASTER PLAN AGAINST THE SACRED SUNTANNED HE AND SHE OF MAN

The Suntanned Male and Female United

No, the pale male had never experienced
such an expression of contoured
shaped and formed femininity
Nothing that he had ever encountered
could match the experiences that he would witness
of this magnificent suntanned expression of the essence
of divinity
Imagine that beautiful, brown-eyed virgin
Totally innocent of pale toxicity
And so from the first moment
the pale male had first sneaked a peak
at this voluscious suntanned female
as she delighted in the suntanned male
treating him with honor and a joy complete
rubbing him down with oil and fruit juices
from head to feet
and then licking, sucking and sapping it all off of him
like he was indeed her most glorious treat
The pale male's only experience
From what he could relate
had come from the thrill of the kill and the blood spill
from the murder and rape to steal and take
from the victim or the prey whom he would defeat
or the feeble or weak friend or foe whom he would eat
What the pale male was now seeing
would totally blow his mind
creating a stimulating arousal of an unknown kind
You see, he was used to a dog-like hump from behind
a snatch or a grab in raging and raping force

FULFILLING THE SACRED ANCESTRAL PROPHECY OF THE TRIPLE NINE: UNVEILING THE PROPHETIC 2012 MELTDOWN OF THE LOST AND ASTRAY PALE STATE OF MIND

leaving a wound or a scab
no warmth of any kind
and no compassion, no emotional entwine
Thus, is the truth and the consequence
of the mutated pale state of mind
And it could easily be animal or Man, He or She
dead or alive
because there would be nothing going on intimately
among those born and bred from the cold and pale cave-
dwelling tribes
And his cold and selfish, vicious greed
is now what this pale male would lust to feed
Yes, indeed, this pale male somehow knew
that he would have to destabilize
destroy and discredit the suntanned male
If he even wanted to sniff or smell
or in any way partake of this hot, soft
sensuous and wet, solarized suntanned female
And the pale male could also see that this suntanned male
was bringing this suntanned female a thrill
far beyond anything that he had ever heard
or seen a pale female express or feel
So the pale male would apply those values
that were deep-seated
in his mutated and degenerated DNA trait
And so he would murder and rape, steal and take
Because the suntanned female and the suntanned male
were united in such a natural and innate ancestral way
that they would never, of their own free will, forsake
And once he had raped
and experienced the essence of this feminine kind

CHAPTER FIVE: RUNNING THE PALE MASTER PLAN AGAINST THE SACRED SUNTANNED HE AND SHE OF MAN

Hot, sticky and wet and yet so magnificently sublime
The pale male knew full well
that he would have to mastermind
a partnership of crime
You see, he could use force to rape and take her body
But in order to feel half of what that ancestral male would feel
He would have to quickly wheel and deal
And her mind of thought and reasoning
He would have to steal
Reducing her divine spirit consciousness to nil
Yeah, he would have to plot and scheme to get her to see the suntanned male as the blame
In order to maintain and to remain in control of this sex and violence game
that caused him deep-seated satisfaction
although it caused her much misery, aches and pains

Cold and Pale Games

The suntanned Children's brains
and the spirit of their soul
would be contaminated and infiltrated
by the nature of that bloodthirsty mentality
that was stale and pale and ice cold
that opposite energy
that the Children of the Sun would consume
from that first moment that that pale sperm cell
was ejaculated into the suntanned, solarized womb
And through much self-hate, bitterness and spite
she would give birth to another imitation of life

FULFILLING THE SACRED ANCESTRAL PROPHECY OF THE TRIPLE NINE: UNVEILING THE PROPHETIC 2012 MELTDOWN OF THE LOST AND ASTRAY PALE STATE OF MIND

And so, for generation after generation, the pale male
would push his reality of fear and fright
as it was born and bred within the white blight
Yeah, the pale male was doing his thing
bringing all that he could of what paleness could bring
Masterminding the cold and pale games
of sex and violence and war and crime
in order to divide and conquer and to destabilize
the divine spirit conscious state of mind
of the sacred ancestral suntanned vibe
Making sure that not a single thought or memory
of the sacred ancestral spirit presence would survive
This would be the pale curse
that the pale male would bring forward
from the moment that he had first arrived
And the thoughts, the attitudes, the values and beliefs
of this pale thief
would be upheld, maintained and well-disguised
under the pale-male-warlord deity and its many guises of
disguise and deceptions and lies
It would be a heck of an experience
for this cold and pale male
who would gang bang and then
would use shackles and chains
to implement his enslavement game
And then to invade and enslave the mind
through the use of sex and violence and war and crime
You see after running this cold and pale game
of misery, aches and pain
time and time, over and over again
Offspring, mixed breeds and half-breeds

CHAPTER FIVE: RUNNING THE PALE MASTER PLAN AGAINST THE SACRED SUNTANNED HE AND SHE OF MAN

would start to waver and bend
seeking and searching to integrate and assimilate
in a desperate attempt to blend in
This would be a cruel and deadly game
It would oftentimes have a change of name
Giving the appearance that things had changed
Yet, the only thing that would truly change
is that the pale male would change the way he would play this game
Be it the Semite, Hittite and Aryan clan
Be it Judaism, Hinduism, Christianity
or the Muslim plan
Be it socialism, capitalism or a communistic fate
they would indeed be the same game with another name, at any rate
hell and damnation
against the suntanned He and She of Man
would be the vicious master plan
And this would be how the pale male would claim
and maintain his fortune and fame
And the pale-male-war-god deity would be the image
that he would claim is running this game
And so from the first time the pale male
had the opportunity to gang bang
he would find himself caught up
in the addictions and afflictions
of running this cold and pale game

<u>The Pale False and Fake Superiority Trait</u>

You see, from the moment that he had encountered
this sleek and athletic suntanned male

FULFILLING THE SACRED ANCESTRAL PROPHECY OF THE TRIPLE NINE: UNVEILING THE PROPHETIC 2012 MELTDOWN OF THE LOST AND ASTRAY PALE STATE OF MIND

and had seen his tail
and how well he was hung
The pale male would take that short and brief look
at his own self
and within his mind
his own personal insecurities would self-define
With being a host
consuming of that opposite energy
he would reverse the truth
and claim the white man's burden of manifest destiny
And out of this cold and pale game
he would find ways and means to get paid
Buying, selling, misusing and abusing
the sacred ancestral ones as his god-ordained slaves
Declaring the suntanned Children
to be the savage heathens
who needed their souls to be saved
and further stating that the reason the suntanned male
was so well-endowed and hung
was because he was akin to King Kong
or that other gorilla that was dark and well hung
that they would call by name as Mighty Joe Young
And so while he was busy about the task
of stripping, ripping and raping the suntanned female
He would use this approach and otherwise
in an attempt to revise and downsize
the mental, physical and spiritual essence of the
suntanned male
But the DNA tracks and traces
of the suntanned He and She of Man
were so strong that even sometimes

CHAPTER FIVE: RUNNING THE PALE MASTER PLAN AGAINST THE SACRED SUNTANNED HE AND SHE OF MAN

this did not work too well
Although through time the suntanned Children
would indeed begin to turn mentally, physically and
spiritually pale
And to maintain the pale false and fake superiority trait
the pale male would practice the game of racial hate
while introducing the suntanned Children to self-hate
And he would do everything he could
to keep that pale female away from the suntanned male
He would declare the suntanned male as an infidel
and a big-dicked demon from hell
who would use his long, hard tool to ruin and gain
control of the pale female
And everywhere he would roam
he would describe the suntanned male
as a monkey with a long tail
And he would declare the suntanned male
as a three-legged monster
who had no greater desire than to bang and claim
the pale female
And this would be the base, root and foundation
that would govern and administrate many a pale nation
and that would orchestrate, dictate and influence
every global relation
Yeah, the disciples and followers
of the lost and astray pale state of mind
were cold, blood-spilling, wheeling and dealing m.f.ers
with no ancestral feeling
And even the most compassionate acts of this blood-spilling, pale pack would be chilling
And each and everyone who had consumed of this lost
and astray pale state of mind

FULFILLING THE SACRED ANCESTRAL PROPHECY OF THE TRIPLE NINE: UNVEILING THE PROPHETIC 2012 MELTDOWN OF THE LOST AND ASTRAY PALE STATE OF MIND

would require deep-seated healing
Or the facts of hell and damnation and doom and gloom
would continue to manifest
from the deviant and violent sex bred from the violence
of war and crime
that would breed, seed and feed the final, fatal decline
Although all that would be seen
and that would come to be
was already foretold
there would be nothing beyond the experience
that could express the coming
of the mutating and degenerating paleness
of that freezing mental and spiritless cold
that that opposite energy would unfold
as it continued its downward-spiral roll

Verse Two: A Painful Story to Tell

A Turning Point

And this would be such a painful story to tell
The sacred ancestral male would be raided and invaded
and slaughtered as an infidel
While the sacred ancestral mother spirit
would be left to lead the sacred suntanned Children
deep into the pits of hell
of this cold-blooded, bloodstained trail
And although we would emerge in splendor and glory
Divine Children of the Sun
there would be a turning point to this story
And the turning point would come in a flurry
Snow storms, freezing ice

CHAPTER FIVE: RUNNING THE PALE MASTER PLAN AGAINST THE SACRED SUNTANNED HE AND SHE OF MAN

catching the lost and astray Children of the Sun off track
Because they did not listen to the sacred ancestral advice
And nature would talk, yes, nature would talk well
But the ancestral Children had lost their connection
and would mutate and degenerate
and become the dreadful character of this story
that the I in I now tell
You see, the changing tide of the environment
would give warning
but apparently those who were in the lead
did not take heed
And so all of the Children who were lost and astray
would face truth and consequences
And yes, they would have to pay
They would face 360 degrees change
totally opposite in how they would live
and how they would feed
Yes, they would indeed go 360 degrees
Away from their divine and innate way to live
and their divine and innate way to feed
And after these lost and astray Children
had degenerated and mutated
within the deep freeze of this white blight
they would emerge into a stale and pale mentality
Consuming of a death-culture reality
And this death-consuming reality
would strip and rip all the life energy
out of the mental, physical and spiritual whole
Manifesting lust, lies, illusions, confusion, death and
deadly destruction everywhere it would roll

FULFILLING THE SACRED ANCESTRAL PROPHECY OF THE TRIPLE NINE: UNVEILING THE PROPHETIC 2012 MELTDOWN OF THE LOST AND ASTRAY PALE STATE OF MIND

Nearly 6,000 Years

And this mentality would uphold the death blows
of the cold for nearly 6,000 years
before it brought Billie Holiday her tears
And playing within this stale and pale game
would certainly get the blame for John Coltrane
pushing it into his main vein
DOA, deadly on arrival, and it don't play
And ODing certainly is not tribal
Although it severely threatens
the suntanned Children's survival
And Madame Walker must have been insane
If she thought you could burn and fry and perm and dye
this lifeless and esteemless energy
into an integrated and acceptable change
Leaving burnt stains on the brain
And ruptured pores and skin sores
I think it was somewhere within
this stale and pale state of mind
that the ancestral motherspirit
would sink into a decline
surrendering, taking flight
into the attitudes and the behaviors
of the white-blight plight
And every time you trace
this stale and pale bloodstained track
it would lead you right back
To a cold and pale mentality where
raiding, raping, murdering and enslaving
would become a pale reality

CHAPTER FIVE: RUNNING THE PALE MASTER PLAN AGAINST THE SACRED SUNTANNED HE AND SHE OF MAN

Organized and programmed to occur
by any means and many ways
Until the white blight would become something to crave,
an investment to buy, sell or trade
And this is how those addicted to the white blight
would behave from the crib to the grave
And the pale Children would exert their will
And they would use their cold-blooded and deadly skills
And the lands of the Children of the Sun
would become their killing field
So, so many personalities and so many Emmet Tills
And the Children of the pale mentality
had created so much vengeance and hate
And their racist ideology made it clear
that their vengeance and hate
Was against those suntanned Children
who maintained their solarized ancestral trait
I guess somewhere within this stale and pale mentality
of vengeance, jealousy, wrath and greed and hate
these pale Children would scorn and curse
these suntanned Children for not experiencing
the same cold and pale, deep-freeze fate
You see, this pale mentality would cause
anyone to lose their mind
And by mere association, assimilation or integration
would cause one to become so entwined
that to rape, raid, murder and enslave
would be just a matter of time
And those of the pale mentality
would work so hard to control the hands that rock the crib
because gaining control of the ancestral mother spirit

FULFILLING THE SACRED ANCESTRAL PROPHECY OF THE TRIPLE NINE: UNVEILING THE PROPHETIC 2012 MELTDOWN OF THE LOST AND ASTRAY PALE STATE OF MIND

would mean gaining control
of each and every life that she would give
After dividing and conquering and inflicting
a devastating wound and scar
Those of the pale mentality would declare
that all is fair in love and war
And they would work hard to blind the mind
with the idea that between love and hate
exists a very thin line
And they would fake and pretend
and they would act like some kind of Jinn
And they would walk this thin line so well
that the mesmerized and the hypnotized
really could not tell
where they were at within this bloodstained trail
As those of that pale mentality would continue to lead
their disciples and followers deeper into the pits of hell

Power Would Concede Nothing Without a Struggle

You see, the pale Children had goals and objectives
and they had every intent on accomplishing them this time
You see, deeply encoded within their DNA
were memories of that night of day
when they first went lost and astray
And the energy encoded would be full of hell,
remembering how they would first rebel
against the Most Supreme Seen and Unseen
And then turn to the energy that is pale
the manifestation of a war god who was male

CHAPTER FIVE: RUNNING THE PALE MASTER PLAN AGAINST THE SACRED SUNTANNED HE AND SHE OF MAN

Yes, this energy was predatorial, and it was slick and sly
and it would hide and slip around
And this energy would have to be detoxed and purged
But it would be so difficult to deal with this energy
unless one would focus on divine action instead of words
And the Divine Children of the Sun
did not follow them the first time around
Supreme thanks, praise and appreciation
because these lost and astray Children
ended up stale and pale and locked down
within ice-cold caves
where they would mutate and degenerate pound for pound
And they would consume of this energy bite for bite
And the energy that they would consume
would make room for the energy of the white blight
And they would gain the power, strength and might
of the energy that is opposite of the Essence of Life
Power would concede nothing without a struggle
And would automatically create stress, strain and strife
And so the focus would become to put shackles and
chains on the suntanned Children's mind
to ensure that they follow them this time
And the Children of the Sun
would be enslaved and controlled
And the place the pale ones would take them
would be cold and pale as hell
But it would be heavenly for the Children who were pale
You see, historically the objective was to dethrone
the suntanned Children and to orchestrate their downfall
and then quickly self-install
But, you see, historically

FULFILLING THE SACRED ANCESTRAL PROPHECY OF THE TRIPLE NINE: UNVEILING THE PROPHETIC 2012 MELTDOWN OF THE LOST AND ASTRAY PALE STATE OF MIND

every time this tactic was attempted
The pale Children would run into a brick wall
You see, the sacred ancestral spirit presence
of the High Priest had warned
And the priestesses and priests had advised
the Children of the Sun to take heed
And the bas relief would read
that these pale Children were savage
and would pillage, rape, raid, kill and ravage
And, indeed, off of blood and guts and bones and skin
they would feed
And the High Priest had warned
the Divine Children of the Sun to forever reject
that cold-blooded, stale and pale-male-war god
which these pale Children would project

A New Beginning and a New Ending As Well

And so these pale Children would eventually begin to see
that unless they were able to break down
that sacred ancestral brick wall
They would never, ever be able to self-install
And unless they were able to get control of the hands
that rock the crib of this sacred ancestral family tree
they would have done nothing at all
You see, the sacred ancestral mother spirit
was divinely connected with the most supreme seen and
unseen essence of femininity
And so this pale-male-war god, huh
she would never decree
And so these pale Children would raid, rape
murder and enslave

CHAPTER FIVE: RUNNING THE PALE MASTER PLAN AGAINST THE SACRED SUNTANNED HE AND SHE OF MAN

And they would buy, sell and trade
and they would plot, scheme and connive
and finally they would come up with means and ways
And the family of the ancestral mother spirit
would mix and mingle until finally she would get a tingle
And the sacred ancestral ones could sense and see
that something stank and something would smell
As these pale Children would orchestrate
a new beginning and a new ending as well
As Julius Caesar would take the hands of Cleopatra
and lead her down this bloodstained trail
deep into the cold-blooded pits of his stale and pale hell
They had murdered the father
yes, her ancestral father spirit was gone
And with no High Priest
she was now left to make all the decisions wrong
And after all the plots, scheming, conniving
and the sugar-coated lies had drawn her inside
Her sacred ancestral spirit would not be able to survive
And through the suffering
she would bring about her own demise
by committing suicide
She had started to turn mentally and physically pale
but apparently, she was not taking to that energy too well
You see, she was the product
of generations and generations of invasions
of the pale persuasion
And although she was light-bright and damn near white,
her sacred ancestral spirit
had not completely submerged into the white blight
And so her decision was before she would submit
to this white-lady syndrome and become a clone

FULFILLING THE SACRED ANCESTRAL PROPHECY OF THE TRIPLE NINE: UNVEILING THE PROPHETIC 2012 MELTDOWN OF THE LOST AND ASTRAY PALE STATE OF MIND

She would return back home
in shame and disgrace
and face what she would have to face
and be stoned
This was before this white-blight was full grown
and overblown
nearly two-thousand years before Billie Holliday
would get it on and feed her jones to be stoned

Verse Three: The White Blight and the White-Lady Syndrome

This is dedicated to a few brothers who died on death row
Some who would be strung out on the end of a tree
Some that would be strung out on the end of stuff
that would cause them to OD
Yeah, some who would hang from the end of a rope
Some who would hang from the end
of an addiction to dope
Some addicted to lies and a deceptive footnote
Some addicted to a false ray of hope
Worshipping a god that spooks folks
Yeah, this story is dedicated to daughters and mothers, too
And most especially
this story is dedicated to you, Sister True

CHAPTER FIVE: RUNNING THE PALE MASTER PLAN AGAINST THE SACRED SUNTANNED HE AND SHE OF MAN

It's Just a Program

Fatherhood, brotherhood, sisterhood, motherhood
Yeah, it seems like the entire neighborhood is full of rats
and stray pussy cats
And dogs chasing after the big dog in reverse
who first implemented the black curse
And every since we took that first trip
Our sacred ancestral culture has started to flip
And we went through changes
and we done changed everything
And the only thing we got in return was
misery, aches and pains
And a fantasy and an illusion and delusions
And we all had a few dreams deferred
And we changed our name
We got a new name
You see, we changed everything that was important
to our sacred ancestral presence
as the Divine Children of the Sun
and here we come again changing into deception
Crappin' with our mouth flappin'
Adapting the addictions and the afflictions
of the white-lady syndrome which the white blight brings
Denying, yet identifying with, the deep-freeze ice cold
Big, bad and bold
Infected, disconnected
broken down ancestral spirit decode
And the cute sister and the smooth brother
He think she think they think they really on a roll
Because of the stuff and things

FULFILLING THE SACRED ANCESTRAL PROPHECY OF THE TRIPLE NINE: UNVEILING THE PROPHETIC 2012 MELTDOWN OF THE LOST AND ASTRAY PALE STATE OF MIND

They are now able to buy and sell
He looked her in the eyes and she smiled
and her body began to shake
And he got a smell, and what is it about anyway
as his ego would begin to swell
And he threw down a smooth rap
And she said, yes, she would let him tap
As they both became entrapped
in the white-lady syndrome mishap
Yeah, he was beginning to adapt
playing with her luscious thighs
He was now wearing a masterful disguise
of brother man on the rise
Yeah, he had become a predator
and he would plot, scheme and connive
Superficially and artificially positioning himself
within the deceit of this man-made hell
And what would cause his ego to swell
Was it because of that slam dunk after that high lob
Or was it that hole in one or that blow job
And what was it that made his ego swell
Was it her complexion
Was it because she was fine and stacked as hell
Or was it because she gave up some tail
Yeah, what is it that's making this weak and feeble
manchild feel that he's doing so well
As he becomes even more lost and astray
in the tracks and traces of this bloodstained trail
Young brother's minds sho nuff deaf, dumb and blind
Too many invitations to ejaculate
into the front or the behind

CHAPTER FIVE: RUNNING THE PALE MASTER PLAN AGAINST THE SACRED SUNTANNED HE AND SHE OF MAN

And if nobody is there, he would dream of a nightmare
And take that opportunity to ejaculate into the air
And if he couldn't get off on a nightmare
he'd simply turn on the TV
because there'd be somebody's wide open thighs
sitting there
You see, the other day, as he was about to play
This brown-eyed, brown-skinned woman
walked up to him
and had something soft and luscious to say
And there they were standing there
She reflecting the image of himself
and he seeing her as his worst nightmare
And it must have been his studdish charm
Or that sister did not see that drop-dead blonde on his arm
Anyway, he was addicted to being lost and astray
And this is how he would play
Because that dark-eyed, brown-skinned woman
was just another victim of prey
Since the white-lady syndrome was his mainstay
Yeah, he was addicted
but not to the same average substances as a dope fiend
And it seemed that nothing else
would give him the same thrill
Yeah, he know the deal
But the deal he know just ain't real
In fact, the real deal is that he don't even know
what he's supposed to feel
But he do know he can fire the pill
and he can play some ball
And he can dance and sing

FULFILLING THE SACRED ANCESTRAL PROPHECY OF THE TRIPLE NINE: UNVEILING THE PROPHETIC 2012 MELTDOWN OF THE LOST AND ASTRAY PALE STATE OF MIND

and strut up and down the street, looking discreet
or up and down a college or a business hall
yeah, he can play some ball
Though his mind would stutter and stall
As a result of that cold-blooded, deep-freeze fall
And the sacred ancestral spirit presence
that he can no longer recall
One may see this addiction as a different thing
But it's the same old white-lady syndrome
that drove John Coltrane insane
And she really played John Coltrane
had him begging for a Love Supreme as he OD'd in vain
And suffice it to say, Emmet Till
got caught up in harm's way
As that same old white-lady syndrome
caused him to become a victim of prey
And that same old white-lady syndrome
had Jimi Hendrix in a daze
Popping technicolor pills because a purple haze
is what he was trying to feel
And as the energy of the white blight
would continue to grow
She would become the snow and ice
that little boy blue would blow
And because they went down so damn low
She would become the white thing that the thug rappers
would use to thug rap themselves into fortune and fame
And then she would transform into the smoke
that would cause the dread man to choke
As he took her home, a gigolo, bought and paid for
to assist her to get her groove on

CHAPTER FIVE: RUNNING THE PALE MASTER PLAN AGAINST THE SACRED SUNTANNED HE AND SHE OF MAN

And hey, don't get me wrong
because a fine white sister all right with me
So long as she's focused on resurrecting
our most supreme ancestral presence of whole life energy
But we not talking about a fine white sister for true
We talking about that mental and physical dope
Yeah, we talking about those stale and pale white lies
that have affected Sister True and Brother Man too
Yeah, we talking about a cold-blooded and serious
white lady here, my dear
One that breeds inferiority, insecurity and fright and fear
And you know, the white-lady syndrome
is not limited to the complexion of white
We talking about anyone
of any color, shape, form or fashion
that upholds or maintains this white blight
And guess what, it's just a program

Verse Four: Spreading the Pale Plague into the Chattel Slavery Days

And this thing grew from the phase
when the suntanned Children were invaded, raided,
captured, raped and enslaved
and bought and raped and then sold and raped
and then again raped and sold for trade
And where a blood brother was used as a stud
to produce more black slaves
and where a well-programmed
and well-orchestrated mentality
would become one's reality
From the crib to the grave

FULFILLING THE SACRED ANCESTRAL PROPHECY OF THE TRIPLE NINE: UNVEILING THE PROPHETIC 2012 MELTDOWN OF THE LOST AND ASTRAY PALE STATE OF MIND

all the way into these days
And master would rape and take
and master would breed in hate and self-hate
and the half-breeds that master would seed
master would rape and trade and forsake
Master's energy would be very pale
and it was mass confusion that master would create
For master, mass confusion was innate
And to streamline this mass confusion
that he was orchestrating to create
master would put the white lady
high on a pedestal as his mate
And a hangsman's noose would be a nigger's fate
If it would even appear
that with her he had the idea to sexually relate
You see, the white woman was profiled
as being godly, pure and fair
Possessing the heavenly gift of angel hair
And the pale-male-war god was seen as white
And the controller and the keeper of this great white blight
And so to be born with melanination
and suntanned pigmentation was seen as a curse
And to go forward and multiply this nappy-headed birth was seen as even worse
Imagine the relationship of a suntanned male and female
and the suffocating mental decay
Imagine being in a relationship with absolutely no stability and where you could be used and abused any time
Of night or day with nothing to say

CHAPTER FIVE: RUNNING THE PALE MASTER PLAN AGAINST THE SACRED SUNTANNED HE AND SHE OF MAN

Imagine being a luscious, suntanned female
born, bred and fed to be a victim of prey
Imagine the lust, lies, illusions, confusion
death and deadly destruction that this pale male
would ejaculate into this dark-eyed, brown-skinned prey
Misusing and sexually abusing
the suntanned male's mother, sister, daughter or his mate,
breeding hate and self-hate
Imagine being forced by course
to worship the skin that is fair and straight hair
And no longer knowing of any ancestral beauty to
declare
Imagine how many brown-skinned sisters
who would just sit there and stare
wishing that they had blue eyes and blonde hair
Imagine the different ways and means
that she would submit or perform sexually, or otherwise
to go there
Programmed and seeking to feed
the pale male's lustful greed
anytime and anywhere
Imagine the requests of the mind of conquest
knowing that she would give
everything that she could give
and when she gave, she would give her very best
Imagine the jive of this master of disguise
Imagine how he would slip, slide and hide
Then imagine the lies that he would tell to that white lady
who just could not match this suntanned daughter's
soft and sensuous and sexy solarized vibe
no matter how hard she tried
Then imagine the many lonely days and nights

FULFILLING THE SACRED ANCESTRAL PROPHECY OF THE TRIPLE NINE: UNVEILING THE PROPHETIC 2012 MELTDOWN OF THE LOST AND ASTRAY PALE STATE OF MIND

and the many lustful tears that this white lady cried
Imagine how her lustful pleasure
would be disregarded and denied
And although there was always a suntanned
nappy headed man there somewhere
she'd better not dare
Or it would be death upon her
and that nappy-headed Negro man
Because such a relationship
was socially and legally banned
especially not that white lady
that he bought and paid for and stored away
until he was ready to pray
You see, master's objective was for her to nurture his lie
And to go forward and multiply his pale-male-war god cry
At that time if she had had the chance
to openly experience this Negro man
It would have interrupted his master plan
And so the pale male would hang, rape, murder, burn
and castrate, imprison and kill
Applying any means necessary to deter her will
desire and determination
to feel that suntanned man's
deep-seated solarized penetration

Master Program

But now that the pale male has established
a master program
and gained greater control of this thang
The pale male has changed the way he plays this game

CHAPTER FIVE: RUNNING THE PALE MASTER PLAN AGAINST THE SACRED SUNTANNED HE AND SHE OF MAN

You see, now, he would pimp, push, prostitute or ho
that white lady to maintain greater financial control
and capital gain
He pushed her off on John Coltrane
And she left her chalk-white traces
all up inside his main vein
And that same old two-bit ho
Would have Jimi Hendrix begging for mo'
And he would use every ounce and every trace
to play that bass
And with his eyes closed, he would look that white lady
straight in the face from up inside his nose
And from the street sales to the prison cells
gangster rappers had rose
And they would talk a lot of smack and they would
smack on a lot of coke and crack
And they would profile as gangsters
and they would be ice cold
And within them and among them
the white-lady syndrome would be pushed
bought and sold
And sometimes she would be subtle
and she'd leave her remains as ash
Stroking, smoking and choking
buying and selling for cash
And yo and yo, these brothers are serious
up and down the street, chasing that white lady
And little boy blue would think the white lady's nice
So he would become addicted to snow and ice
And after the blood of freedom was spilled
all up and down this bloodstained track
The children of the children who were free at last

FULFILLING THE SACRED ANCESTRAL PROPHECY OF THE TRIPLE NINE: UNVEILING THE PROPHETIC 2012 MELTDOWN OF THE LOST AND ASTRAY PALE STATE OF MIND

Would be introduced to crack
Yeah, the pale male was a cold-blooded predator
a pimp, a pusher, who knew how to use a ho'
And he would prostitute this white lady in a way
that would make her user beg for mo'
And he would erect her in the halls of justice
and she would symbolize justice as being blind
guess that's why she couldn't truly see
who was really committing the crime
And just to be safe, justice would profile the darker race
And even if the dark-skinned man did not do the crime
it was a guarantee that he would do some time
And she would stand there looking statuesque
surrounded by polluted water and air
representing liberty and conquest
Yeah, the pale male would profile the white lady
at her very best
As he orchestrates and manipulates
this white-blight syndrome
that will never be nothing less

Verse Five: The Protection Divide

And the game of inferiority and superiority
had been played very well
And the playing of this card would reverse
the divine thought and reasoning
of the suntanned male and female
As she and he would seek to produce offspring
who would become a major player
in expanding this bloodstained trail

CHAPTER FIVE: RUNNING THE PALE MASTER PLAN AGAINST THE SACRED SUNTANNED HE AND SHE OF MAN

And many would claim that their son or daughter is
doing very well, riding the tide of success
within this man-made hell
However, with a true focus on reality
you could see through the façades
and the pretense and the false success tales
that the mass majority had miserably failed
Remaining trapped
in the cold and dank pits of this bloodstained trail
Yeah, they had been sold a bill of goods in the hood
And the hood program would not allow a suntanned
sister to knock on wood
From jump street, he was well programmed
and the program did not skip a beat
Addressing every thought, attitude and behavior
from the stuff that one drink to the stuff that one eat
It started when he was a little baby
and began with the blanket in which he was wrapped
Yeah, all of the stuff and things
was part of a major scheme
and it had its own commercial theme
And it would be so subtle how it had came
and it would appear that there was
absolutely no one to blame
Yet a little child was being zapped, sapped and trapped
and driven totally insane
And although it was not by osmosis, like magic
a little child was being fed mental comatosis
And like a light beam, it would appear
as though it was coming out of thin air
Because, at first, the little child was not even there
And so mama had absolutely no reason to fret

FULFILLING THE SACRED ANCESTRAL PROPHECY OF THE TRIPLE NINE: UNVEILING THE PROPHETIC 2012 MELTDOWN OF THE LOST AND ASTRAY PALE STATE OF MIND

as she tuned into the programs on her TV set
Yet, it's a sure bet
what mama would consume
is what these offspring would get
And he would succumb and he would reject
and he would seek another outlet
And as soon as he was able to get it on
The little boy would grow to the man
Who would seek the white-lady syndrome
And there would be so many options
there would be so many drugs
And there would be so many cute females
With whom he could fall in love
And there would be so many opportunities
to become a thug
And so many religious and social programs
on which he could tug
Yeah there would be so many ways
for a brother to get paid
And so much stuff to buy, sell or trade
And so many females begging to be laid
And if one could mastermind
the ways and means to get paid
And if one could become schooled
on the proper use of one's tools
One could tap into all 666 ways
of being mentally and physically screwed
And although this white-blight
is a cold-blooded game of misery, aches and pains
There would be too many options to gain fortune and
fame for one to have any desire to want to change

CHAPTER FIVE: RUNNING THE PALE MASTER PLAN AGAINST THE SACRED SUNTANNED HE AND SHE OF MAN

When one is young, it is the lust-busting fun
in which one aspires
And when one matures
it's about hanging on until one can retire
And it seems that one never, ever brings anything
whole and true to the table
Just a lot of conversations and insinuations
from a mind that's unstable and disabled
Talking loud and proud and saying absolutely nothing
beyond the story of the dog in reverse
that lives in the clouds
Continuing to uphold the gray ghost that spook folks
And the lost and astray mind is really a joke
As one claims and proclaims
to be of a consciousness higher, and as it plays out
it's just another brother proving himself as a liar
Playing social and religious games
that allow him to falsely claim himself as a Black messiah
Still honoring the stale and pale-male-war-god syndrome
that was used to raid, invade, murder, rape and enslave
and then to buy and sell
his dark and lovely ancestors for trade
Still full of explanations, justifications and
rationalizations that have distorted and retarded
the suntanned family community situation
for generation after generation
Still consuming of the same toxic habits and addictions
that continue to cause mental, physical
and spiritual disease and affliction
This is how he would grow
because this is what he would know

FULFILLING THE SACRED ANCESTRAL PROPHECY OF THE TRIPLE NINE: UNVEILING THE PROPHETIC 2012 MELTDOWN OF THE LOST AND ASTRAY PALE STATE OF MIND

Chasing after a ho as a stud, a pimp or a gigolo
or going down low as a homo
You see, this game was cold, and to survive within it
one would have to pay the toll
And after all, he was not the only domesticated creature
with a hole
He was now moving into the fast lane
big, bad and bold
And this was a dog-eat-dog game
of misery, aches and pains
and the top dog do not care how he roll
And you could actually begin to hear a brother man
playing his hand
as he begin to stark and to bark
A true sign that he was the carrier
of this pale opposite energy birth mark
Although he was born of melaninated skin
that ranges from light-bright to dark
Remember that he was told that his darker ancestors
were turned black and torn apart
because a son would happen to see
his broke down and drunken father
laying within the bowels of Noah's Ark
Imagine how this thing would unfold
Imagine all of those animals that had a hole
And imagine all of that urine and that ka-ka that would roll
Imagine the collections upon the floor
the piles and the bile and the waste
Imagine the funk and the stink and the flies
and the maggots and the smell;

CHAPTER FIVE: RUNNING THE PALE MASTER PLAN AGAINST THE SACRED SUNTANNED HE AND SHE OF MAN

imagine seeing one's drunk and broken down father
laying face-down with this stuff as a pillow base
Imagine the stench in the air
that actually stunk more than a skunk
Imagine what this stale and pale dude would eat
while he was drunk
Imagine trying to trace the taste
Imagine that old drunk and broken down disciple
Then imagine the bitterness and the anger
and the disgrace
that his old pale-male-war god must have faced
in order to place the black curse
said to be the base of the darker race
All because an innocent son would see
his stale and pale father laying there
bent, broken and drunk
Face down in all that rot and that stench and that funk
Imagine all of this being overlooked
within the telling of this Noah's Ark story
How could one overlook forty days
and forty nights of encaged funk?
Imagine the depraved and mentally enslaved state of
mind that could conceive, retrieve, or believe this bunk
Imagine an innocent child being fed
these kinds of stories by the chunk
Yeah, the superiority and inferiority game
had been played very well
And Man, He and She, was now lost and astray
in the bottomless pit of this bloodstained trail
And Mama would stare and sit there
as the programmed conditions would cause her
to become his worst nightmare

FULFILLING THE SACRED ANCESTRAL PROPHECY OF THE TRIPLE NINE: UNVEILING THE PROPHETIC 2012 MELTDOWN OF THE LOST AND ASTRAY PALE STATE OF MIND

And Mama would become so bitter and so fussy
and so hard to bear that even when he was there
most of the time, he did not even want to be there
And as time would go on
their relationship would grow worse and worse
And they would learn to despise the idea
that they were part of a color syndrome of a curse
And she was steeped knee-deep
in the syndrome of the white blight
because the pale male had used her as a personal whore
to change his financial status to being rich from being poor
You see, historically, the suntanned mother
has been used to increase his financial gain
And she has been used very effective here within
and throughout the rein of the chattel slavery game
Yeah, the pale male would orchestrate a stock market
And the suntanned female would be used
to multiply the stock
Yeah, the suntanned female was a real treasure
used to multiply his financial gain
and then used to multiply his sexual pleasure
And now that the suntanned mother's son
felt that he was full grown
footloose and fancy-free
with a mind of his own
He would invest all of his energy into the pale tone
Leaving the suntanned mother spirit sick, fat
and obese and all alone
Because he was bathed, baptized in filth
with the ghost of the white-lady syndrome

CHAPTER FIVE: RUNNING THE PALE MASTER PLAN AGAINST THE SACRED SUNTANNED HE AND SHE OF MAN

And within this white blight, there were too many habits,
addictions, distractions, beliefs, rituals
privileges and rights for anyone
except a divine and sacred few to have enough guts
to break the chain and make enough change
to detox and purge and to take flight
Departing this stale and pale game
that multiplies false, fake and pretentious insanity
360 degrees

Verse Six: Indulging in the Treats and the Tricks of the Triple-Six Fix

An Analysis of a Very Serious Time

With Man, He and She, being taken so far off track
And with this white-blight syndrome
being so vicious, cruel and whack
It would seem almost impossible
to get the ancestral mother spirit forwarded again
and on track
Or to get that sacred ancestral father spirit free
forwarding divine guidance and protection
in order to secure that sacred nurturer of whole life
energy
And unquestionably, divine spirit consciousness
is an absolute necessity
in order to facilitate the divine resurrection
of Man, He and She
With the mother being the first teacher from birth
she would go forward and multiply
all that she consumed for better or worse

FULFILLING THE SACRED ANCESTRAL PROPHECY OF THE TRIPLE NINE: UNVEILING THE PROPHETIC 2012 MELTDOWN OF THE LOST AND ASTRAY PALE STATE OF MIND

And any positive and affirmative effort
that she would attempt to make would be in vain
until she detoxed and purged
this cold-blooded stale and pale game
And without the divine guidance and protection
of the sacred ancestral masculine energy
She would remain stuck and stagnant
wherever she might be
You see, the masters of animal husbandry
well understood the nature
of the domesticating property
This is why the stud bull's feet are chained
and his feet will remain chained for the rest of his life
or until he has been bent or broken enough
where there can be a smooth transition of those chains
from his feet to his brain
Otherwise that old stud bull will make a break
taking all of those heifers and those offspring with him
as they escape
Yeah, in order to gain and maintain control
over anything that they encountered
these pale lost and astray Children
had learned to do whatever it takes
And sometimes as a predator and a scavenger
it was absolutely necessary to pretend and to fake
And, you see, being cunning and conniving
well, that was just a simple predator trait
And lust, lies, illusions, confusion
death and deadly destruction, huh
that was just how a predator would relate
And the hunting and herding culture

CHAPTER FIVE: RUNNING THE PALE MASTER PLAN AGAINST THE SACRED SUNTANNED HE AND SHE OF MAN

well that was the birthplace of animal husbandry
And the death-consuming culture
well, that is what it has come to be
And there would just not be the same regard
for the earth, the wind, the rain and the sun
or the fruit or the tree
And there definitely would not be the same regard
for the resurrection of the whole life energy
And forwarding lies and deceptions
well, that would be a predator's truth
Just as the consumption of the dead of the rot
and the stench and funk of flesh and bones and blood
and skin would actually be a scavenger's fruit
And since one is merely a sum total
of the energy which one consume
And with the adverse effects
of this stale and pale, death-consuming mentality
looking Man, He and She, straight in the face
It is the nature of the I in I to establish
and to bring about a saving grace
And come hell or high water
and regardless of what you wish to believe
The nature of this self-destruct vibration
has recycled 360 degrees
And it can be easily tracked and traced
And the nature of this self-destruct mechanism
is what Man, He and She, now face
And what remained of the ancestral mother spirit
Well, there she was, sitting there
disconnected from her roots, foundation and base
Caught up in the stale and pale mentality
of this white blight and its social economic

FULFILLING THE SACRED ANCESTRAL PROPHECY OF THE TRIPLE NINE: UNVEILING THE PROPHETIC 2012 MELTDOWN OF THE LOST AND ASTRAY PALE STATE OF MIND

religion and race
And there she was sitting there
with a vague and empty face
no divine spirit consciousness to trace
Nothing whole, natural and true to declare
sitting there, a lost and astray mind
focused and pondering within toxic and polluted air
And with a sour frown, she would grin and bear
trying to figure out why life had treated her so unfair
And it would be so difficult for her to see the things
that she would do that would be the catalyst
to keep her life empty, lonely, sad and blue
Frustrating as hell to her and to her children
and to her man too
You see, if mama only knew
she would not have groomed her son to grow
in the way in which he had grew
You see, his focus was now so far away
from those of her kind now that he had grown
In fact, his focus was now on the white-lady syndrome
And if he achieved or acquired financial gain or success
You'd best believe that it would be
the white-lady syndrome
in which he would consume and invest
And if he had to settle for anything less
you'd better believe that it would definitely
pass the white-lady syndrome test
And it seems that absolutely no one understood the truth,
the consequences and the fatality of this thing
Not even that pale male who had changed
the way he was now playing this game

CHAPTER FIVE: RUNNING THE PALE MASTER PLAN AGAINST THE SACRED SUNTANNED HE AND SHE OF MAN

You see, what in prior time was considered a crime
was now considered an instrument
used to maintain greater control and financial gain
within these modern times
And so regarding the white-lady plots
ploys and endeavors
The pale male had grown more sophisticated and clever
In fact, he was so deeply indulged in financial gain
and greater control that he felt
that she could do whatever, whenever, however,
wherever with whoever she wish to roll
After all, she was not the only domesticated creature
who had a hole
Since the suntanned female
had grown so sick, fat and obese
The pale male's interest
in the suntanned male had increased
In fact, with this well-tanned and bronzed he-man
the pale male had always wanted a piece
Ever since he had first viewed him as a well-hung
and studded beast
It would not surprise him at all
that the pale female's desires were the same
And now that the suntanned female
was overused and well-drained
The pale male would join the pale female
in focusing on that suntanned man
who had grown cocky, arrogant and vain
feeling that he was now Mr. Thing
You see, the pale male had long admired
how the suntanned male would bang that wench
Oftentimes lining them up one after another

FULFILLING THE SACRED ANCESTRAL PROPHECY OF THE TRIPLE NINE: UNVEILING THE PROPHETIC 2012 MELTDOWN OF THE LOST AND ASTRAY PALE STATE OF MIND

without a flinch
Yeah, the suntanned male was known to be
big, bad, bold and strong, an athlete
Quick and fast on his feet
He would be used
yeah, he would be used to fight a battle
He would be used to fight a war
He would be used to build everything
from a monkey wrench to a motor car
Yeah, he would get paid
You see, the pale male would pay a nigger to do his thing
He would pay him to dance; he would pay him to sing
He would pay him to bump and grind it out and bang
Yeah, the suntanned male would gain fortune and fame
on many different things
But let us make it clear, the suntanned male did not know
how to function outside of this stale and pale mentality
of this deep-freeze atmosphere
This is what he would know
and this is how he would grow
And when it comes to dealing with
the ancestral family community
It would definitely show
You see, the suntanned male had grown so far out of
sync, out of focus and off track
That for a few dollars more
anyone could get him to do anything that they would like
But so what; now, he was playing the game
of financial gain
And at least he had retained some fortune and fame
Even if he was now caught up

CHAPTER FIVE: RUNNING THE PALE MASTER PLAN AGAINST THE SACRED SUNTANNED HE AND SHE OF MAN

in the cold and stale pale game of misery, aches and pain
And mama, well, mama prayed for this
It's just that mama didn't know who she was praying to
or what she was praying for
And now mama was left sitting there
festering in dread—sick, fat and obese
as her hostility, bitterness and anger would increase
leaving the suntanned female empty, lonely, sad and blue
Left to dominate, to control and then to screw
So whether it was shackles and chains
that were installed or whether the suntanned male
was placed behind prison walls
Whether he had become educated and sophisticated,
having the master pale program installed
Or whether it was drugs, alcohol or addiction that was
imprisoning his mind while pumping it to his butt
Keeping him in a rut, whether he nip, sip, or suck
Or be used in the same manner as was the eunuch
So after the many raping raids of domination and control
and the many ways and means to enslave
the suntanned female would become a partner in this
crime against her own ancestral kind
As integration, assimilation, and the vibrations
of the pale, melting pot syndrome
would dominate and control
every thought and reasoning that she would bring home
It was indeed becoming crystal clear
that the sacred suntanned female
had been converted into a clone or a worker drone
And so be it perming, frying, wig-wearing
or bleaching her skin
she would do any and every thing she could

FULFILLING THE SACRED ANCESTRAL PROPHECY OF THE TRIPLE NINE: UNVEILING THE PROPHETIC 2012 MELTDOWN OF THE LOST AND ASTRAY PALE STATE OF MIND

in an attempt to blend in
Be it painting or blood staining her lips, fingernails
and toes or talking out her nose
Or learning to walk with a hump
or a bend like her cave-dwelling kin
or wearing tinted contacts in an attempt to reflect
that paleness definitely resides within her DNA track
Oblivious and unaware of the fact
that she's glorifying
the cold and pale, raping and raiding invasions
of the blood spilling pack
Venomous and aggressive, talking a lot of yakkety yak
Giving birth to offspring who are addicted to crack
Or freebase or coke or snow and ice
or a cross or crucifixion or some other
social economic, religious addiction
And what would be more whack
Is that she had bought into these lies
and she would be waiting for the dead to arise
Or for Gabriel to blow his horn
so she could die and go to heaven
and get some slack

Verse Seven: Sister True

Tell me true, Sister, what do you want to do?
You've been well paid to play this game
From the time you were transformed into a slave
Remember all of these times in the big house, yeah
You thought you had it made
And then there was all of those times
that I was ready to depart

CHAPTER FIVE: RUNNING THE PALE MASTER PLAN AGAINST THE SACRED SUNTANNED HE AND SHE OF MAN

But your life, true, I wanted to save
Remember the innocent conversation with your master
And how quickly he took my brethrens to the grave
Remember the nearly fatal wounds
that was inflicted upon the I
As I laid there in misery, aches and pains and a daze
And so you tell me true, what you going to do?
Because before I again suffer
those same misery, aches and pains
I'll do this thing without you
Hey, Sister True, I wish that you would know
what I know about you
You see, you have not always been out of align
out of sync, out of focus
in this death-consuming state of mind
And even in this ice-cold, deep-freeze state of mind
You remained sensuous and loving, sometimes
And it seems bipolar is doing it to you
One day you are joyful and happy, too
But the slightest touch of your ego
takes you very low
and makes the best man want to up and go
Before your venomous and hateful rage misbehave
It's clear that this is the consequence
of the cold-blooded slavery days
Or the adverse effects of the cold-blooded Muslim raids
I've seen you in the north, the south, the west and the east
And I've seen how this cold-blooded invasion mentality
has festered in you
Destabilizing your sacred ancestral spirit presence
Sister True

FULFILLING THE SACRED ANCESTRAL PROPHECY OF THE TRIPLE NINE: UNVEILING THE PROPHETIC 2012 MELTDOWN OF THE LOST AND ASTRAY PALE STATE OF MIND

Hey, Sister True, do you remember
when you were totally into I and I was totally into you
And our sacred ancestral presence was all that we knew?
Do you remember the herbs
and do you remember the spice?
And do you remember how we would consume
of the fruits of the trees of life?
Do you remember that mango sap mishap?
I mean the time you wasted it in my lap
And we were both surprised
when we looked into each other's eyes
As you licked that mango sap from my hand
you made my nature rise
And I was much obliged
And I had nothing to hide
And you, baby, you came straight forward
with no disguise
And like a heartbeat, our bodies would vibe
And juices would move from the soft and mellow groove
of your hips
And just as we would touch, lip to lip
Our heads would bow, and you would take a dip
And what a trip as your tongue continued to track
that mango trail
My nature would swell
And the nature of your body heat
I could feel it in your feet
And your soft and sweet sensuous female smell
would tell the whole tale
And like hot lava, you would boil
And if I did not move very quickly

CHAPTER FIVE: RUNNING THE PALE MASTER PLAN AGAINST THE SACRED SUNTANNED HE AND SHE OF MAN

the entire story would spoil
Yeah, you were speaking in tongues
And I was in such a groove
all I could do was to want some
And fortunately, I would move fast and quick
You see, one more touch from your lips and your tongue
And, baby, baby, baby that would have been it
And I had to be hard and firm, and I had to be strong
Because the best was yet to come and get this groove on
As quick as I was able to move
was as quick as I was able to groove
And your passion was soft and wet
And it was clear that you was not ready
to stop this expression yet
And you took me to my peak, and I was ready to roll
But somehow I was able to draw on my calmness
and I was able to hold
And just as you was ready to take another trip
Tongue and lip, your mouth would burn
But somehow I was able to make the table turn
And just one more touch, tongue or cheek
And I would not have been able to stand up
as my semen began to leak
Yeah, I was able to take the turn
Somehow I was able to survive the coming tide
And now it was your turn to yearn
But I still had to change my focus
quick and fast in order to last
Because, girl, you too much
you little fine such and such
Soft and wet and hot as you can be
Fitting the I in I to a "T"

FULFILLING THE SACRED ANCESTRAL PROPHECY OF THE TRIPLE NINE: UNVEILING THE PROPHETIC 2012 MELTDOWN OF THE LOST AND ASTRAY PALE STATE OF MIND

You hear me?
I started with those beautiful toes
And decided I was going to work my way up to your nose
But, by the time I got front and center
you was already on a roll
And what I remember is how your thighs would tremor
And how your hips would rock
And how your body was actually too hot to trot
And our divine union was much too old
For you and I to be carrying on
like this the first time we got it on
As I started to leave the center and headed up for the top
I would stop and hit your time clock
And I guess that must have been it
As your body would begin to tremor
And your pulse would begin to throb
And hey, I wanted to be where you was, baby
Because now I was feeling robbed
Yeah, I knew you
And I was on another mission, because I wasn't through
And then, it started to rain
Just as I took my second aim
And you came, sweet, wet and juicy
Succulent like sugar cane
And that really inspired the I in I to do my thing
And you would smell so sweet
intensifying your body heat
Feeling so good was the I in I
Bringing joy to the sacred ancestral mother spirit of Man
And that is why I wasn't through, Sister True

CHAPTER FIVE: RUNNING THE PALE MASTER PLAN AGAINST THE SACRED SUNTANNED HE AND SHE OF MAN

And it was all part of the plan
and now I could take my place
Positioning myself as a He Man
And groove off of your sensuous move
Until my juices had ran
And coming again, well, that was just you, Sister True
Grooving off the sensation and vibration
of causing the I in I to come too
Ooooh, Sister True, if you knew what I knew about you
This death-consuming culture
would have long been through with you
Hey, Sister True, do you remember the times
when you were naturally fine
With all that natural hair up on your head
Twisted or froed or natty dread
No paint on your toes and no stuff on your lips
Except for the juices of that mango that you sipped
while taking that trip
An ancestral sparkle in your eyes
and a beautiful, spirit-inspired smile
Hey, native child, you had your own style, naturally
And all of this is what would get to me
But now, sometimes, Sister True
I actually break down and cry
Watching and witnessing how you've been ripped, mangled and torn
And broken down, honoring and worshipping
this cold-blooded, deep-freeze lie
Toxic sprays and all kind of toxic smells
and toxic chemicals within the hair
Spreading even more toxic pollutants within the air
Stuff on your lips

FULFILLING THE SACRED ANCESTRAL PROPHECY OF THE TRIPLE NINE: UNVEILING THE PROPHETIC 2012 MELTDOWN OF THE LOST AND ASTRAY PALE STATE OF MIND

Tattoos on your hips
It's like your mind is gone, because your brain took a trip to the clone zone
Yeah, Sister True, this stuff is all up inside of you
And it's deep stone to the bone
And you've grown
and think you've got a mind of your own
When in truth and reality
you have a mind that that white-lady syndrome own
Ah, Sister True, it's a program, ma'am
And that's why you can't truly see
Who the I in I am
But it's down to the wire
and you're going to have to decide
what you're going to do, Sister True
Are you going to continue to support this insanity
and hold it up
Consuming of an energy
that keeps you weak and feeble and in a rut?
Hey, Sister True, I know what you could do
If you only knew what I know about you
Sister True, there's just enough spirit conscious energy left in you to get you through
However, it is up to you to decide what you gonna do
You see, if you decide that you wanna stay and play
Hey, you've got that say
And although, the I in I do indeed desire that you would let go
of that death-consuming culture and join the I in I in this sacred ancestral spirit flow
do not underestimate or misconstrue

CHAPTER FIVE: RUNNING THE PALE MASTER PLAN AGAINST THE SACRED SUNTANNED HE AND SHE OF MAN

my total and absolute alliance to this most supreme
ancestral gathering of a sacred few
Sister True, the I in I have absolutely no desire
to do this thing alone
But, if you decide to stay and play, I'm gone

Verse Eight: Ancestral Spirit Call

In the midst of the toxins that would pollute the water
and the soil and the smog and the filth in the air
The pale mentality had become Man, He and She's,
worst nightmare
And the solution to this mental pollution had gone above
and beyond simply a global affair
Yet the pale ones showed no regret, and with Man, He
and She's, life on the line
The earth would continue to be drilled and peeled and
strip mined
And with the earth continuing to be ripped, stripped
and raped
And left in a state of the disciples and the followers of
that pale trait
The offspring seeds of the suntanned breed
will continue to feed on the lusting greed
and would come to believe that they did indeed succeed
in causing the pale ones to concede
as they now jockey for the position to assume power
while taking the lead
And the more this suntanned male would jell
the more this suntanned male's head would swell
And the more the suntanned male would become as
pale as hell

FULFILLING THE SACRED ANCESTRAL PROPHECY OF THE TRIPLE NINE: UNVEILING THE PROPHETIC 2012 MELTDOWN OF THE LOST AND ASTRAY PALE STATE OF MIND

And the more his thoughts, attitudes and behaviors would start to stank and smell
And the suntanned female would become addicted, afflicted and sick, fat and obese as hell
You see, her storyline was that she had been well-groomed and primed
To become the major partner in this hellish, palish partnership of crime
For generation after generation she had played this pale game so well
But now she had become addicted, afflicted and sick, fat and obese as hell
No, mother was not doing too well
For generation upon generation, she had been pushed and pulled and tugged and drug down this bloodstained trail
For generations upon generations, she had been forced to consume of the toxic rot and funk and smell
And for generations upon generations, she had been ripped, stripped and raped and tricked and deceived like hell
And so after generations upon generations of blood, sweat and tears
And after much grueling misery, aches and pains and suffering fright and fears
she would become fully anointed within this hellish, palish partnership of crime amongst wailing cries and hollering cheers
And her offsprings would dance and sing to the pale-male-wargod theme
And from many places and spaces, they would come and they would cheese and grin and smile

CHAPTER FIVE: RUNNING THE PALE MASTER PLAN AGAINST THE SACRED SUNTANNED HE AND SHE OF MAN

profiling the latest fashions, hair flair that Helene Curtis would declare, yeah, they would style
And in the midst of the toxic pollutions within the water, soil and air
they would sit and stare wondering if this was another dream deferred or the hoped and prayed-for ending to a cold-blooded, pale nightmare
But come what may
this permed, fried and dyed mother spirit would feel that this was indeed her day
Becoming even more aligned within this hellish, palish partnership of crime, feeling that these were just the dues that one would have to pay if one wanted to play
You see, now mama sister was well programmed
to the max
moving in the fast lane and on the fast track
because the Willie Lynch syndrome had been
precise and exact
And generation after generation would uphold and maintain this hell and damnation
without an ounce of reparation
And dying and going to heaven would be her ultimate salvation
And as for Brother Man, well, yeah, he was becoming seriously bland
Although melanin would secure his golden tan
And as far as the eye could see
both He and She was divided and conquered unconditionally
And with all of this being that and all of that being this
Everything that could have been said would have already been said

FULFILLING THE SACRED ANCESTRAL PROPHECY OF THE TRIPLE NINE: UNVEILING THE PROPHETIC 2012 MELTDOWN OF THE LOST AND ASTRAY PALE STATE OF MIND

And everything that could have been told would have already been told
As the era of 2012 would begin to unfold
You see, according to the ancient ones who had told this story very well
As we begin to slowdrag into the era of 2012
the bottom is scheduled to fall out of hell
And although the earth-shift change would indeed be to blame
The true culprit of this thing would be the lust, lies, illusions, confusion, death and deadly destruction brought forward through the misery, aches and pains inflicted by those disciples and followers of this cold-blooded, pale game
And almost everyone would be completely deaf, dumb and blind about the coming of the true signs of the time related to the era of the cycle of the triple nine
And both the haves and the have nots would be on this time clock
And no matter how hard they would try, there was nothing they could do to make it stop
You see, the pale ones were about fortune and fame, supply and demand, regardless of the level and degree of misery, aches and pain that the supply might brang
And you see, they were not about to change one single, solitary thang
So long as the demand for the supply would cause that cash register to ring
So imagine this, and imagine the coming of the era of 2012

CHAPTER FIVE: RUNNING THE PALE MASTER PLAN AGAINST THE SACRED SUNTANNED HE AND SHE OF MAN

Yes, imagine the idea that the bottom was about to fall out of hell
Imagine the chaos and the conflict that would run up and down that bloodstained trail
Imagine the rot and the stank and the funky smell
Yes, imagine this for true
Then imagine what the lost and astray pale state of mind might do
Imagine the pale female
and imagine that somewhere deep, deep within a lost and astray ancestral mother spirit would dwell
And she would have been born of the pale and mutated and degenerated sperm cell
And the multiplication of that mutation and degeneration would fertilize the egg that would give birth to the pale male
And then imagine the pale male
and imagine that somewhere deep, deep, deep within a lost and astray ancestral father spirit would dwell
Imagine the suffering grueling pains
and the violations committed by a state of mind that was beyond being homicidal, psychotic and insane
Then imagine what each and every birth born of this cruel and cold-blooded hurt would bring
Yes, imagine this manifestation
and then imagine the continuation of the mutation and degeneration
Yeah, imagine the vicious and cruel and deadly acts beyond insanity
inflicted against all of humanity

FULFILLING THE SACRED ANCESTRAL PROPHECY OF THE TRIPLE NINE: UNVEILING THE PROPHETIC 2012 MELTDOWN OF THE LOST AND ASTRAY PALE STATE OF MIND

Pushing this pale game over and over again not truly
wanting nothing to change except a furthering and a
continuation
of the ways and means to manifest deadly force in order
to maintain control and domination
Imagine this mental mindset
And it is indeed a true bet
that you will know and understand exactly where
we are now at
When it comes to enhancing the whole life essence of all
living things upon the Earth on which Man, He
and She, dwell
the pale male have truly failed
Although he would indeed succeed in rip, stripping and
raping the earth and polluting the air, water and soil
And he would indeed succeed in pushing the hunting and
herding fatality of the death-consuming cultural reality
And he would indeed succeed in pushing the mass
majority of Man, He and She, into a mentality
dominated, controlled and fueled by that cold and pale
opposite energy
And out of the urgent request of the Most
Supreme Unseen
It would now be left with the sacred ancestral spirit
presence of masculine and feminine energy to
gain control
and break through this freezing cold, deep-freeze mold
And the deadly grip of that pale stranglehold
Resurrecting a divine and sacred few so that a greater
story can indeed be told
And so as we continue to plant this seed

CHAPTER FIVE: RUNNING THE PALE MASTER PLAN AGAINST THE SACRED SUNTANNED HE AND SHE OF MAN

We do indeed encourage that you take heed
And know fo' sho that you steeped head-deep in a helluva program
And power has absolutely no intentions to concede
And so Brother Man and Sister True
This piece is dedicated to each of you
It is indeed up to you
To detox and purge this cold and pale doo doo
In order to get a divine and sacred few through
so that a greater story can indeed be told
beyond this sorrowful hellish, palish woe

Chapter 5 Innerlude:
Helluva Program

**Song 8 from "Supernatural Healing Serum: Dose Three,"
Kwatamani musical CD release, September 2006**

<u>Royal Priestess vocals:</u>
*Your entire life lays before you
And all that you ever knew
in the death consumption culture is exposed
as illusions, delusions and fantasies
All that you thought was true
What a joy to know the holistic living truth
about Supreme Love and have the opportunity
to regain and reclaim all that was lost
all that was stolen, forgotten, taken
rejected and denied then
In the glory of your divine origin
How can you release the deceptions
of a mind lost and astray?
How can you release the habits of toxic consumption?*

<u>High Priest vocals:</u>
*It was so harmonious and peaceful
during the coming forth of day by night
Divine union, divine consumption
going forward to multiply divinity
Yes, Man, He and She, really had this thing right
And so it was and so it would continue to be
until the coming of fear and fright
Led by the raping rage, gut and blood-spilling strength
and might of the lost and astray Children of the Sun*

FULFILLING THE SACRED ANCESTRAL PROPHECY OF THE TRIPLE NINE: UNVEILING THE PROPHETIC 2012 MELTDOWN OF THE LOST AND ASTRAY PALE STATE OF MIND

who identified themselves as white
Yes, it was harmonious and peaceful upon the seen
With the Most Supreme Unseen
harmonizing in an ancestral theme
Tilling the soil and harvesting
the fruits of the trees of the land
Glorifying in the divinity of the He and She of Man
Sisters and brothers working gallantly
to give each other a helping hand
Multiplying through the warmth of each other and the sun
Which feeds whole life energy
into them through their glorious melaninated tan
And when you add this to the whole life consumption
of the fruits of the trees of the land
What would be multiplied over and over again
is the Most Supreme Spirit Presence of He and She
of Man
Therefore, conflict, confusion; lust, lies, and illusions,
death and deadly destruction would definitely be banned
Among the Divine Children of the Sun with a golden tan
It was indeed a glorious time
of the coming forth of day by night
When the Divine Children of the Sun
knew nothing about the ice-cold, deep-freeze mentality
Or the freezing frost bite
or the degenerated pale breed
who was, in fact, a mutated offspring seed
Who had become disconnected
from their whole life basic need
Therefore becoming a blood-spilling power

CHAPTER 5 INNERLUDE: HELLUVA PROGRAM

who would rape, murder, steal and kill
in a split second, hour by hour
And would transmit this vibration
to every encounter and every relation
living for this vibration and the blood rush
and the adrenalin feel
heavily addicted to the thrill of the kill
This would cause this terrorizing encounter and vibration
to be very real
so a flesh- and bones- and blood-
and guts-consuming culture would emerge
out of this ordeal
So consuming of the rot and stink and the funk
of this vibration would be beyond explanation
And would indeed be the base, root and foundation
of expanding mental, physical and spiritual
contamination
This would be passed on from generation after generation
transmitted into the thought and reasoning of every head
that encountered this war-god tribe
who were the worshippers and consumers of the dead
This would leave the mother and the father spirit
of every generation with this cold-blooded vengeance
and wrath and deep-freeze infestation
Ripped, mangled scarred and tarred
raped, murdered, enslaved, family torn apart
Seed after seed, mother spirit breed and feed
mixed breeds, cross breeds, half-breed seeds
Completely deprived of their basic needs
and a dehumanized and emasculated man child
grow up weak, feeble and buck wild
Reflecting the epitome

FULFILLING THE SACRED ANCESTRAL PROPHECY OF THE TRIPLE NINE: UNVEILING THE PROPHETIC 2012 MELTDOWN OF THE LOST AND ASTRAY PALE STATE OF MIND

of the death-consumption-culture style
Caught up in a life, trapped in hostile bitterness
anger and spite
Out of sync and out of focus
with the original ancestral culture
that once flourished in the Indus Valley
along the Tigris, the Euphrates
and up and down the Nile
And generation after degeneration
after more degeneration, the death-consumption culture
would become the adaptation
And the lust, lies, illusions, confusion
of this manifestation would become the roots
and the backbone of this stale and pale infatuation
This would be declared as the proper ways and means
to establish civilized religion and education
And so the pale offspring seed of mutation
and degeneration would henceforth declare themselves
as the superior breed
And the highest evolution of mankind
And through a slick and cunning education vibration
they would mastermind this massively deceptive
vibration and transmit it into a state of mind
And so more and more generations of degeneration
of degenerated generations would integrate and
assimilate into this cold-blooded, deep-freeze
state of mind
Until the sacred suntanned Children
would become spiritually deaf, dumb and blind
and a weak and feeble carbon copy
of these pale Children of mind

CHAPTER 5 INNERLUDE: HELLUVA PROGRAM

And this would be the baggage
that the sacred suntanned Children would tote
As they strive and struggle to have the opportunity to
vote, and they would see this casting a vote
as a cure to their political ills
and the social economic discomfort
that they would feel
And so casting a vote would become
their last ray of hope, instead of connecting
with the most supreme ancestral presence
encoded in the original DNA
that the Most Supreme Unseen first wrote
And so, instead of striving and struggling to achieve
divine spirit consciousness
these lost and astray Children would be tricked
and deceived into believing that the power
truly would come from a vote
And so they would vote
and drug and alcohol addictions
would continue to be massive in the street
And the sick, fat and obese would continue
to consume of flesh and bones and blood of meat
and cooked and depleted and devitalized fruits,
vegetables, seeds and nuts and other toxic treats
And they would vote
while mental, physical and spiritual disorder
would continue to be borne and bred as a norm
And the ancestral mother and father spirit
would continue to be treated with scorn
And the Children of the Sun would continue to live
as though they're half dead, homosexuality, bestiality,
perming and frying their head

FULFILLING THE SACRED ANCESTRAL PROPHECY OF THE TRIPLE NINE: UNVEILING THE PROPHETIC 2012 MELTDOWN OF THE LOST AND ASTRAY PALE STATE OF MIND

Living large, eating like a pig, growing very big
wearing false hair and wig
And then there are those who would change their mood
and move into a cultural groove, they change their name,
play fortune and fame, seeking the same thang
with another name, trying to culturize this thang
Innate ancestral character and traits
they would deny, ignoring their basic needs
in an attempt to breed a paler seed
ducking and dodging the sun
Indulging in cold-blooded, deep-freeze
melaninated fun by the ton
Living their life like a worker drone clone
buying into all kinds of plots and schemes
to have their melaninated tan dethroned
Yes, the suntanned Children have joined the ranks
of the civilized, and the lies would be civil
organized and revised
And the social, political, economic structure
would declare these lies to be true
And regarding that that is divinely true
there would be no clue
So now, the suntanned Children have joined
the pale Children to uphold the ranks of the social order
of the thrill of the kill and the bloodspill
ignoring the Supreme Spirit of Truth
and the whole-life lessons that have come their way
would take them even farther lost and astray
causing them to have even more dues to pay
Although the initial degeneration and mutation
occurred in the ice-cold, deep freeze

CHAPTER 5 INNERLUDE: HELLUVA PROGRAM

this modern new-age degeneration and mutation
occurs in the sunshine and in an environment
surrounded by trees
The death consumption culture would be
the degeneration and the mutation base
and the plague of this degeneration and mutation
would be played out in the pale and deceptive ideology
of religion and race
The ignorancy of the pale, racist ideology would declare
that all of Man, He and She
evolved separately and that white is the superior race
Ignoring the holistic living truth
that all of Man, He and She
evolved from a single family base
that the DNA would trace
to the Most Supreme ancestral race
Down in the old Ethiopian land
of the Divine Children of the Sun with a golden tan
and that the white supremacist ideology of race
could also easily be traced
to the deep-freeze, cave-dwelling clan
of the Caucasus Mountain region and the frozen ice land
that entrapped the lost and astray Children of the Sun
who mutated and degenerated
and lost their spiritual essence and their golden tan
and came out running this deep-freeze
sex and violence scam
And be they blonde or bald or natty, natty dread
there'd be a massive addiction to this
deep-freeze mentality and the culture
that consumes of the dead
and the ghosts and goblins of the dead

FULFILLING THE SACRED ANCESTRAL PROPHECY OF THE TRIPLE NINE: UNVEILING THE PROPHETIC 2012 MELTDOWN OF THE LOST AND ASTRAY PALE STATE OF MIND

would grow stronger and stronger up inside their head
and the whole vibration of bip bam, thank you ma'am
would gain a whole new meaning
in this sex and violence scam
And upon the seen, you could hear the ego scream
"Do you know who I am,"
as the lost and astray mind gets deeper and deeper
in running this cold-blooded, deep-freeze scam
And in the midst of wailing cries and the hollering
scream, you could hear the most supreme ancestral
presence say, "Dammmnnn….what a helluva program."

Chapter Six: Religions and the Deities of Death

Chapter 6 Prelude:
Something to Step to

Song 6 from "12th Hour Prophecy: Pale Curse and the Solarized Energy Shift," Kwatamani musical CD release, 2008

<u>Royal Priestess vocals:</u>
*So you say you need something to step to
better watch what you say and who you say it to
Cause the High Priest Kwatamani
will give you something to step to*

<u>High Priest vocals:</u>
Yeah, this piece here, well this a love song
Syncopated and orchestrated for you to step on
For the big, bad and bold who think they're full grown
Footloose and fancy free with a mind of their own
For the bad mamma-jammas who stone cold to the bone
Doing the wrong thing right and the right thing wrong
Take a few minutes, groove with this groove
And let this smooth love song take you to school
Where truth lyrics are the golden rule
Moving through the streets, always on the run
Pistol Pete carrying heat and every other daughter or son has become a master con
Like a predator or a leech, sucking you like a sponge
Stealing your life energy, leaving you with none
And you better move fast and quick, better stay on the run
Cause every bad, mamma-jamma out there got a gun
Kicking ass and taking aim is a gang-banger's fun
And the way the story is wrote, hardly anybody can cope

FULFILLING THE SACRED ANCESTRAL PROPHECY OF THE TRIPLE NINE: UNVEILING THE PROPHETIC 2012 MELTDOWN OF THE LOST AND ASTRAY PALE STATE OF MIND

So everybody seeking, searching out a ray of hope
Trying to relieve the mental stress and strain and the
misery aches and pains from the baggage they tote
Some would sniff and snort and smoke some dope
Some would preach and teach and fool some folks
Some would seek and search a hole to stroke
Some would beat their meat, some would seek out dead
and devitalized something to eat
Hell, oh yeah, this stale and pale game
is stone cold to the bone
And the suntanned Children won't leave this thing alone
Just can't seem to figure out where it went wrong
And why this stale and pale game
has been going on for so long
No, I ain't going to end this love song
here in the midst of this doo doo
Leaving you empty, ignorant, sad and blue
I'm a take a moment and let the priestess sing to you
And then I'm a come back
and give you something to step to

<u>Royal Priestess vocals:</u>
Mothers, fathers, sons and daughters
Game playing within an insane game
Ducking and dodging each other headed for self-
destruction in the fast lane
And with absolutely nothing divine to step to
Deadly destruction has a point-blank aim
And our sacred spiritual essence
is what this pale game will claim
High Priest Kwatamani, High Priest Kwatamani

CHAPTER 6 PRELUDE: SOMETHING TO STEP TO

the ancestral mother spirit is requesting
that you give us more divine spirit insight to step to

<u>High Priest vocals:</u>
Aaaw, sing it, baby
If I didn't say it before, I now say to you
Get natural, raw and rare and take a breath of fresh air
And let this supreme truth talk to you
There's sum deep-seated programs that you must let go
And we don't have any time to waste anymo'
Without hoop or holler and a lot of to-do
use this supreme truth to step to
Who betrayed the Garden Culture, Abel or Cain?
Who made the burnt offering in their god's name?
Who is the god of the folks
who used Brother Cain as a scapegoat?
Who are the disciples and the followers who would take
the supreme truth and have it rewrote establishing a pale-
male-war god culture who would rape, murder
enslave and spook folks?
Who would orchestrate truth to deceive anyone who
would come to believe the triple-six alliance
about Adam and Eve?
And the triple-six god said, in the beginning was the
word
And there'd be a declaration of war
against the keepers of the word
And in truth and reality, the keepers of the word
were the keepers of the Most Supreme Truth
far beyond the syllables of a word
And the keepers of Supreme Truth far beyond the word
was raided, invaded, murdered, raped, and enslaved
And the word was stolen, and the truth was reversed

FULFILLING THE SACRED ANCESTRAL PROPHECY OF THE TRIPLE NINE: UNVEILING THE PROPHETIC 2012 MELTDOWN OF THE LOST AND ASTRAY PALE STATE OF MIND

And the word would become deception
and deception would become the word
And this is exactly what Adam and Eve heard
And a ventriloquist-like voice was projected
and Eve heard the word
And after being tricked and deceived
Adam would hear the other voice
that pointed the finger at Eve
And she would be seen as evil, always ready to follow
disorder, leading Man into temptation
profiled as the devil's daughter
And woman would be cursed to give birth
in toiling suffering pains upon the earth
You see, here before, the thing was man made
And Eve was born out of Adam's rib cage
Oh yeah, let us not forget that they were led out of the
Sacred Garden Culture
and into a culture of war and crime
And they would learn to hunt and herd and slaughter and
kill flesh and blood is how they would dine
What kind of god is this that would declare this opposite-
energy culture as divine, choosing of the slaughter and
the burnt flesh of death instead of the fruits of the trees of
life, and declaring this burnt offering
as its first-choice way to dine?
Who betrayed the Garden Culture, Abel or Cain?
Who declared a burnt offering in their god's name?
What kind of energy is the possessor of this god?
And what is the worship of the folks
who declared Brother Cain a scapegoat?
Now, take this Truth and step on

CHAPTER 6 PRELUDE: SOMETHING TO STEP TO

<u>Royal Priestess vocals:</u>
So you say you need something to step to
better watch what you say and who you say it to
Cause the High Priest Kwatamani
will give you something to step to

Chapter Six: Religions and the Deities of Death

The First and the Second Coming

Ever since the emergence of the opposite energy upon the seen, the disciples and followers of that foreign and toxic energy have gained control through violent force, terror tactics and the resulting fright and fear. For a very long time, ever since this unfortunate cold and pale emergence, Man, He and She, has been misinterpreting and misunderstanding the nature of events based on the appearance of things. There are actually two separate and different origins that have occurred upon the planet Earth. The first coming was the emergence of the divine order of earth, wind, rain and sun. The first coming was the sacred ancestral spirit presence of the Divine Children of the Sun and the Sacred Garden Culture from which we come.

This original and Most Supreme Seen presence reflected the whole life energy of the Most Supreme Unseen presence as the Essence of Life and Supreme Love. This first coming expressed the Divine Union of One as the most supreme ancestral spirit essence of masculinity and femininity. This first coming was suntanned Man, He and She; consumers of raw and living fruits, vegetables, seeds and nuts; as the original inhabitants of planet Earth.

The second coming is an entirely separate and different story. The second coming was the mutated and degenerated breeds of mankind who emerged from the

FULFILLING THE SACRED ANCESTRAL PROPHECY OF THE TRIPLE NINE: UNVEILING THE PROPHETIC 2012 MELTDOWN OF THE LOST AND ASTRAY PALE STATE OF MIND

white-blight ordeals of the Caucasus mountain and steppe regions after the last ice age. This story of mutation and degeneration has actually become the dominant frame of reference throughout the planet and is known as truth within the death-consuming culture. The deceptions and misinterpretations of "western education" and "western religion" and every other branch, be it north, south, east or west, are based on the confusions regarding this second coming. The "western" social economic structure is based on the cold and pale nature of this second coming. This is the only way to describe those who originally descended from the opposite energy. In fact, the entire planet is still suffering from the adverse effects and consequences of the cold and brutal encounters that were the breeding ground for what is today called "western civilization."

What has happened upon the planet Earth over the several thousands of years since the second coming is an energy shift into the opposite energy of the toxic parallel. The history and the existing accounts of vicious invasions and bloody conquests by the mutated and degenerated breeds of mankind are more telling than one could ever imagine

It has only been a matter of time for the long-awaited return of the first coming to appear once again upon the seen. The sacred ancestral prophecy of the Triple Nine has been in place to bring divine clarity regarding this long-awaited resurrection of the sacred ancestral spirit presence of the Divine Children of the Sun and the Sacred Garden Culture from which we come. One must begin to see the foreign and toxic nature of the

CHAPTER SIX: RELIGIONS AND THE DEITIES OF DEATH

energy that one consumes within this death culture of the hunting and herding mentality. One must begin to acknowledge how one has consumed the opposite energy and how it has actually invaded, conquered, raped, and enslaved one's life energy. One must begin to see how one has integrated, assimilated, and adopted a deceptive identity of self and how one's lost and astray mind has claimed superiority over divine spirit consciousness.

Always remember that the mutated and degenerated breed belongs to the hunting and herding culture where male-domination is maintained by killing one's opponent, adversary or enemy in warfare. The very nature of these early nomadic clans and tribes would be to uphold their pale-male-warlord deities. Within the cold and freezing experiences of those northern lands, this would be all that they would know or be able to conceive of. And so when these pale breeds of warring clans would encounter the suntanned He and She of Man, they would view the suntanned presence of masculinity as the ultimate threat. You see, the suntanned Children in no way resembled anything that the mutated and degenerated breeds could identify with or relate to from their experiences in the northern cold.

All that the pale ones would encounter during their first invasions into the sacred suntanned lands would be stunning, but all that the nomadic warring clans could do within their nature was to kill and destroy in order to dominate and control. And these violent invaders had no knowledge, wisdom and understanding on how to re-build all that they had destroyed, so all that they left behind was ruins and remnants of that which had existed. In fact, for many, many generations these lost and astray

FULFILLING THE SACRED ANCESTRAL PROPHECY OF THE TRIPLE NINE: UNVEILING THE PROPHETIC 2012 MELTDOWN OF THE LOST AND ASTRAY PALE STATE OF MIND

pale Children would reside within the ruins and remains of their own destructive patterns and would become grave robbers, collecting the relics, treasures and remnants for trade. The lusting greed to possess power, strength and material wealth as the might of the warlord has manifested many cold-blooded, ruthless ways where terrorizing fear is used to instill submission and one has no thought about quickly slaughtering one's challenger. While all that the warring nomadic invaders could bring with them were the violent expressions of the energy that they consumed, what they met when they came face to face with the Divine Children of the Sun was the solarized expressions of whole life energy. And the sacred ancestral spirit presence of the Divine Children of the Sun would be seen as an opposition to all that pale-male-warlord deity represented. You see, the pale-male-warlord deity was a vengeful and jealous god who would have no other god before him, so conquest was seen as a necessity and the Children of the Sun would be forced to submit or die. It is unquestionable to the pale ones that the pale male warlord deity was indeed a god of love; that is, a love for the way of life that these nomadic hunting and herding warring tribes would honor and uphold.

Religion: A Way of Life

Religion within the divine parallel is a far different practice than what has come to be known and called religion within the toxic parallel of the cold and pale opposite energy. The Divine Children of the Sun did not experience religion as a set of rituals or a belief system, a

CHAPTER SIX: RELIGIONS AND THE DEITIES OF DEATH

dogma or doctrine or the mere physical acts of worship. In fact, the entire way of life within the Sacred Garden Culture from which we come was a sacred expression of the Divine Union of One between the Most Supreme Seen and Unseen Essence of Life and Supreme Love. There was no separation between one's spirit presence and all other aspects of one's existence within the divine social economic family community. Leadership was defined by one's strength and ability to embody the expressions of divine spirit consciousness. All life creations and matters of such were honored, respected and considered of value within the divine order of whole life energy. So the concept of religion would actually be translated in the divine parallel as a holistic living way of life with no division between the most supreme seen presence and the most supreme unseen ancestral spirit presence of masculinity and femininity.

The transformations of whole life energy within divine spirit consciousness included no place for the idea of death and dying. Life was known to be an eternal circle where one's most supreme ancestral responsibilities within the unseen were carried forward upon the seen. The whole purpose of the life cycle is to manifest greater levels of divine spirit consciousness, taking one into the Most High state of being. This was the only way that Man, He and She, could re-cycle back into a most supreme unseen ancestral spirit presence. Therefore, one's earthly or seen responsibilities to maintain the glory of earth, wind, rain and sun and the Sacred Garden Culture from which we come was a divine and innate privilege, obligation and requirement for re-

FULFILLING THE SACRED ANCESTRAL PROPHECY OF THE TRIPLE NINE: UNVEILING THE PROPHETIC 2012 MELTDOWN OF THE LOST AND ASTRAY PALE STATE OF MIND

cycling back into the Most Supreme Unseen ancestral spirit presence of masculinity and femininity.

We should make it clear right here that the Sacred Garden Culture from which we come has always maintained and upheld the way of life that honors earth, wind, rain and sun. To instigate the pollution of air, water and soil would forever remain a contradiction to the Essence of Life as well as a conflict of interest to Supreme Love. Likewise, to instigate the pollution of the whole life temple of Man, He and She, would also be a grave contradiction and conflict of interest. The sacred solarized presence of Man, He and She, was glorified, and it was well-comprehended that melanin expression was vital for the whole life consumption of solar energy. And if this cycle of divine consumption within whole life energy was ever broken, severe consequences would cause Man, He and She, to exit divine spirit consciousness and enter a toxic parallel.

The Divine Children of the Sun practice a garden-based, veganic consumption of raw and living fruits, vegetables, seeds and nuts that affirms, preserves, and respects all life. Killing, slaughter, murder, war and blood spill are not, and have never been, a part of the sacred ancestral spirit presence of the Divine Children of the Sun and shall never be. These cold and pale acts of violence, violation and destruction are the very nature of the energy that is opposite of Supreme Love and the Essence of Life.

We must make note that many of the religious beliefs within the toxic parallel only serve to reflect the depleted, devitalized and self-destructive nature of the

CHAPTER SIX: RELIGIONS AND THE DEITIES OF DEATH

opposite energy. There is absolutely no way that the Divine Children of the Sun would ever submit to the deception that a pale-male-warlord deity was superior to the Most Supreme Seen and Unseen essence of masculinity and femininity as the Divine Union of One.

The only reason that the savage and brutal nomadic tribes that descended from the Caucasus mountain and steppe region did not extinguish themselves within the cold and pale chaos of their white-blight mentality is because they encountered the sacred ancestral spirit presence of the Divine Children of the Sun and the Sacred Garden Culture from which we come. And the sacred ancestral spirit energy that was able to transmit into their pale consciousness was enough to prevent their total self-destruction. Until their encounters with the Divine Children of the Sun, the mutated and degenerated breeds were completely cold-hearted and had no sense of compassion for anyone or anything of life. And in the process of the brutal, cruel and blood-lusting invasions, these lost and astray pale Children ripped apart and sought to devour with beastly greed the Sacred Garden Culture from which we come. While the lost and astray pale Children prospered from their ruthless invasions, their prosperity forced the sacred suntanned Children into a state of severe danger. Prosperity among these pale breeds was equated with lusting greed, the thrill of the kill and blood spill.

While the dominant patterns of the opposite energy can now be seen through the historical movements of the disciples and followers within the toxic parallel, there was a time when the cold-blooded patterns of destruction were not clearly recognized, comprehended or exposed

FULFILLING THE SACRED ANCESTRAL PROPHECY OF THE TRIPLE NINE: UNVEILING THE PROPHETIC 2012 MELTDOWN OF THE LOST AND ASTRAY PALE STATE OF MIND

as an energy that is opposite of Supreme Love and the Essence of Life. Even up until these present days, there are those who do not comprehend the well-defined toxic nature of those who consume from the death culture of that pale opposite energy. In fact, it is still not fully comprehended as to what we mean by death-consuming culture even though the toxic habits, sickness, afflictions and disease run rampant. These toxic habits, attitudes and beliefs have emerged into an acceptable way of life, sanctioned by the dominant religious orders. Indeed, over thousands of years this unwhole and depleted energy has shown itself through different names and disguises. If one begins to look carefully one can actually begin to detect the presence of this cold and pale energy throughout the death-consuming culture.

Now we come to that most difficult element within the detoxing and purging process. Unquestionably, releasing one's addiction to the religions of the death-consuming culture is that most difficult element. Why? Clearly and precisely, because the religious orders of the death-consuming culture have been integrated, assimilated and molded into a way of life. To make matters worse, the disciples and followers of that opposite energy have utilized sex and violence, war and crime to push the religious ideologies of the pale-male-war-god deities deep into the mental mindset of the most precious gift that the Divine Children of the Sun have, i.e. the ancestral mother spirit. The ordeal has been one of the most horrendous experiences faced by Man, He and She. The most cruel, gruesome and vicious acts of

CHAPTER SIX: RELIGIONS AND THE DEITIES OF DEATH

sex and violence, war and crime imagineable have been used to spread this massive plague of deception.

The deception is that this deity of the opposite energy is the all-mighty creator of every living thing upon the Earth. As the all-mighty and omnipotent creator of every living thing, the disciples and followers claim to have absolute right to seek, search and destroy anyone who is identified as a non-believer in that particular deity. The nature of these belief systems has caused massive destruction of massive populations without an ounce of sympathy and compassion for those victimized. Ever since the disciples and followers of that opposite energy harnessed enough strength to depart the deep-freeze regions of the Caucasus mountains and steppe regions, blood spill has marked their trail. From the east to the west, these cold and savage predators invaded, raided, raped, slaughtered, burned and pillaged their way southward into the Fertile Crescent.

Upon entering the rich and vibrant, fertile and peacefully organized land of the sacred suntanned He and She of Man, chaos has indeed has been the mark of this beastly mentality born and bred from the mutation and degeneration of that opposite energy. The brutal invading nomadic tribes carried their violent way of life, their religious rituals of slaughter and blood sacrifice, and the vengeful wrath of their pale-male-warlord deities who blessed victory in the battlefield.

The first suntanned populations to feel the wrath of those nomadic warring clans were the Children of the Sun who inhabited what has been called Old Europe to the west and those suntanned Children of the eastern regions presently called the Asiatic lands. However, it

FULFILLING THE SACRED ANCESTRAL PROPHECY OF THE TRIPLE NINE: UNVEILING THE PROPHETIC 2012 MELTDOWN OF THE LOST AND ASTRAY PALE STATE OF MIND

seems that once that pale plague of mutating deception was introduced into divine social order, then lust, lies, illusions, confusion, death and deadly destruction would spread like a virus.

Research indicates that a period of global warming caused a tremendous amount of ice from the polar ice caps and mountain glaciers to begin to melt at the end of the last ice age. Studies show that sea levels began to slowly rise. Findings reveal that between 5,000 and 6,000 BCE water levels had increased by as much as 300 feet in certain flooded areas within the Caucasus mountain and steppe regions. With the thawing ice and flooding, came waves of vicious nomadic tribes with their violent hunting and herding culture and their pale-male-warlord deities.

The initial attacks and raging raids against that first generation of suntanned populations would leave settled garden communities ripped apart, raped, burned, stripped and destabilized. As was the warring nomadic custom, any captured males would be slaughtered, and oftentimes the captives would be consumed as a meal or presented as a sacrifice to the warlord deity. The suntanned females who survived these attacks would be gang raped, and those who survived this horror would be all that remained of a village scene once the bloodthirsty horde had departed. Oftentimes, this gang-raping ordeal would breed offspring seeds of the mutated and degenerated breed. The ancestral suntanned mother would be left to struggle through this ordeal alone as she would begin to breed an entirely new kind of offspring seed within an entirely new kind of social disorder.

CHAPTER SIX: RELIGIONS AND THE DEITIES OF DEATH

These offspring would be born within the corruption and chaos of a severely disrupted garden culture. The males among these generations who were bred by that opposite energy would have less of a connection with the sacred ancestral spirit presence of the Divine Children of the Sun and the Sacred Garden Culture from which we come. In other words, they would take on a new way of life, new beliefs, attitudes and behaviors. The religious practices that would emerge out of the invader culture would begin to displace the sacred ancestral ways of life.

Let's be clear here: every single Man, He and She, upon the earth function within some sort of religion, that is, within some way of life, regardless if one is atheist, communist, metaphysical or any other declaration of a scientific frame of reference. The I in I hope that this point is very well understood. Regardless of the frame of reference, the nature of the dogma preached, or the doctrine otherwise expounded upon, the individual can only be within one parallel of energy or the other. One is either in alignment with our most supreme ancestral spirit presence as it exists within the divine parallel of divine spirit consciousness or one is in alignment with the thoughts and reasoning of the toxic parallel and the various attitudes, values, beliefs and behaviors as manifested within the death-consuming culture.

The genetic strain of the invader father would leave the contamination of the white blight and the consequences of the deep-freeze ordeal imprinted within these offspring born of this ordeal. This kind and type of experience would go on for generation after generation, and would even enter into what is called the 21st century.

FULFILLING THE SACRED ANCESTRAL PROPHECY OF THE TRIPLE NINE: UNVEILING THE PROPHETIC 2012 MELTDOWN OF THE LOST AND ASTRAY PALE STATE OF MIND

The ancestral tradition of the Children of the Sun opens its arms to the offspring, and this new pale ordeal would at first be treated in the same regard. So long as the ancestral suntanned mother spirit provided the ancestral connection for the offspring, these suntanned communities would embrace all offspring born off of her. Although this would serve as a saving grace for many offspring born of the invasion ordeal, it would also breed massive division and strife as the offspring born out of the mutating and degenerating seed would carry violent strains of pale disorder within the DNA.

Many of these offspring seeds would indeed have access to the sacred temples and would hold other ancestral privileges and social links. If that ancestral mother had royal links or lineages, the offspring born from her would automatically inherit off of her. If that ancestral mother was a priestess, her offspring would have certain ancestral rights to sacred ancestral history and records kept within the temple as a natural fact of birth. These offspring would have access to the rites by the course of being born, bred and raised off of that mother spirit. It should be clear then that through time, those offspring who continued to identify with the invading, raping and raiding father's way of life would serve as primary agents to harness information. In fact, these offspring would begin to link up with those breeds of the invading fathers and would begin to formulate new invader tribes and clans.

You see, these offspring kind and kin born off of the pale mutated seed would begin to stand out simply by the nature of their attitudes and behaviors. The sacred

CHAPTER SIX: RELIGIONS AND THE DEITIES OF DEATH

ancestral mother and father had no idea of the degree of mutation and degeneration that was bred within the DNA trait of these half-breed or semi-breed offspring. So it would be very difficult for them to understand these strange and unusual attitudes and behaviors that would be displayed by these offspring who were born from an ancestral mother spirit. As a matter of fact, within those deep-seated family community settings, the nature of the extended family vibration would offset many of these toxic attitudes and behaviors. However, after generations upon generations of continuously in-breeding off of the nature of the opposite energy, there would be absolutely nothing left within the sacred suntanned social order that could contain this new breed of kin.

The Dominant Religious Orders of the Toxic Parallel

This breakdown of ancestral social order would then begin to breed a new way of life, and off of that would be born new religious orders that would directly identify with the pale-male-war-god deity. With the sacred ancestral temples disrupted, destroyed and contaminated, it would then become easier to intrude upon the mental mindset of the suntanned Children. The Divine Union of One between the Most Supreme Seen and Unseen would be broken and divided as more and more of the Children of the Sun began to consume of the opposite energy. Once the disconnection occurred, all that could be experienced is a state of mind that is reduced to calling upon the deities of the toxic parallel.

The mutated and degenerated breeds of mankind upheld deities that reflected and reinforced their brutally violent way of life. These various pale-male-warlord

FULFILLING THE SACRED ANCESTRAL PROPHECY OF THE TRIPLE NINE: UNVEILING THE PROPHETIC 2012 MELTDOWN OF THE LOST AND ASTRAY PALE STATE OF MIND

deities have been given many, many different names throughout the cold-blooded history of vicious invasions, constant violence and bloodshed. Today these dominant religions have maintained the vibrations and sensations of the white-blight ordeal. The energy that formulated these deities was cold and pale and the opposite of the Essence of Life and Supreme Love, and the patterns of this energy remain the same game with a different name.

In each dominant pattern of religious order within the toxic parallel there is a pale male deity of vengeance, wrath and fierce aggression who was called upon to protect his loyal disciples and followers by blessing them with victory in battle. These battles were attacks, invasions and acts of violent aggression against other populations that are labeled as non-believers, heathens, infidels, etc. The nature of the energy called upon has not changed over time, indeed, the energy that is opposite of Supreme Love and the Essence of Life. The rites and rituals within these dominant religious orders began with acts of slaughter, blood spill, burnt offerings and human and animal sacrifices that define the nature of the energy that is opposite of Supreme Love and the Essence of Life. While the rituals and sacraments of worship are now said to be symbolic in some instances, i.e. eating the flesh and drinking the blood of the deity; nevertheless, the nature of the opposite energy does not change.

As a matter of fact, the first acts of creation performed by each of these pale-male-warlord deities exist outside of the Divine Union of One. Where there is no supreme ancestral essence of femininity joined in the Divine Union of One with the supreme ancestral essence

CHAPTER SIX: RELIGIONS AND THE DEITIES OF DEATH

of masculinity there is no supreme Essence of Life and Supreme Love. Therefore, while these pale-male-warlord deities certainly have been able to amass strength and might within the consciousness of multitudes of disciples and followers, these worshippers are in reality bowing in servitude to the energy that is opposite of Supreme Love and the Essence of Life. The recorded history of these religions speaks for itself. Crusades, holy wars, inquisitions, witch-burning, genocidal religious purging, righteous proclamations to sanction slavery, suicide bombings and missionary acts of invasion and conquest all committed in the name of the pale-male-warlord deity of one's belief.

It would be a waste of energy to name the numerous clans and tribes of warring nomadic invaders. The basic fact that needs to be comprehended is that these clans of nomadic warlords did indeed attack and invade the stable garden communities of the suntanned He and She of Man. This basic fact is hard to swallow by those who maintain that the pale breeds of mutation and degeneration were the bearers of great civilization as they descended from their white-blight ordeals. There were so many clans, so many tribes, so many attacks, throughout centuries and centuries before the history keepers and storytellers even began to record their bloodstained trail. Therefore, there is no need to debate the details. One must reason within self regarding the nature of the environment that would support the Sacred Garden Culture and the suntanned presence that must reflect a solarized relationship. One must then reason with the nature of the environment that would support the ice-cold deep freeze and the mutation and degeneration that would occur in such a solar-deficient relationship.

The differences in skin tones were not at all as significant as the changes in attitudes, values, and behaviors, especially the adoption of consumption patterns of the hunting and herding culture. In fact, the color syndrome would not become an issue until these lost and astray Children began to seek what were seen as the advantages of the conquering and dominating warrior tribes and clans. These offspring would become addicted to the death-consuming patterns of eating slaughtered animal flesh and drinking animal milk and blood. Instead of reasoning with the holistic living truth about Supreme Love and the Essence of Life, these mixed breeds would begin to identify with physical characteristics and traits that reflected mutation and degeneration as a mark of distinction.

Secret Societies and Sacred Orders

These disruptive and disturbing changes upon the seen gave even greater strength to the secret societies within the Sacred Ancestral Temple of Kwa Ta Man I. The secret societies reflected sacred ancestral orders established within the Sacred Garden Culture to maintain the structures of the divine social economic community. These sacred ancestral orders had always been divinely guided and protected and divinely nurtured to insure that the essence of the sacred ancestral spirit presence of the Divine Children of the Sun and the Sacred Garden Culture from which we come remained whole and clean upon the seen. The High Priest and the sacred order of

CHAPTER SIX: RELIGIONS AND THE DEITIES OF DEATH

royal priestesses and priests were ordained to keep the Most Supreme Seen and Unseen Essence of Life and Supreme Love in tact and in place. The Essence was kept whole and clean within the sacred ancestral temples, regardless of the conflict, confusion, lust, lies, illusions, death and deadly destruction inflicted against the Sacred Garden Culture. These secret societies of the Essence would later come to be known as the Sacred Order of the Essence.

There would be many attempts throughout the history of the cold and pale invasions to co-opt and destabilize this most supreme ancestral order. It eventually became known that the strength and will of the Divine Children of the Sun and the Sacred Garden Culture from which we come was held within the sacred ancestral spirit presence of the Essence of Life and Supreme Love. Therefore, in time, the High Priest of the Sacred Ancestral Temple as well as the royal priestesses and priests as the keepers of this sacred order were hunted down, and many temples within the Sacred Garden Culture were raided, robbed, burned and destroyed. However, the Sacred Order of the Essence was a stronghold unseen and unknown by the outsider culture. The High Priest, royal priestesses and priests would remain totally aligned within divine spirit consciousness, regardless of the most violent threats and acts. We make it clear that this most sacred order of the Essence unquestionably represented the Divine Union of One of the most supreme ancestral spirit presence of masculine and feminine energy.

The keepers of the Sacred Order of the Essence would remain within the Most Supreme Unseen as a result of a massive disconnection from the Essence of Life and Supreme Love upon the seen. Even within the harsh realities of conflict, confusion, lust, lies, illusions, death and deadly destruction upon the seen, all that was necessary was for the Children of the Sun to remain whole and clean within the Essence of Life and Supreme Love, and the disconnection would not have been possible. Divine communication would have continued in a steady flow from the Most Supreme Unseen to the seen. However, once fright and fear had penetrated the mind of thought and reasoning, divine spirit consciousness would become inaccessible. Once disconnected, the Children of the Sun would be left vulnerable to the vicious and violent attacks of the disciples and followers of the opposite energy.

This state of spiritual disconnection would leave the social economic communities of the garden culture without the divine guidance, protection and nurturing of the Most Supreme Unseen upon the seen. With no voice of divine guidance, protection and nurturing upon the seen, individuals were left to interpret and translate the nature of events upon the seen and the movement of energy in their lives with no real comprehension and no focus on the essence of divine spirit consciousness. Physical events would indeed begin to overwhelm the Children of the Sun. Conflict and confusion in leadership positions fed more and more into the opposite energy as division and strife became a daily reality within the conquered and divided minds of those who survived within the remaining garden culture.

CHAPTER SIX: RELIGIONS AND THE DEITIES OF DEATH

The lost and astray pale Children would inflict a level and degree of toxic energy upon the Children of the Sun that was very similar to the white blight of toxic energy that they had experienced in their deep-freeze cave-dwelling ordeal. And the same consequences of mutation and degeneration that occurred in the deep freeze, would begin to manifest in the garden lands of the suntanned Man, He and She, during these bloody storms of invasion inflicted by the nomadic tribes.

The same devastating energy shift into paleness that began in the deep freeze of the white blight continued to spread as that energy that is opposite of Supreme Love and the Essence of Life invaded the Sacred Garden Culture. That pale opposite energy would have the opportunity to dig even deeper into a more focused earthly host. The cold and pale nature would intensify as these disciples and followers would invade, raid and attack with slaughtering, raping rage in brutal efforts to enslave, dominate and control the Essence of Life and Supreme Love.

The Children of the Sun would endure attack after attack, and these vicious invasions inflicted by the nomadic outsider tribes would cause severe destabilization and disruption in the sacred ancestral way of life. The Children of the Sun became lost and astray in a vicious downward cycle of the energy that is opposite of the Essence of Life and Supreme Love. They began to worship in contradiction and confusion as they became more and more acquainted with the pale-male-warlord deities and the ways and means of the death-consuming culture.

FULFILLING THE SACRED ANCESTRAL PROPHECY OF THE TRIPLE NINE: UNVEILING THE PROPHETIC 2012 MELTDOWN OF THE LOST AND ASTRAY PALE STATE OF MIND

There was no absolutely no way for the nomadic invaders to penetrate the secret societies of the sacred ancestral temples and the Sacred Order of the Essence. The priests of the opposite energy would only know of the spirit of the toxic unseen. Not even Alexander with his massive army and all his claims to greatness was able to penetrate the secret society of the Sacred Order of the Essence within the sacred temples. Neither he nor any of the priests and oracles with whom he communicated could penetrate the Essence, because they stood outside of the divine parallel.

The protective measures put in place by the Supreme Laws of the universe have indeed maintained the divine order of whole life energy. Divine union, divine consumption and going forward to multiply divinity in the offspring stand as the spiritual locks to keep all those cold and pale imposters and their disciples and followers forever confined to the toxic parallel. Although the knowledge base and the wealth of the sacred ancestral temples was raided, robbed and claimed by the mutated and degenerated breeds, all that was stolen could only be translated and interpreted through the limitations of the lost and astray pale state of mind. Throughout the history of the mutated and degenerated breeds of mankind, all that the cold and pale invaders and temple raiders could do was fabricate a pale imitation of what little they could comprehend.

As a result, the religious orders of the toxic parallel would establish their own secret orders and societies to conjure and invoke and call upon that pale opposite energy. They would build shrines and carry holy boxes

CHAPTER SIX: RELIGIONS AND THE DEITIES OF DEATH

called arks and make sacrificial alters for slaughter and mix their pagan, heathen, and blood-cult ways with the bits and pieces that they could steal from the remnants of the sacred ancestral temples. The holy books of the outsiders were actually extracted from the papyrus of the sacred ancestral scribes and the bas reliefs that were stolen from the ruins of the sacred ancestral temples. Additonally, the various stories that would be translated into pale thought and reasoning were ancient accounts of Enki and Ninhursag, Osiris and Auset, other representations of the Divine Union of One. The only difference was that the outsiders would add their pale-male-war-god deity to the top of the order.

The High Priest and others of the Sacred Order of the Essence would identify these invader warring clans and all of the descendants of that pale state of mind as the outsiders, simply because their laws, rules, attitudes and beliefs, i.e. their way of life, was outside of the Sacred Order of the Essence. A few of the names given were Hebrew, tamhou…and from this would branch the warring tribes and clans of the death-consuming culture, such as Semites, Hittites, and others. As the branches would continue to break through time, the names would be too many to mention. In modern times, these offspring of the warring tribes and clans would simply declare themselves as the Semitic groups and the Aryan groups, and offshoots of the Hittites that would be called Asiatic. The esoteric and occult practices of the toxic unseen are all within the same energy that has misled so many who call upon some form of a pale monotheistic male warlord as a god of love. Then the atheists simply honor and deify the cold and pale state of mind without the trappings of a religious dogma, doctrine or denomination.

There would be no way for the pale opposite energy to install itself within the first coming of the divine origin of Man, He and She. Even the disciples and followers of the pale-male-warlord deities, could not re-write themselves into the supreme telling of the Divine Union of One. The very nature of the opposite energy and all those born and bred of the toxic parallel stands as an outsider presence, a foreign imposter and a stranger to the holistic living truth about supreme love, in other words a *Genesis Two* that would re-tell the story from the pale male warlord point of view. The pale-male-warlord deity had no way to penetrate the original expressions of a supreme beginning in *Genesis One*. The supreme laws of whole life energy stand as the spiritual lock. The first genesis tells of divine union, divine consumption and going forward to multiply divinity in the offspring.

Genesis Two reveals the contamination and corruption of an opposite energy lurking around the garden. There is no divine union in the second coming as the pale male deity creates a solitary male who is alone and lonely after the animals could no longer serve his companionship needs. And where the female was created as a last resort and an afterthought. There is no divine consumption as temptation would lead to disobedience and the acts of forbidden consumption. However, this forbidden consumption would later be ratified and further clarified as the actual way of life of the pale-male-warlord deity. The truth would be exposed in the second generation of offspring as the first son's

CHAPTER SIX: RELIGIONS AND THE DEITIES OF DEATH

offering of the fruits of the tree of life would be rejected, and his younger brother's burnt offering of flesh would be accepted by the pale-male-warlord deity. This would be the stamp and seal of approval that would anoint the death-consuming culture as the dominant way of life. A way of life that would be spread like a plague through deadly force using the hunting and herding methods of animal husbandry that they had mastered through time.

Therefore, the way of life of the pale-male-warlord deity would intrude and invade upon the sacred suntanned Children's mind through continuous, repeated applications of physical pain to inflict fright and fear. The death-consuming culture as way of life was encoded in the bloodspilling acts of sex and violence, war and crime. The tricks and deception to breed, seed and to feed conflict, confusion, lust, lies, illusions, death and deadly destruction would be the defining factors of the way of life that would be protected and maintained by the invading warring tribes and clans.

There is no forward multiplication of divinity where a pale-male-warlord deity curses his creation from the onset and birth is cursed in toiling suffering pains and the ground is cursed to cause sorrow in all who eat from it. Not only that, the offspring are divided and conquered, and brother ends up killing brother. Of course, the pale-male-warlord deity who was born and bred out of the mindset of a hunting and herding culture would love the smell of blood and burning flesh, taking the burnt offering with great honor. Clearly, the telling in the second genesis reflects the coming of a cold and pale state of mind led by a pale-male-warlord deity.

FULFILLING THE SACRED ANCESTRAL PROPHECY OF THE TRIPLE NINE: UNVEILING THE PROPHETIC 2012 MELTDOWN OF THE LOST AND ASTRAY PALE STATE OF MIND

The second coming is indeed the coming of lust, lies, illusions, confusion, death and deadly destruction. This second coming marks the coming of each and every deity within the toxic parallel as worshipped by the dominant religions, and each and every sect and cult and spiritual belief system that maintains the principles and practices of the death-consuming culture. The names of religions are numerous within the toxic parallel and while each deity or spirit entity or god or "supreme being" is seen as separate and distinct by the followers and disciples who are true believers, the energy in any example one examines will reveal itself to be the energy that is opposite of Supreme Love and the Essence of Life. The bottom line that determines the nature of the energy worshipped, the nature of the deity, in any religion is the attitudes, beliefs, values and behaviors that one practices as a way of life. This way of life extends beyond the individual who may declare that the religion itself is beyond contamination while it is not comprehended that the entire religious system or way of life was originally conceived and birthed within the energy that is opposite of Supreme Love and the Essence of Life. The question is often asked how the religious orders of the death-consuming culture and their "holy texts" have become so widespread and dominant and gained so many disciples and followers if they are not, indeed, righteous and ordained by god. It is not comprehended that when one inflicts violent, bloodspilling acts of "submit or die" upon humble populations, all those who reject the doctrines are slaughtered, and all those who submit are left to join the ranks of loyal disciples and followers, becoming even more aggressive in pushing the belief systems of the pale-male-warlord deity. The I in I say to each of you very clearly that this is indeed the time of the revealing or revelations as it is often called. This second coming would play itself out on a grand scale in each of the dominant religions that occupy the north, south, east and west as the stage becomes set for the final conflict among the disciples and followers of the toxic parallel. Although this fits within the prophecy of the era of 2012, is this the revealing that the I in I am now bringing forward? Remember, we are dealing with the first coming within the divine parallel and this is the second phase of emergence of the sacred ancestral prophecy of the Triple Nine.

The Favor and Blessings of the Pale-Male-Warlord Deity

The benefits and blessings of material gain would be seen by many as the signs of favor by an all-mighty pale-male-warlord deity. Within the history of the dominant religions, blood spill, animal sacrifices and burnt offerings were used to appease these deities of the death-consuming culture and gain favor. However, the real sacrifice that has been offered to that opposite energy is one's sacred ancestral spirit presence. And while it may appear that the pale-male-warlord deities have chosen those who are worthy to receive the blessings of the death-consuming culture, these special disciples and followers are in line to receive the truth and the consequences of the toxic parallel. Keep in mind that the religious concepts of the toxic parallel have absolutely no connection with divine spirit consciousness. The concept

FULFILLING THE SACRED ANCESTRAL PROPHECY OF THE TRIPLE NINE: UNVEILING THE PROPHETIC 2012 MELTDOWN OF THE LOST AND ASTRAY PALE STATE OF MIND

of a Chosen People comes from the historical experiences of warring clans and tribes who would call on any power available to defeat their enemies, subdue their prey and gain domination and control. The will of this pale-male-warlord deity would be perceived as adding strength to the goals of the disciples and followers. To be favored by this all-mighty deity would mean that the tribe was in a better position to receive protection, good fortune, and success in conquest, in hunting and on the battlefield. It was reasoned that blessings from the deity would secure material wealth and advantages, and would elevate the believers into a position of privilege where they could maintain their strength and might over others. And because of the nature of the freezing cold environmental experiences which were filled with danger, uncertainty, and scarcity, the need for some sense of security was projected into the concept of a deity or being that was greater than one's physical self. This powerful, merciful male warlord deity would stand beyond one's harsh, cold and cruel experiences, and that mental image would provide hope in the face of daily crisis and struggle. In fact, this deity was seen as the bringer of these cruel circumstances. It was reasoned that the deity brought these suffering pains because someone had not made the proper sacrifices, had not followed the proper rituals and rites and was not properly obedient to the particular deity. Therefore, it was imagined that if one could please the deity, then blessings of mercy would come upon one, if not in the present upon the seen, then in the hereafter.

CHAPTER SIX: RELIGIONS AND THE DEITIES OF DEATH

The hope of these religious beliefs born and bred within the deep-freeze ordeals would present the fantasized image of a greater experience, a paradise, a heaven, a new world after one dies. The concept of a divine paradise that is far beyond one's day-to-day earthly experiences began as the memory of the Sacred Garden Culture. The Children of the Sun who became lost and astray in the deep freeze were confronted by earthly experiences that were vastly different from what was known in the warm and sunny garden environments of the suntanned Man, He and She. It is not surprising that the concepts of hell originate from the Norse mythology of Hel which tells of an icy and frozen underworld. These Norse or nordic or northern breeds of mankind who were the cave-dwellers of the ice ages, indeed, were bred in the cold and freezing pits of hellish suffering.

Unfortunately, the lost and astray mind in its disconnected state has nothing to call upon except itself; it can only tap into its own imagination and its own ability to create illusions, delusions, fantasies and dreams. These dreams are often nightmares, horror stories and grim and gruesome fairytales. And the fear of the dark that grew in the cold and pale dank caves of the white blight ordeal really was the fright and fear of paleness which resulted from the lack of connection to Most Supreme Unseen. This fright and fear was multiplied by the threat of predators who lurked in the shadows of those caves, hidden yet present.

All of these terrorizing and horrifying true-life experiences were indeed imprinted in the tribal consciousness and collective memory of the mutated and degenerated breeds of mankind. The energies of these collective thoughts and experiences would indeed be the breeding ground of each and every one of the cold and pale warlord deities. The anxieties, insecurities, stresses and strains of the lost and astray pale state of mind would be the reflection and expression of the religious orders of the toxic parallel.

All that one could dream of within the toxic parallel would be the product of one's experiences and one's imagination, which is defined by the nature of the opposite energy that is consumed. Having no frame of reference other than what has already been amassed before one's birth within the death-consuming culture, one can only conceive of lust, lies, illusions, confusion, death and deadly destruction.

The descendants of the pale opposite energy manifested an entire way of life, belief system and social order that is recorded in their religious history of warfare, and their political history of warfare and their social economic history of warfare. Of course, this history is encoded in the mutation and degeneration of their DNA profile. The mutated and degenerated breeds of mankind have repeated the same violent and destructive historical patterns. And as long as one practices the same things over and over again, while expecting different results, one is practicing insanity, and therefore one will breed, seed and feed the insanity of a lost and astray state of mind.

The history of these pale breeds of mankind has continued to repeat itself over and over again while the concepts of their religious, political and social economic

CHAPTER SIX: RELIGIONS AND THE DEITIES OF DEATH

orders project the hope of a different result. Not only that, the history also shows clearly that the vicious nomadic tribes and clans have worked aggressively to spread this pale opposite energy like a plague or a virus in each and every encounter with each and every suntanned population that has been encountered.

The first place that the plague is spread begins in one's own consciousness. The inner state of division that occurs when one breaks away from and opposes the vibrations and sensations of one's sacred ancestral spirit presence is truly spiritual warfare. Therefore, there is a tremendous amount of anger, bitterness, guilt and shame that forms within the lost and astray pale state of mind. Through time this state of division has been translated and structured into an ideology of paleness that is called white racism. And white racism is then covertly maintained through integration and assimilation into a melting pot syndrome where the attitudes, values, beliefs and behaviors of the paleness ideology are upheld as the dominant way of life that all others should aspire to. The tribalism of the warring cave clans transferred into the consciousness of a fierce and divisive group identity that is set above all others.

Superiority within the earliest generations of the mutated and degenerated breeds was simply defined as the swiftest ability to kill and destroy in order to dominate and control. It would indeed stand to reason that the deity who would be considered the most superior, the all-mighty and the all omnipotent would be the grand master of these characteristics and traits. Therefore, the most violent and aggressive male within the white-blight ordeal was the most successful killer, scavenger and hunter. Those who banded with him would be in a greater position to secure a meal from the kill. Those who were indifferent or who did not totally submit to the warlord's will would either be slaughtered, or left out in the cold to starve or freeze. It mattered not whether the individual was male, female or child. This would be the breeding ground for the concept of submit or die.

These violent and aggressive males would also be able to gain dominance within the social order through the slaughter and subjugation of rival males. Subjugation of rival males would allow free access to the females who were then vulnerable to sexual assault, domination and control. Thus, arrived the phrase that to the victor goes the spoils and the "booty." Those who banded together with these brutal and ruthless warlords would loyally claim the clan identity as their strength under the leadership of the top warlord. This hierarchy of violent male dominance was the model of superiority that became the powerbase of the pale-male-warlord deity.

The clan or tribal identity allowed one to easily target those who did not belong to the group. Tribal warfare was the norm within the deep-freeze environment. Most historical accounts take it as a matter of fact that these cold and pale breeds of mankind were of a violent, fierce and warlike nature, and their brutal tactics are often praised as great charismatic leadership and brilliant strategy. Although these toxic vibrations are not of the natural and innate presence of Man, He and She, they were and remain a normal expression of the

CHAPTER SIX: RELIGIONS AND THE DEITIES OF DEATH

mutation and degeneration that was born and bred within the toxic parallel.

The test of time now makes the attitudes, values and behaviors of this opposite energy much easier to identify and detect. The test of time is really about whether or not the lessons of the first coming and the lessons of the second coming have been learned.

The concepts of force and violent restraint to control and dominate were unknown within the Sacred Garden Culture. One remained within divine order, not because of external means, but because of one's sacred ancestral spirit connection within the Divine Union of One. The greatest acts of discipline came from imparting divine knowledge, wisdom and understanding. The major objective was to always go forward and multiply a greater presence of divine oneness and unification upon the earth to prepare a place for one's emergence from the unseen back upon the seen. It was comprehended within the Sacred Ancestral Temple of Kwa Ta Man I that to deviate away from the divine order of one's most supreme ancestral Seen and Unseen being would automatically tap into an energy of thought and reasoning that was totally disconnected from Supreme Love and the Essence of Life. The challenge was to bring forward this comprehension from the Most Supreme Unseen to the seen, and those of the Sacred Order of the Essence worked to bring forward every possible expression.

In other words, it has always been very clear to the keepers of the Sacred Ancestral Temple that, without the essence of a holistic living presence, Man, He and She, would drift into a disconnected state of being. In a state of disconnection, one would begin to wonder about one's

FULFILLING THE SACRED ANCESTRAL PROPHECY OF THE TRIPLE NINE: UNVEILING THE PROPHETIC 2012 MELTDOWN OF THE LOST AND ASTRAY PALE STATE OF MIND

true existence, one's true origin, one's true creator and the true meaning of life.

Without that most supreme connection within the Divine Union of One, one would be very easily misled. One would wander into the toxic thoughts and behaviors that cause the worship of a monotheistic male warlord deity. You see, within the divine parallel it is an absolute truth that the Divine Union of One is the most supreme unification of masculine and feminine energy manifesting upon the seen as Man, He and She. Without this sacred ancestral comprehension, the breeds of mankind would become so out of sync, out of focus and out of alignment that sexuality would have no connection with one's sacred ancestral spirit presence.

Sexual expression would be reduced to a physical act with mental fantasies that serve as entertainment to satisfy a lustful thrill. Man, He and She, would come together for acts of procreation and recreation that had no relationship with the whole life expressions of the Divine Union of One, and the experiences of divine innercourse would sound like an impossible dream. Within the toxic parallel, sexual energies would be tied to acts of violence and violation, and it would not matter if one were heterosexual or homosexual; practicing bestiality, necrophilia, pedophilia, sadomasochism or using manmade sex toys. Therefore, within the dominant religions of the death-consuming culture, sexuality would be viewed with suspicion and condemnation. From fornication to the so-called carnal nature of mankind to celibacy, the religious views within the death-consuming

CHAPTER SIX: RELIGIONS AND THE DEITIES OF DEATH

culture are that sexuality, in general, is a source of temptation that must be suppressed.

The stage was being set from the Most Supreme Unseen so that the weak link upon the seen could be strengthened and the whole life presence of Man, He and She, upon the seen could be secured. The weak link was a breakdown in thought and reasoning and the resulting lack of divine clarity and comprehension. The Sacred Ancestral Temple of Kwa Ta Man I provided the sacred core of communication from the Most Supreme Unseen to the seen. This source of divine spirit consciousness came directly from the Sacred Order of the Essence and circulated through the entire physical presence of the Sacred Garden Culture from which we come. As the divine social economic family community grew and grew, the physical distance between extended families increased, and some moved further and further away from the sacred core of focus and communication within divine spirit consciousness.

As one became more distant from the sacred core physically, one would be left to deal with new and different circumstances that called for different responses. However, it was a tremendous challenge to comprehend that the Supreme Laws are absolute regardless of the circumstances, and yet one still has to reason with how to translate and apply those Supreme Laws to the day-to-day circumstances of one's environment without disconnecting from a holistic living way of life. This function of providing a sacred communication network to establish the divine laws of a holistic living way of life is fulfilled within the Sacred Ancestral Temple of Kwa Ta Man I.

FULFILLING THE SACRED ANCESTRAL PROPHECY OF THE TRIPLE NINE: UNVEILING THE PROPHETIC 2012 MELTDOWN OF THE LOST AND ASTRAY PALE STATE OF MIND

It was at this time that mind consciousness began to supersede divine spirit consciousness, leaving one in an attempt to figure things out on one's own based on the physical appearance of things. New experiences that appeared different were not reasoned with in a whole and clean manner, and it became assumed that somehow the Supreme Laws were not absolute and could be applied differently in different circumstances. However, regardless of the different circumstances encountered, the level and degree of divine clarity needed to connect with divine spirit consciousness would not change. The flow of communication would be just as strong and vibrant as it was in the divine origin of Man, He and She. In fact, there has never been a break, nor will there ever be a break, within the whole life energy of divine spirit consciousness as it circulates from the Most Supreme Unseen to the seen. The break occurred in the thoughts and reasoning of Man, He and She, and this break was the entry point for the opposite energy.

The divine and innate responsibility of sacred ancestral leadership calls for immediate focus, concentration and dedication to tune into the most supreme ancestral communication link. This link was indeed available and has never been broken up until this day. By tuning into this most supreme ancestral communication link, the Divine Children of the Sun would not have allowed themselves to become lost and astray. You see, in a disconnected state, one moves individually, and an egotistical state of mind begins to manifest the I-me-my-mine syndrome, and one becomes

CHAPTER SIX: RELIGIONS AND THE DEITIES OF DEATH

more stubborn and steadfast in proving one's self to be right.

The instant that one becomes distracted, is the exact instant that one becomes disconnected from divine spirit consciousness. Instead of being able to observe the nature of the toxic disorder along one's pathway, one begins to step right into the toxic parallel. If one had remained within the central core of divine social economic family community, there would be enough checks and balances to correct one's distracted state of mind quickly. As one became more distant from the central core of a holistic living way of life, the first voice of divine spirit consciousness would often be heard, but it would be overridden by that second voice that reflected the pale state of disconnection. Thus, distraction in one's thought and reasoning established a weak link in the divine communication network between the Most Supreme Unseen and the seen. The weak link is the manifestation of that pale mental state of thought and reasoning.

The lessons are many. Regardless of the circumstances encountered, the Supreme Laws of the universe remain absolute. Regardless of any toxic disorder that arises, we must move fast and quick to establish divine order, and this must be done without any hesitation. We must never allow the mind to function or reason outside of the discipline and focus of divine spirit consciousness. In fact, divine spirit consciousness must be the root, base and foundation of our way of life, a holistic living way of life to maintain the sacred ancestral spirit presence of the Divine Children of the Sun and the Sacred Garden Culture from which we come.

Chapter 6 Innerlude:
Submit or Die
Original version 1996, unreleased

<u>*Royal Priestess vocals:*</u>
This is dedicated to the ones we love
Dedicated to the ones we love
Love, the ones we love

<u>High Priest vocals:</u>
Uuh! This is dedicated to the sacred suntanned He and She of Man
Who refused to submit to that pale-male-war god's master plan
This is dedicated to those who refuse to deny their most supreme ancestral spirit essence in order to uphold and to maintain this stale and pale lie
This is dedicated to the ones we love
Who have been mentally, physically and spiritually persecuted beyond and above
Ripped, mangled and torn by opposing predatory energy, a beast of scorn
This is dedicated to rid you of that toxic energy fed to you from the time that you were born
And through this dedication, the I in I now come to ensure that you are informed
And now that you're deep within this vibration and its tone
Let's take the holistic living truth on home

FULFILLING THE SACRED ANCESTRAL PROPHECY OF THE TRIPLE NINE: UNVEILING THE PROPHETIC 2012 MELTDOWN OF THE LOST AND ASTRAY PALE STATE OF MIND

<u>Royal Priestess vocals:</u>
This is for the Divine and Sacred Few
And Sacred Few
Who cannot pretend
A pale male god of war can only create more and more of what he created before
Rape, slaughter, raids, crusades under the religious cry, submit or die

<u>High Priest vocals:</u>
Uuh! "Submit or die," the historic religious cry
That caused the Children of the Sun to submit to that pale male war god and hope to die
And she would cry, and he would sigh
And you could tell that this was the entry to the gates of hell
How the Children of the Sun hollered and yelled
As the old pale male's disciples and followers screamed and hollered, "Kill the infidel!"
"Off with their heads!"
So many was left slaughtered and dead
A mother, a child
There was no alibi
Placing chains on the feet and hands until the pains would break the spirit that remained
And the pains would continue and it would drive one insane
Until one had suffered enough mental and physical pain to submit or die
And he would come like a thief in the night

CHAPTER 6 INNERLUDE: SUBMIT OR DIE

Until that suntanned female would give birth to a child
with no spirit insight
Who would submit or die to uphold and maintain this
white blight
Submit or die, a pale Judaism cry
They would seek and search out the male first born
Whom they would curse, ridicule and scorn
Leaving dark skinned families in dread
As death angels celebrate passing over, leaving behind
the scared and the dead
And there'd be nothing humane to feel
Because it was their god's will to kill
Submit or die
A pale Hindu cry
And every time they would cut off another head
Another Black male was dead
Another Black male of the Black Untouchable
family trail
Submitted to the death culture of hell by these invader
Children who were pale
And there'd be nothing humane to feel
Because it was their god's will to kill
Submit or die
A pale Christian cry
A new testament of the Judaism cry
And they would go down upon every dark land
To enslave and control
every child, every woman, every man
Sold
Converting those heathens
A soul to be saved
And those who would not submit

FULFILLING THE SACRED ANCESTRAL PROPHECY OF THE TRIPLE NINE: UNVEILING THE PROPHETIC 2012 MELTDOWN OF THE LOST AND ASTRAY PALE STATE OF MIND

Send 'em to the grave
And there'd be nothing humane to feel
Because it was their god's will to kill
Submit or die
A pale Muslim cry
Declaring holy wars and jihads
Leaving a bloodstained trail of beheaded infidels and eunuchs and concubines
Dreadful fright and fear left in the mind
And there'd be nothing humane to feel
Because it was their god's will to kill
Submit or die, submit or die
Thus would be the nature of every pale invader seal
And there would be nothing humane to feel
Because it was their god's will to kill

Royal Priestess vocals:
Uuh!
When the disciples, followers and believers kneel to pray they say
Thy will be done, thy will be done, thy will be done
To a god of wrath and vengeance
A god of wrath and vengeance
A jealous god who declares that he's a god of love
A jealous god who declares that he's a god of love
What kind of love, what kind of love is this god made of?
What kind of love is this god made of?

High Priest vocals:
Uuh! Mental and physical pollution invading the earth, water and air

CHAPTER 6 INNERLUDE: SUBMIT OR DIE

A living dead nightmare that the sacred ancestral spirit can't bear
Homosexuality, bestiality, necrophiliac
Sex and violence on the attack
Gone completely whack
Living in dread, half alive and half dead
Sick, fat and obese
Make up made over permed and fried head
Drugs, alcohol, materialistic addiction
Collaborating while in deep-seated competition
And under this stale and pale spiritless condition
What do you expect out of the generation next?
Born, bred and spoon fed off of this death culture and its pale-male-war-god complex
This piece is dedicated to the resurrection of the sacred ancestral presence of the Divine Children of the Sun and the Sacred Garden Culture from which we come
Uuh!

Chapter Seven:
The White Blight Zone

Chapter 7 Prelude:
What's Up

Song 7 from "12th Hour Prophecy: The Pale Curse and the Solarized Energy Shift," Kwatamani musical CD release, 2008

<u>Royal Priestess vocals:</u>
Thing's are getting bad, and it's so sad
Children of the Sun, jumping on every passing fad
in the white-blight zone
Don't get mad; you've been had
Why not leave this pale, cold-blooded game alone?
Just leave it alone

<u>High Priest vocals:</u>
What's up? What's going on?
How are you getting your groove on?
How's life rolling for you in the white-blight zone?
And what it look like as you strut and stroll the
bloodstained tracks and trails of this civilized hell?
Pollution in the air, water toxic as hell
Something stale and pale is starting to stank and smell
Heard this thick-talking thug who was toting around a
monkey on his back that was so heavy
that it had to be drug
Saying that life is a bitch
and everything that he do is a death wish
Ain't nothin' got nothin' to do with love
And said I'd betta get out of his way
'cause he is a bad-ass thug
And he iced the last dude that made him feel bugged
And if it ain't Johnny Law, it's the undercover prankster

FULFILLING THE SACRED ANCESTRAL PROPHECY OF THE TRIPLE NINE: UNVEILING THE PROPHETIC 2012 MELTDOWN OF THE LOST AND ASTRAY PALE STATE OF MIND

Stressing you out to be dealt with by another gangster
Who's selling that stuff
that made that bad-ass thug so tough
And cold-blooded as hell, although it appear to be a bluff
As the mass majority of the tough-ass males
are fresh out of a prison cell
The melting-pot social center
used to turn the suntanned male pale
Just as it did in the cold and freezing pits of hell
When the lost and astray Children learned to cave dwell
Giving each other flack, running in the same
kind of packs
Stuck and stagnant in the same kind of pissy corners,
using sex and violence to revive
the same kind of doggish acts
And where the top dog is deified
for being the toughest-assed thug who ever died
And what is this all about, Children of the Sun,
melanated skin, yet pale as hell from deep within?
Reverse and then twist, 'cause the lesson was
truly missed
Male-to-male, female-to-female, all up in it
Correction in action, hot and deep passion
Reversed and twist, some seeking a death-wish kiss
And then it's back out on the streets with this cold-
blooded, cave-dwelling vibe that becomes more
intensified as it is being multiplied
Heartless and maddening insane rage; caged and
uncaged, same mutation and degeneration game
different time frame
Same cold paleness in the brain

CHAPTER 7 PRELUDE: WHAT'S UP

death-consuming culture, simple and plain
Cocky, arrogant and vain
and the Children of the Sun are singing
about how they loving this thang
And the top dog is sitting above it all
wheeling and dealing, got his money from the underdog
And I'll be damned if this pale thang is not the same,
except now it's being pushed and pulled by a paper game
Cash and carry, paper money
wheeling and dealing, m.o.b.
And ain't nothing funny, when a ganster is pimping,
leaning, scheming trying to get that money
And thugs wearing pants that sag below the waist
Showing that rump like they trying to sell a taste
or just been had
Yeah, these lost and astray Children really got it bad
And it's become a status symbol to be a gangster
or a thug
Blowing that blow, going down low
Pushing a thuggish thug, 'cause ain't nothing
got nothing to do with love

<u>Royal Priestess vocals:</u>
Ain't got nothing to do with love
With a gangsta lean, what do you mean?
Ain't got nothing to do with love
What are you made of?
Sister, sister running around
It sure ain't love you found
Allowing another brother, another brother
another brother
Using you as a place to throw down

FULFILLING THE SACRED ANCESTRAL PROPHECY OF THE TRIPLE NINE: UNVEILING THE PROPHETIC 2012 MELTDOWN OF THE LOST AND ASTRAY PALE STATE OF MIND

<u>High Priest vocals:</u>
And what is it with this hellish, palish, freakish game
That you continue to claim
while you seek and search for green paper and purple
rain, claiming it as your thing
as you continue to die in vain, just like Coltrane
And in the midst of that chalk-white powder
riding his main vein
He would holler, yell and scream for a Love Supreme
And the peeps would lean, and the gangster
would scream
Creaming in his jeans over a violent movie scene
And time after time, you continue to die in vain
Pimping, leaning, scheming
pushing, tugging, drugging
Trying to obtain the fantasies, dreams and delusions
of this pale game
And if stuff and thangs just happen to catch you just right
You will indeed feed off of the nut-busting, lusting greed
And although your natural and innate DNA code
do not instinctly roll with the freezing ice and frost bite,
you quickly claim part ownership within this white blight
As you continue to consume of the hell and damnation
and the doom and the gloom
that's about to blow the bottom out of hell very soon
An although the official chattel slavery days
are indeed long gone
The application and the adaptation
of the Willie Lynch syndrome
coupled with the truth and the consequence
of being beat, hung, roped, bound

CHAPTER 7 PRELUDE: WHAT'S UP

shackled and chained, tied down
raped until the misery, aches and pains make it very easy
to reinstall the shackles and the chains on your brain
And so, if you're a thug, pushing and pulling
toting that monkey on your back
Or a gangsta, pushing and pulling, selling ganga or crack
or a prostitute or a ho
pushing or pulling selling that mojo
Or whether you're sophisticated and educated
feeling you got class, grace and style, bourgeoisie as hell,
fronting, faking and pretending
shucking, cheesing and grinning
saying nothing, talking loud, having much debate
while trying to relate to a pale trait
Having no idea about who was raped, murdered
shackled, chained, tied down
bought and sold pound for pound
having no conceptual reality
about how the thing has gone down
Why the pale ones took the course
of deadly force to make sure daddy was not around
Like a stud bull, he was shackled and chained
and tied down
Like a domesticated animal
the shackles and the chains continue to remain
on his brain
Like a heifer or a bitch, she continue to produce misfits,
counterfeits, living a life that contradicts
Programmed like clones
seeking to be successful and well known
within the white-blight zone
She remained vague and empty

FULFILLING THE SACRED ANCESTRAL PROPHECY OF THE TRIPLE NINE: UNVEILING THE PROPHETIC 2012 MELTDOWN OF THE LOST AND ASTRAY PALE STATE OF MIND

sad and blue and all alone
and he's become an institutional rolling stone
whether he's at home or gone
And regardless of the level and degree of achievement
within this white-blight flight
And their offspring continue to be pushed in a hole
as the Pied Piper plays the game
to continue to make this thing roll
while pimps in business suits and capitalistic thugs
collect the toll
And like crabs in the bucket
continue to push, pull and tug
The educated elite, the sophisticated discreet
and those who run the street
Continue to function like pimps, pushers
prostitutes and hos
users, consumers and gigolos who thief
Gang-banging thugs and kiss and hug and snug and rub
And do the most freakish thangs
in this cold-blooded, hellish, palish game
Where ain't nothing got nothing to do with love

Chapter Seven: The White Blight Zone

As the I in I have often stated, "Consume this energy, and set your spirit free." However, it is clear from the many comments and questions we have received, that there are many individuals who do not even realize that the spirit essence of their being is calling to be set free. For this reason, there is a need to explore the nature of freedom as it relates to divine spirit consciousness.

The deception that keeps so many individuals in confusion within the toxic parallel is the deception that their personal experiences and expressions are different and individualized. Breeding concepts such as "different strokes for different folks" and "to each his own." However, the laws of energy consumption are an absolute statement that each and every individual within the death-consuming culture is consuming of the same opposite energy. The first divided state of being that caused the lost and astray Children of the Sun to become disconnected from their sacred ancestral spirit presence is the same state of being that expresses the division, separation and conflict that defines the existence of modern Man, He and She.

When the I in I asks, "What's up, what's going on. How do you get your groove on in the white blight zone?" the point being made is that the mass majority of Man, He and She, is now grooving in the modern white-blight zone. Indeed, to the physical eye, all these appearances look like separate, individual and quite different expressions. Nevertheless, these different expressions reflect the same type and kind of mental mutation and degeneration that was born and bred within the Caucasus deep-freeze experiences. When the I in I echo, "Consume this energy, and set your spirit free" the call is to free one's sacred ancestral spirit presence from the toxic consequences that come from consuming the pale opposite energy.

Herd Mentality of the Hunting and Herding Culture

The mass majority of Man, He and She, indulge in a distinct herd mentality where one becomes defined by one's group association. These group associations form mental categories that have nothing to do with divine spirit consciousness and only serve to keep one conforming to the dominant thought patterns of the death-consuming culture. The concept of freedom within the toxic parallel actually has no meaning other than to refer to a mental range of movement that is available in selecting one group association or another. Freedom to move from one group association to another within the death-consuming culture is the freedom to determine the manner in which one will consume of the pale opposite energy.

The attitudes and values of the social order determine which group associations are highly prized and which group associations are degraded, ridiculed and scorned. Within the toxic parallel, there is no sense of wholeness where a common ground of unity can be expressed or manifested. This is to be expected, because the fueling source of the death-consuming culture is an unwhole energy, a energy that is opposite of the Essence

CHAPTER SEVEN: THE WHITE BLIGHT ZONE

of Life and Supreme Love. Therefore, tribalism, racism, sexism, and all such expressions of fierce group loyalty are a reflection of the fragmentation and separatism of an unwhole state of being where every part is in conflict within itself and with every other part.

There are even those who have a group affiliation of solitary membership forming a "community of one." These loners and lonely drifters have become so dominated by the separatism and individualism of the I-me-my-mine-mind syndrome that they represent the extreme alienation and disconnection of the social order at large. In fact, one becomes so alienated and disconnected within their thoughts and reasoning that they can not even see the toxicity emerging from deep within that keeps them from fulfilling the basic needs of life itself. In reality, any group within the death-consuming culture can only be a group of disconnected and unwhole individuals who band together for a greater sense of strength. This is the nature of the disciples and followers of the pale opposite energy.

The group association, group identity and group behaviors of a small group of lost and astray Children of the Sun who fell prey to the opposite energy have, in turn, become the means for spreading the consumption of that same opposite energy throughout the planet. Instead of the practices and principles of divine union, where all parts work together for the benefit of the whole, a new kind of opposite state of being emerged. The disciples and followers express the nature of the opposite energy very well in the selfish, hostile, competitive, divisive, us-vs.-them mentalities that are born and bred within the hunting and herding culture. The divisions are clearly

FULFILLING THE SACRED ANCESTRAL PROPHECY OF THE TRIPLE NINE: UNVEILING THE PROPHETIC 2012 MELTDOWN OF THE LOST AND ASTRAY PALE STATE OF MIND

outlined as the hunters and the hunted, the masters and the slaves, the conquerors and the conquered, the winners and the losers, the victors and the defeated, the have's and the have not's, the rich and the poor, and the lines of division go on and on within the toxic parallel. And the rules of engagement within the death-consuming culture are "take your position, come out fighting and winner take all."

Depending on one's early mental conditioning and one's exposure to various toxic consumption patterns within the death-consuming culture, one will work to fit into a particular group and will eagerly claim a tag and label. This herd mentality is well-bred within the animal husbandry ways and means of the hunting and herding culture. And those who are the powerbrokers of the social order built by the opposite energy, even refer to the masses of Man, He and She, as sheep and cows and even lambs to the slaughter, describing the masses of Man, He and She, as basically dumb, gullible, unaware and easy to control and manipulate.

The techniques of animal husbandry were first used by the mutated and degenerated breeds of mankind as they became skilled at hunting and developing techniques to herd and control large groups of animals that were bred for consumption. All the while, the mass majority of Man, He and She, runs around claiming freedom and seeking freedom within the confines of the death-consuming culture. Unfortunately, these aspiring free thinkers and free spirits and rebels without a cause, can not even see how their every move and every thought and every bright idea is predetermined and prefabricated

CHAPTER SEVEN: THE WHITE BLIGHT ZONE

within the pale opposite energy. The massive deception keeps these individuals investing their time, money and life energy deeper in the toxic parallel, thus ensuring their further entrapment in the mental prisons of lust, lies, illusions, confusion, death and deadly destruction. And the pale opposite energy keeps on sucking the life energy of the sacred ancestral spirit presence and giving fuel to the fires of cunning plots and schemes of the cold lost and astray mind.

Within this herd mentality, there are several major groups. Every individual who consumes of the pale opposite energy fits into one of these death-consuming culture groups or is in the process of transitioning from one group to another. One major group is populated by individuals who have realized that they live within the chaos and conflict of a violent and cold-blooded way of life. These individuals represent the hard-core expressions of the death-consuming culture, and they actually embrace the thrills of the kill that stimulated those first cave-dwelling lost and astray Children. The members who represent this particular pattern of the opposite energy are labeled as hunters, soldiers of fortune, members of hate groups who advocate and instigate brutality, serial killers and other kinds of killers, violent criminals, warmongering politicians and dictators; rapists, pornography addicts and other sexual predators; the profiteers of the death industries, horror-movie fans and those who enact the real-life horrors, meat-eaters; and other intentional consumers of lust, lies, illusions, confusion, death and deadly destruction. This list, indeed, goes on and on. These types of personalities form the general profile of a special-interest group who

FULFILLING THE SACRED ANCESTRAL PROPHECY OF THE TRIPLE NINE: UNVEILING THE PROPHETIC 2012 MELTDOWN OF THE LOST AND ASTRAY PALE STATE OF MIND

whole-heartedly supports and upholds the vibrations of the toxic parallel as those who capitalize and profit from toxic consumption and those who are the loyal, addicted and habitual consumers. This group of individuals is truly at home within the opposite energy, and seeks more of the vibrations and sensations of lust, lies, illusions, confusion, death and deadly destruction.

The Appearance of Change

Other individuals who make their way of life within the ways and means of the toxic parallel claim to be seeking a better life based on some form of change within the death consumption culture. Individuals of this mindset uphold the social, religious, educational and political institutions of the death-consuming culture with the hope for a better day. These individuals are activists, social reformers, preachers and teachers, business people, everyday people, and others who seek to re-form the social order in the midst of the cold-blooded and vicious predatory values that define the nature of the hunting and herding culture. These reformers call upon some aspect of life-affirming values to redeem the social ills of the death-consuming culture. However, life-affirming values have no basis within the hunting and herding mentality of the opposite energy where slaughter, enslavement and feasting on the remains of other creatures defines the way of life.

Whatever life-affirming values, practices and principles that have managed to survive in the memory of Man, He and She, originated from the sacred ancestral spirit presence of the Divine Children of the Sun and the

CHAPTER SEVEN: THE WHITE BLIGHT ZONE

Sacred Garden Culture from which we come. The value that is placed on peace and unity, a sense of cooperation, family and community is the value that is rooted in the Sacred Garden Culture way of life. The opposing values of war, conflict and hostile aggression, conflict and violence have everything to do with the death-consuming culture. Even though members of this group are self-proclaimed to be the intellects, scholars, educated and enlightened among the mass populations of the toxic parallel, many are still unable to comprehend that life-affirming values can only manifest within the whole life energy. That is to say, only whole life energy truly affirms life and enables Man, He and She, to manifest the affirmative expressions of the Essence of Life and Supreme Love. Unfortunately, these well-intentioned reformers continue to consume of the opposite energy while expecting to see different results. The nature of that toxic energy and the depleted way of life that manifests from all those who consume of that toxic energy has not changed over thousands of years. Today the vicious, cruel and ruthless nature of the opposite energy remains the same as when it first emerged upon the planet.

    The historical patterns that have manifested within the vibrations of lust, lies, illusions, confusion, death and deadly destruction may look very different to today's modern consumers of the opposite energy. Based on the atrocities that were committed by those within the pale lost and astray state of mind, many individuals attempt to distance themselves from the violent, brutal nature of those who historically invaded, raped, enslaved and conquered throughout the planet. Regardless of the denials, those who consume depleted and devitalized food substances are still consuming the opposite energy. Whether the food substances are animal flesh or devitalized fruits and vegetables, the end result of consuming within the toxic parallel remains the same. Additionally, those who do not undergo an intense detoxing and purging process to release the vibrations of lust, lies, illusions, confusion, death and deadly destruction that have amassed within the death-consuming culture are, in effect, still consuming of the pale lost and astray state of mind.

Because there has been no whole life change, individuals continue to maintain the ways and means of the death-consuming culture. The thoughts, attitudes and behaviors of today still express the same energy that was born and bred within the deep-freeze, ice-age ordeals. These days, the nature of the opposite energy may be disguised in sophisticated and civilized expressions that are more acceptable to the disciples and followers of the death-consuming culture. And because the appearance is different, many have fallen for the deception that things really have changed. Nevertheless, the same opposite energy that fueled the violent and brutal nomadic invasions against the Sacred Garden Culture continues to be the fueling source for the hunting and herding culture of present day Man, He and She.

Therefore, individuals who have enough presence to desire a better existence tend to fall into sub-groups of those who end up making little change in their life or no change at all. Likewise, the larger social order of today's death-consuming culture still bears the marks of the vicious and brutal vibrations and sensations of the ice-age, cave-dwelling ordeals, because the energy consumption has not changed. For example, the atrocities of war are still a reality within the death-consuming culture. Violent crimes, war, massive disease and physical afflictions, mental disorders, widespread slaughter and mistreatment of animals, environmental destabilization, abusive relationships, self-destructive addictions and other expressions of the opposite energy are still current events within the toxic parallel.

Even though there may be a call for change, a hope for a better way and the movement toward a new and improved experience, one's personal investments of time, money and energy remain rooted in the belief systems of the death-consuming culture. The remedies, solutions and answers offered by the opposite energy become all-consuming and the individual does not ever dare to venture outside of the ways and means of the toxic parallel. This is why the mere appearance of change can pacify many individuals while the nature of their toxic consumption remains the same in some degree or percentage or aspect. And because the concept of wholeness is beyond the reasoning of the pale lost and astray state of mind, one remains unable to address the mental, physical and spiritual requirements of whole life change.

Crying for a Little Relief

Those who cry for change in the death-consuming culture are crying for a little relief or the desire to see their personal agendas taken as priority. In effect these individuals are calling for some small token or gesture of change. For the most part, they desire to maintain their favorite and familiar habits within the death consumption culture. Surface change is actually encouraged within the mental mindset of the toxic parallel. Many feel victorious when their surface changes are implemented, and will join together in a group to declare, "We did it. We won." What has truly changed is the face, place, and style of toxic consumption that keeps the opposite energy still circulating, manifesting its nature of lust, lies, illusions, confusion, death and deadly destruction. These superficial changes keep one wandering from one new appearance to another without ever consuming enough whole life energy to address the core issues regarding one's essence. In fact, one can continue many old habits while feeling satisfied that one has really changed.

Mental and physical conditions can improve temporarily and even appear to be different and new. When these kinds of minor changes occur, one is lulled into a state of false security within the toxic parallel. Once an individual no longer feels a pressing sense of urgency to change his or her situation in life, then he or she has little motivation to let go of the fantasies, illusions, delusions and dreams of the cold and pale state of mind. In this way, it is within the interest of the powerbrokers, disciples and followers who benefit and profit from the current social orders and belief systems within the death-consuming culture to support causes and movements that deal with surface change.

When the pressures of day-to-day survival became too much for the lost and astray Children of the ice-age, deep-freeze ordeals, the disconnected mind simply

CHAPTER SEVEN: THE WHITE BLIGHT ZONE

collapsed into distraction and emotional breakdowns. Without the ability to address whole life change within the toxic parallel, every so often toxic build-up from consumption of the energy that is opposite of the Essence of Life and Supreme Love causes mental explosions. The disciples and followers of the opposite energy struggle with depression, rage, frustration, emptiness, confusion, self-doubt, insecurities, and even suicidal and homicidal tendencies. This toxic build-up explains why so many individuals become alcoholic, drug-addicted, abusive, selfish and arrogant, and mean; why, they can be compulsive liars, sexually frigid and impotent, and so on. While these individuals project so much intensity into correcting and fixing others and advocating for social change, their personal lives can be really chaotic, vague and filled with disorder.

The amazing thing is that everyone within the toxic parallel fits into one profile of the lost and astray state of mind or another. There are many individuals who will insist that they are not really within the toxic parallel. Many will become offended and insulted, because their sacred cow is being debunked. Many will immediately see how these group profiles apply to others but will refuse to see how they, too, fit neatly into one of the herds. In fact, many will insist that even though they have never detoxed and purged from prior consumption of the opposite energy, they have somehow managed to escape the toxic parallel through their knowledge, wisdom and understanding. Regardless of their many contradictions, they will truly feel as if the supreme laws of the universe do not apply to them. Moreover, these individuals do not even recognize the significance and

FULFILLING THE SACRED ANCESTRAL PROPHECY OF THE TRIPLE NINE: UNVEILING THE PROPHETIC 2012 MELTDOWN OF THE LOST AND ASTRAY PALE STATE OF MIND

absolute implications of the supreme laws of the universe, because they are still stuck giving honor to the ways and means of the death-consuming culture.

Many individuals hold a deep and abiding respect for what they consider to be the bold and commanding presence of the mutated and degenerated conquering tribes who slaughtered, raped, pillaged and enslaved. There is an admiration for the powerbrokers of the death-consuming culture, because, after all, they are the movers and the shakers, the high achievers, the captains of industry, the heroes, and on and on. And there is a secret desire within the lost and astray pale state of mind to get a hold of a little of that power, too. The real motivation for change oftentimes is really an attempt to make a little room in the winner's circle for the individuals in question, to share in the power so coveted within the pale lost and astray state of mind. Whether the power be in the form of religious power with one's particular pale-male-war god as the monotheistic top dog, or political power with one's candidate in office, or economic power with one's financial position well-cushioned, or social power with one's social agenda as the main platform, the issues of power within the death-consuming culture keep one invested in the power plays of the opposite energy.

These demonstrations, campaigns and pep rallies keep the masses pacified while the nature of the death-consuming culture has never changed, and will not ever change, from the vibrations and sensations of lust, lies, illusions, confusion, death and deadly destruction. So whether it is a new face, a new political party or a new social program, the same old cold and pale nature is expressed in different terms. Unfortunately, these change agents of the death-consuming culture mislead many who fall within the third and most significant group.

On the Fringe of the Social Order

There exists an often overlooked group of individuals within the death-consuming culture who have a different mindset from the mass population of Man, He and She. While they seek change and relief from the oppressive and suffocating nature of the opposite energy, these individuals make every attempt to look beyond the current formulas and strategies offered within the toxic parallel. These progressive-minded individuals often populate groups that are on the fringe of the social order, often referred to as alternative, conscious, counter-culture and radical. In no way do these groups represent anything more than one more option within the death-consuming culture. Nevertheless, those who have become disillusioned, frustrated and weary of the contradictions, deceptions and confusion that plague the death-consuming culture do not have many places to turn. Often these individuals have no clue about what they really need to do. They know that they need to detox and purge the nature of the opposite energy that they have consumed, but they are not sure about what that means in simple terms. Yet and still, they continue to seek a connection in order to provide a greater source of meaning, purpose and clarity in their lives.

The remnants of the Sacred Garden Culture are pieced together in bits and pieces within the beliefs and practices of these individuals. Regardless of race, creed, color or national origin, they are drawn towards

FULFILLING THE SACRED ANCESTRAL PROPHECY OF THE TRIPLE NINE: UNVEILING THE PROPHETIC 2012 MELTDOWN OF THE LOST AND ASTRAY PALE STATE OF MIND

organizations and activities that express a caring concern for the environment and all living things, a caring concern for healthy consumption patterns, a caring concern for wholesome spiritual values, a caring concern for peaceful family and community relationships, and a caring concern for traditional culture and ancestral connection. If they continue in this forward direction, eventually they will encounter an entirely different energy that has emerged upon the planet. They will encounter the presence of divine spirit consciousness of thought and reasoning that will certainly lead them far away from the status quo of the toxic parallel.

The messages within the Sacred Temple of Kwa Ta Man I are brought forward to catch the attention of the sacred few. There is a spark of recognition within these spirits when they encounter the holistic living truth about Supreme Love. However, the level and degree of confusion is so massive that many of those with a Sacred-Few vibration end up wandering back into the tricks and traps of the death-consuming culture. Without a divine connection to the sacred ancestral spirit presence, they soon run out of fuel in the dead end called "I've been there and done that."

The first phase of the Gathering Time was set forth to learn the lessons that have caused so many struggling spirits to sink back into the empty promises and deceptions of the death consumption culture. Many individuals who vowed that they would never again become the willing pawns to the energy that is opposite of Supreme Love and the Essence of Life have unfortunately fallen by the wayside. The evidence of the

CHAPTER SEVEN: THE WHITE BLIGHT ZONE

past decade as well as previous generations has shown that partial change and the superficial appearance of change really equals no change at all. It becomes so convenient to reach for the familiar mental habits and old patterns of mental and physical consumption that defined one's personality and character disorders within the toxic parallel.

Who really wants to be told that they have to detox their vibrations of arrogance in order to enter divine spirit consciousness when they can so easily find someone within the death-consuming culture to not only support their arrogance, but even place them in a position of receiving attention and praise? Who really wants to face their old emotional insecurities and work to become totally accountable for their energy consumption when the option of remaining within the familiar excuses and righteous justifications of the opposite energy is still wide open to offer trinklets and ornaments and other materialistic awards?

While many individuals have established a pattern of joining organizations and social movements with the purpose of seeking status and power and gaining some level of control over others, the common goals that one pursues within the toxic parallel will certainly not be met within the whole life energy. Therefore, it can take a matter of months or years for someone who encounters the Kwatamani vibration to go through his or her bag of tricks until the tricks run out and the individual departs. This personal bag of tricks contains all of the ways and means that an individual has used in the past to get his or her way within the death consumption culture. The I in I have seen all kinds of bags and all kinds of tricks, such as

FULFILLING THE SACRED ANCESTRAL PROPHECY OF THE TRIPLE NINE: UNVEILING THE PROPHETIC 2012 MELTDOWN OF THE LOST AND ASTRAY PALE STATE OF MIND

whining, using flattery, making demands, pretending to be super loyal, repeating the right words, asking what appears to be insightful questions, talking plenty about one's spiritual elevation and other claims and behaviors that are supposed to be impressive or effective.

After finally realizing that the goals and objectives of the lost and astray mind will not be met within the whole life energy, a frustrated individual will find one way or another to return to his or her fantasies, delusions, illusions, and dreams within the death consumption culture.

One may first assume that one is prepared to tackle the necessary phases of detoxing and purging until one comes face to face with one's most secret personal fears and most humiliating shame and most hurtful memories. Instead of using every bit of spirit strength to deal with the consequences of one's past encounters within the energy that is opposite of Supreme Love and the Essence of Life, one soon surrenders to the weight of toxic overload within one's consciousness. One surrenders to consuming the same opposite energy that caused the problems in the first place. The Supreme Laws are quickly forgotten and dismissed, especially the ones that state that the whole life energy can not exist within the same space as the energy that is opposite of Supreme Love, and the Essence of Life and that power concedes absolutely nothing without a struggle.

Unless the situation becomes so critical that there is a massive movement towards resurrecting the sacred ancestral spirit presence of the Divine Children of the Sun and the Sacred Garden Culture from which we come,

CHAPTER SEVEN: THE WHITE BLIGHT ZONE

it will continue that: 1. Only a few individuals will ever gather enough willpower and inner focus to embark upon the exit route from the toxic parallel. 2. And then only a few of those will actually have the tenacity and strength to endure the process. 3. And only a few among the few will even have the desire to consume of whole life energy and release their addictions to the devitalized and depleted food substances and other forms of toxic mental, physical and spiritual consumption within the death-consuming culture.

The momentary enthusiasm of finding truth soon wears off as soon as one picks up a few new words, concepts, symbols and maybe special clothing. All along these many winding paths, one can encounter the truth and yet remain completely unchanged maintaining one's same character flaws and disorders, emotional damage and inner weaknesses. After the thrill is gone, one soon crosses over to the next path that catches one's attention. As soon as the going gets tough or one is challenged to actually address the truth within self, one quickly sidesteps the issue and heads down another path. The vibrations of disappointment, frustration and emptiness are the baggage that one carries on this and many other journeys to the truth.

The Truth Shall Set You Free

Let's take a few minutes to examine the statement "the truth shall set you free." Free to do what? Free to be what? First, one moves within the energy that is opposite of Supreme Love and the Essence of Life under the illusion that one is experiencing a level and degree of freedom. All the while the individual is obeying every demand, whimper and whine of the lost and astray pale state of mind like a well-trained animal. Secondly, one thinks and reasons from a position of assuming that one has free will. Individuals take great pride in the belief that they are the controllers of their own fate. The self-determination of many individuals within the death-consuming culture is expressed in their personal plans for the weekend, what they choose to wear or eat and how they behave in their relationships. And while the shackles and chains are gone from the feet and hands, the shackles and chains have become even tighter on the brain.

It is difficult for many individuals to see how the opposite energy actually dictates, "You will do as I say," because the voice they hear giving the directives is their own lost and astray state of mind as it expresses the thoughts and vibrations of lust, lies, illusions, confusion, death and deadly destruction. Therefore, when a bright idea or an emotional reaction pops into an individual's head, they are certain that they have freely generated their own thought. The supreme laws of energy consumption are beyond their comprehension, and there is no way for them to reason with the fact that the energy that they consume actually sends the signals that manifest in their brains as thoughts, sensations and images.

The concepts of self-control and restraint are rather unappealing to the lost and astray pale state of mind, because the practices and principles of the toxic parallel are in place to promote lust, lies, illusions, confusion, death and deadly destruction. One has been conditioned to see discipline, obedience and order as methods to

CHAPTER SEVEN: THE WHITE BLIGHT ZONE

restrict one's freedom while concepts of independence, liberation and self-determination are used to describe the free-spirit ideal within the toxic parallel. The one requirement of the opposite energy is "Consume me, and do whatever you please within the toxic parallel." The death-consuming culture is the evidence that one can basically eat, drink, sniff, snort or smoke whatever one pleases; say whatever one pleases, do whatever one pleases; and have sex with whoever, whatever, however, whenever, and wherever one pleases within the toxic parallel. And if anyone has anything to say about that, an individual will quickly declare that there are many paths to the truth and each person has his or her own journey to travel.

The idea of having many paths to the truth is usually given as a rationale for justifying one's personal decisions and defending one's position. Within this reasoning process, each individual is then able to assert the freedom to believe or behave how he or she pleases regardless of the level and degree of contradiction in maintaining optimum mental, physical and spiritual health and well-being. These individuals feel very righteous about criticizing and condemning anyone who promotes the restricted acts and requirements of living a natural and innately disciplined way of life. They uphold the freedom of choice and the pleasures of life that they freely pursue while quickly projecting cocky, arrogant and vain behaviors.

Nevertheless, these same individual suppress the vague and nagging feelings of being entrapped. Sometimes this entrapped vibration expresses itself in the manifestation of being stuck in a nerve-wracking job,

FULFILLING THE SACRED ANCESTRAL PROPHECY OF THE TRIPLE NINE: UNVEILING THE PROPHETIC 2012 MELTDOWN OF THE LOST AND ASTRAY PALE STATE OF MIND

stuck in a nerve-wracking relationship, or stuck in a nerve-wracking circumstance that squeezes one between a rock and a hard place. Or stuck and stagnant in the consequences of near-fatal violence produced by freely chosen sexual encounters; entrapped in the suffering of physical afflictions such as venereal disease, AIDS, cancer...; entrapped in the addictions that keep one hustling to buy another shot, another snort, another hit; entrapped in the beauty standards that keep one piling those chemical toxins and hot irons on one's head to be obedient to the images of paleness...

As a matter of fact, many of the impulsive acts of reckless, rebellious, stubborn and wild behaviors are used to defy the feelings of being unable to free one's self from the mental worries, pressures and demands within the cold paleness produced by the death-consuming culture. In truth and reality, individuals are entrapped in the toxic parallel. They are entrapped by the conflicts and turmoil and frustrations that mark their personal lives and trouble their minds within the opposite energy.

Their life presence is actually being dominated by a pale lost and astray state of mind. The bossy and demanding appetites of the ego keep many individuals performing tricks and jumping through hoops to keep that bloated ego well-stroked and well-fed. It is amazing to watch individuals parade around declaring their freedom and independent thinking and then watch how easily a simple word can trigger a reaction. In the same way that a dog is conditioned to respond to the ringing of a bell or a command to attack, the pale lost and astray mind is deeply conditioned by the vibrations and

CHAPTER SEVEN: THE WHITE BLIGHT ZONE

sensations of the opposite energy. When the opposite energy commands its disciples and followers to jump, the lost and astray mind jumps quickly to its limit, and then asks, "how high" as it prepares to stretch just a little further if necessary.

While it is often spoken about in the terms of a conspiracy syndrome within the death-consuming culture, the techniques of mind-control and brainwashing are very effective methods used to produce the herd mentalities that are at work in the lives of the mass majority of Man, He and She. What we mean by "brainwashing" is the methods used by the disciples and followers of the opposite energy to erase the last memories of sacred ancestral spirit presence from one's consciousness. Fright, fear, violence, religious indoctrination, mass media programming, chemical and substance abuse; and miseducation are just a few of the cold and pale brainwashing methods that have been historically used and are still currently in use. Therefore, the concept of freedom within the toxic parallel becomes one of those deceptive terms that has no real meaning except to keep the fantasies, illusions, delusions and dreams in full production within the mental consciousness of so many.

All information gathered by the disciples and followers of the death-consuming culture becomes the powerbase of deceit serving as ammunition to support, maintain and advance the strength of the cold and pale state of mind. Because the mental and physical presence of Man, He and She, has been reduced to a disconnected state of being, data, facts and figures can be manipulated to project a favorable version of the truth. Without a

FULFILLING THE SACRED ANCESTRAL PROPHECY OF THE TRIPLE NINE: UNVEILING THE PROPHETIC 2012 MELTDOWN OF THE LOST AND ASTRAY PALE STATE OF MIND

connection to divine spirit consciousness, an individual can be easily misled and deceived by superficial displays of knowledge enacted by the pale lost and astray mind.

The ultimate goal of acquiring knowledge is to thereby gain control over life itself, to gain control of the spirit presence and dominate the unseen movement of energy that forms the seen.

Any truth that one encounters within the energy that is opposite of Supreme Love and the Essence of Life will certainly set one free to experience a greater level and degree of sensations and vibrations within the toxic parallel, i.e. the vibrations and sensations of the energies that are opposite of Supreme Love and the Essence of Life. The more entrenched one becomes within the intellectual, scientific and religious truths of the death consumption culture, the more free the lost and astray mind is to run amuck and the more entrapped the sacred ancestral spirit presence becomes.

The idea of being free within the energy that is opposite of Supreme Love and the Essence of Life means that one is allowed a wide range of choices in one's expression, because no matter which path is chosen, one still remains within the mental mindset of the toxic parallel. And guess what? Within the melting-pot syndrome of the paleness ideology, there has not been even one ounce of focus on stepping away from the cold and pale mindset that is fueled by the energy that is opposite of Supreme Love and the Essence of Life. On the contrary, the goal and objective continue to be for the mass majority of Man, He and She, to assimilate and integrate into a cold and pale melting-pot state of mind.

CHAPTER SEVEN: THE WHITE BLIGHT ZONE

Yes, the melting-pot syndrome dictates, dominates and rules the social, economic and religious environment by any means necessary. And the new name for this pale melting-pot syndrome is globalization. In other words, the melting-pot syndrome simply means melting into a pale state of mind.

The Subconscious: Far Below Whole Life Awareness

The subconscious serves to keep one's mental consciousness comfortably unaware of the nature of the opposite energy that one consumes. Those internal practices of subtle self-deception allow one to project the appearance of all those desirable qualities that one wishes to possess while deep down inside there is a core of insecurity, self-doubt and self-loathing. One engages in massive cover-ups to protect this toxic core. The greatest deception is that one insists on pretending that one is not a carrier of the energy that is opposite of Supreme Love and the Essence of Life while knowing inside that one is truly immersed in the lust, lies, illusions, confusion, death and deadly destruction of daily encounters within the toxic parallel. One's conscious and subconscious consumption continues to reflect unwholesome patterns and tendencies.

It is common for an individual to deny carrying undesirable vibrations and project them away from self, blaming someone or something else. This habit of placing blame outside of self is the way the opposite energy remains well-disguised within each and every host. Fault-finding and criticizing others prevents many individuals from having to deal with their own flaws, defects, weaknesses and shortcomings. Having a subconscious within the toxic parallel means that the mass majority of Man, He and She, actually function within a severe lack of awareness that distorts and dulls their thinking and reasoning processes. One is not able to reason with the foul eruptions of the energy that is opposite of Supreme Love and the Essence of Life that often leave an individual asking, "Why did I just do that?" So, what is unknown and unseen becomes shrouded in paleness as far as the pale lost and astray mind is concerned. And one can pretend to be innocent and blameless in matters regarding one's own conduct and behaviors. And one can avoid confronting and addressing such inner matters of consciousness for an entire lifetime.

On the other hand, individuals defend and protect their consumption of the opposite energy as if those vibrations and sensations are the very core of their identity. The state of division that keeps Man, He and She, lost and astray in a pale state of mind is based on consuming from a core of energy that is opposite of Supreme Love and the Essence of Life. This toxic core was laid in the consciousness of Man, He and She, just like a parasite that feeds off of its host. So long as one consumes of this toxic core, the opposite energy is able to remain active, injecting more of the vibrations of lust, lies, illusions, confusion, death and deadly destruction, and sucking more and more of one's life energy. This toxic core has managed to embed itself within the consciousness and life presence of Man, He and She. And the mass majority of individuals have forgotten and rejected their true identity as a spirit being while

CHAPTER SEVEN: THE WHITE BLIGHT ZONE

becoming entrapped in the lost and astray pale state of mind. In truth and reality, the lost and astray mind is nothing more than disconnected thoughts and reasoning produced by a brain that is fueled by the opposite energy.

As one approaches the core of the energy that is opposite of Supreme Love and the Essence of Life, the hardcore ugliness of the opposite energy begins to be seen for what it is. When one wonders how all of the atrocities and cruelty and slaughter and torture and hate can exist within the consciousness of Man, He and She, one is simply identifying the nature of the energy that is opposite of Supreme Love and the Essence of Life. It is a chilling reality that all of Man, He and She, within the toxic parallel are consuming of the exact same energy that is opposite of Supreme Love and the Essence of Life that has fueled and continues to fuel wars, massacres, brutal rape, genocide and the destruction of the precious nonrenewable natural resources.

Even the highest consciousness within the toxic parallel cannot escape the reality that one is still entrapped within vibrations of lust, lies, illusions, confusion, death and deadly destruction. However, those who are busy pursuing their personal schemes of fortune and fame rarely stop to consider the true nature of their own consciousness anyway. They are too busy trying to make that buck and get a slice of that pie before they die. And regardless of the artificial colors, flavors and smells, someone will say, "Hell, it's pie; you got to die of something."

What is not so easily comprehended is that the consciousness of the mass majority of Man, He and She, is dominated at this time upon the planet by the energy that is opposite of Supreme Love and the Essence of Life. There is no time to debate the existence of the toxic parallel or to argue with individuals who insist that they do not reside within the toxic parallel. Time will reveal the divine wisdom of this sacred text as the energy that is opposite of Supreme Love and the Essence of Life plays itself out in each and every individual who continues to consume of that opposite energy. It is indeed about that time when Man, He and She, must become consciously aware of the energy that he and/or she consumes.

The Highs of the Low

Individuals may wonder why they can experience feelings within the toxic parallel that have been identified as happiness or joy or even love. "If the parallel is so toxic, then how come I am still walking around feeling all right? It must not be that bad after all..." The energy that is opposite of Supreme Love and the Essence of Life is less than whole, and every experience generated within the toxic parallel is less than whole. The so-called "good" feelings that one may experience with the toxic parallel are short-lived, inconsistent and sporadic. However, that does not stop the lost and astray mind from constantly seeking to tap into a state of being high within lowness. There is a definite limit within the toxic parallel regarding the nature of one's energy level. In truth and reality, the highs of the toxic parallel are actually very weak and low level energy expressions.

The highs of the toxic parallel are temporary and addictive, because one becomes desperate to experience more and more of the high while the returns are less and

CHAPTER SEVEN: THE WHITE BLIGHT ZONE

less with many adverse side effects Therefore, one must constantly seek new or more frequent ways to induce the artificial highs of the death consumption culture. Entertainment and recreational drugs are the greatest pacifiers within the energy that is opposite of Supreme Love and the Essence of Life. Music, movies and magazines... the performing and visual arts of the death-consuming culture... theatrical productions, parades and holiday celebrations... sex and violence, war and crime... in other words, lust, lies, illusions, confusion, death and deadly destruction... The best way to keep the mass majority of Man, He and She, lulled into the dullness of the cold and pale state of mind is to keep the pacifiers widely available and widely consumed.

The same vibrations of rushing adrenalin, quickened pulse and fast breathing that cause the fight-or-flight response within the lost and astray mind during the Ice Age mutation and degeneration form the same basic pattern of the so-called highs within the modern death consumption culture. Mass hysteria, giddiness, orgies; drug-crazed, booty calls and down-low and other forms of entertainment sex; war games, religious euphoria, spirit possessions, killing frenzies and other mob mentalities are all related within the energy that is opposite of Supreme Love and the Essence of Life.

The same vibrations that cause sports fans to holler in breathless anticipation of the next play and movie-goers to jump in excitement at an onscreen explosions and church-goers to weep and wail with screaming prayers and concert-goers to dance in a trance to loud thumping music and soldiers to fire their guns with whooping yells of ecstasy are the exact same vibrations

FULFILLING THE SACRED ANCESTRAL PROPHECY OF THE TRIPLE NINE: UNVEILING THE PROPHETIC 2012 MELTDOWN OF THE LOST AND ASTRAY PALE STATE OF MIND

that keep individuals feeling that they are experiencing the joys of life within the toxic parallel.

The manic agitation and speeded-up body responses and high anxiety reflect the mental stress of encountering violence and life-threatening attacks on a daily basis from the cave-dwelling origin of the cold and pale state of mind. These feelings of excitement and adrenalin rush and thrilling chills are the basis of the highs that are valued and pursued within the energy that is opposite of Supreme Love and the Essence of Life. These vibrations are then entangled in the sex and violence and the war and crime of the death consumption culture. Yes, a death-consuming culture that breeds, seeds and feeds from the hardcore paleness of lust, lies, illusions, confusion, death and deadly destruction.

Music concerts, movies, sports events and religious services all allow individuals to tap into the vicarious thrill of watching someone else and then imagining what they must be experiencing. Remember, pleasure, happiness and joy within the toxic parallel have many perverse expressions. Roman gladiators fought to the death as spectators yelled in glee at the death blow. Lynch mobs in the south gathered round crackling fires with grinning excitement as suntanned males were burned alive. And as the charred remains of a human being smoldered in the ashes, men, women and children feasted in celebration at picnics. Soldiers raided and plundered a small village in the midst of brutal war games, gang raping a young village girl with hollers of frenzied and brutal lust.

CHAPTER SEVEN: THE WHITE BLIGHT ZONE

Even up until today, mass populations gather in patriotic sentiments of pleasure to watch colorful pageants and firework displays, celebrating war and the thrill of victory. These are the vibrations that fuel the toxic parallel and contaminate every vibration of joy, happiness, and pleasure that are experienced within the death consumption culture. When wide-eyed movie-goers sit in darkened theaters and watch reenactments of horror and brutality while munching popcorn, the giddy delight and morbid fascination are bound together within the same toxic parallel. During a hunting expedition that thrill of killing an aloof or hard-to-capture animal brings an adrenalin rush that makes an individual feel like a victorious conqueror. The intense surge and feeling of adrenalin in one's blood system become addictive, regardless of the adverse effects. From the adrenalin rush and other hormonal responses to stress, other addictive patterns are formed, such as addictions to drugs, alcohol, depleted food substances and other chemical substances to maintain a high.

Unfortunately, this low state of being which entangles one within the energy that is opposite of Supreme Love and the Essence of Life is a pale and poor substitute for a whole life connection to the Most Supreme Unseen. Within the death consumption culture, there are so many who willingly settle for so little. Yes, one can experience the temporary highs and the artificial stimulants and intoxicating substances that cause one to feel good within the toxic parallel. As a matter fact, feeling good and having a good time can become one's primary pursuit and major pastime. Most individuals are aware of the behaviors and consumption patterns that aid in the "feel-good" vibration, and these are readily available to soothe the nerves of those who romp and stomp within the energy that is opposite of Supreme Love and the Essence of Life.

The I in I have had many individuals insist that their chemical addictions and smoke inhalations and favorite treats are necessary for their sense of well-being. As a matter of fact, individuals have insisted that their smoking of marijuana or consumption of certain mushrooms or usage of chemical substances take them on a spiritual high. These individuals are not able to realize that their brains are being bombarded by artificial stimulants and intoxicants and that drug-induced highs are a dime a dozen within the death consumption culture.

Artificial highs within the toxic parallel are common. The reason that these highs are artificial is because they have to be constantly maintained from outside of self or they will not last. Much like the feelings that one may experience from an over-inflated ego, the artificial highs require a great deal of attention and energy to maintain.

The I in I simply state that the toxic parallel is definitely a haven for those who worship the toxic unseen and call upon the deities of lust, lies, illusion, confusion, death and deadly destruction within the energy that is opposite of Supreme Love and the Essence of Life. There are vibrations that can be invoked and conjured within the toxic parallel; there are states of consciousness within the toxic parallel that are a definite trip deep into the twilight zone of the energy that is opposite of Supreme Love and the Essence of Life. And what does

CHAPTER SEVEN: THE WHITE BLIGHT ZONE

this have to do with divine spirit consciousness anyway? Nothing at all. Please do not deceive one's self.

Chapter 7 Innerlude:
Divided Union

Song 8 from "12th Hour Prophecy: The Pale Curse and Solarized Energy Shift," Kwatamani musical CD release, 2008

<u>Royal Priestess vocals:</u>
Same old, same old, taking-care-of-business thangs to do
Did you ever stop to wonder what's ailing you?
Staying in line, keeping that mind thinking it's in control
Paying the hellish, pale toll

<u>High Priest vocals:</u>
And time would tick fast and quick
And the Earth's temperature would start to rise
But, it would be business as usual
within the last phase of the pale days
You see, the mesmerized had become so hypnotized by
the deceptions and the lies that they could not imagine
that they were indulging in the last rituals and rites
of the white blight
And although there was a massive increase
in the toxic rot and the foul stench
The idolizers and worshippers of this white blight
was in it to win it
and was not about to give up an inch
You see, it was about profit and gain and fortune and
fame and dog eat dog, vicious, cruel and vain
And there was nothing going on but the rent outside the
fast lane, while the meek, weak and feeble was focusing
on getting a piece of that pie in the sky

FULFILLING THE SACRED ANCESTRAL PROPHECY OF THE TRIPLE NINE: UNVEILING THE PROPHETIC 2012 MELTDOWN OF THE LOST AND ASTRAY PALE STATE OF MIND

The wheelers and the dealers was focusing on getting a
piece of that bad mamma jamma right now
Beg, borrow, steal or buy, and the suntanned Children
were about it, 'bout it, 'bout it baby, yeah
They were getting it on, stone cold to the bone
pushing the values, attitudes and behaviors
of this white-blight zone
And would use any means necessary
to get their groove on
And life would move fast and furious
and would come and go in a blink
And since there was no ancestral link
There would be no ancestral future thoughts
for one to think
And this would be a bad mother for you
full of blinkety-blinks
And living for the moment would be how low
Man, He and She, would sink
And the I-me-my syndrome
was the trademark of the white-blight zone
And the lusting selfish greed
would replace natural and innate basic needs
And whole foods and sunshine and tender loving care
would be replaced by false fads and do-dads and things
and stuff to eat, use and wear
So, the sacred ancestral relationship of Man, He and She,
would no longer have anything to do
with a Love Supreme
You see, it was paleness to the max
and those cold-blooded
Caucasus ways and means to behave

CHAPTER 7 INNERLUDE: DIVIDED UNION

have been carried around like a monkey on the back
And would be unloaded
through every cold-blooded pale act
And could be traced through the trails
of every cold, pale, bloodstained track
That would produce sex and violence to re-enact
transvex, homosex, necrophiliac
bestiality, S & M, and be it rough, raped or straight,
it would be bip-bam, quick, fast and in a haste
And everybody afflicted and addicted
to this pale, civilized state of mind
would see sex and violence, war and crime as prime time
And it would be business as usual, same old, same old
And the Children of the Sun of every kin and every kind
would continue to indulge in the lies and the deceptions
of a lost and astray pale state of mind

<u>Royal Priestess vocals:</u>
Same old, same old
Same old, same old
Wheeling and dealing, rocking and reeling
Rocking and reeling
Seeking that feeling, seeking that feeling
Begging, borrowing and stealing
Stealing yourself blind, yourself blind
Lost and astray in a pale state of mind
Pale state of mind

<u>High Priest vocals:</u>
It'd be business as usual, same old, same old
And it would be a crime to see the Children of the Sun
Deaf, dumb and blind to the signs of the times
And unless there was a quick and fast turnabout

FULFILLING THE SACRED ANCESTRAL PROPHECY OF THE TRIPLE NINE: UNVEILING THE PROPHETIC 2012 MELTDOWN OF THE LOST AND ASTRAY PALE STATE OF MIND

This pale thang here would be all over but the shout
And the fat lady was already singing
about the misery, aches and pains
And the empty, lonely blues
that this pale game was bringing
And the shackles and the chains
that was clamped down
on the Children of the Sun's brains
was causing excruciating pain
And the helplessness and hopelessness of the insane pain
was keeping the addicted and afflicted playing this game
And since there was no ancestral link beyond the rotten, foul funk of this toxic stink
There would be no future thoughts to think
regarding the person, place and things
of an ancestral link
There would be no divine relationship
with the earth, wind, rain and sun
the rainforest or its trees
And therefore, there would be no whole-life concern
regarding the air that we breathe
And with no divine spirit consciousness
and disconnected from the Most Supreme Unseen help
Living for the moment would be all that left
And within this reference, there would be no need for the divine union of Man, He and She, to be honored and kept
And this would be the tool the pale opposite energy
would use to get into its groove
Implementing a sexual freedom concept where he get it on with he and she get it on with she
And he and she get it on with their pets intimately

CHAPTER 7 INNERLUDE: DIVIDED UNION

And the crimes of a dominating state of mind would trace
their tracks to a death act through necrophiliac
And the joys and pleasures of inflicting pain
is how S & M came
And the monotheistic deity would thrive off the pale
curse, and take the Sacred Garden Culture
and turn it in reverse
Seeding freakish and unnatural relationships
genetically modifying the spirit-worth of birth
And so from the experimentation of animal husbandry
the hunter and herder culture would consume
Making room for cloning and stem-cell research
as that opposite energy
prepare the pathway for doom and gloom

Chapter Eight:
Sacred Ancestral Prophecy

Chapter 8 Prelude:
Hear We Stand

Song 9 from "Conjuring Sacred Ancestral Consciousness," Kwatamani musical CD, 2007

<u>Royal Priestess vocals:</u>
Here we stand
We have the opportunity to turn this thing around
Turn this thing around
There is a divine master plan, let's turn this thing around
Return the original glory of the suntanned Man
And through it all, despite the fall, we rise
Let's turn this thing around
No more time for lies and alibis, we rise
Here we stand...And still here we stand

<u>High Priest vocals:</u>
Here we stand as we are
with a chance to make things right
Yet the mass majority are deep in a coma-like sleep
consuming toxic fear and fright
Descendants coming from an ancestry divine
Addicted, hung up in a deep-freeze state of mind
Leaving a toxic scar, declaring war on air water and earth
degenerating into a fatal physical decline
Air conditioning millions of acres
turning solarized lands ice cold
Moving a selfish and greed ideology
having no concern how it takes its toll
And this is how the pale mind works and play
This is how the Children of the Sun

FULFILLING THE SACRED ANCESTRAL PROPHECY OF THE TRIPLE NINE: UNVEILING THE PROPHETIC 2012 MELTDOWN OF THE LOST AND ASTRAY PALE STATE OF MIND

who went lost and astray spend their day
And it does not matter the color of one's skin
Everybody playing the pale game, desperate to win
And although this game is cold, stale and pale
and was born and bred in the caves
of the deep-freeze pits of hell
Now most everybody walk this bloodstained trail
playing this cold-blooded game very well
Although the rules to fail or pass
is anchored in the game of color, caste and class
Everybody's struggling not to be last
From the whitest of the white and the blackest of the
black and everybody in between
Talking that smack to get ahead of the pack
Moving real fast to the fast track
Why point the finger when it's self
that one should blame?
Continuing to do the same thing
hoping that things will change
Mass populations growing sick and obese
on the greed of how they feed
Out of sync and out of focus with their own basic needs
Striving to get there fast and quick
amassing heart attacks, diabetes, cancer and AIDS
Struggling for a materialistic gain
living their life in misery, aches and pains
Trying to turn a trick, making self very sick
Offspring grow fat, obese and sick
What a shame, what a crime
But then crime is determined by how it's defined
Is crime then properly defined

CHAPTER 8 PRELUDE: HEAR WE STAND

By glorifying this bloodstained trail so you can buy and
sell these toxic tastes and smells
Or is crime the time spent when caught!?
If you declare war, you can take crime far
and it will be how gallant you fought
Although many a negro has been sent to death row
it's not considered a crime
what Columbus did to the Taino
And the Conquistador is still considered a hero
It's not seen as a crime to deplete the rainforest
and to rape the earthly land
It wasn't seen as a crime for the religious fanatics to rape
and enslave the Children of the Sun with a golden tan
It was not seen as a crime to hunt down
the Australian aborigine seed
killing them, then stuffing them like they do animals,
killing another suntanned breed
Crime was well-defined when Tasmania's suntanned
breed was wiped off of the planet Earth
by the plague of the white man's disease
And although the slave ship Jesus
was truly the name of a slave ship
that took many Children of the Sun on a slave trip
It seems that the born-again vibe
that caused the Jesus ship to arrive
is still taking Children of the Sun on a slave trip
Bottom line, there is no shame
in these social economic religious games
that are still not considered a crime
And the storyline
to these death-consumption-culture crimes
will put Man, He and She, in a bind

FULFILLING THE SACRED ANCESTRAL PROPHECY OF THE TRIPLE NINE: UNVEILING THE PROPHETIC 2012 MELTDOWN OF THE LOST AND ASTRAY PALE STATE OF MIND

Causing them to integrate into the deep-freeze mentality
of a lost and astray mind
And, it's a battle between the east and the west
with both sides running nuclear bomb tests
And nobody knows what will be destroyed next
by this lost and astray mind with a god complex
Yet, we've got to address this thang that's causing all life
on earth much pain

Royal Priestess vocals:
Here we stand, here we stand
We have the opportunity to turn this thing around
We have the opportunity to turn this thing around
With the Most Supreme Spirit of Love
And of a consciousness divine, we must let actions
speak louder than words
We must let actions speak louder than words
And meltdown this deep-freeze state of mind
Let's turn this thing around
And, here we stand

Chapter Eight: Sacred Ancestral Prophecy

There are many who will comfortably return to their everyday concerns, their habits and familiar routines within the death-consuming culture never to give another thought to the resurrection of the sacred ancestral spirit presence of the Divine Children of the Sun and the Sacred Garden Culture from which we come. As a matter of fact, to even entertain such a thought about resurrection would cause grave disturbance in the individual's thoughts and reasoning. While one continues to socialize and maintain close associations within the culture of death consumption, it becomes a conflict of interest to even consider whole life change.

Nevertheless, for those readers who have continued through these pages, it has been a heck of an experience consuming all of this supreme truth to arrive to this point. The impact of that supreme truth will not allow one to sit idle and continue to repeat one's same old toxic consumption patterns without rubbing against the conscious contradictions of one's self-deception.

Beyond Speculation

Let us reason with what is known within divine spirit consciousness with a certainty that exceeds the speculations of the lost and astray pale state of mind. Please remember that there are unseen energy movements that come before every manifestation upon the seen. In fact, there is no physical event that does not first begin within an unseen parallel of energy. However,

FULFILLING THE SACRED ANCESTRAL PROPHECY OF THE TRIPLE NINE: UNVEILING THE PROPHETIC 2012 MELTDOWN OF THE LOST AND ASTRAY PALE STATE OF MIND

it is quite a challenge for individuals entrapped within the lost and astray pale state of mind to reason with anything that is beyond the physical senses. The state of disconnection causes one to move without a focus or direction on anything except the most superficial and shallow kinds of observations.

Understandably the vast majority of Man, He and She, reside in a confused state where disorientation, chaos, and disorder are the prevailing winds that blow the thoughts to and fro. Unfortunately, individuals who exist within the paleness of the toxic parallel can not even reason with how deficient and incomplete and unwhole they really are. Instead, these individuals are arrogant in their ignorance and boastful of their pale lost and astray mental tricks that somehow feed a bloated and unstable self-image.

Only through a divine intervention could the communication link between the Most Supreme Unseen and the seen presence of Man, He and She, be re-connected. The lost and astray pale state of mind is actually conditioned to defend against any possible resurrection of the sacred ancestral spirit presence of the Divine Children of the Sun and the Sacred Garden Culture from which we come. Nevertheless, there are those individuals who have a spark of spirit life, and these spirits are struggling to make contact with whole life energy. While they may still continue patterns of toxic consumption, those habits and behaviors have never really provided a sense of deep inner satisfaction. One is not able to do this thing alone; one cannot undertake an escape from the toxic parallel without the divine

CHAPTER EIGHT: SACRED ANCESTRAL PROPHECY

intervention of the Most Supreme Seen and Unseen Essence of Life and Supreme Love.

Those individuals who are entrapped within the opposite energy have absolutely no idea what to expect or how to anticipate what the resurrection of the sacred ancestral spirit presence of the Divine Children of the Sun and the Sacred Garden Culture from which we come will look like. Scattered pieces of prophecy have been handed down through generations and preserved through many distortions and misinterpretations. There are some who are busy calculating dates and times based on calendars and charts left by ancient populations who, themselves, eventually faced the adversities of the pale invaders. There are those who use scientific theory and hypothesis formulated within a pale frame of mind to interpret data and figures regarding the shifting earth changes. There are some who tune into the outer reaches of the lost and astray pale state of mind to channel what they refer to as galactic beings who can tell Man, He and She, about upcoming earthly events. There are some who cling to a religious doctrine and scriptural account of a second coming, an Armageddon or apocalyptic event without truly understanding the first coming of the energy that is opposite of Supreme Love and the Essence of Life. There are many who have a political analysis about the global happenings that will usher in a new world order. And there are the skeptics and the alarmists and all the disciples and followers in between, mixing and mingling within the toxic vibrations of lust, lies, illusions, confusion, death and deadly destruction.

The resurrection of the sacred ancestral spirit presence of the Divine Children of the Sun and the

FULFILLING THE SACRED ANCESTRAL PROPHECY OF THE TRIPLE NINE: UNVEILING THE PROPHETIC 2012 MELTDOWN OF THE LOST AND ASTRAY PALE STATE OF MIND

Sacred Garden Culture from which we come is not about revolution or a military coup or the overthrow of a government; it is not about holy wars and genocidal massacres of religious purging; it is not about scientific "discoveries" and outer-space adventures. And while it may appear that the movement of energy that is being orchestrated by the Most Supreme Unseen has some connection with the other occurrences that may or may not unfold during the era of 2012, there are indeed two separate and very different energy cycles at work. All those who continue to associate and participate within the confines of the death-consuming culture will definitely experience manifestations of the opposite energy in its most characteristic expressions. The nature and character of the opposite energy has been exposed over the last several millennia.

Those who were the first hosts of this opposite energy certainly bear the greatest burden of detoxing and purging in any hopes of resurrecting their sacred ancestral spirit presence. Let there be no mistake, the first hosts have declared themselves to be white and have upheld so-called "white" racist ideologies of social, economic and religious order within the death-consuming culture. This in no way excuses the absolute burden of responsibility upon those who have been historically victimized by the first hosts of the opposite energy. We state clearly that it is the divine duty, obligation and responsibility of each and every Man, He and She, to come forward with the greatest level of consciousness in order to detox and purge the attitudes, values, beliefs and

CHAPTER EIGHT: SACRED ANCESTRAL PROPHECY

behaviors of the opposite energy and its death-consuming culture.

The massive deception that was played by the conquering nomadic pale tribes, and all their descendants who have inherited the opposite energy as a birthright, is that the lesser state being that manifests through the consumption of an inferior and toxic energy is really superior. Not only do the descendants of the white-blight ordeal insist that their origin of the deep freeze is superior, they also insist that their origin is of the highest evolution of Man, He and She. As these Children of the Sun mutated and degenerated into flesh-eating, carnivorous and cannibalistic beings in the ice-cold caves; as they turned pale with a cold-blooded lust for violent domination; as they continued to degenerate into nomadic warring cave clans, and then nomadic warlord invaders; the ability to kill and destroy was all that they wielded in their bloodstained hands. The ability to inflict fright, fear, misery, aches and pain through lust, lies, illusions, confusion, death and deadly destruction is all that they wield today as the disciples and followers of that same opposite energy. And the destructive acts of greed and exploitation are covered up by material gains and petty rewards for those who become the willing disciples and followers of the cold and pale state of mind. And in the course of rationalizing, justifying and excusing their schemes of manipulation and domination, these disciples and followers have joined with the original hosts to become masters and grand masters of deceit.

The global issues that are facing Man, He and She, really are about an energy crisis. In truth and reality, the

FULFILLING THE SACRED ANCESTRAL PROPHECY OF THE TRIPLE NINE: UNVEILING THE PROPHETIC 2012 MELTDOWN OF THE LOST AND ASTRAY PALE STATE OF MIND

toxic nature of the opposite energy is being exposed through the failures and errors of the overall globalized death-consuming culture. The nature of Man, He and She, within the toxic parallel is a mirror reflection of the energy that is opposite of Supreme Love and the Essence of Life. Thus, the energy crisis reflects the crisis of toxic energy consumption. With this amazing cry for change that is rising up from mass populations, there is a recognition that the death-consuming culture can not continue on its present course without facing more intense and grave consequences.

The sincere intentions and honest efforts to reach for a better state of existence have little or nothing to do with the nature of the opposite energy that one consumes on a moment-by-moment basis. It is not possible for Man, He and She, to continue polluting his or her mental, physical and spiritual presence without severe consequence. It is not possible for Man, He and She, to continue polluting the earth, water and air without severe consequence. The supreme laws of the universe remain supreme. One must reap from what one sows. Within the toxic parallel, toxic energy consumed is toxic energy manifested is toxic energy multiplied over and over again, on a personal level, family level, community level, national level and global level. And these cycles of toxic consumption have been going on for thousands of years, ever since the opposite energy first entered the consciousness of Man, He and She, causing the lost and astray Children of the Sun to mutate and degenerate, ending up in a pale deep-freeze state of being.

CHAPTER EIGHT: SACRED ANCESTRAL PROPHECY

When an imbalance or disturbance occurs in the physical body, systems are in place to preserve the life presence. At the first sign of invasion by a foreign substance, mechanisms are activated to restore proper function and order to the body. Therefore, as the first warnings regarding the depleted and unwhole energy were sent forward by the Most Supreme Seen and Unseen, it was also foreseen that a divine intervention would come to be. Nevertheless, if the opposite energy ever entered the consciousness of Man, He and She, then this depleted and devitalized energy would have to run its course. When the crushing weight of that toxic energy would become almost unbearable, a collective cry for help would amass from the Sacred Few who would truly and sincerely desire, from the gut-level of their essence, to have nothing else to do with that death-consuming culture or its cold and pale nature.

You see, the Most Supreme Unseen has never left us to do this thing alone. Nevertheless, the mass majority of Man, He and She, have actually allowed the lost and astray pale state of mind to dominate and control their presence, thereby rejecting, blocking, refusing and denying any hopes of resurrecting their sacred ancestral spirit presence. The ages upon ages of violent attack and brutal savage raping raids against the sacred ancestral spirit presence of the Divine Children of the Sun and the Sacred Garden Culture from which we come caused a tremendous amount of pollution, contamination, and corruption within the consciousness of Man, He and She. The fright, fear and terror caused by this bloody onslaught can never be underestimated, and the mental breakdown that caused widespread spiritual

FULFILLING THE SACRED ANCESTRAL PROPHECY OF THE TRIPLE NINE: UNVEILING THE PROPHETIC 2012 MELTDOWN OF THE LOST AND ASTRAY PALE STATE OF MIND

disconnection is the most profound tragedy upon the planet.

One can now see suntanned females, bleaching their hair to blonde or perming their hair to reflect the desired traits of paleness. One can see suntanned individuals readily adopting speech patterns, affectations, gestures and clothing styles to emulate paleness. One can see suntanned individuals mutating and degenerating into obese and disease-ridden monstrosities. One can see suntanned individuals buying into the social orders that promote paleness, advance paleness and erect paleness as the highest order of being upon the planet. One can see suntanned individuals worshipping the pale-male-war god of choice and dreaming of heavenly paleness. One can then see how the suntanned Man, He and She, has become paler than pale within a consciousness that is completely disconnected from the sacred ancestral spirit presence of the Divine Children of the Sun and the Sacred Garden Culture from which we come. And one can begin to comprehend that the issues of greatest concern go beyond the concepts of race, creed, sex, religion or the color of one's skin and address the core of one's innermost essence.

The supreme patience of the Most Supreme Unseen infuses this sacred ancestral prophecy with a strength that is unstoppable. The Most Supreme Unseen has always been present. Every time there was a disconnection from divine spirit consciousness and a return path to the seen became blocked, the Most Supreme Unseen was still present to go forward to multiply the divinity of whole life energy, seen and unseen. So while Man, He and She,

CHAPTER EIGHT: SACRED ANCESTRAL PROPHECY

was in the midst of rapid decline because of the plague of toxic consumption that was spread by the mutated and degenerated pale breeds of mankind, the Most Supreme Unseen was still present, manifesting the glory of earth, wind, rain and sun.

Divine union, divine consumption, and the forward multiplication of divinity continued within the Most Supreme Unseen, becoming more and more intense, re-circulating again and again within the unseen, amassing into an overwhelming unstoppable magnitude of whole life energy. Just as no Man, He and She, can stop the sun from shining nor stop the changing of the tides, the natural movement of the Most Supreme Seen and Unseen Essence of Life and Supreme Love can not be stopped. One will either be with the flow of the Essence of Life and Supreme Love or one will go against the flow and function opposite of the Essence of Life and Supreme Love.

Current Affairs and Global Issues

A quick survey of current affairs and global issues will reveal a wide range of problems that are plaguing Man, He and She. Some may call it global warming and become overwhelmed by predictions and future projections about what might happen. We call it the meltdown of the opposite energy. These unseen movements have nothing to do with underground conspiracies or plots and schemes to overthrow a power base or any of the other common exploits within the death-consuming culture. Neither does it have anything to do with a color-coded Illuminati syndrome to replace the old guard of the death-consuming culture. The Most

FULFILLING THE SACRED ANCESTRAL PROPHECY OF THE TRIPLE NINE: UNVEILING THE PROPHETIC 2012 MELTDOWN OF THE LOST AND ASTRAY PALE STATE OF MIND

Supreme Unseen has been moving in divine order to penetrate the veils of deception that have kept so many of Man, He and She, enslaved, entrapped and endangered within the toxic parallel.

The opposite energy has dominated the consciousness of mass populations through the manipulations of a select group of privileged grand masters of deceit and overseers. These individuals have stolen, lied, slaughtered, enslaved and destroyed to monopolize the natural resources of the planet, utilizing deadly force through armed police, security agencies and military might, and reinforcing massive programs of deception through mass communications media.

A consciousness that would allow one to pollute the air, water and soil of one's living environment is not a whole life consciousness. And if the general population of Man, He and She, is quick to point the finger at political leaders or corporate leaders or any other leaders, one must realize that these leaders are a mere reflection of the followers who support, maintain and willingly consume from the death-consuming culture. The insanity of dumping toxic waste in the water that one has to drink and emitting toxic fumes and smoke in the air that one has to breathe, and spreading massive amounts of toxic chemicals and inorganic pesticides, insecticides and fertilizers into the soil from which one has to plant and eat reflects a consciousness that is headed for self-destruction.

And in the midst of global toxic consumption, the signs of severe imbalances and disturbance upon the planet are becoming more pronounced.

CHAPTER EIGHT: SACRED ANCESTRAL PROPHECY

(CNN) -- Between 1.5 trillion and 2 trillion tons of ice in Greenland, Antarctica and Alaska have melted at an accelerating rate since 2003, according to NASA scientists, in the latest signs of what they say is global warming...

"The ice tells us in a very real way how the climate is changing," said Luthcke, who will present his findings this week at the American Geophysical Union conference in San Francisco, California...

"A few degrees of change [in temperature] can increase the amount of mass loss, and that contributes to sea level rise and changes in ocean current," Luthcke said.

In the past five years, Greenland has lost between 150 gigatons and 160 gigatons each year, (one gigaton equals one billion tons) or enough to raise global sea levels about .5 mm per year, said Zwally, who will also present his findings at the conference this week...

"Every few extra inches of sea level have very significant economic impacts, because they change the sea level, increase flooding and storm damage," said, Zwally, ICESat Project Scientist. "It's a warning sign."

Melting ice, especially in Greenland and the Arctic, is also thought to contribute to global warming, Zwally said. When the vast ice sheets and glaciers melt, they lose their reflective power, and instead, oceans and land absorb the heat, causing the Arctic waters and the atmosphere to warm faster.

"The best estimates are that sea levels will rise about 18 to 36 inches by the end of the century, but because of what's going on and how fast things are changing, there's a lot of uncertainty," he said.

Ice melting across globe at accelerating rate, NASA says, www.CNN.com. December 16, 2008.

FULFILLING THE SACRED ANCESTRAL PROPHECY OF THE TRIPLE NINE: UNVEILING THE PROPHETIC 2012 MELTDOWN OF THE LOST AND ASTRAY PALE STATE OF MIND

Regardless of all the differences among Man, He and She, that have been exploited, manipulated and capitalized upon, one's basic needs remain one and the same, and we all share this one planet Earth. We have expressed these basic needs as food, sunshine and tender loving care. Equally, we all share the same common ancestry and the same duty, obligation and responsibility to uphold all that we have been given from our most supreme ancestral spirit presence that manifested as the Divine Children of the Sun and the Sacred Garden Culture from which we come. Yet, because of the break into a separate parallel, a toxic parallel, the Earth and the universe of Man, He and She, has become so threatened and violated that the voice of the Most Supreme Seen and Unseen Essence of Life and Supreme Love has been forced to speak loud and clear. In addressing the three categories of need, we have addressed one's mental, physical and spiritual consumption, one's living environment and one's relationships within the divine order of earth, wind, rain and sun. In order to sustain one's life presence, these needs must be addressed. What is becoming more and more obvious is that the way of life that is practiced, upheld and glorified as the death-consuming culture is failing miserably to provide for the basic needs of Man, He and She.

Each critical issue appears to be a separate and unique problem. Nevertheless, whether one is looking at environmental issues, global warming and climate changes, the energy crisis, economic crisis, terrorism, war and global conflicts; racial issues and/or social sexual issues be they hetero, homo or some other sex-

CHAPTER EIGHT: SACRED ANCESTRAL PROPHECY

related profile; famine and food supply issues, poverty, epidemics… within any of these global problems, certain patterns emerge. The patterns of crisis that emerge on a global scale all relate to patterns of the pale, toxic and unwhole energy that is consumed by mass populations of Man, He and She. This depleting energy is opposite of the Essence of Life and Supreme Love. And these patterns of toxic energy consumption are the way of life that defines every group and sub-group within the death consumption culture. As foretold in ancient ancestral prophecy, it was only a matter of time before the manifestations of the opposite energy would start to expose the depletion, destruction and self-destruction that is inherent in the nature of that toxic energy.

Crisis for the Consumers of the Death Culture

How is it possible to speak of food shortages and famine and starvation and poverty and thousands upon thousands of hungry children dying every day while millions upon millions suffer from malnutrition upon the planet Earth? There is a difference between starvation and malnutrition. For example, many populations within the U.S.A. are suffering from malnutrition while they are fat and obese. What this means is that the glutting mentality of mass populations is provided plenty to eat, junk food and other dead and devitalized food substances of the death consuming culture. Amazing as it may seem, this "well-fed" population can be evaluated as one of the most malnourished upon the planet. Then, there is starvation which is an entirely different matter. Starvation exists when there is little or no food to eat, regardless of whether it is depleted and devitalized food

FULFILLING THE SACRED ANCESTRAL PROPHECY OF THE TRIPLE NINE: UNVEILING THE PROPHETIC 2012 MELTDOWN OF THE LOST AND ASTRAY PALE STATE OF MIND

substance or not. Starvation means that one is not getting enough of any kind of food substance to consume.

When one looks behind the scene, the root, base and foundation of capitalizing plots and schemes are truly dictating things. This lacking can only occur when led by those of pale thought and reasoning who would prefer to dump, burn and/or otherwise destroy billions of tons of food in order to control prices and manipulate supply and demand. It is not about addressing the basic needs of Man, He and She; it is about capital gain, baby. These are the reasons why drug addiction is so widespread and why mass populations consume of toxic, dead and devitalized food substances that become the key to massive mental and physical sickness, disease and disorder. Yeah, it's about capital gain, supply and demand, regardless of the truth, regardless of the consequences. And so the over- and under-the-counter drug dealers have to make that cash, regardless of those who are adversely affected. Who within this kind of hellish, palish thinking would want mass populations to consume of whole life energy, i.e. raw and living fruits, vegetables, seeds and nuts? And the program is so well installed that we have had millions of mass consumers say to us directly and indirectly, "That's too healthy for me."

There is no need to think that the medical and hospital industries and the pharmaceutical companies that support, and are supported by, these industries would be in favor of a mass population that rejects the death-consuming culture. It is actually financially healthy and considered to be a sound investment to maintain a

CHAPTER EIGHT: SACRED ANCESTRAL PROPHECY

consumer base that is addicted to attitudes, behaviors and consumption patterns that produce heart attacks, cancer, diabetes, obesity and the rest of the list that is so long that it would take an entire chapter just to name them. Within such a scheme of profit that fuels a capital-oriented system of death consumption, who really wants to see a Sacred Garden Culture manifest?

The death-consuming culture is defined by conspicuous consumption patterns of greed, waste and excess. Spending priorities reflect the cold and pale values of material gain, luxury and the creature comforts of the privileged classes while the crisis of poverty around the world shows the gap. Satisfying the lustful greed of those global money brokers who control major corporate interests is more important within the death-consuming culture than conserving and protecting the nonrenewable resources of the planet Earth. Draining the earth of fossil fuels; stripping the earth of trees and destroying the rainforests; dumping toxic wastes into the waters and filling the air with smog, smoke and carbon emissions is simply a matter of course and business as usual for the captains of industry who dominate and control the death-consuming culture.

Ever since the pale Children emerged out of the deep freeze and spread the plague of pale deception throughout the planet, there has been a global downward spiral regarding earth care and maintenance. This downward spiral is producing a new type and kind of white-blight zone where the soil is depleted and contaminated with toxic chemicals, the water and air is polluted by toxic waste, the forests and rainforests are cut down and destroyed, and natural mineral resources are stripped, ripped and raped from the earth. Whereas the freezing conditions of the ice age prevented trees from growing, the deep-freeze mentality of those who consume of the opposite energy is manipulating earth conditions so that the trees are cut down and massive deforestation is leaving barren and depleted lands.

Deforestation is a common act to fulfill the death-consuming-culture attitudes, values and behaviors as promoted by the beef and dairy industry and corporate interests. For example, trees are cut down by huge lumber industry interests; trees are cut down by beef industry interests to provide pasture; and trees are cut down by huge agri-business interests to produce animal feed and biodiesel concerns. The natural cycles of carbon and water and oxygen that sustain life upon the planet have been interrupted by pollution, contamination and toxic overload. Many down side effects have befallen the planet since the coming of the Caucasoid civilizing attitudes, values and beliefs that perpetuate, uphold and maintain pale domination and control. For the sake of time, let's call this pale civilized order, the power base of deceit.

A dominant group of individuals sit at the top of every social order within the globalized death-consuming culture. These wealthy elite are the powerbrokers and captains of industry with enough financial pull and political clout to run the programs and policies of the opposite energy on a global scale. Those who populate the privileged ranks of masters and grand masters of deceit continue to command the exploitation of the earth's natural resources—renewable and nonrenewable

CHAPTER EIGHT: SACRED ANCESTRAL PROPHECY

—with the same plundering vibrations that destabilized the Sacred Garden Culture from which we come. The same historical attitudes of selfish greed and waste continue today as the natural resources of the Earth are squandered with no care about maintaining and sustaining the ecological balance of the planet.

There is no concept of compassion within the profit motive of those of the lost and astray pale state of mind regarding how to conserve and preserve the non-renewable natural resources. No real care about ripping, stripping and raping the earth's surface by strip mining mineral deposits and drilling for fossil fuel deposits. No real thought about depleting the earth's ecology systems, causing craters, sinkholes and destroying the natural balance of the earth's layers and formations. And there is no way for those of the lost and astray pale state of mind to tune into the environmental vibrations that regulate the divine order of earth, wind, rain and sun. So, regardless of the consequences, massive air-conditioned skyscrapers, industrial complexes and manufacturing plants, as well as air-conditioned offices and homes, are burning energy at a tremendous rate. Despite the fact that excessive car emissions have been identified as contributing to the greenhouse effect and global warming, vehicles continue to clog the cities and highways with traffic jams as single passengers luxuriate in air-conditioned comfort. And the automobile industries continue to avoid the mass manufacture of cleaner-running transportation for the general consumer, because they are tied into, and controlled by, a network of profiteers who are totally focused on capital gain, regardless of the true consequences of this insane

FULFILLING THE SACRED ANCESTRAL PROPHECY OF THE TRIPLE NINE: UNVEILING THE PROPHETIC 2012 MELTDOWN OF THE LOST AND ASTRAY PALE STATE OF MIND

capitalizing game. Oil companies are continuing to profit by the barrel. And the mass-consumer attitude reflects a disposable society where aerosol sprays fill the air with fluorocarbons and foam plastic fast food containers fill the land fills with the throw-away convenience of the death-consuming culture.

How will the powerbrokers, money brokers and corporate giants of the death-consuming culture deal with the intense earth-shifting changes? What will these dominating pale Children who mutated and degenerated in the deep freeze do to maintain their positions of advantage, privilege and economic control? Well, based on the nature of their consumption within the toxic parallel, these individuals will burn the last ounce of fossil fuels if that last ounce will maintain their creature comforts as the global heat intensifies. The powerbrokers will horde and drain the last energy reserves in the midst of famine, drought or any other environmental conditions that might become a threat to survival. And of course, the rot of the prey will still need to be refrigerated.

There will be no concern for anyone or anything else upon the planet; there will be no concern for future generations from these mutated and degenerated offspring seeds who control the military might and deadly force of the globalized death-consuming culture. An increase in massive destruction is just a few seconds away in the trigger-happy agitation and hostile aggression of the lost and astray pale state of mind. Pushing a final fatal button of destruction and self-destruction is just a matter of time. The aim now is to

CHAPTER EIGHT: SACRED ANCESTRAL PROPHECY

find any quick-fix solution to keep the cash registers ringing just a little longer in the death-consuming culture. For example, to deal with depletions in the ozone layer and the increase in ultraviolet rays which cause skin cancers in those who do not have a strong melanin presence, melanin becomes a commodity.

> ...A senior research scientist in the department of dermatology at the Yale School of Medicine, recently was awarded a U.S. patent entitled Cosmetic Melanins for producing and composing synthetic melanins that may be used in cosmetic products.
> Through its Office of Cooperative Research, Yale licensed the Melasyn technology originating in a medical school laboratory to Vion Pharmaceuticals, Inc. of New Haven. This month, Vion announced an exclusive world-wide licensing agreement with San-Mar Laboratories of Elmsford, NY., to manufacture and market products containing Melasyn.
> ...The Yale laboratory work behind the patenting and licensing offers interesting insight into the process of research and development of potential new products. "It started several years ago with our basic research on skin enzymes that produce melanin," Dr. Pawelek explains....
> "We were motivated by the thought that melanin naturally protects our skin from cancer induced by ultraviolet light. Perhaps, we reasoned, synthetic melanin would do the same," he says. "If we could design a melanin that produced a natural-appearing tan, we believed that people might be attracted to the product through its cosmetic qualities and simultaneously apply a sun-protectant, affording them added sun protection and potentially reducing the incidence of sun-induced skin cancer," hopes Dr. Pawelek, a cancer biologist who studies melanoma. Skin cancers are the most prevalent type of cancer in

the world, so even a small reduction in their incidence would make an impact on a significant number of people.

"We have, in fact, shown that Melasyn protects the skin of mice from ultraviolet light," he notes. "Now, controlled clinical studies are needed in order to be able to claim its protective effects in humans, and those will take months. In the meantime, we hope that its excellence as a cosmetic self-tanner will be sufficient to promote use."

Frank Penna, executive vice president of San-Mar Laboratories, states, "We are very excited about the Melasyn technology. Its potential applications are quite varied, from cosmetics to sunscreens." San-Mar intends to aggressively pursue commercial development.

The Melasyn technology grew out of Vion's cancer research collaborations with Dr. Pawelek and his Yale colleagues...

Yale Scientist Invents Cosmetic Melanin, Liquid Melanin Moves Closer To Marketplace, ScienceDaily (Feb. 26, 1998) http://www.sciencedaily.com/releases/1998/02/980226075340.htm

We make note that this research, which was stated to be a profound discovery, has not reduced skin cancer that the non-melaninated populations face as we move into the era of 2012. Yet and still, massive pollution and toxicity still spread the pale plague of self-destruction while business continues as usual as though all is well within the social orders controlled by the disciples and followers of the death-consuming culture of paleness.

CHAPTER EIGHT: SACRED ANCESTRAL PROPHECY

Fossil Fuels

Natural resources such as coal, petroleum, and natural gas take millions of years to form naturally and cannot be replaced as fast as they are being consumed. Let us continue to review what should definitely be self-evident by now.

> The burning of fossil fuels produces around 21.3 billion tons (21.3 gigatons) of carbon dioxide per year, but it is estimated that natural processes can only absorb about half of that amount, so there is a net increase of 10.65 billion tones of atmospheric carbon dioxide per year...Carbon dioxide is one of the greenhouse gases that enhances radiative forcing and contributes to global warming, causing the average surface temperature of the Earth to rise in response, which climate scientists agree will cause major adverse effects, including reduced biodiversity...
>
> In the United States, more than 90% of greenhouse gas emissions come from the combustion of fossil fuels. Combustion of fossil fuels also produces other air pollutants, such as nitrogen oxides, sulfur dioxide, volatile organic compounds and heavy metals.
>
> According to Environment Canada:
>
> "The electricity sector is unique among industrial sectors in its very large contribution to emissions associated with nearly all air issues. Electricity generation produces a large share of Canadian nitrogen oxides and sulphur dioxide emissions, which contribute to smog and acid rain and the formation of fine particulate matter. It is the largest uncontrolled industrial source of mercury emissions in Canada. Fossil fuel-fired electric power plants also emit carbon dioxide, which may contribute to climate change. In addition, the sector has significant impacts on water

and habitat and species. In particular, hydro dams and transmission lines have significant effects on water and biodiversity."

Combustion of fossil fuels generates sulfuric, carbonic, and nitric acids, which fall to Earth as acid rain, impacting both natural areas and the built environment... Fossil fuels also contain radioactive materials, mainly uranium and thorium, that are released into the atmosphere. In 2000, about 12,000 metric tons of thorium and 5,000 metric tons of uranium were released worldwide from burning coal. It is estimated that during 1982, US coal burning released 155 times as much radioactivity into the atmosphere as the Three Mile Island incident...

Harvesting, processing, and distributing fossil fuels can also create environmental concerns. Coal mining methods, particularly mountaintop removal and strip mining, have negative environmental impacts, and offshore oil drilling poses a hazard to aquatic organisms. Oil refineries also have negative environmental impacts, including air and water pollution. Transportation of coal requires the use of diesel-powered locomotives, while crude oil is typically transported by tanker ships, each of which requires the combustion of additional fossil fuels.

Fossil fuel from *Wikipedia, the free encyclopedia*
http://en.wikipedia.org/wiki/Fossil_fuels

Giant corporations dominate the economic arena of the death-consuming culture in banking, food, pharmaceuticals, railroads, publishing, petrochemicals, utilities, forestry, real estate, insurance, data, entertainment, health care, weapons, and so on. These massive corporate bodies dominate and influence the laws and policies of the death-consuming culture to

CHAPTER EIGHT: SACRED ANCESTRAL PROPHECY

benefit their profit motives and capital gain, regardless of consequences upon mass populations and regardless of the adverse effects upon our glorious planet. Yes, these massive corporate bodies are made up of the wealthiest legions within the toxic parallel who selfishly exploit the natural nonrenewable resources and dominate land use on a global scale. Most importantly, these economic entities form a collective powerbase of deceit that keep the plots and schemes of toxic consumption going strong. As a result, these corporate entities are major players in the death-consuming culture with devastating effects on the natural environment: global warming, greenhouse gases, rising sea level, animal habitat destruction, species extinction, decline of creatures that aid plant pollination, overgrazing of land, environmental effects of meat production, desertification, illegal logging, deforestation, soil erosion, soil contamination by toxic chemicals, soil salinization, nuclear meltdown and radioactive materials, ozone depletion, noise pollution, acid rain, ocean dumping, oil spills, water crisis, exploitation of natural resources, acid mine drainage, mountaintop removal mining, chlorofluorocarbons, DDT, Dioxin, heavy metals, herbicides, pesticides, and toxic waste.

Coming Out of the Cold

What has become clear to the I in I over time is that there are a few born and bred off of that mutated and degenerated DNA strain who do indeed have a desire to re-emerge into divine spirit consciousness. However, we make it very clear that the mass majority of those Children who mutated and degenerated and turned pale have a constituted agreement to maintain that paleness

FULFILLING THE SACRED ANCESTRAL PROPHECY OF THE TRIPLE NINE: UNVEILING THE PROPHETIC 2012 MELTDOWN OF THE LOST AND ASTRAY PALE STATE OF MIND

until death do they part. In fact, it is their belief that they are truly a superior species of mankind. The I in I make note of the term mankind. Let us not be deceived by all this. It is very clear that there are certain advantages that one seeks based upon one's allegiance to the lost and astray pale state of mind and maintaining a close association with the paleness ideology. It serves in many ways as a means to identify one's self and identify that pale culture, upholding and maintaining it to a level where it will provide those who hold the grips of power with a certain sense of security, because they can surround themselves with those who are identified as themselves and therefore become insulated by the vibrations and sensations of the opposite energy. Sort of like a shield of frozen numbness for those who have become most adapted to the toxic vibrations of lust, lies, illusions, confusion, death and deadly destruction of the toxic parallel. However, there are those who have come to recognize that they too are captured slaves who just appear to be in a profile that is a little different than those who were overtly and officially declared as legal property. Nevertheless, these lost and astray pale Children have spent a lot of time orchestrating cunning tricks and deception in order to persuade the suntanned Children to take a position of inferiority and have indeed been very successful at doing this.

It is well understood that there may be a few pale lost Children who have a focus on resurrecting the sacred ancestral spirit presence of the Divine Children of the Sun and the Sacred Garden Culture from which we come. Just as there are a few among the melaninated breeds of

CHAPTER EIGHT: SACRED ANCESTRAL PROPHECY

mankind. As for the mass majority of the suntanned Children who have adopted, integrated and assimilated into becoming cold-blooded disciples and followers of the death-consuming culture, it is clear that they have taken flight far away from their ancestral spirit presence and would rather fight than switch into anything other than paleness.

We are very clear that no racist ideology shall stand up in the long run. We are also very clear that there must be a true divine melting forward into the essence of the most supreme ancestral spirit presence of the Divine Children of the Sun and the Sacred Garden Culture from which we come. Therefore, there is absolutely no room for the hunting and herding culture that masterminded animal husbandry. The hunting and herding culture was produced by a mutated and degenerated breed of mankind, a vicious and cunning predator who seeks, searches and destroys as a way of life.

The technology and current developments in telecommunications are coming forward to assist the communication elements of the Children of the Sun in order to provide access to the Holistic Living Truth upon the seen. The mechanisms and tools reflect the innovation and expression of that Most Supreme Essence of Life and Supreme Love. However, the signals and ideas that are sparked from the life energy are immediately translated through the lost and astray pale state of mind. While the tools can be used for wholesome benefit or harm, the manifestations within the death-consuming culture would be to serve the interests of the disciples and followers of the energy that is opposite of Supreme Love and the Essence of Life.

FULFILLING THE SACRED ANCESTRAL PROPHECY OF THE TRIPLE NINE: UNVEILING THE PROPHETIC 2012 MELTDOWN OF THE LOST AND ASTRAY PALE STATE OF MIND

Every mechanism and machine that would manifest, the opposite energy would adapt the technology to serve the vibrations and sensations of the death consumption culture.

Mind pollution keeps the toxic vibrations of lust, lies, illusions, confusion, death and deadly destruction as the major contamination within the toxic parallel, perpetuating the lost and astray pale state of mind. And there is definitely money to be made by catering to the lowest and most wretched appetites of the death-consuming culture. As a matter of fact, mega-corporations maintain their economic edge by stimulating and satisfying toxic consumption and creating a ever-increasing target audience of addicted, mesmerized and loyal consumers.

> Electronics giant Sony has sparked a major row over animal cruelty and the ethics of the computer industry by using a freshly slaughtered goat to promote a violent video game.
>
> The corpse of the decapitated animal was the centrepiece of a party to celebrate the launch of the God Of War II game for the company's PlayStation 2 console. Guests at the event were even invited to reach inside the goat's still-warm carcass to eat offal from its stomach.
>
> Critics condemned the entertainment giant, which produces scores of Hollywood blockbusters each year, for its "blood lust" and said the grotesque "sacrifice" highlighted increasing concerns over the content of video games and the lengths to which the industry will go to exploit youngsters. At the event, guests competed to see who could eat the most offal procured

CHAPTER EIGHT: SACRED ANCESTRAL PROPHECY

elsewhere and intended to resemble the goat's intestines from its stomach....

The article, based on a Sony Press release, shows more vivid pictures from the event under headlines such as Topless Girls! and Flesh Eating! It asks readers how far they would go to get hold of Sony's next-generation console, the PlayStation 3.

"How about eating still warm intestines uncoiled from the carcass of a freshly slaughtered goat? At the party to celebrate God Of War II's European release, members of the Press were invited to do just that . . ."

...Sony describes it as "an adult-rated, fast-paced bloodbath and enormous fun to boot", adding that it is "bigger, better and as brutal as ever". One reviewer said the title featured "the most brutal, visceral combat of any action game".

...Sony, based in Japan and run by Welshman Sir Howard Stringer, is one of the largest media organisations in the world, boasting global revenues of £40billion from electronics, video games, music, television programmes and feature films including Spider-Man 3 and Casino Royale.

It is regarded, along with Coca-Cola, Nike and Mercedes-Benz, as one of the world's most valuable brands.

Slaughter: Horror at Sony's depraved promotion stunt with decapitated goat, last updated at 17:43 01 May 2007
http://www.dailymail.co.uk/news/article-451414/Slaughter-Horror-Sonys-depraved-promotion-stunt-decapitated-goat.html

As a matter of fact, those who are the powerbrokers, disciples and followers of the opposite energy will indeed pollute, contaminate, destabilize, rape and defile any and all living things, as well as the Earth herself, for the lust of money, power and domination. While physical destruction and all manner of wicked, foul and wretched deeds have been, and will continue to be, enacted upon the seen by the disciples and followers of the opposite energy, the consistent and tenacious movement of the Most Supreme Unseen Essence of Life and Supreme Love has been at work. This unseen movement is hidden from the greedy, lustful and vicious plots of the capitalizing hunters and herders who stalk the planet as the power brokers of the death-consuming culture.

Stem Cells

Many years of detailed study of the biology of mouse stem cells led to the discovery, in 1998, of how to isolate stem cells from human embryos and grow the cells in the laboratory. These are called human embryonic stem cells. The embryos used in these studies were created for infertility purposes through in vitro fertilization procedures and when they were no longer needed for that purpose, they were donated for research with the informed consent of the donor.

.... In the 3- to 5-day-old embryo, called a blastocyst, stem cells in developing tissues give rise to the multiple specialized cell types that make up the heart, lung, skin, and other tissues. In some adult tissues, such as bone marrow, muscle, and brain, discrete populations of adult stem cells generate replacements for cells that are lost through normal wear and tear, injury, or disease. It has been hypothesized by scientists that stem cells may, at some point in the future, become the basis for treating diseases such as Parkinson's disease, diabetes, and heart disease.

...As scientists learn more about stem cells, it may become possible to use the cells not just in cell-based

CHAPTER EIGHT: SACRED ANCESTRAL PROPHECY

> therapies, but also for screening new drugs and toxins and understanding birth defects.
> *Stem Cell Information,* The National Institutes of Health Resource for stem cell research, http://stemcells.nih.gov/info/basics/

Within the toxic parallel, there is no stopping the momentum of toxic consumption that has been festering since the coming of the opposite energy. The disciples and followers of the death-consuming culture have only become more reactionary, more fanatical and more toxic in their thinking and reasoning as the degeneration and depletion continues mentally, physically and spiritually. And instead of addressing whole life solutions, the powerbrokers and money brokers continue to search within the contaminated intellect of the pale lost and astray state of mind to unravel the secrets of life and find a way to secure their existence in the midst of a solarized global shift. Therefore, stem cell research, cloning, genetic engineering, melanin research and so forth are attempts to unlock the hidden codes of life, solve the unseen mysteries, and dominate life itself. This opposite energy has used every way and means to penetrate the Most Supreme Seen and Unseen Essence of Life and Supreme Love, and still there is no entry. There will never be an entry into the divine parallel of whole life energy unless one enters through divine spirit consciousness, and that is an impossible act for any of Man, He and She, who maintain acts of toxic mental, physical and spiritual consumption. Nevertheless, even those scientific research projects that are presented in such charitable and benevolent terms end up being another instrument to serve the greedy, selfish and controlling schemes of the masters and grand masters of

FULFILLING THE SACRED ANCESTRAL PROPHECY OF THE TRIPLE NINE: UNVEILING THE PROPHETIC 2012 MELTDOWN OF THE LOST AND ASTRAY PALE STATE OF MIND

deceit who sit at the helm of the death-consuming culture.

Even though it is not acknowledged, the disciples and followers of this opposite energy are preparing for the hell and damnation, and doom and gloom that is definitely scheduled to come very soon. And the sensationalists and alarmists are busy wondering if this apocalypse syndrome will be televised during prime time or hyped as the latest blockbuster movie or whether it will be featured after the late night news. In fact, it is virtually unimaginable that such an insidious mentality could be so widespread even during the final days and times of the lost and astray pale state of mind.

The powerbrokers and money brokers and stockbrokers are rewarded well within the toxic parallel, and their number-one priority is to maintain the death-consuming culture at all costs. Regardless of the national identity; regardless of the social economic, political or religious structure; there is a globalized pale mentality that is shared by all those who profit most from the systems, structures, production, manufacturing, and consumption patterns of the death-consuming culture. The same vibrations of domination, conquest, enslavement, exploitation and subjugation that emerged in those first mutated and degenerated pale breeds who survived the deep-freeze ordeals of the white blight continue today as a modern inheritance within a power base of deceit. Natural resources have been, and continue to be, exploited; suntanned populations have been, and continue to be, systematically subjugated, exterminated and exploited. The capital gains from these

CHAPTER EIGHT: SACRED ANCESTRAL PROPHECY

celebrated exploits have been, and continue to be, greedily horded from generation to generation within the pale mentality of a depleted and toxic energy that is opposite of Supreme Love and the Essence of Life.

And business as usual continues to fuel global issues of depletion and deterioration. Big business and the corporate entities of the death-consuming culture seem to have taken on a life of their own, within an economy based on the consumption of depleted and devitalized energy. Issues such as global warming, earth-shift changes, new-age consciousness, population control, global conflict and war, energy crisis and food production loom large on the radar of concerns. And in the midst of social issues at large, the question would remain, "Would Man, He and She, continue to follow the direction of those lost and astray pale Children who mutated and degenerated into cold-blooded predators?"

>...Scientists have monitored sea ice conditions for about 50 years with the help of satellites. Changes in the past decade have been alarming to climate researchers and oceanographers...
>
> "It is the second lowest on record. ... If anything, it is reinforcing the long-term trend. We are still losing the ice cover at a rate of 10 percent per decade now, and that is quite an increase from five years ago," Meier said. "We are still heading toward an ice cover that is going to melt completely in the summertime in the Arctic."
>
> Artic ice helps regulate and temper the climate in many other parts of the world. The less ice there is, the more dramatic the impact. Huge sheets of ice reflect solar radiation, keeping our planet cool. When that ice melts, huge expanses of darker, open ocean water absorb the heat instead, warming things up.

FULFILLING THE SACRED ANCESTRAL PROPHECY OF THE TRIPLE NINE: UNVEILING THE PROPHETIC 2012 MELTDOWN OF THE LOST AND ASTRAY PALE STATE OF MIND

Although few humans live in the Arctic, the disappearance of this ice cover can have effects far beyond the few residents and the wildlife of this harsh region. Ice cover loss can influence winds and precipitation on other continents, possibly leading to less rain in the western United States and creating more in Europe.

"That warming is going to spread to the lower latitudes, to the United States, and it's going to affect storm systems and storm tracks, the jet stream; that's going to affect crops and all sorts of things," Meier predicted.

...The best known consequence of disappearing sea ice in the Arctic is the loss of the polar bear habitat. "The Arctic sea ice melt is a disaster for the polar bears," according to Kassie Siegel, staff attorney for the Center for Biological Diversity. "They are dependent on the Arctic sea ice for all of their essential behaviors, and as the ice melts and global warming transforms the Arctic, polar bears are starving, drowning, even resorting to cannibalism because they don't have access to their usual food sources."

Scientists have noticed increasing reports of starving Arctic polar bears attacking and feeding on one another in recent years. In one documented 2004 incident in northern Alaska, a male bear broke into a female's den and killed her.

In May, the U.S. Department of Interior listed the polar bear as a "threatened" species under the Endangered Species Act. In a news release, U.S. Interior Secretary Dirk Kempthorne stated, "loss of sea ice threatens and will likely continue to threaten polar bear habitat. This loss of habitat puts polar bears at risk of becoming endangered in the foreseeable future, the standard established by the ESA for designating a threatened species."

CHAPTER EIGHT: SACRED ANCESTRAL PROPHECY

> What is the future for Arctic sea ice? Some scientists believe that in just five years, the Arctic may be ice-free during the summer.
>
> "The Arctic is kind of the early warning system of the climate," Meier said. "It is the canary in the coal mine, and the canary is definitely in trouble."
>
> *Polar bears resort to cannibalism as Arctic ice shrinks,* December 5, 2008, CNN.com

The adverse effects that are now being caused by the changing Artic environment provide insight into what did occur with the Children of the Sun who became lost and astray in the northern regions of the planet during the deep freeze of the most recent ice age periods. We can comprehend that the polar bear adapted to its polar environment, mutating and degenerating from its former presence as the herbivorous solarized brown bear during freezing periods within the Artic regions. The polar bear survived in the ice-cold environment by becoming a pale reflection of the snow and ice, becoming a hunter of seals and transitioning to a death-consuming state of being. As the ice continues to melt, the Artic seals are swimming away, leaving the polar bear to either face starvation or become a cannibal to survive. We have historical accounts of this exact same desperate hunt for food that caused the lost and astray Children of the Sun to become flesh-eating scavengers, predators and cannibals during the coming of the ice in the white-blight ordeal of the deep freeze.

> The study reviewed three examples of polar bears preying on each other from January to April 2004 north of Alaska and western Canada, including the first-ever reported killing of a female in a den shortly after it gave birth.

FULFILLING THE SACRED ANCESTRAL PROPHECY OF THE TRIPLE NINE: UNVEILING THE PROPHETIC 2012 MELTDOWN OF THE LOST AND ASTRAY PALE STATE OF MIND

Polar bears feed primarily on ringed seals and use sea ice for feeding, mating and giving birth...

Environmentalists contend shrinking polar ice due to global warming may lead to the disappearance of polar bears before the end of the century.

The Center for Biological Diversity of Joshua Tree, Calif., in February 2005 petitioned the federal government to list polar bears as threatened under the federal Endangered Species Act.

Cannibalism demonstrates the effect on bears, said Kassie Siegal, lead author of the petition. "It's very important new information," she said. "It shows in a really graphic way how severe the problem of global warming is for polar bears."

Deborah Williams of Alaska Conservation Solutions, a group aimed at pursuing solutions for climate change, said the study represents the "bloody fingerprints" of global warming.

"This is not a Coca-Cola commercial," she said, referring to animated polar bears used in advertising for the soft drink giant. "This represents the brutal downside of global warming."

...Researchers discovered the first kill in January 2004. A male bear had pounced on a den, killed a female and dragged it 245 feet away, where it ate part of the carcass. Females are about half the size of males.

"In the face of the den's outer wall were deep impressions of where the predatory bear had pounded its forepaws to collapse the den roof, just as polar bears collapse the snow over ringed seal lairs," the paper said.

"From the tracks, it appeared that the predatory bear broke through the roof of the den, held the female in place while inflicting multiple bites to the head and

CHAPTER EIGHT: SACRED ANCESTRAL PROPHECY

neck. When the den collapsed, two cubs were buried, and suffocated, in the snow rubble."

In April 2004, while following bear footprints on sea ice near Herschel Island, Yukon Territory, scientists discovered the partially eaten carcass of an adult female. Footprints indicated it had been with a cub.

The male did not follow the cub, indicating it had killed for food instead of breeding.

A few days later, Canadian researchers found the remains of a yearling that had been stalked and killed by a predatory bear, the scientists said.

CBS News Anchorage Alaska
http://www.cbsnews.com/stories/2006/06/13/ap/tech/

The polar bear is now being forced to adapt as its polar habitat warms in the penetrating heat of solarized radiation. And with its pale polarized coloration, the polar bear faces additional hardships in the growing heat. The best option for the polar bear, as a breed, is to transition into the genetic presence of its origin as a herbivorous brown bear through natural selection and mating. In any event, the polar existence of this polar bear, as it has been known, is definitely ending. The food source is disappearing, and the polar bear is becoming a cannibal. Once the hostile aggression and mental conditioning of cannibalistic behaviors become dominant, extinction is inevitable. Once the polar bear has become conditioned to killing other bears, what would happen if the polar bear then attempted to migrate away from its ice-cold environment? Well, this pale cold-blooded predator would prey on others of its kind or any other victim of prey that it is capable of hunting down, trapping and consuming.

FULFILLING THE SACRED ANCESTRAL PROPHECY OF THE TRIPLE NINE: UNVEILING THE PROPHETIC 2012 MELTDOWN OF THE LOST AND ASTRAY PALE STATE OF MIND

This scenario should provide a clear-cut comprehension of what happened when those lost and astray pale Children mutated and degenerated in the deep freeze. It should be clear that these lost and astray pale Children turned the entire life population of the planet into their victim of prey. And as the ice began to melt, the vicious nomadic tribes of this pale predatorial breed of mankind rode the high waters and inflicted hell upon the Children of the Sun and the Sacred Garden Culture from which we come. It should also be clear that the consumption patterns during those freezing days when animal carcass was hard to come by also included the pale Children of the Caucasoid stock indeed consuming of each other.

It must also be comprehended that this cannibalistic way of life would be carried with the mutated and degenerated breeds as they invaded the Sacred Garden Culture of the Divine Children of the Sun. Through their various ways and means of indulging in toxic consumption, these lost and astray pale Children would spread cold and pale attitudes and behaviors through their various belief systems and the forces of sex and violence, war and crime that they used to pollute every land of the Children of the Sun with the golden tan. Unlike the polar bear, the pale Children of that deep-freeze experience have amassed enough comprehension to survive just a little bit longer while steeped knee-deep in paleness. However, they are very well aware that it is just a matter of time until hell and damnation, doom and gloom will seal the fate of the pale mentality upon the earth. And how will the lost and astray pale Children born and bred

CHAPTER EIGHT: SACRED ANCESTRAL PROPHECY

from the opposite energy begin to deal with the solarized state of being as it is now manifesting again upon the planet?

Chapter 8 Innerlude:
Change of Tide

Song 8 from "Supernatural Healing Serum: Dose Two," Kwatamani musical CD release, 2006

<u>Royal Priestess vocals:</u>
Can you feel the movement in the air?
If you don't focus, you won't know it's there
Nowhere to run, nowhere to hide
Changing tide, changing tide
What is seen will give you a clue
The death-consumption culture is just about through
The final moments of the death-consumption ride
Will be washed away in the changing tide
Changing, changing, changing tide
Changing, changing, changing tide
Changing, changing, changing tide

When you look upon the shore
You'll see something that you didn't see before
From the deep darkness of the Most Supreme Unseen
Divine intervention, divine intervention
is the changing tide I mean
Changing, changing, changing tide
Changing tide
Changing, changing, changing tide

<u>High Priest vocals:</u>
Hurricane, earthquake, tornadoes and desert storm
Know for a fact that you have been warned
Mental, physical sickness and disease

FULFILLING THE SACRED ANCESTRAL PROPHECY OF THE TRIPLE NINE: UNVEILING THE PROPHETIC 2012 MELTDOWN OF THE LOST AND ASTRAY PALE STATE OF MIND

Spirit ripped and torn
Cartoons doomed the baby boom
Generation next, hooked on porn
And out of this, the crack baby would be born
It's starting to get hot upon the earth
And the polar bear is starting to bite the dirt
And the seals want to live, swimming away quickly
so they don't be killed
It is a necessity that the Children of the Sun
get with this changing tide
And the I in I have come to escort you
through this most exposing ride
So vibe with the inner essence
beyond the deceptive conclusion
Of the fantasies, delusions and illusions
of the deep-freeze vibe
Pulsate with the earth, wind, rain and sun
And understand the holistic living truth
about the great flood
Know and understand that ignoring this change of tide
has already caused a man-beast
to leave a blood-stained trail
Throughout the rich and fertile soil
of the sacred garden culture mud
Too, too many suntanned Children
have already had to grin and bear
Because all things are fair in war and love
among the blue bloods
And too many suntanned Children
have already been given too much hell
By the Children who were semi pale

CHAPTER 8 INNERLUDE: CHANGING TIDE

who swept their ancestry under the rug
After they first appeared after the flood
Remember the ice-cold, deep-freeze breed
a vibration that contradicts the divine growth of a seed
Remember that the first concept of hell
began in the ice-cold deep freeze
where the Children of the Sun first turned pale
Remember the vicious and deadly blight
Remember the fear and fright
Remember how the frost bite
Remember the lost and astray mind
went spiritually deaf, dumb and blind
Ignoring the vital change of tide sign
Remember the connection, remember the connection
The death consumption culture and
the ice-cold, deep-freeze infection
Remember that the triple six is the energy
That is opposite of the triple nine
But what we're talking about here
is resurrecting from the ice-cold
deep-freeze state of mind
There's no doubt that there's a mark of the beast
and that the vicious, cold-blooded and heartless vibration
has been released
The scent of the beast is marked
by the funk and the stench of a plot and scheme
of a cold-blooded vibration like a Willie Lynch
The mark of the beast has been alive and well
ever since it first came out of the ice-cold, deep-freeze
where the Children of the Sun turned pale
And no matter how many times
you traced this bloodstained trail

FULFILLING THE SACRED ANCESTRAL PROPHECY OF THE TRIPLE NINE: UNVEILING THE PROPHETIC 2012 MELTDOWN OF THE LOST AND ASTRAY PALE STATE OF MIND

it would lead you deep into the pits of hell
where the Children of the Sun turned pale
Chain reaction, mass corruption, lust, lies, illusions,
confusion, death and deadly destruction
Kind of remind you of the story of Satan
and the ways and the means of the Children of the Sun
with the golden tan
And as the story goes, the devil descended from hell,
worshipping a war god who was pale
And as the devil descended
down upon the fertile earthly land
it would rape, murder, steal and take
and give birth to the energy of Satan
And lust, lies, illusions, confusion
death and deadly destruction
would be planted in every land
of the Children of the Sun with the golden tan
And although the Children of the Sun with the golden tan
were the original host of every Man, He and She
The Children of the Sun would cease
to consume of the fruits of the tree
Disconnecting themselves
from the whole life ancestral divinity
And so as the offsprings and the friends and the kin begin
to consume of the flesh and the blood
and the bones and skin
the devil would have successfully given birth
to the Satanic Jinn
The Children of the Sun who had never honored sin
would now begin to waver and bend
As the glory of the Sacred Garden Culture

CHAPTER 8 INNERLUDE: CHANGING TIDE

would begin to come to an end
The death consumption culture would be spread
among He and She, friend and kin
as the ice-cold, deep-freeze mentality
would be ushered in
And so, regardless of the color of their skin, in essence,
the deep-freeze mentality would be the beast of sin
The energy of one's consumption would set the course
and would be the breeding force
of the energy of the beast of sin within
And the death consumption culture
would bring many pains to the seen
And Man, He and She, would holler and scream
And divine intervention, divine intervention
and a change of tide, a change of tide would arrive
This change of tide begin when the masters
and the grand masters of deceit
begin to distort the holistic living truth
and replace it with the energy of the beast of sin
In fact, this change of tide begin exactly when
the Children of the Sun begin to get off track
It was late, in fact, by the time the Children of the Sun
began to encounter the trans-Saharan
and trans-Atlantic slave trade
It was already late by the time the Black Untouchables
encountered the Aryan, Hindu wave
It was already late by the time the Southern Africans
encountered the Boers
turning the sacred suntanned Children into whores
It was late by the time the rest of Africa
encountered the European, colonial plan
distorting and polluting the original man

FULFILLING THE SACRED ANCESTRAL PROPHECY OF THE TRIPLE NINE: UNVEILING THE PROPHETIC 2012 MELTDOWN OF THE LOST AND ASTRAY PALE STATE OF MIND

It was late by the time Egypt and Sudan
and the rest of the solarized land
had encountered the Semite clan
It was already late by the time
the Australian aborigines encountered their fate
with the Caucasian trait
It was too, too late for the Taino
by the time they encountered Christopher Columbus
and his conquistador manifesto
It would be too late by the time the Children of the Sun
learned to crave the ways and the means
of the Children who mutated in the caves
By this time, too many would seek out the war god
and the Crusades and the Holy Wars
in order for their soul to be saved
Although there would be a change of tide
the Children of the Sun would position themselves to ride
the tides of lies
And although this story is old and has already been told
it seems that this ice-cold, deep-freeze mentality
and this death-consumption culture
has now really begin an ice-cold roll
And no matter how many times you trace
the origin of this bloodstained trail
the stench and the smell
would lead you deep
into the vicious and the deadly and the cold vibration
of the ice-cold, deep-freeze mentality
where the Children of the Sun turned pale
And in the midst of the toxic and vicious
and cold-blooded vibe

CHAPTER 8 INNERLUDE: CHANGING TIDE

has come a glorious change of tide
And this change of tide
has not come a minute to soon
as the lost and astray mind
prepare themselves for doom and gloom
Hurricane, tornadoes, earthquakes and desert storm
Know for a fact that you have been warned
Mental, physical sickness and disease
causing your spirit to be ripped and torn
Cartoons doomed the baby boom
And the generation next hooked on porn
And out of this, a crack baby would be born
It's starting to get hot upon the earth
And the toxic fumes cause harm and hurt
And the water and the air and the things and stuff
become very confused
And it must be the stuff that you use
And it would be the season
for divine spirit conscious reason
If the Children of the Sun truly wanted to heal
they would move away
from the attitudes and the behaviors of the killing field
And move into a divine spirit consciousness ordeal
Because this divine intervention
and this change of tide is for real

Chapter Nine:
The Changing of the Guard

Chapter 9 Prelude:
Lies in Disguise

Song 9 from "12th Hour Prophecy: The Pale Curse and the Solarized Energy Shift," Kwatamani CD release, 2008

<u>Royal Priestess vocals:</u>
Time to recognize the lies that began in division
isolation, separation, frustration
frustration, disconnection from the whole
As the essence of divine oneness unfolds

<u>High Priest vocals:</u>
As it is during these times, the Children divine
would have much to retrieve in order to relieve
themselves from the massive lies and deceptions
they had come to believe
While being entrapped within the cobwebs of hell
That those of the pale, opposite energy
had masterfully weaved
And being of the former and following
degenerated and spiritless leadership of the latter
Would cause one to huff and puff and bluff
and grow bigger and fatter
much chitter and chatter
Striking with the deadly force of a mamba
a viper or a puff adder
Although all of Man, He and She
had emerged from a Love Supreme
of the Most Supreme ancestral presence, seen and
unseen, honoring of earth, wind, rain and sun
whole and clean
Those of that blood-spilling, pale opposite energy would
emerge upon the scene

FULFILLING THE SACRED ANCESTRAL PROPHECY OF THE TRIPLE NINE: UNVEILING THE PROPHETIC 2012 MELTDOWN OF THE LOST AND ASTRAY PALE STATE OF MIND

cold-blooded, pale and unclean
You see, that cold and pale opposite energy
did indeed succeed
to enslave, mutate, degenerate the seed
that would germinate into a pale breed
You see, that cold and pale opposite energy
was of nothingness, of lifeless matter
feasting off the essence of life
Utilizing fantasies, illusions, delusions to entice
one to idolize and worship the energies opposite of life
And so a death culture would be born
and out of that would manifest a beast of scorn
And the ancestral essence of Man, He and She
would be ripped, mangled and torn
And a spiritless breed would be born
from the ejaculation of this pale seed
And they would go forward
to multiply a semi-pale breed
Born of the invasions, murder, rape, theft and enslavement
And the victims of this cold, invasive, pale mentality
would consume of the content of this pale opposite energy
And this would cause the former
to be enslaved by the latter by decree
And the pale Children who had originally
fell to the cold-blooded, opposite energies of hell
would deify and would ritualize
the pale-male-war-god deity
A jealous god of vengeance, war and wrath
the conceptual reality of this opposite energy

CHAPTER 9 PRELUDE: LIES IN DISGUISE

And they would push this deity
upon the Children of the Sun who were forced to
self-deny
And even worse
their dark skin was said to be a curse
ordained by the god of the pale Children
with a blood thirst
And so the suntanned Children
would be forced to submit
to the deception and the lie
of the pale-male-war-god cry or die
And the rituals and the rites of this raping
and murdering, and enslaving pale plight
would produce semi Semites and Hittites
and Creoles and mestizos
And dark whites and light brights
and would turn Melanesians into Polynesians
dividing to conquer to maintain non-cohesion
Using the lightness of skin to maintain pale allegiance

Royal Priestess vocals:
Disconnected from the Most Supreme Unseen
There is no Love Supreme
Divide and conquer
To break down self-esteem

High Priest vocals:
From the earliest days of the cold-blooded, pale craze
From the deep-freeze pits of the Caucasus cave
Melting down into the regions of the steppes
and the secret well-kept
is that many dark and lovely civilizations
would continue to fall
And to avoid this mishap

FULFILLING THE SACRED ANCESTRAL PROPHECY OF THE TRIPLE NINE: UNVEILING THE PROPHETIC 2012 MELTDOWN OF THE LOST AND ASTRAY PALE STATE OF MIND

the dark and lovely Children would build a wall
But the raping rage and the murder, raid and invades
had already seeded a new breed of color-coded kin
And the raping raids and invasions
by the great, great grandfathers
of the Huns and the Genghis Khans cold-blooded kin
would continue as if it had no end
And the dark and lovely Asiatic He and She of Man
would continue to be raided and raped and invaded
and used for all reasons
And what was sent around
is exactly what would come back around
during this twelfth-hour-prophesied show down
From the north to the south, the east versus the west
and it would be a hell of a contest
And the Ta and the Tat would look upon this
and the ancestors would not be pleased
Because those of this cold pale mentality would concede
nothing without this struggle
In fact, there would be nothing less than lust, lies
illusions, confusion, death and deadly destruction
that this opposite energy would concede
So the hell and damnation of doom and gloom
would continue to fester and seed
And the sacred ancestral soothsayers had come and gone
and come again
and the Za and the Xia and the Olmeks had much to
reveal and the Children of the Sun had much to retrieve
And the Mayan calendar would make note of this
And as the bottom would begin to fall out
Of the western economic base

CHAPTER 9 PRELUDE: LIES IN DISGUISE

Fright and fear would cause the Mayan calendar
to be tracked and traced
And although the pale ones were cunning
sly, slick and wicked and quick
They could not see Supreme Truth
through those pale deceptions of their eyes
And so the supreme truth of this sacred ancestral
prophecy they could not hide
And so in the midst of a cover up
a quick fix, a new deal
they could not find a red or blue pill to cure this ill
And in the midst of all of this and that going on
The sacred ancestors and the essence of the earth
Wind, rain and sun would put the pale ones on trial
And they were guilty as hell
yet they would declare themselves innocent
with that hellish, palish smile
And the sun would rise and as the ice would begin to
melt, Mother Nature would warm with tears in her eyes
And the wind and the rain would share the Earth's pains
And the Most Supreme Unseen would sympathize
and ordain the coming of a sacred one
to expose the deceptions and the lies
of the pale-male-war-god cry
And the earth, wind, rain and sun would unify
with a spiritual surge to detox and purge
this cold, pale opposite energy
And as it was again in the Unseen
so it would come to be in the Seen
during this twelfth hour prophecy

Chapter Nine:
The Changing of the Guard

Recycling and Reciprocation

The sacred ancestral spirit presence of the Divine Children of the Sun moves within the Supreme Laws of whole life energy, which maintains the divine order of the universe of Man, He and She. The recycling and reciprocating nature of whole life energy is key within the Most Supreme Seen and Unseen Essence of Life and Supreme Love. Every cycle of life upon the seen bears this pattern of a recycling and reciprocating nature. The planting of a seed which bears the root which grows into the tree that bears the fruit that bears the seed which will reproduce the essence of that tree again is one expression of this circle of life that goes around and comes back around from the unseen to the seen, earthly bound. For example, that sweet and juicy mango that one may enjoy today contains the same essence of the mango as it has been within its own existence since its first ancestral presence upon the earth. And so long as all of the necessary elements and environmental factors are present, that mango tree will continue to reproduce itself time and time again. And that ancient mango tree that was enjoyed by ourselves as the Divine Children of the Sun did not die and go to some mango heaven to be permanently frozen and stagnant within some pale heavenly bliss on the right-hand side of the throne of some pale-male-war-god deity. That ancient mango tree continues to live today within every mango tree growing and bearing fruit and being divinely and innately true to the essence of being a mango.

Perhaps, one may feel that as long as one does not return to the seen with the exact same name, and the exact same physical features, profile and memories, then one will no longer exist as one's self. This feeling is produced by the thoughts and reasoning of a lost and astray pale state of mind that can only claim a physical existence within the personality traits, body features and limited experiences of a single lifetime. Once this single lifetime ends, then what has come to be called the ego is finished, slipping back into the nothingness that is the opposite energy. No sense of a continuing presence within the Most Supreme Seen and Unseen Essence of Life and Supreme Love, no connection to one's sacred ancestral spirit presence. Nothing. This is why individuals who consume of the opposite energy are haunted by a vague and empty feeling that they will truly die. Simply put, the energy that is opposite of Supreme Love and the Essence of Life is the nothingness of a lifeless state of being, or as many refer to it – death.

In fact, this single-life vibration is fortified by the selfish greed that feeds the I-me-my-mine syndrome. Oftentimes, one can hear an individual claiming and declaring that "my spirit told me this" or "my mind made me do that" with the same sense of possession that really says that the individual is deep within the toxic parallel of a separated and disconnected state of being. In these cases, the physical identity actually claims the focus of the individual, and a physical focus means that the individual has no real sense of their unseen essence.

CHAPTER NINE: THE CHANGING OF THE GUARD

Thus, without the ability to emerge into a divine spirit conscious state of being where the collective mass of one's mental and physical presence is a reflection of sacred ancestral spirit presence, one is left to claim a superficial, artificial and deceptive identity within the tags and labels of the opposite energy. As a result of one's indulgence and association with the toxic parallel of the death culture, one truly has no comprehension of whole life presence. And one's lifetime becomes the private, personal possession of a pale state of mind that becomes very stubborn, spoiled and demanding when it can not have its way. Therefore, the body and the brain and the spirit are actually dominated and controlled by the vibrations and sensations of the opposite energy that speaks through the thoughts and reasoning of an insanely jealous, greedy, vengeful and violent state of mind. As we have said, the single-life concept is unquestionably of the toxic parallel and shows no regard for the glory of earth, wind, rain and sun; any other living thing, or the Most Supreme Seen and Unseen Essence of Life and Supreme Love.

Let us make it clear that as one goes through the toxic cycle provided by the opposite energy, one is pulled off track and becomes derailed into the nothingness of a cycle that projects an imitation and a deception of the cycle of life. Instead of the circular movement of life, one encounters a straight flat line, a linear extension of time that goes from a beginning to a definite end. As one travels this timeline within the toxic parallel, one eventually comes to the end of the line where one falls off into the bottomless pit of nothingness. However, the mental programs of the lost and astray pale state of mind include the projections of a heaven and a hell to keep the manipulations of the opposite energy going strong. The story goes that if one has lived a good and righteous life within the death-consuming culture one can expect to go to heaven to sit on the right-hand side of one's lord. Of course, one has to go through the rituals of being saved and becoming a loyal disciple and follower of the pale-male-war-god deity of one's choice. And, of course, there are financial dues to be paid and other gestures of loyalty to be enacted within the death-consuming culture. And if one performs within the rules of the death-consuming culture, one then receives a special ticket to enter the pearly gates of this cold and pale heavenly bliss within the toxic parallel. If one rebels against these particular belief systems and instead becomes a renegade, a lawless disciple and follower of the opposite energy, one will be condemned to hell to burn in the fiery pits of the same toxic parallel. These fantasies are induced to keep the consumers of the opposite energy pacified and lulled into a frozen state of numbness as they continue to be depleted, drained and controlled.

Let us continue this forward movement and just maybe a Sacred Few will reach the safety zone of divine clarity through divine spirit consciousness. Although this straight-line thinking or flat-world mentality is projected to be the gospel of truth by those who consume of the death culture, this limited frame of reference does not even begin to approach divine reality. In truth and reality, the host who has been absorbed within the toxic parallel actually disappears into the nothingness of the depleted and unwhole energy that he or she consumed

CHAPTER NINE: THE CHANGING OF THE GUARD

and manifested while within the body of flesh and mind of thought.

What the I in I am saying is that the cycle of life continues to exist, except that the separated and disconnected spirit presence becomes entrapped in the toxic parallel. The concepts of heaven and hell are pale projections that have formed within the lost and astray pale state of mind in a weak and feeble attempt to reason with what actually happens to that entrapped life presence. Individuals cannot help but worry and wonder about what happens when the physical body is finished. When one leaves the seen, one can only be absorbed into the unseen toxic vibrations and sensations that one has consumed. And within this vicious cycle of toxic consumption, all that one manifests upon the seen becomes one's energy pathway to emerge again. Lust, lies, illusions, confusion, death and deadly destruction; and the manifestation of sex and violence, war and crime are glorified and sugar-coated by the fantasies, illusions, delusions and dreams that the lost and astray pale state of mind conjures up as part of its false, fake and pretentious existence in the body of flesh and mind of thought. The I in I am sure that if the lost and astray Children of the Sun—be they blonde or bald or natty, natty dread, regardless of the color of their skin—comprehended that the toxic attitudes, behaviors and beliefs that they consume await them nine times worse once they leave the seen, there would be a different kind of movement going on.

As a result of not having full comprehension, one can spend an entire lifetime preparing and focusing on that day when one will meet one's maker. So many are

FULFILLING THE SACRED ANCESTRAL PROPHECY OF THE TRIPLE NINE: UNVEILING THE PROPHETIC 2012 MELTDOWN OF THE LOST AND ASTRAY PALE STATE OF MIND

unaware that their maker is the sum total of the energy that they have consumed, and the sum total of that energy is none other than the energy that is the opposite of Supreme Love and the Essence of Life. If this could be comprehended even a little bit, then one could better reason with the nature of the opposite energy. One could also better reason with why such concepts as "There is a thin line between love and hate" and "All is fair in love and war" are the full expressions of a pale-male-warlord deity that is, indeed, declared as a vengeful and jealous god while also being declared as a god of love.

Within the cycles of toxic consumption, the life presence of an individual becomes weaker and weaker each time that life presence attempts to emerge upon the seen. With increasing depletion and deterioration, that individual becomes so weak and feeble that they become totally possessed by that opposite energy. This is when the lost and astray pale state of mind really swells and bloats into the most hideous and gruesome forms of brutal, vicious, blood-thirsty and merciless kinds of personalities within the death-consuming culture. Without an infusion of whole life energy, it does not take long for a spirit presence to be completely drained and sucked into the nothingness of the toxic parallel, never again to be seen or unseen. So it is possible for a spirit to be depleted to the point of being completely extinguished.

We are not here to explain where the toxic parallel came from in the unseen or how it came to be. It is enough to comprehend that the toxic parallel does indeed exist and must be confronted because of the historical

CHAPTER NINE: THE CHANGING OF THE GUARD

acts that allowed this wretched, foul, toxic energy to seep into the whole life presence of Man, He and She. By now, individuals must call upon enough gut-level sense to begin reasoning with the events that are unfolding around them. One must examine the happenings of the past that have been documented, and even celebrated, within the death-consuming culture and begin to connect the dots of a very glaring pattern of lust, lies, illusions, confusion, death and deadly destruction. Violence and violation. Slaughter, rape, conquest, and enslavement. These toxic acts are not the exception to the rule within the toxic parallel; these toxic and foul acts are indeed the rule. They are the defining acts of the energy that is opposite of the Essence of Life and Supreme Love. And the entire toxic parallel is within a cycle of collapsing back into the nothingness of its origin. All those spirits who are entrapped within the sucking, draining pull of the toxic parallel, entangled in all those destructive and self-destructive vibrations and sensations that continue to fester and feed on themselves, will be committing spiritual suicide.

Spirits Who Choose To Live

We know that there are spirits who choose to live. The Divine Children of the Sun honor each and every cycle of life as part of a greater unseen process that regenerates within the Most Supreme Seen and Unseen Essence of Life and Supreme Love. Within the process of re-cycling whole life energy, the Divine Children of the Sun comprehend the importance of maintaining a wholesome and healthy relationship with earth, wind, rain and sun. As we were speaking of mangoes, in order

FULFILLING THE SACRED ANCESTRAL PROPHECY OF THE TRIPLE NINE: UNVEILING THE PROPHETIC 2012 MELTDOWN OF THE LOST AND ASTRAY PALE STATE OF MIND

for that glorious mango tree to fulfill its role in maintaining its own life presence, it produces leaves that fall to the ground to create organic fertilizer along with those mangoes that drop and decompose, returning to the soil. And this enriched soil becomes the compost bed to receive the seeds that will carry forward the essence of that ancestral mango tree once again upon the seen. To further the process, the mango tree absorbs the carbon dioxide of our breathing and recycles it by producing oxygen. In this way, the mango tree filters the air in a reciprocating exchange that supports the systems and cycles of earth, wind, rain and sun, again and again. In fact, the mango tree represents a grand essence contributing to the divine union of earth, wind, rain and sun.

The Divine Children of the Sun uphold the utmost care and respect for the earth, wind, rain and sun in recognition that we are intimately inter-connected within the cycles of life that sustain our presence, seen and unseen. And we, as the Divine Children of the Sun, embody that supreme Essence of Life and Supreme Love that unifies with earth, wind, rain and sun in the same manner as within the life cycle of the mango tree. Just a different expression of the same whole life energy.

For this reason, we must uphold, honor and respect the growth of a mango tree and every other tree in order to maintain the divine union of Man, He and She, with the fruits of the trees of life. In this way, Sister True's great, great grandchildren can enjoy mango sap with even more refined pleasure than Sister True did. And because of Brother Man's participation, his great, great

CHAPTER NINE: THE CHANGING OF THE GUARD

grandchildren can also experience a greater fullness of the ooh's and the aah's of a love supreme expressed within a matured encounter of the Divine Union of One. As both Sister True and Brother Man, too, continue to divinely evolve into a greater level and degree of divine spirit consciousness as Man, He and She, their ancestral return will be ensured through the forward multiplication of their offspring. The reciprocating nature of whole life energy is clearly seen again and again within the way of life that defines the Sacred Garden Culture from which we come.

Within the sacred body temple of Man, He and She, a sweet and juicy mango is received as a true communion of life and is consumed with holistic living satisfaction. From every sensory stimulation, the vivid colors and scents of ripeness, the soft and juicy sensation of the fruit as it drips into the mouth, and the sweet essence of that unique mango taste are all received with appreciation. From the process of ingestion to the river of life that goes around and comes around with every pulsing beat of the heart to deliver fuel and nutrients throughout the body and carry away waste, the entire body unifies with the essence of that mango. The body receives every possible energy of divine fuel, every energy of earth, wind, rain and sun that the raw and living fruits, vegetables, seeds and nuts offer; and transforms that whole life energy into a greater presence within divine spirit consciousness as Man, He and She. Even the waste matter is released again to the earth, to be recycled back into the soil as compost to fertilize and enrich the garden from which our food grows in order that we may continue to consume again from the cycle of life. Thus, a warm and loving

FULFILLING THE SACRED ANCESTRAL PROPHECY OF THE TRIPLE NINE: UNVEILING THE PROPHETIC 2012 MELTDOWN OF THE LOST AND ASTRAY PALE STATE OF MIND

sense of connection, respect and appreciation defines every relationship that is formulated within whole life energy, infusing every vibration and sensation that one experiences within the divine parallel.

The essence of life itself is reproduced with the divine union of Man, He and She, that brings forward a seed of life to reproduce itself again and again. The monthly cycle of ovulation is a reminder that the nature of life is renewal and birth as represented in the nurturing essence of the sacred ancestral mother spirit. And as day follows night, and then as night leads day back into night again with every rotation of the earth, it is well-comprehended that the movement of the sacred ancestral spirit presence of Man, He and She, is of the Most Supreme Unseen emerging upon the seen only to return again to the unseen in an eternal recycling process of whole life energy.

Every Man, He and She, carry some remnant of the ancestral DNA codes that were originally expressed within the radiant suntanned presence of the Divine Children of the Sun. However, the consumption of the opposite energy has caused a tremendous amount of mutation and degeneration of the DNA, leaving a genetic weakening and depletion of the whole life presence of Man, He and She. We should make note that we are using the concept of DNA here, because it is a more familiar term at this time. However, any physical factor of life, even the genetic codes that help to build cells, contain essential elements of whole life energy, which are brain, body and spirit. When one of these elements is missing, then an unwhole state of being develops and the

CHAPTER NINE: THE CHANGING OF THE GUARD

living presence is reduced to a physical existence with no connection to the Most Supreme Seen and Unseen Essence of Life and Supreme Love. Therefore, it is possible to tamper with DNA codes through genetic engineering, cloning and other types of lost and astray, pale scientific research and end up with spiritless beings. In fact, the mass majority of Man, He and She, have already become so depleted of life energy through toxic consumption that they are indeed populating a clone zone of the living dead, i.e. spiritless beings, who function on programmed and conditioned responses that have been encoded through severe mutation and degeneration.

This tendency to tamper with nature reflects the inability of the lost and astray pale state of mind to penetrate the inner reaches of divine spirit consciousness. Since the unwhole energy cannot penetrate the divine parallel, all that it can do is lurk in the outer zone, probing, poking, and seeking any means of entry. This opposite-energy approach reveals a complete disconnection from the life cycle of the seed.

Upon the seen, that opposite energy and its disciples and followers have been to able inflict terrorizing fright and fear and the pains and misery of violent force in order to dominate and control. Torture can be used to make someone confess or surrender information. Denying access to food and water can be used to make a person submit. In fact, the age-old cry of "Submit or die" is one of the clearest expressions of the vicious tactics and methods used by the disciples and followers of that opposite energy to gain domination and control. Please be reminded that the ultimate aim of the opposite energy is to dominate and control the Essence of Life. However,

FULFILLING THE SACRED ANCESTRAL PROPHECY OF THE TRIPLE NINE: UNVEILING THE PROPHETIC 2012 MELTDOWN OF THE LOST AND ASTRAY PALE STATE OF MIND

there is absolutely no way for the lost and astray pale state of mind to penetrate the Most Supreme Seen and Unseen Essence of Life and Supreme Love.

So, while the scientific tampering continues within the death-consuming culture, there are unseen consequences, adverse effects, mishaps and fatal errors that will occur as a result. And the genetic contamination that can occur from splicing sections of genetic coding and inserting them into completely different organisms, is beyond what the lost and astray pale state of mind can foresee. And the best that can be engineered is a terminator seed that does not even reproduce just to satisfy the greed and profit motive of corporate giants, seeking to dominate and control the seed market. In truth and reality, that terminator seed is indeed a reflection of that linear frame of thought that projects a closed timeline with a beginning and a definite ending, and that is all. This cold and pale outlook reflects the attitudes and beliefs of a disconnected state of being, a temporary and fleeting existence with no greater context of meaning and purpose than a single, brief moment in time. In order not to dwell on this bleak and barren existence, the cold and pale state of mind chooses to remain lost and astray in fantasies, illusions, delusions and dreams, entertaining and amusing itself to pass the time, indulging in as much ego gratification as possible and hording as much material stuff and things as one can afford even though it is readily acknowledged that "you can't take it with you."

CHAPTER NINE: THE CHANGING OF THE GUARD

More than a Cause

Maintaining the earthly lands, honoring the trees and the green plants and every living creature is more than a cause or a social agenda within the Sacred Garden Culture. A holistic living way of life far surpasses the various environmental issues that have formulated into a campaign of activism to save the planet. We are not talking about a political platform, nor do we have an alliance with the "green," eco-friendly initiatives that have popped up within the death-consuming culture to capitalize on new products and a new consumer trend. You see, the toxic parallel is notorious for its pale imitations of life and the superficial efforts of the disciples and followers of the death-consuming culture who have no sense of direction except to become more entrenched in the deceptions of the lost and astray pale state of mind. Regardless of the social climate, the major death industries continue business as usual with only minor adjustments made for those seeking an alternative, while ambitious new entrepreneurs seek to ride the waves of current trends, hoping to cash in on popular demand. So, while recycling and composting, and window-box herb gardens have gained mainstream attention, and bio-degradable products and natural fiber garments are marketed for the environmentally conscious, the death-consuming culture is still very much at the forefront of dictating general tastes, values, attitudes and behaviors.

Sustainable living, organic produce, and even raw and living foods are now the buzz with those who consider themselves to be of a more enlightened mindset. Nevertheless, their so-called conscious lifestyle choices

FULFILLING THE SACRED ANCESTRAL PROPHECY OF THE TRIPLE NINE: UNVEILING THE PROPHETIC 2012 MELTDOWN OF THE LOST AND ASTRAY PALE STATE OF MIND

simply reflect the diversity within the death-consuming culture where many dominating and controlling games of ego gratification lurk in many shapes, forms and fashions. Sometimes, it is not as easy to recognize how one can be progressive and affirmative in one part of one's daily affairs while remaining so cold, stale, pale and stagnant in another.

Notice how many of those exotic tropical fruits and nuts, everything from cacao to noni, and those lovely, vibrant, handmade natural-fiber creations are produced in the suntanned lands of rainforests and garden-culture remnants. And those who capitalize on the natural resources of these suntanned lands aggressively export raw materials to what they call the first world in order to profit from the labor, mineral wealth and fertile land of the suntanned, He and She of Man. The idea is to package and sell whatever can be hyped to a greedy and ego-driven consumer base within the death-consuming culture. If one can promise vitality and vigor in a bottle, then the only question becomes, "How much does it cost?" If someone can sell the idea of a tropical paradise and then put a price tag on it, there is always someone with disposable income to buy it. And while the lost and astray pale state of mind figures that it can merchandise its way into a tropical paradise vibration, the supreme essence of the Sacred Garden Culture is not for sale.

And while it may appear that the opposite energy is winning so far, that is only because one is still looking with eyes that are very accustomed to being tricked and deceived by the superficial appearance of things within the death-consuming culture. You see, the energy that is

CHAPTER NINE: THE CHANGING OF THE GUARD

opposite of Supreme Love and the Essence of Life has never been able to sustain itself; it has always been within a process of depletion that constantly uses some kind of host to supply its energy boost. How can we expect whole and divine solutions from those disciples and followers who are aligned with the opposite energy? How is it even possible to look at any of the social economic, political and religious orders of the death-consuming culture and not immediately begin to recognize the massive disorder, depletion, and toxic consumption that have formulated every thought and reasoning within these cold and pale power bases of deceit since their origin?

Checks and Balances

The onset of the first manifestations of disorder upon the planet began with a misdirection that occurred and a disconnection. Who can really afford to sit idle and point the finger at someone else while feeling satisfied that the blame falls outside of self? We cannot support the division that is fueled by portraying either the male in isolation or the female in isolation as the villain, the scapegoat or the cause of the problem. Let us not play that cold and pale game that continues to fuel the bitter accusations, impatient demands, and the self-deceptions while keeping one just as confused as ever, entrenched in a divided and conquered state of being. Let us be whole and clean while examining the divine and innate responsibilities that were certainly neglected so that we can begin to reclaim the Divine Union of One and get on with correcting this thing.

FULFILLING THE SACRED ANCESTRAL PROPHECY OF THE TRIPLE NINE: UNVEILING THE PROPHETIC 2012 MELTDOWN OF THE LOST AND ASTRAY PALE STATE OF MIND

Yes, one can easily reason that somewhere along the way, the masculine presence misguided the sacred ancestral mother spirit and this caused a tremendous downward spiral. And just as easily one can reason that somewhere along the way the mother spirit nurtured an imbalance that was allowed to manifest. Let us make no mistake here, we are speaking about those very first instances of distraction among the Children of the Sun who became lost and astray. Make no mistake about it, their distraction interrupted the flow of whole life energy and led to disobedience. Disobeying the supreme laws of divine guidance, protection and nurturing created a tremendous downward spiral that is still in motion up until today. We must be clear that the initial error of being absent from one's innate responsibility to provide divine guidance and protection was an error committed by the masculine presence. Equally, for the disorder to be nurtured rather than rejected, the feminine presence also committed an error. These errors could only manifest with the participation of both the masculine and feminine presence.

In order for toxic disorder to manifest there must be a toxic union between the masculine and feminine presence as they join together in their disconnected state of being. The pale master plan of the energy that is opposite of Supreme Love and the Essence of Life was to do anything and everything necessary to break the bond of the Divine Union of One between the Most Supreme Seen and Unseen presence of masculine and feminine energy. What must be divinely clear is that a toxic union, which is really a state of division, would be the only way

CHAPTER NINE: THE CHANGING OF THE GUARD

to instigate that downward spiral which is indeed the nature of that opposite energy and its death-consuming culture. The truth and the consequences of this divided state of being are the defining factors of the toxic parallel.

Let us be reminded that this is a spiritual war and the greatest weapon of that opposite energy is fright and fear. The greatest tools available to the disciples and followers of this opposite energy are lust, lies, illusions, confusion, death and deadly destruction.

What all the facts and factors of history tell us is that this downward spiral first began as an inherited trait in those lost and astray Children of the Sun who mutated and degenerated in the freezing ice. In fact, the grueling and suffering pains of mutation and degeneration and the freezing circumstances were the primary consequence of ancestral disobedience to the whole life presence of Man, He and She. Although there is an ancestral kinship that linked the Divine Children of the Sun with the lost and astray pale Children, the mutation and degeneration totally disconnected these pale breeds from any level and degree of divine spirit consciousness. That is to say, these pale breeds became totally disconnected from their Most Supreme Seen and Unseen ancestral state of being. In other words, that opposite energy was able to implement the pale curse against the lost and astray Children of the Sun, dividing them from their divinity. And what would occur is truly a horrifying telling; however, the inherited traits of lust, lies, illusions, confusion, death and deadly destruction is what these lost and astray pale Children would bring to the table in order

FULFILLING THE SACRED ANCESTRAL PROPHECY OF THE TRIPLE NINE: UNVEILING THE PROPHETIC 2012 MELTDOWN OF THE LOST AND ASTRAY PALE STATE OF MIND

to destabilize the Sacred Garden Culture from which we come.

The sacred suntanned Man, He and She, were caught completely off guard during the initial circumstance when the pale outsider invasion culture pushed the issue of submit or die. Nevertheless, the sacred suntanned Man, He and She, still had a divine duty, obligation and responsibility to uphold their sacred ancestral spirit presence. As painful as it has been to comprehend, the slightest surrender to the opposite energy would simply fuel the downward spiral. This surrender creates a vicious circle that has now finally come back around to the point where; unless the Children of the Sun learn their lessons, retrieve their blessings, and move back into the essence of the Divine Union of One; it will indeed be all over, regardless of the dance, the song, the praying cries or the wailing or the grueling and agonizing shout. You see, the blessing is that the Most Supreme Seen and Unseen essence of masculine and feminine energy is now giving Man, He and She, the opportunity to detox, purge and release the cold and pale death-consuming factors of the toxic parallel and its opposite energy. Or witness the downward spiral as it accelerates its crash-course collision into a DEAD END.

The vibrations of being too permissive and passive, and becoming slack in one's focus clearly befell both the masculine and feminine presence. In truth and reality, the transmission of whole life energy from the masculine presence to the feminine presence to the offspring had to be compromised in each instance in order for the error to be reproduced and continue to manifest. The initial

CHAPTER NINE: THE CHANGING OF THE GUARD

wondering and pondering of the lost and astray state of mind that led to distraction could have been stopped by the masculine presence who corrected himself or the feminine presence who corrected herself. The distraction could have stopped with that son who corrected himself and realigned with the principles of divine guidance and protection or that daughter who corrected herself by providing an absolute focus on divine nurturing within the checks and balances of the divine social economic family community. The point is that no one took the challenge of correcting him or her self, and, instead, the wondering and pondering in each individual led to growing confusion. Therefore, the first step in the detoxing and purging process is to reclaim one's accountability right now for one's own actions. One can always claim that one didn't know any better or that one just did not comprehend as an excuse to relieve one from the weight of one's responsibilities that call for immediate corrective actions. Perhaps, that reasoning worked in the past when the opposite energy was an unknown threat, but we know better now.

You see, the supreme nurturing essence of the universe is the sacred ancestral mother spirit, and she will manifest based upon the patterns of energy that she consumes. And every manifestation upon the seen will bear that nature, which is why the terms Mother Nature and Mother Earth have still remained as concepts up until these days. Therefore, each and every toxic experience, every toxic relationship and each toxic ejaculation will breed, seed and feed more and more out-of-sync vibrations within her existence, and these toxic vibrations will be what is nurtured to manifest upon the seen. This

FULFILLING THE SACRED ANCESTRAL PROPHECY OF THE TRIPLE NINE: UNVEILING THE PROPHETIC 2012 MELTDOWN OF THE LOST AND ASTRAY PALE STATE OF MIND

process of toxic reproduction has been happening long enough upon the planet for the patterns to be recognized so that they can be consciously stopped.

The ancestral mother spirit, in her misguided and misdirected state of being, has been turned out by that opposite energy. One can see the gruesome transformation upon the physical seen in the many ways that the suntanned female has been turned out by the pale male as the dominating and controlling masculine presence of the death-consuming culture. Regardless of whether it was a modern-day social, political welfare program, an integration platform, colonialism or neo-colonialism, slavery or neo-slavery; it would not matter whether she was a functional whore, prostitute or concubine or a successful career-oriented mother; the female would find ways to function within these labels with a primary focus on securing the survival of the offspring. Even if this survival meant breeding a more docile and submissive slave or citizen. Once this was understood by those of the hunter and herder mentality and the animal-husbandry strategies, the feminine presence was targeted for brutal violation, rape and subjugation through such syndromes as the Genghis-Khan and Willie-Lynch techniques of physical and mental conquest and enslavement. The consequences of these kinds of hellish pale-ish ordeals would dominate and control the suntanned female and be the primary programming factors that would govern her existence and each and every offspring born off of her. This would be the state of affairs of the Children of the Sun up until this

CHAPTER NINE: THE CHANGING OF THE GUARD

very day. As it is, we are deep-seated in this pale mess, trying desperately to find ways and means to recover.

Let us see how the opportunity to re-align is again being offered and again being rejected by the disciples and followers of the death-consuming culture, regardless of one being blonde or bald or natty, natty dread, and regardless of the color of one's skin. The I in I bring this forward at this point in time, because ignorance is the primary supporter of the lost and astray pale state of mind. The Most Supreme Unseen ancestral spirit presence is, within this text, providing the energy and elements to meltdown ignorance and deception. Let us see what those of the lost and astray pale state of mind would do with this supreme truth. Here is a good example. In 1999, the I in I prophesied that the second cycle of the Triple Nine of the Divine Gathering of the Sacred Few would be an amazing time.

Deliverance

And now a divine set-up has occurred to expose just how far that opposite energy will go to disrupt, detour and defer the vibrations of divine change that were amassing to move large populations towards a greater consumption of thought and reasoning regarding divine spirit consciousness. The level and degree of divine change that is inevitable was camouflaged in a color-coded disguise and covered with deceptions and lies, and then presented as the appearance of change to keep the death-consuming culture in popular demand as cries of victory and celebration are still fresh in the memory. It is difficult for the lost and astray pale state of mind to reason with the Holistic Living Truth about Supreme

FULFILLING THE SACRED ANCESTRAL PROPHECY OF THE TRIPLE NINE: UNVEILING THE PROPHETIC 2012 MELTDOWN OF THE LOST AND ASTRAY PALE STATE OF MIND

Love and to comprehend that every act to defer or detour whole life energy will only accelerate the forward movement of divine spirit consciousness.

The Most Supreme Seen and Unseen Essence of Life and Supreme Love will not settle for token gestures and token positionings. Man, He and She, will have to come forward whole and clean or suffer the pale consequences of indulging deeper and deeper into attitudes, values and beliefs of lust, lies, illusions, confusion, death and deadly destruction. It is absolutely horrifying to imagine such a pale state of mind that would play on the hopes and dreams of mass populations of Man, He and She, with such vicious intent, especially under these present-day circumstances when the essence of life upon the entire planet Earth is at stake. Even more shameful and disgraceful to watch is the herd mentality at work as mass populations become pawns in the cold and pale games that are being orchestrated to amass a greater level and degree of power, control and fortune and fame. The full horror of it all is yet to be witnessed or experienced within the toxic parallel. After all, where does the lost and astray mind go from here when the fanfare and ceremonies are done, when this much-publicized last shot at the appearance of change proves to be just another hoax played against the consciousness of Man, He and She?

This is why we say that unless the consciousness of Man, He and She, can move from that pale state of being and enter the safety zone of divine spirit consciousness, there is no way to overcome the numbing passivity of the adverse effects that the death-consuming culture breeds,

CHAPTER NINE: THE CHANGING OF THE GUARD

seeds and feeds. It should be clear that the energy that is opposite of Supreme Love and the Essence of Life is indeed of a depleted consciousness, a lost and astray pale consciousness of thought and reasoning. It is not coincidental that the sacred ancestral prophecy of the Triple Nine runs parallel with the time of master maneuvers and manipulations to avoid that which is expected and projected to come during the era of 2012.

There should not be any complications in reasoning with these facts after reading this text. It should be clear to the reader that there are two parallels of existence. The toxic parallel of the lost and astray pale state of mind breeds, seeds and feeds off of the death-consuming culture. The toxic parallel is the opposite of the divine parallel of divine spirit conscious state of mind that breeds, seeds and feeds off of the Sacred Garden Culture. While what the I in I say will not win any popularity contests among the disciples and followers of the death-consuming culture, the purpose has never been to appeal to those who are at home within the toxic parallel. This sacred ancestral call is for the Sacred Few who are able to sense the winds of change and are on watch for the signs of this sacred ancestral spiritual uprising, an uprising of divine spirit consciousness, an uprising that is truly focused on resurrecting the sacred ancestral spirit presence of the Divine Children of the Sun and the Sacred Garden Culture from which we come. Let's get back into the flow to see if one can read between the lines as both parallels run their course.

Ancestral prophecies of deliverance and the emergence of a Sacred One who would rescue the suntanned Children from bondage have been whispered

FULFILLING THE SACRED ANCESTRAL PROPHECY OF THE TRIPLE NINE: UNVEILING THE PROPHETIC 2012 MELTDOWN OF THE LOST AND ASTRAY PALE STATE OF MIND

and passed on from generation to generation ever since the coming of the pale ones who brought forward the vicious and brutal energy that is opposite of Supreme Love and the Essence of Life.

Upon the seen, when the social economic political climate heats up to the point that there is massive discontent, the possibility of a social movement occurs that can actually create an opening long enough for an individual to question and challenge the oppressive nature of the pale opposite energy that dominates and controls the death-consuming culture. How long has there been an overt and covert attempt to prevent the rise of a black messiah? How long has the suntanned male been targeted as a threat to the dominant pale male of the death-consuming culture? So what is really going on? Wait, wait, as the I in I recall here; the old saying is that power concedes nothing without a struggle. Is it possible that power has conceded without that great struggle that was projected to occur in a race war? As the I in I understand, power actually concedes nothing except greater plots and schemes to amass a greater level and degree of power. Let's take a fraction of a moment to review the shape of things that have already come:

> Keep in mind that during the time of COINTELPRO's intervention, i.e. covert invasion, into the "black" community, the term "afro" was a statement of Afro-centric beauty and statements such as, "Say it loud, I'm black and I'm proud" were common. A sense of self-love, dignity and pride were beginning to filter through the ice-cold, deep-freeze mentality that was the inherited state of mind from pre-

CHAPTER NINE: THE CHANGING OF THE GUARD

and post-slavery. One need but look around at the suntanned populations of today to see the tragic consequences of esteemlessness both nationally and internationally.

COINTELPRO is the FBI acronym for a series of covert action programs directed against domestic groups. In these programs, the Bureau went beyond the collection of intelligence to secret action defined to "disrupt" and "neutralize" target groups and individuals. COINTELPRO began in 1956, in part because of frustration with Supreme Court rulings limiting the Government's power to proceed overtly against dissident groups; it ended in 1971 with the threat of public exposure. In the intervening 15 years, the Bureau conducted a sophisticated vigilante operation aimed squarely at preventing the exercise of First Amendment rights of speech and association, on the theory that preventing the growth of dangerous groups and the propagation of dangerous ideas would protect the national security and deter violence....

Prior to that time, the Division's investigation of "Negro matters" was limited to instances of alleged Communist infiltration of civil rights groups and to monitoring civil rights protest activity. However, the long, hot summer of 1967 led to intense pressure on the Bureau to do something to contain the problem, and once again, the Bureau heeded the call. The originating letter was sent out to twenty-three field offices on August 25, 1967, describing the program's purpose as...to expose, disrupt, misdirect, discredit, or otherwise neutralize the activities of black nationalist, hate-type organizations and groupings, their leadership, spokesmen, membership, and supporters, and to counter their propensity for violence and civil disorder. Efforts of the various groups to consolidate their forces or to recruit new or youthful adherents must be frustrated.

On March 4, 1968, the program was expanded from twenty-three to forty-one field offices. The letter expanding the program lists five long-range goals for the program:

FULFILLING THE SACRED ANCESTRAL PROPHECY OF THE TRIPLE NINE: UNVEILING THE PROPHETIC 2012 MELTDOWN OF THE LOST AND ASTRAY PALE STATE OF MIND

> (1) to prevent the "coalition of militant black nationalist groups," which might be the first step toward a real "Mau Mau" in America;
> (2) to prevent the rise of a "messiah" who could "unify, and electrify," the movement, naming specifically Martin Luther King, Stokely Carmichael, and Elijah Muhammed;
> (3) to prevent violence on the part of black nationalist groups, by pinpointing "potential troublemakers" and neutralizing them "before they exercise their potential for violence;"
> (4) to prevent groups and leaders from gaining "respectability" by discrediting them to the "responsible" Negro community, to the white community (both the responsible community and the "liberals" -- the distinction is the Bureau's), and to Negro radicals; and
> (5) to prevent the long range growth of these organizations, especially among youth, by developing specific tactics to "prevent these groups from recruiting young people."
> ...Approximately 28% of the Bureau's COINTELPRO efforts were designed to weaken groups by setting members against each other, or to separate groups which might otherwise be allies, and convert them into mutual enemies. ** *citations omitted*
>
> **COINTELPRO: *The FBI'S Covert Action Programs Against American Citizens.* Supplementary Detailed Staff Reports on Intelligence Activities and the Rights of Americans. Book III. Final Report of the Select Committee to Study Governmental Operations with Respect to Intelligence Activities. United States Senate. (under authority of the order of April 14, 1976) Online Source: http://www.icdc.com/~paulwolf/cointelpro/churchfinalreportIIIa.htm.
>
> *Exposing The Ice-Cold, Deep-Freeze Mentality And Whole Life Healing Of Sexual Energy Within The Divine Parallel,* by High Priest Kwatamani, Second Edition, Copyright 2004, 2008. p.97

Although the disciples and followers of a lost and astray pale state of mind have orchestrated a cycle of

CHAPTER NINE: THE CHANGING OF THE GUARD

social economic, political events that give the appearance that things have changed, there is no real change happening in the toxic parallel. This strategy of positioning a charismatic suntanned front man provides just a little more time in the midst of social economic disturbance that indicates that the bottom is falling out of hell. The ray of hope that change is possible within the death-consuming culture keeps the mass populations pacified so that the power brokers and money brokers can quickly set up "Plan B" as they secure their investments and figure out how to preserve their advantage in the midst of earth-shift changes.

These maneuvers have not been, and will not be able to change the reality of global warming which is intensifying at a pace far more rapid than expected, imagined, planned for, or even able to be dealt with in a manner to prevent or deter the changing tide of coming events. Add the impact of global warming with the massive level and degree of social, religious chaos around the world and one has a bomb about to explode. Therefore, it would stand to reason that the lost and astray pale Children would do anything to uphold the death-consuming culture from which they come. Any move that continues to feed the fantasies, delusions and illusions of a dream deferred to keep mass populations pacified would be viewed as expedient and worthwhile. This is simply the nature of those who consume of the opposite energy as they maneuver, manipulate, plot and scheme to maintain their position of domination and control by any means necessary behind the scene, while orchestrating the appearance of things. You see, every act and event within the toxic parallel serves to draw one deeper into the toxic parallel, whether one calls it converting, integrating, assimilating, melting pot…the purpose is to amass a bigger and bigger consumer base of disciples and followers who are then consumed and depleted by the opposite energy. Therefore, the physical characteristics of the disciples or followers of the death-consuming culture do not matter at this point, as long as the lost and astray pale state of mind is leading the way. For this reason, the conscious move towards integration in the suntanned communities has been devastating to the sacred ancestral spirit presence.

Let's follow this line of analysis as we look back a bit into that profound text the *Holistic Living Truth About Supreme Love, Book Two*:

> The real deal is that one continues to reap the same benefits from the social systems that were built on the death consumption vibrations. And all still remains fair in love and war, and to the victor goes the spoils in one's new "survival-of-the-fittest" world. Therefore, what really and truly happens is that one goes in and wreaks havoc, and after murder, rape, steal and take, one creates a system to validate oneself in honor of god and country and establish a new status quo off of the spoils. One then pauses to look in the tearful eyes of the victims and says with great sorrowful gestures, "I'm so sorry for what we did to you." And the next generation joins hands to walk together in oneness to a death consumption shack and pledge allegiance that they will share in continuing the same game with another name.
>
> The assimilators and the integrators grin and smile, feeling like they have finally gotten a piece of the pie that their great grandparents suffered so dearly to taste.

CHAPTER NINE: THE CHANGING OF THE GUARD

> Instead of the assimilators and integrators consuming a whole life vibration in honor of those ancestral ones, they simply perm and fry their hair, and bleach, powder, and plaster their faces while spraying toxic scents all over their bodies as they "dress to kill" or as if they have died. These long lost and astray descendants of the sacred garden culture seek the reparations of a quarter acre and a Lexus. Oh, how well do the I in I remember the voices of those who came before the I in I, begging and wishing to have access to forty acres and a mule to foster a vibration that was encoded deep within their DNA, wishing for a piece of land to plant some collard greens and tomatoes and some of the other essentials of the garden culture. How many times have the I in I heard the modern offspring say, "Who needs to plant a garden nowadays with supermarkets everywhere? Besides, who has time for that? I'd rather be at the shopping mall." And what happened to generation next? The I in I guess that they became the generation X'd who degenerate into an even newer phase of the death consumption culture, i.e. rapping a drug culture as they dig the scene with a gangster lean?
> *The Holistic Living Truth About Supreme Love, Book Two,* Second Edition p. 30

You see, at this point and time, the issue is far beyond paleness. We are talking about a paleness within the thought and reasoning of Man, He and She, regardless of one being blonde or bald or natty, natty dread, regardless of the color of one's skin. A paleness that must be detoxed and purged in order for one to move into a sacred ancestral spirit surge. To learn our lessons, retrieve our blessings and move back into the essence of the Divine Union of One.

FULFILLING THE SACRED ANCESTRAL PROPHECY OF THE TRIPLE NINE: UNVEILING THE PROPHETIC 2012 MELTDOWN OF THE LOST AND ASTRAY PALE STATE OF MIND

In furthering this analysis, it should be clear that this color-coded change in leadership is not designed to be a force of implementing divine social economic change. This appearance of change would be orchestrated and manipulated to be a carbon copy of the same game with another name. The projections, the values, attitudes and beliefs that would be carried forward by this new leadership would be born and bred out of the ideology of the integration and assimilation hype within the melting-pot syndrome of paleness. Let's keep in mind that there is indeed a divine set-up going on that will prove to be far beyond the plots and schemes of the toxic parallel. The greatest obstacle to any divine social economic family community change would be the family unit of the suntanned male who would be placed in a position of authority as the chief executive within the death-consuming culture. As a matter of fact, the image that he projects as an example of success and acceptance within the privileged ranks of the dominant pale male would send a loud and clear message to suntanned populations.

While these occurrences appear be the answer to the dream of the children of the civil rights movement, the answer to their prayers, and the reward for the generations and generations and generations that were enslaved, tortured and slaughtered because of their ancestral suntanned presence, this divine set-up is far beyond a social economic or political agenda of the death-consuming culture.

During this cycle of fulfilling the sacred ancestral prophecy of the era of the Triple Nine, it is clear that a cry for change would be expressed upon the seen as the

CHAPTER NINE: THE CHANGING OF THE GUARD

vibrations of change are intensifying within the unseen. However, as the reign of the opposite energy comes to an end and the masculine presence who has held those reins of domination and control upon the seen works to hold back the changing tide, an idealized presentation of the suntanned masculine presence becomes the sought-after, solarized ray of hope to hold things together. And the suntanned feminine presence who stands by his side will provide the stamp of approval to give every bit of dedication and devotion to making the death consumption culture work to the bitter end. The level and degree of esteemlessness that is being maintained within the toxic parallel as the suntanned male and female integrate and assimilate the pale values, attitudes and behaviors is massive. The esteemlessness would reflect a lack of self-love, a rejection of one's ancestral spirit conscious self, and a rejection of one's natural and innate physical presentation. It is very difficult for the suntanned feminine presence to reason with the fact that the simple act of perming or relaxing or straightening one's hair symbolizes how deeply one has embraced an image of self that opposes one's natural and innate state of being. The statement is very clearly, "I want to be something other than what I am. I want to look more like the images of paleness that have been upheld as more acceptable. I will burn myself, apply toxic chemicals and suffer discomfort; I will do whatever it takes to re-make myself into a paler image." Many suntanned mothers would feel so ashamed of their natural and innate self that they would inflict this shame upon their young infant daughters and any other young suntanned females within their environment. In fact many suntanned female

FULFILLING THE SACRED ANCESTRAL PROPHECY OF THE TRIPLE NINE: UNVEILING THE PROPHETIC 2012 MELTDOWN OF THE LOST AND ASTRAY PALE STATE OF MIND

offspring would have never truly experienced the beauty of their kinky, curly, nappy or any other natural and innate texture of their hair during their entire lifetime. As a matter of fact, many suntanned mothers would introduce the hair-processing techniques at a very young age with products called baby perms. And this act of self-rejection would become a badge of acceptance, sending one more message that only by becoming a carbon copy of paleness will one be allowed to accelerate within the death-consuming culture and its new world order.

Another appearance of change is the noticeable drop in fuel prices globally that occurred in and around the time of changes in leadership within the most dominant social economic and political order upon the earth. However, while the prices began to drop, the drilling of fossil fuels; the pumping, purchasing and burning of fossil fuels did not decrease. So the environmental impacts remain the same while the main attention is on how much less it costs to fill one's tank. The primary issue that Man, He and She, should now be focused on is that the nonrenewable natural resources, that is fossil fuel, is still being depleted from the earth, and the burning of the fuels is still polluting the air and adding to the greenhouse effect as the earth continues to heat up. There seems to be very little concern about the adverse effects of things. There appears to be a focus on extracting more oil from the earth as the ice in the Artic region melts and the oil magnates see a way to continue the rape of the planet. There is no reasoning that the fossil fuels in the earth may be the bonding element or

CHAPTER NINE: THE CHANGING OF THE GUARD

serve some other vital and necessary purpose in maintaining earth's existence. It is too amazing that the mass majority of Man, He and She, have become so passive and mesmerized by the cold-blooded nature of the death-consuming culture that these acts of depletion are not being brought to a screeching halt immediately.

It should now be clear and obvious that those who did not mutate and degenerate within the white-blight zone have neglected their divine duty, obligation and responsibility to take the lead in guiding all of Man, He and She, forward into divine spirit consciousness. As it is, those of the suntanned presence are actually so far behind the signs of the times that, by the time they do indeed catch up with divine spirit conscious reality, there will be no reality again for those beings.

But wait a minute, wait a minute, wait a minute...we're not done yet!

> Oh, how well imprinted are the memories of the good old slavery days. No one should take lightly the effect that all those many mammies had on all those who suckled at her breast and ate from her hand up into Reconstruction and into today. Oh, how the I in I can feel and hear and sense the wailing cries of those many ancestral ones who made this powerful nation what it is in hopes that the sacred spirit of the I in I would one day resurrect the sacred garden culture. The blessings come from the many who struggled in misery, aches and pains and the many others who had thought their lives had gone in vain as they hung as strange fruit on the Tree of Good and Evil. And many tears were cried from the many who swore that they spoke truth while they lied and lied and lied. And many preached deceptive alibis about a righteous god that could not possibly be so while supporting the good

FULFILLING THE SACRED ANCESTRAL PROPHECY OF THE TRIPLE NINE: UNVEILING THE PROPHETIC 2012 MELTDOWN OF THE LOST AND ASTRAY PALE STATE OF MIND

> old slavery days and the lust, lies, illusions, confusion, death and deadly destruction that was a part of the package within the death consumption phase. And, oh, the war-torn pains of the many socio-economic gains on the backs of those who lived in disdain. As death-consuming flesh sellers gained fortune and fame while living life in the fast lane. And to all of those grandmothers and grandfathers that I knew yet never knew, I say in the Most Supreme Spirit of Love, "This one is for you, because in the Most Supreme Spirit of Love, the I in I have come to gather the divine and sacred few."
>
> *The Holistic Living Truth About Supreme Love, Book Two,* Second Edition, p. 312

For this reason, the Most Supreme Unseen ancestral spirit presence of the Divine Children of the Sun has forwarded the I in I upon the seen, whole and clean, to bring forward the holistic living truth about Supreme Love. It is a requirement that an amassment of a Sacred Few among Man, He and She, must move into the safety zone of the divine parallel, quick, fast and in a hurry. However, the only way that one can enter the safety zone is through the indulgement of the mental and physical acts of divine spirit consciousness. Let us be forever mindful of the fact that it requires divine spirit consciousness to resurrect the sacred ancestral spirit presence of the Divine Children of the Sun and the Sacred Garden Culture from which we come.

One may wonder about the nature of the divine set-up. One may ask if the appearance of change should be allowed to play itself out. In truth and reality, the appearance of change, as well as the dynamics of earth-shift changes, will indeed play themselves out, whether one likes it or not. Clearly, events will continue to play themselves out within the fulfilling of the sacred ancestral prophecy of the Triple Nine and the unveiling of the prophetic 2012 meltdown of the lost and astray pale state of mind.

The Known and the Unknown Factors

From divine spirit conscious thought and reasoning, it is indeed self-evident what did, in fact, occur when the lost and astray Children faced the earth-shift changes that brought the coming of the deep freeze. We know that those lost and astray Children continued deeper into the cold rather than changing their direction. Obviously, the wandering suntanned male who was leading those disciples and followers should have recognized the nature of any earth-shift changes that were upon him. But clearly those earth-shift changes were ignored. The truth and the consequences played themselves out in the experiences of freezing cold that would eventually lead to mutation and degeneration of their mental, physical and spiritual state of being.

The ancestral male should have had enough humility to assess the circumstances of the earthly environmental change and then to be strong and firm in making a decision to get their dark behinds up out of that emerging cold. The divine duty, obligation and responsibility of the ancestral male is to sense the weather or climate condition or any other environmental change, tune into his Most Supreme ancestral spirit presence and go the other direction towards the glory and the essence of the sun. And if there were a few stubborn ones who chose to be stagnant and passive and/or who

FULFILLING THE SACRED ANCESTRAL PROPHECY OF THE TRIPLE NINE: UNVEILING THE PROPHETIC 2012 MELTDOWN OF THE LOST AND ASTRAY PALE STATE OF MIND

chose to continue along the pathway of that downward spiral, one who provides divine guidance and divine protection must stay on course.

The ancestral male continues to have the divine duty, obligation and responsibility to focus on a redirection. The circumstance that the lost and astray Children faced during the coming of the freezing ice, truly and sincerely is no different from the circumstances that the offspring of mutation and degeneration now face during this time of global warming. Or the circumstances now faced by the lost and astray suntanned Children, whose ancestral presence has been reduced by the cold and pale acts of sex and violence, war and crime. A subjugation that has reduced the suntanned Man, He and She, to following behind the lost and astray pale state of mind.

A firm decision to totally and absolutely align with divine spirit consciousness must be without any emotional ties that would keep one in a stuck and stagnant position of alignment with those of the energy that is opposite of the Supreme Love and the Essence of Life. Once again, the I in I repeat, there is absolutely no way to tune into the most supreme ancestral spirit presence of Man, He and She, upon the seen without tuning into divine spirit consciousness.

There are instances where it appears that one is just innocent or ignorant in their decision or simply addicted to the attitudes, values and beliefs of all that they have known to be real and true. Nevertheless, the only decision that anyone of a divine spirit conscious focus can make is to keep on pushing a love supreme as a

CHAPTER NINE: THE CHANGING OF THE GUARD

divine example while moving quick, fast and in a hurry to get out of harm's way. One must never fail to realize that it is the nature of harm to cause hurt or harm regardless one's emotional ties to those who are consuming of the harmful nature of toxic, devitalized and depleted energy. As the I am I sure that it was in the days of old, and as the I in I am of the all-knowing that it is today, once one of the sacred ancestral masculine or feminine spirit has made the decision or the commitment to align with divine spirit consciousness, every kind and type of emotional energy of distraction will be presented to him or her in every kind of way and means to cause passivity to keep one stuck and stagnant within the status quo of paleness. As the old saying goes, it is better the devil that you know than that which you don't know.

Within this line of thought and reasoning, it is then no wonder that so many among the mass majority continue to remain stuck and stagnant on that pale and passive pathway that clearly leads one into a downward spiral. It is also clear how the deceptive beliefs projected through the faith-oriented ideologies would keep one steady to the core of that downward spiral while wishing and hoping and praying for a change. And without taking one step towards whole life change, one remains steeped knee-deep in fantasies, illusions, delusions and dreams that the lord will make a way somehow. Unaware that the way made is the way of paleness that rips, strips and rapes the most supreme ancestral spirit presence out of one's existence.

The truth and the consequences of the ancestral male abandoning his natural and innate role by not remaining firm in providing divine guidance and

FULFILLING THE SACRED ANCESTRAL PROPHECY OF THE TRIPLE NINE: UNVEILING THE PROPHETIC 2012 MELTDOWN OF THE LOST AND ASTRAY PALE STATE OF MIND

protection has indeed opened the door to the pathway of the downward spiral. It is amazing that Man, He and She, are facing very similar kinds of circumstances today except that the weather patterns are completely reversed. Instead of the coming of ice glaciers in the northern region, we now face global warming in the same areas and throughout the planet. What will the decision be for those who orchestrate, manipulate and control the mental mindset of the mass populations upon the earth? What will be the decision for the Divine and Sacred Few who are destined to resurrect the sacred ancestral spirit presence of the Divine Children of the Sun and the Sacred Garden Culture from which we come?

And it is a sad state of affairs that the biggest victory for the suntanned Man, He and She, after hundreds of generations of being slaughtered, raped, enslaved and subjugated is to be able to say that a suntanned male has finally been elected to sit at the top of the heap within the death-consuming culture and lead the march for even more opportunities to integrate and assimilate the opposite energy. Yes, a suntanned male is now the leading front man for a superpower entity within the toxic parallel, and mass populations across the globe have viewed this event with great joy, wishing, hoping and praying that things will change. Let's be real here; have the attitudes, values and behaviors of depleted and devitalized consumption all of a sudden changed with the casting of a vote? What is truly being said by majority rule is that the ancestral mother spirit has become so totally lost and astray that she is devoted to nurturing this cold and pale game, and that certain privileged suntanned

CHAPTER NINE: THE CHANGING OF THE GUARD

males have been properly domesticated and can now be trusted to guide and protect this thang like it is his very own. Those who have integrated and assimilated into the toxic parallel, now identify themselves and claim ownership of the pale lost and astray state of mind, assuming full responsibility to guide, protect and nurture the death-consuming culture.

What a statement of conquest for the lineages of the mutated and degenerated pale breeds who literally fought and ate each other for survival a few millennia ago in the white-blight of the ice-age deep freeze. In truth and reality, everything that is conquered by the opposite energy sooner or later ends up depleted, devitalized and lifeless, i.e. dead. It might have been a different story if the suntanned male and female within the toxic parallel had actually been able to maintain greater spirit strength. However, the more that one consumes of the opposite energy, the more one experiences breakdown and deterioration, and the weaker one's spirit-life energy becomes. Therefore, by this time upon the planet, when the mass majority of suntanned males and females have become devoted disciples and followers of the death-consuming culture, their state of weakness and depletion is critical, because they have had no way to refuel within whole life energy for many, many, many generations. Every vestige of sacred ancestral connection, every memory and cultural expression has been tampered with, polluted, corrupted and turned into a pale imitation of life. Just know that there was a tremendous capacity for life energy within the spirit presence of the suntanned He and She of Man, and this vast reserve has been just about

FULFILLING THE SACRED ANCESTRAL PROPHECY OF THE TRIPLE NINE: UNVEILING THE PROPHETIC 2012 MELTDOWN OF THE LOST AND ASTRAY PALE STATE OF MIND

drained bone dry. Where did the suntanned Children get all that soul from in the first place?

As we have said, the opposite energy cannot sustain itself and is constantly on the prowl for an energy boost. This state of depletion is exactly why the lost and astray pale Children have historically been such brutal and vicious killers, thieves, rapists and enslavers, seeking that thrill of the kill and the surge of toxic energy as they feed upon the remains and the life presence of others. As they raided and invaded the lands of the suntanned, He and She of Man, can it not be seen by now that destruction and devastation was all that these original carriers of the opposite energy brought with them out of the melting ice? Nevertheless, the most that any suntanned male, within the death-consuming culture during these days and times, can do is to inspire some fantasy, dream, illusion or delusion about representing a change from the cold and pale nature of the energy that is opposite of the Essence of Life and Supreme Love. As we have said before, there have been many, many examples of a superficial appearance of change within the toxic parallel while the energy of consumption remains one and the same, every time. Therefore, nothing changes except the face who administrates the game and/or the name of the game.

The Sacred Ancestral Ones have been supremely patient within the all-knowing presence of the Most Supreme Seen and Unseen Essence of Life and Supreme Love. The emergence from the unseen to the seen of the I in I as High Priest Kwatamani is indeed the forwarding of the supreme responsibility to resurrect the sacred

CHAPTER NINE: THE CHANGING OF THE GUARD

ancestral spirit presence of the Divine Children of the Sun and the Sacred Garden Culture from which we come. Getting past the mystique and mystery of it all, it is now time for the I in I to state clearly that the sacred ancestral spirit presence of the Divine Children of the Sun has never been, and will never be, conquered by the opposite energy. Resurrection means to reclaim the spirit presence from the depleted and devitalized stranglehold of the opposite energy that stands as a barrier between that spirit presence and the ability to re-connect with the Most Supreme Seen and Unseen Essence of Life and Supreme Love. That is why detoxing and purging is so crucial. In fact, once Man, He and She, has reclaimed their sacred ancestral spirit presence and re-aligned with all that they are, it then becomes very easy to reclaim one's mental and physical existence through the energies of divine spirit consciousness. One must actually expel every aspect of that opposite energy from every fiber of one's mental, physical and spiritual being, vibration by vibration, memory by memory, until one can emerge whole and clean, free from the toxic residue and foul stench of that wretched and depleting energy. As we have said, the energy that is opposite of Supreme Love and the Essence of Life can not penetrate the divine parallel, so, the moment that one consumes of that unwhole energy, one is cast into the wasteland of disconnection. No matter how hard one prays or pleads or promises, one will not be able to enter into the divine parallel unless one has totally and completely rid one self of that opposite energy. Even though one may even believe that because one is regaining a little more spirit strength and spirit sense, one has emerged within divine spirit consciousness, the truth of the matter is that as long as one still maintains even the flashbacks and memory triggers of one's toxic consumption, one is simply working to re-connect to a state of wholeness. Until that time, one has not entered into the sacred sphere of divine spirit consciousness, although one will certainly be able to tell that one is becoming more and more unified within. This is the nature of whole life spiritual healing that is divinely guided, protected and nurtured within the Most Supreme Seen and Unseen Essence of Life and Supreme Love.

Matters of Life and Death

During this prophesied time of earth shift changes, it is of utmost importance to comprehend the nature of the divine parallel and how it differs from all that one has encountered within the toxic parallel. While one can begin to comprehend the presence of this divine parallel, it may be very difficult to relate to the nature of whole life energy as we have described it, because the nature of whole and clean energy is absolutely different from the attitudes, values, and behaviors of the death-consuming culture. For instance, one may assume that comprehending a fresh ripe mango is simple. It is a tropical fruit, it tastes juicy and sweet; one can eat it and be done. A mango is not difficult to comprehend, although one can intellectualize for awhile. The point here is that within the toxic parallel, despite one's best effort, one will remain unable to penetrate the fullness and intensity of that seen and unseen essence that has manifested as mango. The point here is not to glorify the

CHAPTER NINE: THE CHANGING OF THE GUARD

mango, although it is indeed a glorious expression; the point here is to note that any individual who has become conditioned to devitalized and depleted consumption patterns, mentally, physically and spiritually, will be unable to penetrate the vibrations and sensations of whole life energy. Therefore, even the most vivid description will simply be a pale reflection within the thoughts and reasoning of that individual, within the cold and pale parallel of their lost and astray mind. And there is no crossing over from the toxic parallel by mere statements and declarations.

Therefore, how can we expect anyone from within the death consumption culture to be able to guide any matters of life? It is impossible for any consumer of the opposite energy to know anything about anything except the vibrations of lust, lies, illusions, confusion, death and deadly destruction that fill the toxic parallel like an overflowing cesspool. This pattern of depletion repeats itself over and over again. And even if an individual professes to be able to express life matters while consuming of the opposite energy, he or she is only indulging in the fantasies, illusions, delusions and dreams that keep that pale lost and astray mind locked down in deception and insanity.

Thanks to a vast communication network that has extended to the seen, even without knowing the true purpose being served, news is accessible on a wide scale across the planet. Even those with a superficial focus, are now able to reason with the nature of the opposite energy as these events and patterns become more visible and pronounced to the physical eye. So, while the journalists and news reporters and the television

FULFILLING THE SACRED ANCESTRAL PROPHECY OF THE TRIPLE NINE: UNVEILING THE PROPHETIC 2012 MELTDOWN OF THE LOST AND ASTRAY PALE STATE OF MIND

networks and radio stations provide media coverage in a race to keep sensational headlines grabbing attention and captivating the buying public, their purpose is to feed, fuel and expand the appetites of the toxic parallel. However, these news stories provide a graphic exposure of the death-consuming culture in all of its ugly, brutal, greedy and destructive excesses.

There are actually some who continue to hope and expect that there will be a leader from the toxic parallel who will rise up to lead the masses who knows where. Where can any consumer of the toxic parallel go, but deeper into the madness that has repeated itself again and again throughout the brief history of the mutated and degenerated breeds of mankind who were the first hosts of the opposite energy. The very breed of mankind that spread this plague like a cancer throughout the planet.

Within the divine parallel, this supreme telling is news of a completely different nature, a divine nature that expresses the Essence of Life and Supreme Love. Even the most simple example of divine social economic family community carries enough whole life energy to spark divine change upon the planet, because there are those who are locked down behind the fortresses of the toxic parallel, waiting to be rescued and guided to safety. These prisoners of war have been captured by the covert strategies of a whitewash campaign, having survived the tortures and deprivations of being programmed by opposition forces. We must keep in mind that this is a spiritual war, and every covert and overt strategy available has been, and will continue to be, used by the disciples and followers of the energy that is opposite of

CHAPTER NINE: THE CHANGING OF THE GUARD

Supreme Love and the Essence of Life to maintain their position. And what is that position? The position is the death-consuming culture, by any means necessary.

This rescue mission can only be delivered by divine intervention and led by a Sacred One who has actually succeeded in clearing a pathway from the toxic parallel into the safety zone of the Divine Parallel. This safety zone is a whole and clean environment where an individual can to go through the detoxing and purging process in order to emerge within divine spirit consciousness. When these individuals are able to see, know and comprehend that the whole life energy is present upon the earth and that the divine example is present, then an insurmountable spirit surge will inspire movement to identify and connect with these Sacred Few. And as the fulfilling of the Sacred Ancestral Prophecy of the Triple Nine comes to be, divine union and divine consumption go forward to multiply divinity.

While we make every effort to provide a sense of clarity regarding the circular movement of life and the eternal recycling process that is a key to whole life energy, it still may be difficult for individuals to relate this supreme truth within their own life. Nevertheless, for the sake of the Sacred Few, this telling is brought forward from the Most Supreme Seen and Unseen Essence of Life and Supreme Love. The most crucial, critical and significant difference in the universe is whether or not one consumes of whole life energy. If one is not a consumer of whole life energy, then it should now be evident that one is consuming from the death-consuming culture of the toxic parallel. Perhaps, there has been some confusion about where one is at and

FULFILLING THE SACRED ANCESTRAL PROPHECY OF THE TRIPLE NINE: UNVEILING THE PROPHETIC 2012 MELTDOWN OF THE LOST AND ASTRAY PALE STATE OF MIND

where one is headed. Well, as long as one continues to maintain one's current patterns of toxic consumption in any form or fashion, one can be sure that one is within the toxic parallel and one is headed for a more depleted and devitalized state of being.

Every molecule that forms one's cellular structure, every DNA code and every nerve signal that transmits a thought, is directly influenced and affected by the energy of one's consumption. Within the toxic parallel, this means that the opposite energy has contaminated every aspect of one's being, mentally, physically and spiritually. And one is, at this very moment, serving as a host whether one acknowledges this fact or not. Additionally, one has become a conscious or unconscious carrier of a toxic, foul and depleted energy that has a major aim to rob one of that last vestige of sacred ancestral spirit presence while feeding a bloated and self-destructive ego-driven pale state of mind.

It would be a tragedy if Man, He and She, were to align with an energy that is toxic, harmful and destructive to the whole life presence of all matters of life upon the planet Earth and there were no way to escape this doomed fate. Within the toxic parallel, there is no escape, and so the disciples and followers are preparing for the final phases of their doom-and-gloom scenarios while continuing to honor and uphold the vibrations and sensations of lust, lies, illusions, confusion, death and deadly destruction and the pale-male-war-god deities that oversee this pale state of affairs. The conclusion of their story is a violent and destructive collision of all those who bear the toxic nature of the energy that is opposite of

CHAPTER NINE: THE CHANGING OF THE GUARD

the Essence of Life and Supreme Love. However, not everyone is going out like that.

This story has been told before, and the rise and fall of the death-consuming culture is not a new chapter. In the past, there was always another suntanned population to conquer, another land to invade, another host to drag into the pits of the deep-freeze hell of toxic consumption to keep the cold and pale game fueled and on the move. And so the opposite energy was able to spread while draining more and more life energy from the earth. This could not go on indefinitely, a limit would indeed be reached.

The opposite energy is nothing more than a lifeless and depleting disturbance pattern that was not even able to penetrate the existence of Man, He and She without first being allowed in. Once even the smallest opening presented an opportunity, the opposite energy would install itself through applications of pain, fright and fear. You see, the lost and astray pale state of mind is anxiety-ridden, filled with the stress and strain of being disconnected from a whole life energy source, and powerless in the face of physical termination. Because there is no continuation into a Most Supreme Unseen presence for lost and astray pale state of mind, physical existence is a one-time affair. And the concept of death is a real experience within the opposite energy.

Within the toxic parallel, one begins and ends within a linear time span of maybe six or seven decades or so, and then one is finished. This would, indeed, feed a selfish and capitalizing attitude of greed and hording all that one can while one is able to, since there is absolutely nothing else to look forward to except old age and physical decline and death. Why would one be motivated to care for the Earth and future generations when one is planning to be long gone into the dust of time? And if one did imagine a life after death, it would certainly be in some fantasized faraway space and time that does not even resemble the death-consuming culture. The "live-for-today-and-let-tomorrow-take-care-of-itself" attitude denies one's responsibility to be accountable for all that one manifests while upon the seen, because death is seen as the ultimate escape. This is the only reason why an individual would even consider suicide to be an answer to his or her personal problems. Just up and leave, abandoning the mess that one made and leaving the headaches behind for someone else to figure out. Of course, this fixation with death and dying is quite understandable based on the toxic nature of the energy consumed within the death-consuming culture.

The Forward Multiplication of Divinity

The forward multiplication of divinity means that, within the cycle of life, birth is an ongoing process of seen and unseen emergence that moves a spirit presence through phases into maturity and reproduction and then into even greater life cycles to emerge again. Therefore, throughout one's entire being there is a constant regeneration into a more defined and more refined expression of whole life energy. This process of life does not slow down or begin to deteriorate as one becomes physically older. As a matter of fact, as one gains more divine knowledge, wisdom and understanding over time upon the seen, one becomes better able to reason with

CHAPTER NINE: THE CHANGING OF THE GUARD

and connect the patterns of one's own observations and experiences within divine spirit consciousness. One can then express and translate these lessons to allow those who are following in one's footsteps to receive greater divine clarity with fewer stumbles and falls. In this way, reaching the phases of becoming an elder within the divine social economic family community is an honored and much respected asset within the learning and teaching elements of community life. The responsibility of raising the offspring as a multiplication of divinity extends much further than the physical mother and father. And in every instance, the presence of mother spirits and father spirits provide vital support in raising the offspring within a divine spirit conscious state of mind.

Therefore, while we are upon the seen we have every divine duty, obligation and responsibility to focus within divine spirit consciousness and create a greater level and degree of reciprocation with the Most Supreme Seen and Unseen Essence of Life and Supreme Love. This reciprocation allows us to prepare the pathway for our own whole life movement, that is, the movement of our brain, body and spiritual presence, deeper and deeper into the Divine Union of One. And that Divine Union of One of the Most Supreme Seen and Unseen Essence of Life and Supreme Love is indeed the Divine Union of One between the Most Supreme Essence of masculinity and femininity. Two parts to one Supreme Wholeness.

Within divine spirit consciousness, our every expression, mentally, physically and spiritually, creates an offspring vibration that advances the forward multiplication of divinity. Every thought and every behavior contribute to the growth and development of

FULFILLING THE SACRED ANCESTRAL PROPHECY OF THE TRIPLE NINE: UNVEILING THE PROPHETIC 2012 MELTDOWN OF THE LOST AND ASTRAY PALE STATE OF MIND

even greater experiences within the divine parallel. Therefore, the principles and practices of a holistic living way of life form a way of life that, indeed, advances the forward multiplication of divinity in total alignment with the Supreme Laws of whole life energy. And every birthing act, whether it be mental, physical or spiritual, is a sacred act that honors and glorifies the continuous flow of whole life energy from the Most Supreme Unseen to the seen.

The birthing process is truly the manifesting principle of the Divine Union of One wherein the supreme ancestral masculine energy impregnates the supreme ancestral feminine energy to form and manifest all life matters. You see, upon the seen, there is no breathing into dirt and pulling out a rib to make a being; there is no virgin showing up pregnant within the Supreme Laws of the Universe. Perhaps, in the freaky laboratories and disconnected imagination of the pale lost and astray state of mind, such things are conceivable. However, to be conceivable and conceived of by the opposite energy is to be born, bred and baptized in lust, lies, illusions, confusion, death and deadly destruction.

Even with the tremendous amount of tampering and the devastating state of division and disorder between the masculine presence and the feminine presence, there still remains, one and only one, very clear and obvious pattern of conception and birth for Man, He and She. And this divine master plan requires the Divine Union of the sacred masculine and feminine energies. Every Man, He and She, came upon the seen through the exact same arrangement of the masculine presence of a sperm

CHAPTER NINE: THE CHANGING OF THE GUARD

joining with the feminine presence of an egg to make one unified cell of life that then continued to multiply. Likewise, every physical matter came upon the seen through the exact same arrangement of the Most Supreme Unseen masculine essence and feminine essence joining into one unified whole.

Notwithstanding the tampering of the lost and astray pale state of mind, whether that fertilized embryo is incubated in a test tube or even placed within a male's body, the essential elements of the masculine and feminine essence joining together to create life still remain as absolute within divine order. That opposite energy will use any available host to tamper and probe and experiment and work to unravel unseen secrets of life. And that same host will congratulate himself or herself as the ego proudly proclaims, "Look what I did!" In the case of attempting to clone Man, He and She, who can determine what kind of deformed mentality such a spiritless breed of mankind will manifest?

Just look at what mutation and degeneration of the DNA has already produced upon the planet, and that should be enough warning to leave such tampering experiments alone. However, the opposite energy is relentless in its efforts to penetrate the divine parallel. You see, when the spirit presence has been reduced, all one's physical parts may function and one's brain may even function with a level of superficial and artificial intelligence that can be scored on flat and lifeless I.Q. tests, but know for sure that the opposite energy is at the controls, pushing the buttons, running the mental programs and inflicting its depleted, devitalized vibrations on anyone who consumes of it.

FULFILLING THE SACRED ANCESTRAL PROPHECY OF THE TRIPLE NINE: UNVEILING THE PROPHETIC 2012 MELTDOWN OF THE LOST AND ASTRAY PALE STATE OF MIND

All that manifests within the toxic parallel is toxic. However, every manifestation within the divine parallel, every expression, every communication, every behavior, is of whole life energy to beget more whole life energy. And always, the best is yet to come. And within divine spirit consciousness, every expression from the Most Supreme Unseen to the seen is divinely guided, protected and nurtured by that supreme ancestral spirit presence of masculinity and femininity in order for that sacred manifestation to be maintained and sustained upon the seen.

Divine Social Economic Family Community

If one has indeed comprehended the nature of the beast and the nature of each and every disciple and follower who consumes of that cold and pale toxic nature, then one can comprehend why the vibrations of hell and damnation, doom and gloom are so dominant within the mental mindset of so many of Man, He and She. Let us make sure that we understand the methodology that set the pattern for turning the Children of the Sun into a frozen paleness. Let's take a few minutes and trace the vibrations that led Man, He and She, lost and astray. Tracing these vibrations will show exactly how the Children of the Sun got off track and wandered into a cold and pale state of being. And if we use our spirit conscious sense to reason with the truth and the consequences, we will have a clear route to exit the toxic parallel.

The first occurrence that caused a major detour from the movements of divine order was expansion within the

CHAPTER NINE: THE CHANGING OF THE GUARD

divine social economic family community that caused the physical distance between families to increase. And as the various family units became more disconnected from the Tree of Life, that is from the root, foundation and base of their sacred ancestral spirit presence, a new energy of reasoning would begin to manifest. The spreading out of families made direct communication less frequent and caused interruptions or delays in the flow of messages. Also, the second or third-hand translation of a message was prone to be altered in some way, either through omission or misinterpretations, or through the distance of separation. As result, the day-to-day communication link became compromised, and the checks and balances of immediate and ongoing feedback and correction in one's thinking and reasoning became more infrequent. Add all of this to the gradual environmental changes that would somehow be taken for granted or misinterpreted, and the seeds of a confused state of being would find roots. Confusion is one of the elements of the opposite energy and would lay a threshold for full entry.

The masculine presence who maintained his family farther and farther away from the sacred ancestral temples, began a process of possession where his family became his primary focus outside of the essence of the whole because of his insecurity. An air of disregard grew as this masculine presence entertained ideas of proclaiming his manhood by claiming a greater connection to the sacred ancestors than those senior elders afar. This proclaiming would be projected and profiled as elder wisdom, although emerging from an immature mind of thought and reasoning that was not aware of the consequences of disconnecting from one's sacred ancestral spirit presence.

It is a certainty that if the divine messages had been received whole and clean and then heeded, the Children of the Sun would have quickly changed their direction, turning southward to get their dark behinds up out of that emerging hell hole before it would even transform into a freezing ice cold. Nevertheless, by the time messages of divine guidance were received to maintain divine protection, a stubbornness had set in within a state of mind that was quickly becoming lost and astray within the toxic parallel.

The masculine presence was left without his sacred ancestral spirit connection to divine guidance and protection. Therefore he had absolutely nothing divine for the feminine presence to nurture. While the feminine presence did her best to support the movement that the disconnected masculine presence brought forward, she was supporting disorder. Certainly that wayward masculine presence did not reason with the multiplied consequences that he would suffer as he followed his lost and astray state of mind. Little did he know that feeding off of this lost and astray state of mind would automatically provide a lost and astray state of guidance and protection for the mother spirit to nurture and to breed into the offspring. Yes, the masculine presence introduced the opposite energy upon the seen, and the feminine presence nurtured it. And the union of masculinity and femininity became a war zone where lust, lies, illusions confusion, death and deadly destruction were multiplied. Just as sure as every son

CHAPTER NINE: THE CHANGING OF THE GUARD

and daughter born from that lost and astray feminine presence would bear the marks of a lost and astray state of mind, divine nurturing would be aborted, and in its place would commence a foreign and toxic ideology.

The feminine presence was left vulnerable with no divine guidance or protection; the opposite energy secured its entry into the mental and physical presence of Man, He and She. Thus, manifesting the most fatal division that Man, He and She, has ever faced. That fatal division is the disconnection of the mind of thought and reasoning from the sacred ancestral spirit presence, that is, divine spirit consciousness. And the body would be left vulnerable to the whims of the lost and astray pale state of mind.

And the Children of the Sun who became lost and astray spread this cold and pale plague back into the ancestral land, adversely affecting those who had not faced the harsh and cruel conditions of mental, physical and spiritual mutation and degeneration. Yes, the Sacred Garden Culture from which we come would be invaded by mutated and degenerated Children of the Sun who lost their tan, and their primary victims would be the Children of the Sun with the golden tan. The marks of distinction, division and separation have been played out by the cold and pale energy that is indeed opposite of Supreme Love and the Essence of Life.

Melting Down

What had initially occurred is that the masculine presence would sink into a lost and astray state of thought and reasoning thus disconnecting himself from the sacred ancestral energies of divine guidance and

FULFILLING THE SACRED ANCESTRAL PROPHECY OF THE TRIPLE NINE: UNVEILING THE PROPHETIC 2012 MELTDOWN OF THE LOST AND ASTRAY PALE STATE OF MIND

protection. And each cycle of him ejaculating this vibration into the mother spirit would deepen the wound, infecting the open sores that allowed that opposite energy to fester within Man, He and She. Keep in mind that this downward spiral would continue for generations and generations, for thousands of years, deep within the Caucasus caves and would breed an energy so wretched and foul that its most basic patterns would be locked into destruction and self-destruction by any means necessary. If not for that catastrophic event that occurred when the deep-freeze ice began to melt, allowing the hell and damnation of those lost and astray pale Children to ride the tides of hell and high waters into the lands of the Children of the Sun with the golden tan, the nature of that opposite energy would have totally consumed of itself, returning back to the nothingness from which it came.

However, the survivors among the mutated and degenerated Children of the deep-freeze pits of hell did, indeed, emerge upon the seen of the Divine Children of the Sun, bringing the fatal forces of destabilization, depletion, and disruption upon the Sacred Garden Culture from which we come.

Within the toxic parallel, the pale breeds of mankind who descended from the northern regions during the past global warming and meltdown did invade the Sacred Garden Culture lands of the suntanned populations. As a result of the melting ice and the high waters that would flood the Black Sea, the mutated and degenerated ones would carry these cold and pale hunting and herding, predatorial and scavenging values, attitudes and beliefs as a way of life. There was no other comprehension that

CHAPTER NINE: THE CHANGING OF THE GUARD

they could bring. The initial invasions of the lost and astray pale Children would include cannibalism of the suntanned male and female, physically consuming anything and everything else that they would consume. And when their bellies were full, they would commence the hostile, cruel and vicious acts of raping raids, pillaging and burning to dominate and control all that they could possibly dominate and control for as long as they could. As history would tell it, these would be great leaders, heroic warlords and masterful strateticians and generals. Alexander would not just be called Alexander, but Alexander the Great. Julius Caesar would be considered one of the greatest leaders of all time. Just as in the 12th century A.D., an offspring seed like Genghis Khan would be considered a great and masterful warlord. And Machiavelli would be the epitome of great military genius.

Where is all of this going? Let's see how this relates to modern day global warming and the meltdown of the opposite energy. The polar bear is losing its grip. As a result, this cold-blooded pale predator has become a cannibal, starting to consume of the weaker and smaller female and the offspring. The opposite energy is still causing the same patterns to emerge just as it did manifest among the lost and astray pale Children when the pale male began to consume of the female and offspring as smaller and weaker prey. And cannibalism would have continued to reduce the population until the pale male was left with only himself to consume. And when it really got down to it, the decision would be to attack another population, continuing the same process until a death-consuming culture would become their

FULFILLING THE SACRED ANCESTRAL PROPHECY OF THE TRIPLE NINE: UNVEILING THE PROPHETIC 2012 MELTDOWN OF THE LOST AND ASTRAY PALE STATE OF MIND

reality. Clearly, at a particular point in time, the situation would be very similar to modern-day prisons where a more dominant male would attack the weaker male to satisfy his lusting sexual desires, turning them into personal slaves or, when the going got tough, consuming of them as a meal. One thing that should be crystal clear is that homosexuality does not provide the essential elements needed to reproduce. Therefore, through time, attacks on others would continue the multiplication of that deep-freeze paleness. In viewing another set of circumstances in modern times, let us take a moment to analyze the events surrounding the polar bear and the melting glacier ice.

For those who are not aware, the polar bear has become a cold-blooded, pale cannibal; that is, the polar bears are consuming of themselves in a game of survival of the fittest. Let us suppose that the polar bear did have the option of invading the environment of the herbivorous brown bear. What do you think would happen? These cold and pale predators who are now consuming of themselves would indeed take the option to consume of their darker herbivorous kin. The polar bear would certainly prey upon the brown bears and approach the darker male as an adversary. Once their bellies were full, lusting sexual greed would step in and the polar bear would indeed continue their invasion through sexual aggression towards the brown female bear. Before too long an entire herbivorous culture would become so weakened and depleted that it would barely continue to exist. You see, what would happen is the offspring born of the raping raids of the brown female bear would

CHAPTER NINE: THE CHANGING OF THE GUARD

reproduce the characteristics and traits of the polar bear into a new breed of bear. These bears would obviously create warring clans and tribes of bears, and the primary struggle would be to become the most dominant and controlling bear through acts of hostile aggression. The descendants of the brown bear would either be slaughtered and consumed, or would begin to adopt the cold and pale predatorial traits in order to survive the brutal attacks of the pale ones. In a situation like this, even if natural elimination should cause the polar bear to become extinct, those brown or melaninated bears who would have survived the vicious pale attacks would be so adversely affected that the cold and pale characteristics and traits would become their way of life. There is no question that a new breed of bear would produce a predatorial hunter who mixes his consumption of flesh with the consumption of plants. Only if a sacred few among these herbivorous brown bears would gather outside of the invaded environment with a primary focus on preserving their natural and innate way of life would the brown bear survive. The I in I hope that this point is very well taken.

Those intellectual thinkers among Man, He and She, of the cold and pale predatorial mentality certainly sympathize and show great compassion for the circumstances of the polar bear while showing little or no concern for the seals. The poor polar bear becomes easy to identify with as the mighty bear struggles against nature to survive. What about the seal? Who is applauding the escape of the seal? The seal's story is not being told. We must comprehend that up until this era of the Triple Nine, the lost and astray pale state of mind has

FULFILLING THE SACRED ANCESTRAL PROPHECY OF THE TRIPLE NINE: UNVEILING THE PROPHETIC 2012 MELTDOWN OF THE LOST AND ASTRAY PALE STATE OF MIND

dominated and controlled, and does indeed continue to dominate and control, the presentation of history in a way that favors and glorifies the historic raping raids and invasions of sex and violence, war and crime that is the lost and astray pale Children's historic story line.

And the pale invaders would, of course, portray themselves as heroes and brave and valiant warriors. And the admiration and awe for the power to kill that was upheld by the descendants of the deep freeze would twist and tangle inside the minds of the conquered suntanned populations. And the sacred suntanned female who was at first completely repulsed and disgusted by the filthy and gruesome vibrations of lust, lies, illusions, confusion, death and deadly destruction would be turned out. Her fright and fear would be quieted by a frozen numbness that shut out all connections to her sacred ancestral spirit presence. Let us state clearly within divine spirit consciousness that the Divine Children of the Sun and the Sacred Garden Culture from which we come had no place and held no value for the cold and pale way of life that was forced upon the sacred suntanned Man, He and She, through these violating acts of sex and violence, war and crime. Therefore, there was no way for the sacred ancestral spirit presence of the Divine Children of the Sun to comprehend what, within that blood-thirsty hell, was going on. We hope that one comprehends that the female has always been the primary target to dominate, control, abuse and even consume within the pale culture.

Resurrecting the sacred ancestral mother spirit is indeed the nucleus of divine resurrection. The primary issue is detoxing and purging the toxic disorder from the

CHAPTER NINE: THE CHANGING OF THE GUARD

mother spirit due to the destabilization that has been inflicted upon this most precious nurturer of Man, He and She. Since she has been conditioned and programmed to nurture toxic disorder, the ancestral mother spirit must be re-oriented to nurturing divine spirit consciousness. The same tenacity that was used to destabilize her nurturing presence must be re-directed to resurrect this most sacred nurturer out of this deep-freeze, ice-cold mentality.

We must begin to know and understand full well that it is virtually impossible for the ancestral mother spirit to have the ability to resurrect out of this deep-freeze ice cold on her own, by osmosis or by any other miraculous occurrence. What is required is total mental, physical and spiritual focus to the resurrection process itself. And both He and She, must be absolutely attuned to the fact that the resurrection of the most precious nurturing energy, which is the essence of femininity, is the top priority. The divine nurturer is quintessential to the resurrection of the sacred ancestral spirit presence of the Divine Children of the Sun and the Sacred Garden Culture from which we come.

It is not possible for the process of sacred ancestral resurrection to be maintained within the death-consuming culture of the toxic parallel. One must depart the mental and physical surroundings of toxic consumption and begin an intense re-union within the environment of divine social economic family community. Core phases of detoxing and purging are essential and can only be divinely guided, protected and nurtured within whole life energy. One cannot approach these deeper phases without first consuming the sacred texts that have been brought forward from the Most Supreme Seen and

FULFILLING THE SACRED ANCESTRAL PROPHECY OF THE TRIPLE NINE: UNVEILING THE PROPHETIC 2012 MELTDOWN OF THE LOST AND ASTRAY PALE STATE OF MIND

Unseen Essence of Life and Supreme Love. These sacred texts are provided to prepare a capacity for divine clarity and spirit conscious comprehension. One must comprehend the presence of the opposite energy within self and how it expresses, reacts and distracts one's attention away from receiving the whole life healing vibrations of Supreme Truth. One must acknowledge the damage that has occurred as the consequences of one's toxic consumption. And complete dedication and devotion must be given to implementing family structures, social orders and teaching and learning methodologies that will equip one in becoming a vital assistance in this most precious effort of manifesting divine social economic family community through the resurrection of the sacred ancestral spirit presence of the Divine Children of the Sun and the Sacred Garden Culture from which we come.

This is why the Sacred Ancestral Temple of Kwa Ta Man I is of the utmost significance and necessity within the divine social economic family community. This is why the Sacred Ancestral Temple of Kwa Ta Man I is emerging again upon the seen within this second cycle of the divine intervention. The first cycle of nine was for the brain, that is the resurrection of divine spirit conscious thought and reasoning. The groundwork was established for a supreme birthing process within the Kwatamani Royal Family that would allow divine spirit consciousness to be solidified and nurtured upon the seen. A massive wave of divine communication has come forward from the Most Supreme Unseen to complete a series of nine sacred texts that began with

CHAPTER NINE: THE CHANGING OF THE GUARD

"The Divine Gathering of the Sacred Few" in the mid 1960's and a series of nine spoken word musical CD's that began with the initial recordings for the "Advancement of Divinity" series in 1999. These messages have been sent forward for the purpose of providing divine clarity and detailing steps for the beginning phases of detoxing and purging.

The brain thrust of the first cycle would come through the installment of the I in I as the seen presence of High Priest Kwatamani with a full focus on resurrecting the divine union of the Kwatamani Royal Family. And within the fulfilling of this sacred ancestral prophecy of the Triple Nine, the second cycle of embodiment signifies the emergence of the Sacred Ancestral Temple of Kwa Ta Man I in preparation for the expansion of the divine social economic family community as led by the sacred ancestral spirit presence of the I in I as High Priest Kwatamani and the Kwatamani Royal Family. And from that most essential embodiment would come the Sacred Order of the Essence.

We are definitely in place within the land base that was foretold many, many years ago. And the Kwatamani divine social economic family community has been a thriving reality within the continued expansion of the Kwatamani Royal Family, as a second and third generation have emerged to carry forward this divine mission. This prophesied land base has been secured to provide a whole and clean, tropical rain forest environment necessary for resurrecting the sacred ancestral spirit presence of the Divine Children of the Sun and the Sacred Garden Culture from which we come.

Chapter 9 Innerlude:
Emergence of a Divine Intervention

Song 10 from "12th Hour Prophecy: The Pale Curse and the Solarized Energy Shift," Kwatamani musical CD release, 2008

<u>Royal Priestess vocals:</u>
The sacred ancestral key to this divine prophecy
Is that a Divine Intervention would come to be
And the sacred ancestral soothsayer would reveal
This prophecy for all who have eyes to see

<u>High Priest vocals:</u>
And the Ta and the Tat would look upon
all of this and that going on
And the ancestors were not pleased
and would intercede
with divine intervention to melt down
that white-blight zone
Because the Most Supreme Unseen
would never leave us to do this thing alone
You see, the Earth's surface had started to change
Suffering too much misery, aches and pains
as the sacred ancestral motherspirit would do
since the coming of the pale crew
They both had been ripped, stripped and raped
by the cold, pale opposite energies of hell
They both had been ejaculated into by a paleness
that made red blood appear blue
Supreme femininity left grim, bleak and barren
and unfertile to breed the sacred ancestral seed
Only able to produce a pale state of mind

FULFILLING THE SACRED ANCESTRAL PROPHECY OF THE TRIPLE NINE: UNVEILING THE PROPHETIC 2012 MELTDOWN OF THE LOST AND ASTRAY PALE STATE OF MIND

yeah, Mother Earth and the ancestral motherspirit
was in a bind
But that cold, pale, lost and astray mind
and the disciples and the followers of the paleness kind
was about profit regardless of the cost
stuff and thangs and materialistic gain
Deep-seated and focused on gaining fortune and fame
Lusting greed and selfish indeed
beyond any and every thing
Yeah, the nature of that cold, pale, opposite energy
was dominant
And the Earth was being turned into a white-blight zone
And the nature of this death-consuming culture was stone
cold to the bone
And the lost and astray mind would run footloose
and fancy free regardless of how the body
would ache and pain and moan and groan
You see, suffering was how paleness had begin
and those of the pale mentality
was of lust, lies, illusions, confusion
death and deadly destruction
cold and grueling pain, suffering misery
driving the lost and astray mind insane
And out of the nature of this cold-blooded opposite
energy would come the paleness of doom and gloom
And the lost and astray, pale state of mind was working
desperately to consume of this opposite energy
to bring forward doom and gloom
as the cold-blooded, opposite energy would decree
And consuming of this death culture
would provide the fuel for self-destruction

CHAPTER 9 INNERLUDE: EMERGENCE OF A DIVINE INTERVENTION

through mental affliction, physical sickness
and disease and toxic addiction
And once that pale monkey was on your back
it would become a thrill to feel numbed up, zapped out and high
You see, pain was in conflict with the joys and the pleasures of life
But pain became a pleasure game among the children
who mutated and degenerated in the ice
And now that the toxic addictions and affliction
has spread like a plague
The suntanned Children would plead and beg
to be entertained by the pain game
And in their quest to gain fortune and fame
they too would become cold, stale and pale
and addicted to this thang

<u>Royal Priestess vocals:</u>
Fall to the curse
Or rise to the blessing
It all depends on if you learned your lesson

<u>High Priest vocals:</u>
The freaky-deaks and the control freaks
was on the war path deep up inside
their lost and astray minds
And as the thoughts would resurrect deep up inside
their Satanic-inspired god complex
they would ego trip and become vexed
trying to figure out what to do next
Quickly they would attempt to re-organize hell
Restructuring their clone-like social order

FULFILLING THE SACRED ANCESTRAL PROPHECY OF THE TRIPLE NINE: UNVEILING THE PROPHETIC 2012 MELTDOWN OF THE LOST AND ASTRAY PALE STATE OF MIND

through the use of stem cells
Ain't nothing like a control freak being out of control
facing an energy that it cannot control
And it'd be very difficult for the pale ones to face the fact
that melanin would be the saving grace
You see, the melanated ones that they had raped,
murdered and enslaved, misused and abused and tortured
to hell
had become a carbon copy of that cold-blooded, vicious,
opposite energy stale and pale
If all was well, the sacred suntanned Children
would have enough divine spirit consciousness to lead
all of Man, He and She out of this cold-blooded, deep-
freeze pits of hell
But all was not well, in fact the suntanned Children were
still jelling and paling
and had become completely hypnotized and mesmerized
to the deceptions and the deified lies
and the disguise that this opposite energy provide
In fact, the suntanned Children so high on crack and coke
and the stuff that they eat, drink, sniff, snort and smoke
And the social, economic, religious ray of hope
and the fantasies and illusions about the outcome
of a vote
And the struggling pains that came
from trying to be accepted in the games of white folks
and the price for numbing the pain
through the use of over- and under-the-counter dope
Or the passionate aggression to be the control freak
to control the areas where paleness is weak
And due to their indulgement into these pale crimes

CHAPTER 9 INNERLUDE: EMERGENCE OF A DIVINE INTERVENTION

the suntanned Children have become deaf, dumb and
blind and had no reality about the signs of the times
And not even melanin could help rescue
this pale, lost and astray state of mind
You see, the suntanned Children really had no idea about
how close we were to the time
of the clock striking twelve
And really didn't believe that the bottom
was about to fall out of hell
But time was of the essence, there was very little time
left for the Children who were pale
and so they were now on Project Clone and Stem-Cell
You see, the objective was
to acquire the elements of melanin and to get it at any
cost, DNA alteration, hyper-cell growth
manipulating the gene code
Yes, the pale Children would do anything
to keep themselves in control
And although there was much invested time and research
into stars and Mars
There really wasn't much time to go anywhere
You see, global warming was moving very fast
and the pale Children had no idea
how long global warming would last
And so the best they could do was to move quick and fast
becoming body snatchers under Project Stem Cell
And this would become their major task
Cloning our stem cells
to carry out a solarized project would need a female host
a solarized female, and without this element
the entire project would be shot to hell

FULFILLING THE SACRED ANCESTRAL PROPHECY OF THE TRIPLE NINE: UNVEILING THE PROPHETIC 2012 MELTDOWN OF THE LOST AND ASTRAY PALE STATE OF MIND

And they'd have to move quick and fast
before the clock strike twelve

Royal Priestess vocals:
Tick tock, tick tock and the boat would rock
And the waves would roll
As the pale opposite energy takes its toll
Because the sanctity of the motherspirit
has been turned ice cold

<u>High Priest vocals:</u>
Mother Earth or the sacred ancestral motherspirit
yes, the ancestral female was the target
'cause she would give birth to all that's whole and true
And without divine guidance and protection
all that's whole and true is what she could misconstrue
She could be forced and conditioned
to worship deceptions and lies
until all that's whole and true would become a pale blue
And those of that pale, opposite energy
were definitely into tightening up the screw
Inflicting the curse of harm and hurt
into the feminine energy
Until the misery, aches and pains
would eventually cause her to give birth
and to nurture that opposite energy
And then become a worshipper
of that pale-male-war-god deity
And thereafter her most supreme ancestral presence
would become belittled and unwhole
And she would become disconnected from her most
supreme ancestral presence seen and unseen

CHAPTER 9 INNERLUDE: EMERGENCE OF A DIVINE INTERVENTION

The Ta and the Tat, He and She,
of the most supreme essence of Osiris and Auset
Two parts to one whole
And once divided and conquered
there would never be a more sorrowful story told
And she would breed, seed and feed
off that opposite energy and lust, lies, illusions
confusion, death and deadly destruction
would be her offspring's destiny
as doom and gloom and hell and damnation
begin to take its toll
And deceit would be the mark of the beast
and the triple-six elements of lust, lies, illusions,
confusion, death and deadly destruction
was well-programmed and fixed
And brain, body and spirit would be the triple trick
and unless a divine and sacred few
could be pulled out of the mix
that was that and this was the end of this

<u>Royal Priestess vocals:</u>
Unless a Divine and Sacred Few
can be pulled out of the mix
That was that, and this was the end of this

<u>High Priest vocals:</u>
You see, the earth was heating up quick and fast
and the ice was melting as quickly
as it had come in the past
And as the polar ice would melt
the polar caps would shrink
And the polar bear was definitely becoming extinct
And with the pale Children having a polar ancestral link

FULFILLING THE SACRED ANCESTRAL PROPHECY OF THE TRIPLE NINE: UNVEILING THE PROPHETIC 2012 MELTDOWN OF THE LOST AND ASTRAY PALE STATE OF MIND

it would become easy to know what they would think
And for the sake of maintaining their survival
one could only imagine how low they would sink
Yet, all it would take is divine humility
before it's too late
and all things would change in a blink

Royal Priestess vocals:
And the message that was sent around
before the coming of the freezing ice would come again
As the meltdown comes to an end
would the Children heed the advice

High Priest vocals:
But somewhere out there was a Divine and Sacred Few
With a will to hold the Most Supreme
ancestral presence whole and true
Coming in assorted colors, kind and kin
focused on divine oneness from deep within
And the sacred ancestral soothsayer
had called for them to come
And a few would emerge back
into the essence of the Divine Children of the Sun
And they would consume of the fruits of the Trees
of Life
Resurrecting divine spirit consciousness
within the Sacred-Garden-Culture paradise
And they would be led to detox and purge
with an ancestral spirit surge
Learning those lessons, retrieving ancestral blessings
Moving back into the essence of the divine union of one
And the Ta and the Tat would look upon this

CHAPTER 9 INNERLUDE: EMERGENCE OF A DIVINE INTERVENTION

and the ancestors would be pleased

<u>Royal Priestess vocals:</u>
And the ooh's and the aah's of a Love Supreme
Would again be expressed whole and clean

Holistic Living Resource Materials

DVD

Holistic Living DVD Series: Raw & Living Foods Preparation Class
Live Sweet Potato Pie with delicious live potato greens $49.99

Books

Fulfilling The Sacred Ancestral Prophecy of the Triple Nine: Unveiling the Prophetic 2012 Meltdown of the Lost And Astray Pale State of Mind $39.99

Exposing the Ice-Cold, Deep-Freeze Mentality and Whole Life Healing of Sexual Energy within the Divine Parallel...And the Sacred Resurrection of the Divine Garden Culture $39.99
(A classic and historic reading of this text by Royal Priestess Gail Kwatamani available by special order)

The Holistic Living Truth About Supreme Love...And the Sacred Resurrection of the Divine Garden Culture: Book 1-Resurrecting the Divine Body of Flesh & Book 2-Resurrecting Divine Thought and Reasoning $35 ea.
Book 3-Resurrecting Divine Spirit Consciousness $39.99

Raw and Living Foods: The First Divine Act and Requirement of a Holistic Living Way of Life. Raw & Living Fruits, Vegetables, Seeds & Nuts. The Natural Foods for Man, He and She, in the Divine Consumption Plan $29.99

The Divine Gathering of the Sacred Few through a Holistic Living Way of Life
    $25

CD Productions

Truth Lyrics

Supernatural Healing Serum $14.99
Supernatural Healing Serum: Dose Two $14.99
Supernatural Healing Serum: Dose Three $14.99
Conjuring Ancestral Spirit Consciousness $19.99
12th Hour Prophecy: The Pale Curse and the Solarized Energy Shift
    $20.12

TO ORDER: Please visit our website at: www.livefoodsunchild.com

www.ingramcontent.com/pod-product-compliance
Lightning Source LLC
Chambersburg PA
CBHW071431300426
44114CB00013B/1388